GREECE: THE MODERN SEQUEL

This picture of a little girl admiring her new pair of shoes, while still holding on to her old pair, was taken soon after the Second World War and is well known to Greeks. It has been thought to symbolise the attraction of the new, combined with reluctance to be finally parted from the old.

JOHN S. KOLIOPOULOS
THANOS M. VEREMIS

Greece
The Modern Sequel

From 1831 to the Present

NEW YORK UNIVERSITY PRESS
WASHINGTON SQUARE, NEW YORK

First published in the U.S.A. in 2002 by
NEW YORK UNIVERSITY PRESS
Washington Square
New York, NY 10003

Library of Congress Cataloging-in-Publishing Data

Koliopoulos, Giannes.
   Greece : the modern sequel / John S. Koliopoulos, Thanos Veremis.
      p. cm.
   Includes bibliographical references and index.
   ISBN 0-8147-4767-1 (pbk. : alk. paper) –ISBN 0-8147-4766-3 (cloth : alk. paper).
    1. Greece–History–1821– I. Veremis, Thanos. II. Title.

   DF802 .K647 2002
   949.507--dc21   2002016551

Printed in Malaysia

To John K. Campbell
a mentor and friend to
both authors

ACKNOWLEDGEMENTS

This volume was conceived during a long summer afternoon in Hydra. Many subsequent discussions between the authors, the forbearance of their spouses, and the encouragement of friends such as the late P.J. Vatikiotis and John A. Petropulos contributed to its birth. Mark Dragoumis added grace to it with his extensive comments.

Much of the research and writing was facilitated by the Hellenic Foundation for European and Foreign Policy (ELIAMEP). The historical and photographic archives of the Benaki Museum have been generous in their assistance. Views contained in the text were aired with Mark Dragoumis and Theodore Couloumbis, who offered sound advice. The authors owe many thanks to Elpida Vogli, Hilary Sakellariades, Youla Goulimis and Irene Glypti of ELIAMEP, and of course to Christopher Hurst for much editorial work.

Finally, the authors express their appreciatioon for an award by the Eleni Nakou Foundation that covered research and typing expenses.

June 2002   J. S. K.
                                                               T. M. V.

CONTENTS

Acknowledgements   *page* vii

Map   xiii

Introduction   1

Part I. POLITICS AND STATECRAFT

1. A regime to suit the nation   11
2. Government and people   44
   Politics and the public domain   57
   Political leadership   61
   Revolution and defeat: the civil war, 1943–9   68
   The civil-war heritage and post-war politics   98
   KKE, a party like no other   110
   Homo politicus   126

Part II. INSTITUTIONS

3. The Church of Greece   141
4. The military   152
5. Education: The mighty Greek school   157

Part III. THE ECONOMY   165

Part IV. SOCIETY

7. A land of peasants   181
8. The search for a middle class   194

9. Migrants, refugees and diaspora   200
10. Of heroes and heroic deeds   212
    Rhigas Velestinlis (1757–98)   215
11. Crime and impunity   221

Part V. IDEOLOGY

12. Fashioning the new nation   227
13. Demarcating the past   236
14. The return of the Hellenes   242
15. Of Greeks and others   249
    Turkey in Greece   259
16. Europe in Greece   263

Part VI. FOREIGN POLICY

17. Greek foreign policy: From independence to liberation   277
18. The post-war legacy   294
    The years of division   294
    Relations with the West
    Greek-Turkish relations   302
    Relations with the Balkans   305
    After 1974   307
    The Balkans   314
    Turkey   320

Part VII. NATIONAL GEOGRAPHY

19. The frontier and beyond   327
20. A northern boundary   333
21. War for land   342

Part VIII

22. Culture   349

Conclusion   360

Appendix Chronology   364

Bibliography   372

Index   399

ILLUSTRATIONS

The new pair of shoes   *frontispiece*

between pages 210 and 211

Ioannis Kapodistrias (1776–1831), first President of
   independent Greece

Diplomatic corps, early 20th century

Athens, mid-19th century

Thessaloniki burning on the night of 18–19 August, 1917

An Athenian couple, 1885: Eleni and Dimitrios Stavropoulos

Harilaos Trikoupis (1832–96)

The actor Dionysios Tavoularis, representing Rhigas, 1890

The heroic image of Greece: a '*palikari*' from Delphi, 1880

Eleftherios Venizelos (1864–1936)

Constantinos Cavafis (1863–1933)

Ship crowded with refugees from Asia Minor, 1922

First refugee housing in Halkidiki, northern Greece

Ioannis Metaxas reviewing a 4 August parade

29 October 1940: volunteers enlisting at a recruitment centre

29 October 1940: crowds celebrating

Greek forces in the Middle East, 1943

ELAS resistance troops with German prisoners, 1943

Liberation day, 1944

UNRRA relief for a devastated Greece

Omonia Square, Athens, in the 1950s

Dancing in front of the Parthenon—Nelly's (1899–1998)

Maria Callas (1923–77)

George (1888–68) and Andreas Papandreou (1919–96)

Departure of King Constantine and Queen Anne-Marie for the United States, 1967, bidden farewell by the triumvirate of Colonels

Constantine Karamanlis signs the treaty for Greek accession to the European Community, Athens, 28 May 1979

Map © reproduced courtesy of ABC/CLIO, Oxford.

Greece

INTRODUCTION

The thematic, rather than chronological, structure of this book is based on the premise that certain constant factors exist which help to elucidate the attitudes, policies and institutions of present-day Greece. The most fundamental among them in our view is the sense of continuity that the Greek language inspires in its users. Few languages have shown such resilience and durability. Greek-speakers today can understand the second-century BC translation of the Old Testament of the Bible in the '*Koine*', or the language of the New Testament written by the Evangelists in the first century AD.[1]

The very designation of the unitary nation state that emerged at the end of the war of independence as 'Hellas' displays the identity that a Christian Orthodox community owning a linguistic tradition spanning millennia chose for itself. Whereas Serbs and Bulgarians named their nineteenth-century nation states after their medieval kingdoms, 'Hellas' had never been used before to signify a single political entity; it was rather the common culture of people living in the many disparate city states of antiquity—who also, according to Herodotus, were 'of the same stock and of the same speech, and shared common shrines of the gods and rituals and similar customs. ...'

The spreading of Christianity in the East owed much to the Greek language, and the Great Church in Constantinople adopted it as an instrument of religious education. Yet the terms 'Hellas' and 'Hellenic' were associated with their pagan origin and were soon replaced by the official designation of the christianised conquerors of the Hellenised East, the Romans. Thus Greeks became Romans and the Ottomans, who later conquered the eastern

---

[1]M.Z. Kopidakis (ed.), *Istoria tis ellinikis glossas* (History of the Greek language), Athens: ELIA, 1999. See also George Thomson, *To aithales dhendro* (The evergreen tree), Athens: Kedros, 1999, pp. 280–94.

1

Roman Empire, used the term 'Rum' to define the Orthodox *millet*.[2]

Through the good services of a merchant diaspora of secular luminaries, 'Hellas' was adopted as the name of the nation state of the Hellenes. The 'High Culture'[3] of the Hellenic language, which was nurtured by the Orthodox tradition, became the trademark of Hellenism. The choice did not antagonise the Greek-speaking church because the pagan connotation of the term 'Hellenic' was at last purged by four centuries under a regime that used the discourse of the Muslims.[4]

Among the indiosyncracies of the Orthodox East, as compared to the West after the Reformation, one of the most persistent and influential was the perception of cyclical and therefore immutable time. The Orthodox mystics perceived time as a sequence of seasons and, as such, a reaffirmation of God's unchanging will. Concomitant with this notion of time was the absence of the concept of individualism, which was perceived as a manifestation of an egoism that militated against the communal spirit of the Church.[5] The exclusion of individualism from the Orthodox communities protected the parish from undesirable innovations, but it also precluded reform and development in the timeless realm of religious authority.

Such cocooned communities resisted the transition from medieval inertia to the mobility of the post-Reformation era in Europe. Hence

[2]The Latin 'Graeci' (as opposed to the indigenous 'Hellenes') was a designation adopted by the Romans, who first came in contact with people of that name in Epirus. The Latins chose to call the inhabitants of the entire Hellenic world by that name. The Latin Western empire persisted in calling the subjects of the Eastern empire 'Graeci', especially after the schism of the churches in the eleventh century. The term 'Byzantine', replacing Roman, was invented by Hieronymus Wolf between 1576 and 1580, and has caused much confusion to Western scholarship. Samuel Huntington mistook the Byzantine empire for an Asiatic regime and distinguished it from the West as being supposedly not endowed with the rule of law. Of course Roman law reigned in the East for close to 1,000 years, even when it had been totally eclipsed in the West of the Dark Ages by the rule of local warlords. See S. Huntington, 'The West Unique, not Universal', *Foreign Affairs* (Nov.-Dec. 1996), pp. 28–46.

[3]Gellner uses 'High Culture' to define the central education adopted by the emerging states in Europe. He errs in our view when describing the 'third zone' in the East as a territory without 'well-defined and well-sustained High Cultures'. Ernest Gellner, *Encounters with Nationalism*, Oxford: Blackwell, 1995, p. 30.

[4]Paschalis Kitromilides, *Enlightenment, Nationalism, Orthodoxy: Studies in the Culture and Political Thought of Southeastern Europe*, Aldershot:Variorum, 1994.

[5]A creative interpretation of medieval Orthodox theology and its impact on society is attempted by Stelios Ramphos in his *Mia kalokairini eftychia trizei* (A summer happiness is threatened), Athens: Armos, 1999, pp. 62–104.

the existence of the individual separate from the group—whether in the church or in the family, which reproduces the church ideal—was inconceivable throughout the centuries of Ottoman captivity. It was 'group individualism' (if such an apparently contradictory term can be allowed), rather than private individualism, that established the norm in Greek and Balkan communities.[6] However, this absence of emphasis on the self does not confirm, in the case of the Eastern church, the view that communitarian societies are more intolerant than their Western counterparts. Although the notion of individual human rights did not exist when the church was founded, intolerance has, on the whole, been foreign to the Greek Orthodox establishment, which never instituted anything remotely resembling the 'Holy Inquisition'.[7]

If the inertia of the kind described above became the established mindset of the peasant society during the centuries of Ottoman rule, what was the spark that ignited the war of independence and the subsequent establishment of a nation-state endowed with institutions owing their origin to the French Revolution?

The destruction of the medieval Christian aristocracy by the Ottoman Turks and the expropriation of their lands provided the opportunity to the 'Conquering Orthodox Balkan Merchant'[8] to establish his undisputed imprint on cultural and political developments. The routes of trade facilitated the traffic of ideas, while the French Enlightenment that stormed into the Balkans found little resistance from a weak '*ancien régime*'. The church initially provided the finest exponents of the new creed but then shied away when the Jacobins decapitated the religious leadership in France. The execution in 1821 of a large number of metropolitans and of the Patriarch himself by the Ottoman Porte resolved the dilemma for the surviving prelates, who threw in their lot with the revolutionaries.

Although the nation-state was the product of an historical compromise between traditional church values and the importation

---

[6]A.Pollis, 'Political Implications of the Modern Greek Concept of Self', *British Journal of Sociology*, no. 16, 1965, pp. 30–45.

[7]Adamantia Pollis, 'Eastern Orthodoxy and Human Rights', *Human Rights Quarterly*, vol. 15, no. 2 (May 1993), pp. 33–56. According to the author, Eastern Orthodoxy is antagonistic to the notion of human rights. She states that in the teachings of the church 'there is no individualization of the person' and no mention of natural law.

[8]Traian Stoianovich, 'The Conquering Balkan Orthodox Merchant', *Journal of Economic History*, XX (1960), pp. 243–313.

of Western modernity, the spirit of the 'conquering merchant' prevailed. W.H. McNeill explains the orderly movement of internal migrants from the countryside to the urban centres 'resulting from the market orientation of peasant life and the tight-knit organization of Greek nuclear family units'.[9] Familiarity with the workings of the market and the firm structure of the family remain the two stable elements in Greek society that have merged in a creative, if at times tense coexistence. 'It is perhaps this binary phenomenon of market forces, spurring people to movement while anchored on the familial bedrock of traditional values, that may explain the idiosyncrasies of Greece.'[10]

A fundamental question that we should raise at the outset is the exact location of the demarcation line between ancient and modern. How should the student of Greek history approach the notion of modernity? What are the landmarks that signalled the arrival of modern times in the lands inhabited by Greeks or even by those who partook of Greek education? Linguistic continuity in time could be established as a criterion that demarcated ancient from modern history. Some scholars believe[11] that the triumph of Hellenistic Greek, or the Alexandrian *Koine*, which persisted in one form or another till the 1978 educational reform, was indeed the beginning of the transition from ancient to modern times.

In the nineteenth century, before the notion of the Eastern Roman or (Byzantine) empire was firmly equated with the Greek Middle Ages, 'modern' Greece was associated with the era following the Roman conquest of the Greek lands; in other words, it was distinguished from ancient Greece, which 'officially' came to an end in 146 BC, when Corinth fell to the Romans. Anastasios Polyzoidis, the brilliant lawyer who defended Theodoros Kolokotronis, a hero of the Greek Revolution, in 1834 against charges of treason, wrote a two-volume history for use in Greek schools titled *Neohellenika* and subtitled 'Main events and the condition of Greek letters in Greece from the fall of Corinth to the Romans till our recent national struggle for independence (146 BC–AD 1821)'. The work, in tune with the writings

---

[9]William Hardy McNeill, *The Metamorphosis of Greece since World War II*, Oxford: Basil Blackwell, 1978, p. 248.

[10]Thanos Veremis, *The Military in Greek Politics from Independence to Democracy*, London: Hurst, 1997, p. 188.

[11]View held by George Thomson: 'I elliniki glossa archaia kai nea' (The Greek language ancient and modern) in *To aithales dhendro*, p. 282.

of West European writers, added to the same author's two-volume corpus titled *Hellenika*, also written for use in schools, which covered from ancient Greece up to the Roman conquest.[12]

The distinction between ancient Greece and Roman-conquered Greece was the same as that between the independent modern Greek state and not only Frankish and Ottoman Greece but also the Eastern Roman or (Byzantine) empire. What more natural for an illustrious representative of the mature phase of the Greek Enlightenment than to use political independence as a factor distinguishing one period from another in a nation's history? And what more natural for such a representative than to follow Gibbon in considering the Eastern Roman empire as even more inimical to Greek freedom than the Western Roman empire?[13]

Using political independence as a determining factor, but serving a radically different agenda, the foremost Greek historian of the nineteenth century, Konstantinos Paparrigopoulos, placed the stirrings of 'Modern Hellenism' in the fourth of the Latin Crusades, which humbled Byzantium in 1204 and ended the 'political independence' of the Greeks. Ever since the arrogant Latins and the 'infidel' Ottomans destroyed the Eastern Roman empire, the Greeks, according to Paparrigopoulos, never stopped fighting for independence from both. The modern Greek nation-state became the agent for winning back the political independence and unity which had been lost in the thirteenth century, and once they gained their freedom from foreign tutelage the Greeks began developing linguistic, cultural, ideological and social features—such as a popular language, epic poetry, communal self-government and a profound suspicion of the Latin West.[14]

Subsequent historians of Greece did not diverge appreciably from Paparrigopoulos's prescription of the nation's history: 1204 or 1453 have invariably been accepted as the landmarks separating 'modern Greece' from its medieval predecessor. The loss of independence in

[12]Anastasios Polyzoides, *Ta Neohellenika* ... Athens, 1874, 2 vols, and *Hellenika* ..., Athens 1870, 2 vols.

[13]Anastasios Polyzoides, *Geniki historia apo archaeotaton chronon mechri ton kath' imas* (General History from ancient times till our time), ed. by G.P. Kremos, Athens, 1889, vol. I, p. 12.

[14]Konstantinos Paparrigopoulos, *Historia tou hellenikou ethnous* (History of the Hellenic nation), vol. V, Athens 1874, p. 5, and the same author's *Prolegomena* (Prologue) to the 2nd edn of vol. V, ed. by Konstantinos Dimaras, Athens 1970, pp. 84–5, 90–1, 155. See also the same Prologue in the 6th edn of the same work, ed. by Pavlos Karolides, Athens 1930.

either of those years and the development of the features mentioned above have as a rule been advanced as criteria for pushing the beginning of modern Greek times further back than modern times in Western Europe.

It is beyond the scope of this work to present a thorough analysis of periodisation in Greek history. However, the growing knowledge in the last three or four decades of the twentieth century of both late Byzantium and the early centuries of Ottoman rule in the Greek lands has made the student of modern Greece sceptical about the validity of many of the arguments proposed in support of stretching modern times in the Greek lands back to the fifteenth century, let alone to the thirteenth century. A rigorous scrutiny of these arguments gives the impression that they often rest on shaky evidence. For instance, although few would now disagree that the last Byzantine dynasties were Greek in every way, it is questionable whether it could be convincingly argued that their Greekness was modern, in the sense in which modernity is defined below. The reigning dynasties and their administrative, military and fiscal systems were no more modern than the corresponding regimes and their administrative machinery in the West at the same period. Furthermore, the humiliation suffered at the hands of the Western Crusaders provides, in itself, no proof that it was a sufficient cause for a nascent modern sense of identity to arise among the Greeks.

In what sense was Palaeologian high art or Gemistos Plethon's philosophical thinking modern enough to mark a departure from the Middle Ages ? Were the various chronicles and the epic poetry of the same era the precursors of subsequent folk ballads, or the surviving elements of a much older genre ? Was the unquestionable opposition to the Latin West a decisive factor in the development of a modern consciousness, or was it an element that contributed to the process of caving in to Islam? There have been no convincing answers to these and other such questions.

Similar assumptions can be found in the argument that the loss of Greek political independence in either 1204 or 1453 marked the end of medieval times and initiated the forces that prepared the way for modern Greek independence. Few would now argue that the factors that made political independence possible in the nineteenth century were the same (or even similar to) those existing in Greek lands in the thirteenth or fifteenth centuries. The fading memory of a medieval empire would not have sustained a revolutionary movement against the declining Ottomans had there not been a Greek commercial class and a westernised intelligentsia active in it. The movement for national independence and modernity cannot be stretched back to political developments unconnected with the French Revolution. What really 'modernised' Greece and set it on a course that transformed it from an elusive concept into a concrete entity was not only the irrepressible longing of the Greek people for freedom (which romantic historians and poets have read into all kinds of events since the fall of Constantinople), but also—and mainly—the achievement of a group of Greek liberals and radicals dispersed throughout Europe and the Ottoman empire, who were convinced that revolution to overthrow despotic rule was as necessary and as imminent as it had been in France in the years leading up to 1789.

It is in the context of this movement for independence and of its outcome that modern Greece took shape. Before that context had come into existence, the term 'Greece' meant different things to different people; indeed, even those within the revolutionary movement were not in agreement over the place of Greece in time and space. Was it only the cluster of ancient city-states, or did it include the outer stretches of the Greek north? Was it the Greece of classical times or that of the Roman Illyricum? Was it the Eastern Roman empire which the Franks and the Ottoman Turks had destroyed, or was it the empire erected by the Turks on its ruins? And who were the Greeks? Did they include, in addition to those whose mother-tongue was Greek, all the non-Greek-speaking Orthodox Christians named 'Rum' or 'Romans', i.e. Greeks, by the temporal and spiritual authorities under which they lived?

Subsequent attempts, especially by Romantic historians such as Paparrigopoulos, to answer these questions further confused the criteria for locating Greece and the Greeks in time and space by equating 'Hellenism' subsequent to the fall of the Greek city-states to Philip II of Macedon, to the 'Hellenic nation' before the battle of Chaeronia (338 BC). Isocrates's cultural approach to the question was used in support of the theory of the Greek nation's continuity and unity in time and space—at first to silence questions about its survival and later to assert the Greek nation-state's 'historical rights'. Before this daring identification of the Greek nation with Hellenism and of Hellas with the Hellenic *Oecumene*, most educated Greeks viewed their country in the same way as West Europeans with classical training.

For the needs of this introduction and the unravelling of the threads woven into the modern Greek fabric, it is enough to say that by 'modern Greece' we mean the Greek nation-state which emerged

---

Adamantios Koraes (1748–1833)

The leading figure of the Greek Enlightenment. Born in Smyrna, the son of a rich merchant from the island of Chios, Koraes spent time in Amsterdam attempting to pursue the family trade. In 1782–6 he studied medicine at the University of Montpellier and also became a prominent classical scholar. He lived in Paris between 1788 and 1833 and thus witnessed the great changes that occurred during that period at close quarters. He disliked radicalism and became the exponent of a 'middle way' in democratic liberal politics.

Koraes believed that the Greeks would never attain true freedom from the backwardness of Ottoman bondage unless they became versed in the scholarly works of their ancient heritage. The 'Hellenic Library' of ancient Greek authors was his own contribution to the Greek War of Independence, and his development of a formal language for scholars and the state was his lasting testament.

---

from the movement for national independence. This Greece, related to the Hellas of antiquity by language and to the Eastern Roman empire by religion, is a modern construction, no less than, say, Belgium. It is also unique because of the lands in which it was established. Its antecedents–or, rather, certain constructs fashioned by historians working under the influence of romantic nationalism–have been misleading. More often than not, modern Greece has disappointed those in the West who have chosen to make it the subject of their scholarly studies, or their home.[15] Admirers of classical Greece have been apt to look at its modern sequel with a disapproving eye, not only for the poor state of its classical studies and the neglect of its ancient monuments, but also for such generally acceptable practices as replacing non-Greek placenames with Greek ones. Equally, students of Byzantium, when not under the influence of Gibbon's invective against the empire, are bound to ridicule modern Greek efforts to 'Hellenise' it. Finally, orientalists have never really forgiven the Greeks for turning their face away from the Ottoman orient and for seriously trying to discard Eastern aspects of their social organisation. It seems that modern Greece has seldom been accepted for what its founding fathers aimed to make it, or approved for its achievement according to the original blueprint. Perhaps this is because the modern Greeks themselves have not really accepted that they are a modern nation

---

[15]Michel Grodent, *La Grèce n'existe pas*, Brussels: Talus d'approche, 2000.

constructed like all others, or appreciated what they have achieved as a modern nation.

Its modernity thus defined, Greece is explored in this book with the intention of revisiting and perhaps revising a conventional wisdom forged by travellers, observers and historians. Some Western perceptions of today's Greece are mere repetitions of nineteenth-century concepts and notions established as axioms. The more didactic Western works on Southeastern Europe in general, are exercises in complacency and offer little insight into the indigenous phenomena.[16] The lure of the obscure and the picturesque, which the natives often magnify in order to live up to the expectations of their guests, is yet another factor, and a distorting one, in the study of any traditional society.

This new exploration of Greece's modern past comprises a series of flashbacks organised in thematic categories such as Politics, Institutions, the Economy, Society, Ideology, Foreign Policy, Geography and Culture. The chapters and subchapters in each category follow no strict chronological order, but are focused on questions through which it is intended to shed light on vital aspect of the Greek phenomenon. The book also does not pretend to offer a dispassionate analysis. The authors make no effort to conceal their own predilection for the liberal principles that inspired the founding fathers of the Greek state, both the natives and the foreigners. These founding principles are juxtaposed with indigenous norms and practices and the outcome of the clash between opposite forces is assessed in each case.

Discussion of the themes stated above touches upon some aspects of Greek history and leaves out others, perhaps no less important. The book was not meant to be an exhaustive treatment of the subject; rather, it is a commentary on issues raised about Greece in the last decade of the twentieth century and at the same time a rejoinder to debating positions based on premises often obfuscated by nationalism and caricatures fashioned by complacent onlookers. Challenging established notions and certain stereotypes that disfigure Greece is meant to provoke the reader enough to look anew at the country and its people. The reward of such a fresh look might be what the authors have discovered in their own joint venture: that the subject of their study is in many ways more in keeping with modernity than is customarily believed.

---

[16]Maria Todorova, *Imagining the Balkans,* Oxford University Press, 1997.

Part I. POLITICS AND STATECRAFT

1

A REGIME TO SUIT THE NATION

The formation of a revolutionary government in 1821 soon after the first hostile actions against the Ottoman military and civil authorities presumed close co-operation between men who had already exercised some form of authority in the name of the Ottomans. These were called upon to establish a new authority that would be accepted by the Sultan's rebellious subjects and satisfy the country's politicised élites. The long and painful process of government-building was subject to influences and currents not always expressed in the official pronouncements and actions of the revolutionary government. That the new authority was founded on existing nuclei of power was unavoidable in view of the real or presumed power of both the local and the non-resident élites who spoke in the name of the rebels. The immediate objective of this government was to bring the war to a successful end and thus achieve liberation from foreign rule. Rather more pressing was the need to fill the power vacuum left by the abolished authorities and establish a measure of order. As might be expected, the first calls for a government to be put in place were in fact appeals for the establishment of law and order; early references to the 'government' of the land meant the authority entrusted with routine administration and especially the protection of vulnerable peasants from armed marauders.

The First National Assembly that met in late 1821 did not abolish the regional bodies that had come into being soon after the outbreak of the war; indeed, these local assemblies continued to exercise real authority, both because they represented interests easier to accommodate in a regional context than in a national one, and because they were closer to the local power-brokers. They were formed by the same men of local influence who controlled the National Assembly and saw their position strengthened after its convocation.

The War of Independence (1821–8)

War broke out in March 1821 almost simultaneously in the Danubian principalities of Romania under Alexander Ypsilantis, an officer in the Russian army, and in the Peloponnese in southern Greece. The Danubian outbreak had the significance of a general Balkan uprising against Ottoman oppression according to the vision of Rhigas Velestinlis. The rising in the Peloponnese was in keeping with Greek national aspirations and the revival of Hellenism in its birthplace.

Whereas the campaigning in Romania failed dismally and Ypsilantis spent the rest of his life in an Austrian prison, the war in the Peloponnese and its neighbouring islands with a strong commercial tradition was crowned with success. In the battle of Dervenakia in 1822 the commander of the Greek forces, Theodoros Kolokotronis, destroyed an Ottoman army of 30,000 men.

An important factor in the Greek victories of the first two years of the War of Independence was the role of the fleet in the Aegean commanded by Admiral Andreas Miaoulis, of the island of Hydra, who managed to prevent reinforcements reaching the Ottoman garrisons of the Peloponnese by sea. The rough terrain of the hinterland gave the Greek irregulars, using their guerrilla tactics, a clear advantage. However, once the first Greek governments were established and constitutions drawn up, inspired by the model of the French Revolution, a civil war broke out between different localities and factions. Thus the warlords of central Greece joined forces with the islanders against the notables of the Peloponnese.

Civil strife among the Greeks allowed the Ottomans to invite the Egyptian forces under Ibrahim Pasha to quell the rebellion. The naval battle of Navarino in October 1827 between a joint English, Russian and French squadron and an Ottoman-Egyptian force ended with the destruction of the latter. In the spring of the following year Russia declared war on the Porte and marched its forces against Constantinople. The treaty of Adrianople (1829) obliged the Sultan to recognise the autonomy of Greece which, thanks to British-Russian antagonism, was transformed into independence with the London Protocol of 3 February 1830. Within the limited borders of the new state lived only 800,000 Greeks out of an estimated total of 4 million under Ottoman rule. The first President of the independent Greek state was Count Ioannis Kapodistrias, who had formerly been Foreign Minister to the Russian Tsar.

Power and legitimacy, the two major determinants for the acceptance of the rulers by the ruled, were never assumed or exercised by any one party or institution. The *Filiki Etairia* (lit. 'association of friends') was represented as the supreme 'authority', and its nationwide prestige, strengthened by the links the association's agents had forged with powerful and influential men, made it a potential source of power and legitimacy. In contrast to the local power-brokers, who had exercised their authority in the name of the foreign ruler, the association had not been tarnished by any collaboration with the enemy. However, what the local élites, captains and notables lacked in credibility they more than compensated for in real power. The diaspora Greeks, a third source of authority and legitimacy, appeared to exert an influence far greater than their numbers or actual power would have suggesed.

Following the massacre of Turkish officials in the Morea, insecurity of life and property forced local notables to form the initial nuclei of a revolutionary authority: 'Danger alone was guide, leader and rescuer. Saving the people was [our] sole concern,' wrote a Moreot notable.[1] Insecurity and the need to establish a 'regular system' for the necessary contacts with the enemy produced, according to a similar source,[2] the first nuclei of the new government, the 'Ephors' of the first, more or less ephemeral camps. Such was the one set up by the armed company of Karytaena under its chief Kanellos Deliyannis and its captain Theodoros Kolokotronis. In this, as in most such cases, established local authority, as well as concern for the safety of one's 'own' men, strengthened any pre-existing bonds. Kontakis, the local magnate of Hagios Petros and a member of the Etairia, lost no time after the outbreak of hostilities in appointing his own men to command the armed band of his district and in taking over its regular provisioning. At Chrysovitsi the entire *genos* of Karytaena— in this case Deliyannis, his brothers and other lesser notables of the area—'voluntarily' appointed Kolokotronis as 'commander-in-chief and head' of the district's armed men. Deliyannis considered it his prerogative and duty to send military 'diplomas' to members of his family and other relatives, 'according to each one's influence and esteem among our countrymen'. 'None of us chiefs of the districts', he recalled later, 'was prepared to place himself under a chief who

[1] Anagnostis Kontakis, *Apomnimonevmata* (Memoirs), ed. by E.G. Protopsaltis, Athens, 1957, p. 33.
[2] Ambrosios Frantzis, *Epitomi tis historias tis anagenitheisis Hellados* (Short history of regenerated Greece), Athens, 1975 (reissue of Athens 1839 edn), vol. I, p. 424.

lacked an armed following of his own. ... None of us could impose himself on the rest. Everyone was therefore independent of everyone else, since everyone had his own armed men, who had joined the struggle from the beginning. The chief provided them with ammunition, shoes and rations, gave grain for the upkeep of their families and money to those in need.'[3] Before abandoning his hiding-place in Mani and placing himself under his old patron Deliyannis, Kolokotronis sought the assistance of another Moreot notable, Papatsonis, who gave them not only gold but one of his own stallions as well.

'Ephors', '*syncletoi*' (senates), '*cancellariae*' (chancelleries) and '*dieuthynteria*' (directorates) were all extensions of existing structures of local power and authority, now given fashionable new names. They were represented and accepted as the legitimate political organs of the rebels until the time when they would be placed under the Kaltetzae Senate initially and the Peloponnesian Senate afterwards, as well as the Areios Pagos and the Senate of western continental Greece in eastern and west-central Greece respectively. However they were not superseded by any of these upper regional assemblies of notables, and continued to function not only as provisioning agencies but as constituent bodies, always watchful of the special interests they were called on to protect and promote. The seven senators of the Peloponnesian 'System' (Senate) were empowered to manage affairs for the benefit of both private individuals and the common good; to deal with disputes and all issues concerning order and public harmony; to conduct 'our sacred struggle in the way God Almighty directs them and for this purpose consider useful; and to assume all powers, without anyone disobeying their commands or expressing a contrary opinion'.[4] This happened in spite—or because—of the nature of the Senate: it was the 'Assembly of the entire *demos* [people] of the Peloponnesian districts'. The seven-member Senate was essentially a directorate of the Peloponnesian notables and prelates, who had convened with the 'written consent of their districts'. 'Such confidence and such absolute submission to authority show clearly', according to a contemporary observer, 'the kind of devotion the people felt they owed to higher authority.'[5] A

[3]Kanellos Deliyannis, *Apomnimonevmata* (Memoirs), Athens 1957: vol. I, p. 141; vol. II, p. 16; vol. III, p. 265.

[4]*Archeia tis Ellinikis Paligenessias* (Archives of Hellenic Regeneration), vol. I, p. 441; Deliyannis, *Memoirs,* vol. I, p. 223; Palaion Patron Germanos, *Apomnimonevmata peri tis Epanastaseos tis Hellados, 1820–1823* (Memoirs of the Revolution of Greece, 1820–1823), Athens 1837, pp. 42–3.

[5]Philimon, *Greek Revolution*, vol. III, 294.

more careful and less credulous observer would have been able to see that the surrender of all authority to the Senate was not only the result of man's habitual submission to those holding the reins of power, but the expected outcome of the power and influence the senators exercised in their capacity as local notables.

These local and regional 'systems' were neither democratic nor representative in the modern sense, as opponents of the centralised state would like foreign observers to believe. They were representative only in the sense that they stood for well-defined and entrenched local interests, ensuring a balance of power that was not democratic. The emerging centralised state broke them to the extent that those whose interests they represented were gradually divested of the traditional authority they had exercised before. In this sense the new state proved irresistible but, as will be seen later, even as this centralised state was taking over the authority exercised by the '*demogerontes*', ephors, senators and the like, it was being taken over itself by the very forces against which it was fighting. Convinced oligarchs, jealous of the authority, influence and prerogatives they traditionally exercised as local archons and power-brokers, the men of the Greek *ancien régime* were essentially co-opted into the new state system and, most ironically, triumphed over it after 1843, when representative and democratic institutions had been established.

In the senate the local notables were 'representative' in the same sense as they had been in the years of Ottoman rule, i.e. as middlemen operating between the rulers and their subjects. The thirty-seven notables, so invested, were both lay and ecclesiastical, and no less 'legitimate' than the representatives of the same districts to the successive national assemblies; in most cases they were the same people. To Demetrios Ypsilantis's question 'whether the convened patriots in Zarakova had been freely elected by the people and whether they carried their papers of representation'. Palaion Patron Germanos replied that 'such objection is meaningless, as the archons have no difficulty acquiring such papers whenever they wish.'[6]

Those members of the 'Association of Friends' who were banking on Ypsilantis becoming the true representative of the 'Supreme Authority', as well as the Moreot captains, questioned the legitimacy of the Kaltetzae 'system' and did all they could to move the centre of gravity away from this stronghold to a new institution, less 'aristocratic' and more 'democratic', as they maintained. This was the first serious

[6]Deliyannis, *op. cit.*, vol. I, p. 225; Frantzis, *op. cit.*, vol. IV, pp. 90 ff.

conflict between two groups of men representing different interests, but each putting forward exclusive claims to legitimacy. At Vervena first and at Zarakova later the two parties defended their positions with a ferocity that surprised foreign observers, and despite efforts to make them overcome their differences and some minor concessions each made to the other, they remained rigid and unreconciled. The dispute concerned mainly the powers of the two branches of the new government : the legislative and the executive. While Ypsilantis and the captains favoured a strong executive and a weak legislature, the local notables preferred the opposite for obvious reasons and accused their opponents of wanting to establish a new tyranny while they paid lip-service to democracy.[7]

The proposed ways of electing representatives lay at the heart of the dispute. Hypsilantis and his followers, as well as the captains, favoured the election of five ephors 'from the more prestigious and prudent people' of each district, convened for that purpose in the district's principal town. The ephors in their turn would elect from among them the 'ablest' to represent the district in the assembly. The other four would remain in the district to look after recruitment of the district's armed units and the logistics of those units. The representatives of the districts would be 'confirmed' by the 'Plenipotentiary', i.e. Ypsilantis, who would be president both of the assembly and of the council of ministers. As president of the assembly, the 'Plenipotentiary' would also control the judiciary, since the assembly was also the highest court (*Kriterion*) of the land.[8]

The notables would have 'the people of each district' elect their 'ablest' members and provide them with the necessary credentials. They in turn would elect the 'general ephors', six in each district, who would look after local affairs and elect from among their number the 'ablest' to represent the district to the assembly. These representatives, one from each of the twenty-four districts of the Morea, headed by the archon of Mani, Petros Mavromichalis, would meet 'His Highness Prince Ypsilantis' and 'decide in common, by a vote, to manage political and military affairs in such a way that neither the Senate acts without the Prince's approval, nor the Prince without the Senate's approval.' The local notables were prepared to let Ypsilantis assume the presidency of the assembly and even have a double vote, but were determined

---

[7]Philimon, *Greek Revolution*, vol. IV, p. 196.
[8]*Ibid.*, vol. IV, pp. 82–93, 192–8.

that all senators should have one vote each and that decisions would be taken by majority vote.[9]

By limiting the electorate of the ephors to the more 'prestigious' men of the districts, Ypsilantis and the captains aimed to curb the influence of the notables—who, in turn, naturally wished to preserve their political strength intact by insisting on the democratic principle of universal suffrage, because they knew that they would have no difficulty in securing their people's 'consent'. The 'democrats' thus proposed 'aristocratic' procedures and principles. Ypsilantis's assembly was essentially a royal chamber, while that of the local notables was closer to a parliament. Ypsilantis aimed first to concentrate as much power as possible in his own hands in order to be able to proceed with the war unhindered by squabbles among the notables, and secondly to curb the power and influence of the latter, whom he and his supporters identified with the foreign ruler they were fighting to overthrow. The notables naturally wished to preserve their power and influence, and were prepared to accept Ypsilantis only as first among equals. Absent from this confrontation was a third approach to the organisation of the national government—that of men who had brought 'European' ideas to the embattled land, but whose influence was not yet felt. This set included Phanariots such as Alexandros Mavrocordatos and Theodoros Negris; the Heptanesian liberal Ioannis Theotokis; learned men such as Konstantinos Polychroniadis, Gregorios Konstantas, Anthimos Gazis and Ioannis Kolettis; and Philhellenes like Vicente Gallina, who no doubt hoped that in the struggle between the local notables and prelates on one side and Ypsilantis and the captains on the other, there would be no winner. Two more political groups, the archons of the islands and the captains of continental Greece, were also absent. The confrontation was essentially a Moreot one, which appeared to subside in the context of the First National Assembly. However, it created political foundations for the first parties to be formed. It also introduced into the political debate terms like 'democrats' and 'oligarchs' that did not always fit the methods and objectives of those to whom they were applied.

Nevertheless, before clashing over the organisation and control of revolutionary authority, both sides appeared to agree on the need for co-operation. Before forcing the hands of the local notables by

[9] *Ibid.*, vol. IV, pp. 82–3; Germanos, *op. cit.*, pp. 50–2; Frantzis, *op. cit.*, vol. I, pp. 427–8, and vol. II, p. 253; Deliyannis, *op. cit.*, vol. I, pp. 239–40; Photakos, *Apomnimonevmata peri tis Hellenikis Epanastaseos* (Memoirs of the Greek Revolution), Athens, 1858, p. 83.

precipitating events in the Morea, agents of the Association of Friends such as Gregorios Dikaios recognised the notables as the country's natural leaders and expected them to play a leading role in the revolution. This was at least the impression created by the appointment of three ecclesiastical and eight lay notables by the 'Authority' (Ypsilantis) as 'General Commissioners', i.e. ephors responsible for all matters, especially finance. Writing to these men at the time, Dikaios said that the 'Authority' counted on them to set up the new government. He even suggested that they should recommend a role for themselves in the new regime, securing for the 'System of the Notables' more authority over the 'common people' than had been granted to them under the old regime. 'The nation', he warned, 'though now in a position to arrange matters differently and decide everything by decree, does not wish to commit such an injustice to you.'[10]

The notables showed great respect for Ypsilantis when he first came to the Morea before news of the collapse of the revolution in the Principalities reached southern Greece, and was received as the '*hegemon*'. On the Island of Hydra, where he first landed, no one thought of asking him 'what were his social or military credentials, or whether he had any instructions and responsibilities'. According to a reliable observer, everyone hailed him as 'ethnarch' (leader of the nation)'.[11] Everyone's attention was directed to a huge metal trunk, which had to be carried by several men and which everyone took for the Prince's treasure box: 'What a fortune!', they were heard to say, reckoning that the trunk contained a 'Russian grant' to the rebels.[12] The inhabitants of the Moreot town of Stemnitsa called him their '*authentis*' (ruler) while the men besieging Tripolitsa addressed him as '*kyrios pantocrator*' (lord almighty).[13]

This initial recognition of Ypsilantis as the nation's leader quickly receded and turned into suspicion and hostility as soon as people's hopes for Russian assistance were dashed and the unfortunate end to his brother's project in the Principalities became known in southern Greece. Suspicion and hostility increased when the 'Association' provoked the hostility of monarchical Europe, which identified it with the Italian Carbonari, and the exasperation of all Greeks in Western Europe and in Greece proper who counted on West European support

---

[10]Philimon, *Greek Revolution,* vol. IV, pp. 412–14.

[11]*Ibid.,* vol. IV, pp. 414–15.

[12]*Ibid.,* vol. IV, pp. 459–62.

[13]*Ibid.,* vol. III, p. 397, vol. IV, pp. 92–3 and *Society of Friends,* pp. 338–44, 346, 351–3.

for the Revolution. More Greeks turned their back on Ypsilantis when it became apparent that 'Association' members such as Anagnostaras and Anagnostopoulos, who inspired no confidence in the local notables, were able to influence the Prince's decisions. Any value the prince had in the eyes of the notables disappeared when the latter realised that the legitimacy he and the Association offered was much more questionable and fragile than that which they themselves represented. Besides, many of them no doubt thought then that even if Hypsilantis had indeed sacrificed a secure career in the Russian army, they were staking no less themselves and certainly much more than most members of the Association who had no fortunes to lose.

The Senate and the notables continued to exercise real authority, especially after the capture of Tripolitsa in September which strengthened their hand. Their position was further strengthened in October with the addition of two Hydriot notables to the Senate. The National Assembly that was convened in late 1821 turned the Senate into an administrative branch of the central government, though without undermining its position in the Morea; indeed, that position became unassailable when its quarrel with Kolokotronis was terminated as notables and captains established 'a brotherly bond of all those who matter in the country'.[14] The Senate refused to move out of Tripolitsa, as it explained in a letter to the Minister of the Interior, because, among other reasons that kept it in the city, 'the disrespectful attitude of the people required the presence of the government.'[15]

Those who put pressure on the Senate to move out of its power-base were the ministers of the central government, who were desperately trying to give their offices some real authority and see that their orders were carried out. Above all, they strove to collect revenue, which proved extremely difficult. In March 1822 the Senate refused to relinquish national revenues to the central government, maintaining that they were required for its own needs. According to a contemporary source, the Senate did not send revenues to the national government, because the notables had little confidence in the 'newcomers' who were without experience in managing affairs of state.[16] Yet for all their inexperience the newcomers were bent on putting the recalcitrant Peloponnesian Senate out of service, and eventually succeeded in doing so: in 1823 the Second National Assembly finally abolished it along with the other two regional assemblies, the Areios

[14]*Archeia*, vol. I, pp. 460–1. See also Photakos, *op. cit.*, pp. 169, 175–6.
[15]*Ibid.*, p. 449.
[16]Frantzis, *op. cit.*, p. 266.

Pagos and the Senate of western mainland Greece. These had been the work of two men, Alexandros Mavrocordatos and Theodoros Negris. The establishment of revolutionary authority proved a most difficult undertaking in mainland Greece, where the captains were the paramount social force and the people were most exposed to Ottoman attacks from the north. Absent from the region were the established, or potential, nuclei of power and the political relationships that would have allowed the notables in the Morea and the islands to set up a government that both pursued the war of independence and was acceptable to the people. Moreover, proximity to the enemy's power bases vitiated all efforts to bring the captains and their armed followers under central control. It was not until November 1821 that Mavrocordatos, having won the tacit support of the local captains, finally managed to gather at Missolonghi a number of notables of western mainland Greece to elect the region's Senate. What Mavrocordatos had in mind was a regional administrative arm of the central government. The senators, who were picked by the captains to watch over their interests, became easy prey to an astute politician like Mavrocordatos who played one captain off against the other and was thus able to win some respect for the central government. Gradually he and his associates, particularly Nikolaos Louriotis and Georgios Praïdis, succeeded in adding to the initial number of representatives, thus securing the balances necessary to implement central government measures.[17]

However, under a veneer of law and order old conflicts and passions still raged. All that could be hoped by Praïdis, Mavrocordatos's *locum tenens*, and Louriotis, the Senate's secretary, was to avoid open civil strife. They often behaved as if they considered themselves to be the chosen carriers of Western civilisation among savages. When 'the people, too, expressed the wish to take part in the election' and proposed 'a man uncouth, inexperienced and insolent', according to Praïdis, he openly questioned the wisdom of the choice by the captains and notables, and arranged a repeat performance at Aitolikon for their benefit, in which the notables and those of the second class were invited to elect a senator. Predictably the one who had been elected by the archons of the region was re-elected.[18]

The neighbouring district of Valtos presented Praïdis with a dif-

<hr/>

[17]*Mavrocordatos Archive*, vol. I, pp. 124–5, 127–9, 210–12 and vol. II, pp. 43, 66ff.
[18]*Ibid.*, vol. II, pp. 24–6,28, 30.

ferent problem: there were two candidates for one seat in the Senate, each backed by one of the two most powerful military bosses of the region, Georgios Varnakiotis of Kseromeron and Andreas Iskos of Valtos. Praïdis decided that there should be two representatives for the Valtos district, but Mavrocordatos intervened and imposed a single representative, the one backed by Iskos. 'Everywhere discord, disorder and insubordination', was the complaint in April 1822 of Praïdis and two associated senators, Ioannis Trikoupis and Mitsos Frangoulis, the latter being the candidate of the local notables for Aitolikon.[19]

One of the main obstacles preventing the exercise of central government in the region was the system of armatoliks, which was abolished in February 1822 at a special meeting of captains, notables and senators, not without certain concessions by the government. Those present at this solemn but secret meeting accepted the following text: 'Having considered the ignorance of the people in these parts, the depravity of the armed men, and the dangers facing the homeland if no stable government is established, we deem it proper and decide that the aforementioned gentlemen [Georgios Varnakiotis and Andreas Iskos] and members of their families should be able, whenever they wish, to give up the military profession and assume civil offices in the Senate or anywhere else, according to their abilities.'[20] Varnakiotis was in fact named a member of the Senate without his giving up the military profession—this was done to prevent such a powerful captain from openly going over to the Ottomans. 'These people', wrote Varnakiotis about himself and four other captains of the region, 'had a domain of their own, armed bands, and able and honest men, and now that the armatoliks have been abolished, they resent being turned into soldiers with a [monthly] salary of twenty piastres.'[21]

In eastern mainland Greece there were even more suitors than in the western part. Ypsilantis had sent one of his deputies to place the region under his authority, but it was one of Mavrocordatos's men, Theodoros Negris, who managed to secure himself a place in the local political machine. Areios Pagos, which was established by the Salona Assembly in November 1821, was the work of Negris, who provided it with the most advanced and all-embracing constitution in use at the time in Greece. The constitution provided for a

---

[19] *Ibid.*, vol. I, pp. 190–1.
[20] *Ibid.*, pp. 126–7.
[21] *Ibid.*, pp. 248–9.

parliamentary system, which made a clear distinction between the three branches of government. Besides Negris, two other important learned men became associated with Areios Pagos: Gregorios Konstantas and Ioannis Eirenaios. However, this body too did not function or fare much better than the other two, despite its advanced constitution. The people's inexperience of self-government and the local interests opposing its operation do not by themselves explain the serious difficulties that Areios Pagos faced in securing authority for the central government. The Senate, it seems, was undermined by the ministers in the government as much as by local opponents.[22]

One such formidable opponent was Odysseus Androutsos who, like Varnakiotis in the west, felt that he was losing a 'dominion' to newcomers. The capture and occupation of the Acropolis of Athens favoured his designs for a dominant position in eastern mainland Greece. He had his lieutenant Ioannis Gouras, who later worked against him, hold the famous stronghold, while the notables of the region elected him commander-in-chief of all its armies and presented him with a fine sword. In a 'free election' Androutsos, this archon of Athens who was behaving like the pasha he had overthrown, had his friends 'elected' to the city council.[23]

Such arbitrary conduct was not only tolerated and condoned: it was widely practised and considered almost as a necessary and unavoidable evil. Progressives no less than conservatives resorted to such conduct whenever they despaired of the people ever growing out of their servile habits. With few exceptions, references to the basic features of a suitable regime for the country were deeply pessimistic. It would be better if 'subversive' and 'demagogic' theories associated with the French Revolution and particularly with its radical phase were never allowed to reach the people, let alone influence statecraft. Most wished to keep such 'subversive' ideas out for one additional reason: to avoid giving the impression to monarchical Europe that the Greeks were under the influence of Jacobin radicals. However, most observers were convinced that there was no danger of radicalism taking root in Greece. 'But I too am a royalist', Koraes wrote in 1821, 'and I was very glad when the present royal family of the Bourbons returned. I too fought—

[22]Dionysios Sourmelis, *Historia ton Athinon* (History of Athens), Athens 1853, pp. 16, 33–35; *Mavrokordatos Archive*, vol. I, p. 241; *Archeia*, vol. I, pp. 486, 488–9, 492; *Ephimeris ton Athinon*, Nov.-Dec. 1824, where information on the subject, and 10 Jan. 1825, obituary of Negris by Gregorios Konstantas.

[23]Sourmelis, *op. cit.*, pp. 45–6, 49–53.

with all my strength and out of conviction—dangerous theories which threaten orderly society. [...] 'Fortunately', he went on, 'the cause of the Greeks is not the same as that of the French Revolution.'[24] The First National Assembly felt the need to declare, at the end of its deliberations in January 1822, that the war of the Greeks had nothing to do with 'demagogic and subversive principles'.[25] Five years later the Third National Assembly issued a similar declaration: 'This people did not take up arms to base its existence on demagogic foundations, which monarchical Europe considered unacceptable.'[26] In 1830, soon after the July Revolution in France and as liberty was dawning in Greece, Koraes wrote of the mounting opposition to Kapodistrias : 'Our modern Greeks who are eager to mow down the country's weeds must do that in the company of Franco-Greek mowers, so that the clearing is done without subversion, in the peaceful and bloodless manner that is expected of Christians'[27] .

The Greek rebels were not Carbonari, and they were careful that their pronouncements and deeds should not be open to such an interpretation. 'The kings will call us Carbonari, disorderly and mutinous,' Kolokotronis is said to have told the rabble at the Vervena camp, when Ypsilantis's men incited the soldiers to move against the local notables in the summer of 1821.[28] Emmanouil Xanthos, a founding member of the 'Association', was attacked by another member, the merchant Ioannis Melas, for mingling with 'demagogues' trying to 'turn Greece upside down', and maintained that the 'Association' could not possibly be associated with the 'party of the Carbonari'.[29] Writing from Venice in 1823 about rumours that certain persons in Greece were conspiring to entrust the government of the country to Jerome Bonaparte, Dionysios Romas recommended 'eradicating from Greece too the weed of ruin, irreverence and disorder, which aims at overthrowing thrones, holy altars and all legitimate authority in the world'.[30] As might have been expected, royal candidates for the throne of Greece, who were opposed to the Bonapartes, were considered a kind of security against Carbonarism. 'As soon as you establish a monarchical

---

[24]Koraes, *War Bugle*, p. 31.

[25]*Archives of Greek Regeneration*, vol. III, p. 40.

[26]*Geniki Ephemeris*, 21 April 1826. See also Speliades, *op. cit.*, vol. II, p. 555.

[27]Koraes, *Dialogue of two Greeks*, p. 35.

[28]Philimon, *Greek Revolution*, vol. IV, pp. 90, 522.

[29]*Romas Archive*, vol. I, p. 202.

[30]*Ibid.*, vol. I, p. 197.

regime and select a monarch', a supporter of the candidacy of the Duc de Nemours wrote in 1826 from Orléans, 'the slander campaign of your enemies, who are presenting you to the Holy Alliance as Jacobins and Carbonari, will come to an end.'[31]

The supporters of 'prudent' liberty gave the necessary assurances to all those who were afraid that the prolonged 'democratic' form of the regime in Greece night become a permanent system. 'The novel system of liberty', the author of 'Patristic Instruction' had written before the Greek Revolution, 'is nothing but confusion and subversion of all good governance, a road leading to disaster, the latest snare the devil is using to mislead the Orthodox Christians.'[32] For different reasons but using similar terms, various lay leaders were also now condemning the 'novel' system. 'Our constitution is temporary', Mavrocordatos assured one of Metternich's emissaries in 1824.[33] Suggestions to abolish the 'democratic system' were made from many quarters, as will be seen elsewhere. Even terms like 'Areios Pagos', according to Polychroniades, were considered unsuitable because they might present the Greeks to the mighty of Europe as 'friends of untempered democracy'.[34] Speliades, in the aftermath of the destruction caused by civil strife and the invading army of Ibrahim, expressed in 1825 the thought that 'the entire nation realises the need to abolish the democratic system, with which it cannot be governed and which will lead it to certain ruin.'[35] The National Assembly even considered convening a special assembly for the purpose of deciding, along with the Executive, to abolish the 'democratic system' and invite a European prince to ascend the throne.

In this climate obvious suspects like 'Association' agents and unlikely ones such as the captains were all thought to be scheming Jacobins and Carbonari. 'Rascally tricks and Masonic dealings' were all that the former stood for, according to the magnate of Hagios Petros, Yannoulis Kouremenos.[36] The local notables saw that all their old fears and suspicions about the intentions of the 'Association' were now shared

---

[31]*Ibid.,* vol. I, pp. 117.

[32]Anthimos, Patriarch of Jerusalem, *Didaskalia Patriki* (Paternal institution), Constantinople, 1798, reissued by Koraes with his response *Adelphiki Didaskalia* (Brotherly instruction), Rome, 1798, p. 20.

[33]*Mavrocordatos Archive,* vol. IV, p. 610.

[34]*Ibid.,* vol. I, pp. 130–7, vol. IV, p. 661.

[35]Speliades, *op. cit.,* vol. II, p. 349.

[36]Kontakis, *op. cit.,* p. 29.

by other sections of the population, so they vented their resentment against the newcomers, whom they had never held in great esteem anyway. If they associated with these 'scheming rascals', they did so only in order to convince simple folk that the newcomers represented a great power. Deliyannis says that he had once told Dikaios: 'We expect nothing from you—you who do not even own a single tree from which you can be hung. We do not expect you to lead us, who have large families, wealth, extensive lands and all God's blessings, and hesitate to expose the country, our families and relatives to danger.'[37] Soteris Charalampis, another Moreot magnate, had told his peers at the Vostitsa Assembly shortly before the outbreak of the Revolution, and in an effort to boost the unwillingness of notables to follow Dikaios's advice and break relations with the Ottomans: 'Well, let us assume that we kill the Turks; whom shall we then hand power to, whom shall we recognise as our head? As soon as the *raya* take arms they will no longer obey and respect us, and we shall fall into the hands of that man Nikitas, Gregorios's brother, who just a while ago could not hold the fork in his hand and eat.'[38] Gregorios Dikaios and his brother Nikitas, Kolokotronis and his relatives, the Petmezas clan of Kalavryta, the Koumaniotes of Patras and all the other former klephts, all 'adventurers' and 'cut-throats', people without 'hope' or land to stand on, 'roving' and 'rootless' like Kolias Plapoutas and his sons—all these had nothing to lose and everything to gain from a revolution.[39]

They and the *raya* were not to be trusted with authority, because they lacked the qualifications of the 'active' citizen. 'The people', thought Deliyannis, 'never really contemplated freedom, nor do they know what patriotism is ... only the more distinguished and intelligent, who have property, riches and other advantages, exercise influence and move the common people, and can become leaders of men.' And who had contributed more to the struggle—'the so-called Klephts, who have been away in exile for many years? those who carry their homes with them, the ones who came to Greece from abroad and who lack a homeland, the adventurers and the desperate? or the notables and prelates of the Peloponnese, and then the Spetsiots, the Psarians and the Hydriots?'[40] Ypsilantis and perhaps most of his associates

---

[37]Deliyannis, *op. cit.*, vol. I, pp. 99, 112.

[38]Photakos, *Vios tou Papa Flessa* (Life of Papaflessas), Tripolis, 1868, p. 20.

[39]Photakos, *Memoirs*, pp. 4–5; *Romas Archive*, vol. II, p. 599; Deliyannis, *op. cit.*, vol. I, pp. 112, 177; *Mavrocordatos Archive*, vol. IV, p. 243.

[40]Deliyannis, *op. cit.*, vol. I, pp. 99, 173.

thought no better of the common people. He believed that to arm the peasants was unwise if one wanted to avoid the confusion and damage caused by men inexperienced in the use of arms.[41] The 'mob', the 'undisciplined mass', those who thronged to Tripotama of Elis in 1825 to prostrate themselves before the demagogue priest from Ithaca, Father Papoulakis, who exhorted them to discard their arms as well as the costly clothes and jewellery taken from the Turks;[42] the 'Barbatsia', the peasants who ran away when faced with danger;[43] the illiterate, landless and uncouth peasants who looked to Russia not for enlightenment or liberty, according to Koraes, but to intervene with the Sultan and secure for them the right to build churches and the possibility to visit the church of Hagia Sophia in Constantinople one day;[44] the 'simple folk', whom the sudden eclipse of Turkish authority caused to gape at each other in disbelief that they had 'won the arms and the glory of their former masters';[45] the adventurers and opportunists, the riff-raff (*skylologion*) surrounding Kapodistrias[46]— all these, according to conservatives, needed a 'tempered' liberty and a 'prudent' constitution.

Only the nation's 'natural' leaders—the politically 'mature', the existing notables—could establish and maintain such a regime, with the assistance of the enlightened brothers who drew their wisdom not from the prophecies of Agathangelos but from the press of the day.[47] The local notables in the Peloponnese and the captains in mainland Greece had no doubt dragged their feet before deciding to take the road of rebellion; but when they finally took that road and broke with the Ottoman masters, they were unwilling to share power and responsibility with any other group. In contrast to the Greeks who had arrived from abroad, the notables and the captains were obliged to stay in the country to shield the people from the wrath of the Ottomans in case the Revolution collapsed or was suppressed. Unlike those who had come from abroad, the local leaders could not afford

---

[41]Philimon, *Society of Friends*, p. 352.

[42]Frantzis, *op. cit.*, vol. II, pp. 464–5, 468–9; Deliyannis, *op. cit.*, vol. III, p. 95.

[43]*Mavrocordatos Archive*, vol. IV, pp. 398, 402.

[44]Deliyannis, *op. cit.*, vol. III, pp. 187, 194–5; Koraes, *Ti prepei na kamosin oi Graekoi eis tas parousas peristaseis? Dialogos dyo Graekon* ... (What must the Greeks do in the present circumstances? Dialogue of two Greeks ...), Venice, 1805, p. 22.

[45]Photakos, *Memoirs*, p. 29; Kasomoulis, *op. cit.*, vol. I, p. 173; *Romas Archive*, vol. I, pp. 277–278; *Apollon*, 2 May and 3 July 1831.

[46]Koraes, *Dialogue (1831)*, p. 52.

[47]Philimon, *Society of Friends*, p. 217.

to see the Revolution led astray by irresponsible elements. 'Have you gone mad', Iskos asked those who incited the peasants to take arms against the Ottomans, 'going about inciting everyone to come out? Is that the way to win freedom?'[48] War was the preserve of those trained to fight; so was governing and statecraft. The people knew this better than eager newcomers; the armed men of Karytaena waited for the '*Gerontopoula*' (the sons of the '*Geron*', the old man, i.e. Deliyannis) formally to start the Revolution, despite Plapoutas's exhortations not to wait for them.[49]

Koraes, who never ran out of wisdom drawn from the Bible when raising various issues about government with his friends in Greece, knew that its application to human commonwealths on earth had to be tempered by common sense: 'When I praise the equality that religion commands, do not think for a moment that I mean equality for all, but only equality before the law, because the former would lead to anarchy. Commonwealths founded on the rule of law consist of both rulers and ruled, of those who provide the finances for meeting the needs of the polity and those who manage these finances.'[50] 'Prudent' or 'tempered' liberty, 'liberty limited by law', 'the freedom of each citizen to do what the laws do not prohibit, i.e. to do not what he wants but what he wanted when he first united with the other citizens in a commonwealth', the limited freedom that each citizen 'accepted' on joining the commonwealth, and similar terms drawn form the social contract theories of Hobbes, Locke and Rousseau, as well as liberty in the sense 'of living according to the laws of God and men', as religion commanded—one often comes across these expressions in the writings of the men who felt compelled to record their opinion about a regime fit for the modern Greeks. 'Freedom', wrote the *Hellenika Chronika* in 1825, 'is not what the ignorant and the illiterate believe, i.e. to do whatever one wishes or desires, but what one must, i.e. what is in agreement with the law and the common interest.' The Greeks needed such equality as was 'possible and useful', they needed 'freedom' that was 'regulated, prudent and tempered'.[51]

Other references at this time to ways and means of governance pointed in the same direction. Polychroniades recommended in 1822

[48]Kasomoulis, *op. cit.*, vol. I, p. 397.
[49]Frantzis, *op. cit.*, vol. II, pp. 152–3.
[50]Koraes, *Correspondence*, vol. IV, p. 329.
[51]Koraes, *Adelphiki Didaskalia*, pp. 18–19, 40, 53; *Hellenika Chronika*, 22 Nov. 1824, 7 Feb. and 1 Apr. 1825.

'the old system of the notables and prelates', as a model for the new constitution of the country. The notables and prelates 'would form the highest chamber and, assisted by committees of eminent men, would administer all political, legal and religious affairs. This is the system our brothers are accustomed to, and it is one that can develop into a representative system, when the notables are elected by the nation (*genos*). For the time being, concentrate on getting to know the old notables and see that, in your search for modern and perfect systems, you do not end up with nothing at all.'[52] Mavrocordatos recommended as much to Negris, when the latter set his mind on devising an electoral law as part of the new constitution in 1822. Such recommendations, which came from almost all sides, no doubt reflected ideas shared by most of those involved in setting up a government for the new Greek state. In the light of this opinion and contrary to what subsequent writers might lead one to believe, recommendations for a system less dependent on local élites came from convinced adherents of the modern centralised state such as Kapodistrias, who had no illusions about the prospects of a representative system in a country in which the local notables, captains and prelates wielded so much power. However, his efforts came to nothing because of strong opposition from the notables, and because the right to vote was reserved to autochthonous Greeks who possessed land. The newspaper *Apollon*, which reflected the opinion of Hydriot notables, wrote in 1831 that 'although all citizens wished to be active, not everyone could be an active citizen', in the sense that only some possessed the necessary qualifications for that status.[53] Ten years of revolution and a lively debate had obviously not been enough for most people to acquire these qualifications, both material and intellectual. Very few, according to another observer of this period, had reached 'political maturity'.[54] In 1832 a 'most instructive and useful' tract was published. It drew heavily on contemporary conservative opinion stressing the need for societies to depend for their governance on those possessing the necessary qualifications and followed Napoleon's dictum: 'Everything for the people, nothing by the people'.[55]

Property, especially land—both as an inalienable right and as a

[52]*Mavrocordatos Archive*, vol. I, p. 95.

[53]*Ibid.*, vol. II, pp. 283–4; *Archeia*, vol. I, pp. 170–1; Deliyannis, *op. cit.*, vol. III, p. 186; *Apollon*, 1 Aug. and 16 Sep. 1831; *Ethniki Ephemeris*, 6 July 1832.

[54]*Ethniki Ephemeris*, 30 Apr. 1832.

[55]*Ibid.*, 9 July 1832.

necessary qualification for public office—occupies a central place in both public pronouncements and private correspondence of the period. This emphasis can perhaps be explained as the natural reaction of a subject people whose property assets had always been insecure and at the mercy of arbitrary government. Imported views on property ownership and its relation to public office were welcome arguments in support of the effort to make property ownership as important and as secure a qualification for holding office as possible. On the other hand, it would be wrong to interpret this emphasis on property ownership as a nascent or resurgent capitalist mentality and drive, which in fact had never been absent from the Greek lands since early modern times, when Greek merchants claimed a share of Levantine commerce. What was novel was the frequent emphasis on property ownership in the context of the debate on the appropriate regime for the modern Greek state. Naturally, if property ownership was used by already propertied groups to strengthen their entrenched position further, it was also used as a means of undermining the power of these groups by increasing the number of those owning property. Kapodistrias's efforts to facilitate the settlement of as many captains of mainland Greece, Thessaly, Epirus and Macedonia as possible by offering them land should be interpreted as a measure intended not only to tame an unruly and dangerous element but also to extend land ownership in Greece.

Thus there was a high degree of consensus among those involved in forging a national government for the fledgling modern Greek state: that it should be a government founded on the social groups that already exercised influence and some authority, dressed up with as many Western principles and institutions as the ruling groups and the condition of the people allowed. Such a government, as Polychroniades put it, was 'in agreement with our morals and habits, familiar to both the rulers and the ruled, and [had] the merit of not being offensive to the foreign enemies of innovations.'[56] It was a 'Moreot system', akin to the 'democratic government' the local notables had secured from the Turks before the Revolution.[57]

However, this consensus was the outcome of a ten-year debate, which often turned into open civil strife. At first many observers were unable to distinguish a clear political programme amid the pronouncements and actions of the rebels. A foreign observer wrote in

[56]Philimon, *Greek Revolution,* vol. IV, pp. 349–50.
[57]Deliyannis, *op. cit.,* vol. I, p. 18; Archive of Georgakis-Gregorakis, p. 102.

November 1821 that they expressed 'no stable opinion about the principles of the regime they want to establish'.[58] Koraes too was unable to discern a clear direction, and did not hide his fear that the Revolution might have 'started prematurely in a nation that lacks the necessary education to realise its true interests'.[59] With the exception of a handful of Greeks and foreigners, who were projecting their own progressive visions on a people whose traditions and experiences could provide no solid basis for their realisation, most Greeks no doubt expected that the war would lead to the establishment of a kingdom. The popular legends, the teachings of the church and the Greeks' knowledge of the outside world, as well as other factors in Greece shaping people's preferences about the kind of regime under which they wished to live, favoured a monarchy. Even the republican Rhigas perhaps echoed these influences when he wrote: 'And there should be one lord for the homeland.'[60] The 'Society', too, it seems had such a lord in mind 'so that the nation would avoid the strife and demagoguery associated with such political changes.' Homer's *koeranos* (lord), 'absolute but virtuous, just and a friend of the nation's freedom and real happiness', seems to have been the model for a ruler—certainly until a national assembly was convened, but afterwards as well.[61] The Turks of Kyparissia once wondered—and their opponents appeared to agree—how the *raya* would be able to wage war without '*kiralides*' (lords, kings);[62] and the Turks besieged in Monemvasia asked in June 1821 that they might surrender the castle to the 'lord of the Greeks' because they did not trust the Maniots.[63] The 'lord' on this occasion was Demetrios Ypsilantis, who had just arrived in the Peloponnese to represent his brother Alexandros as the '*authentis* [ruler] of the land', as Dikaios and Anagnostaras addressed him.[64] The 'Legal Ordinance [*Nomiki Diataxis*] of eastern mainland Greece',

[58] *Engrapha tou Archeiou tou Vatikanou peri tis Hellenikis Epanastasteos* (Papers from the Vatican Archive on the Greek Revolution), ed. by Georgios Zoras, vol. I, Athens, 1979, pp. 158–9, 186–7.

[59] Koraes, *Correspondence*, vol. IV, p. 320.

[60] *Paternal Instruction*, p. 22; *Rhigas Velestinlis Thourios*, in Vranousis, vol. II, p. 728.

[61] Philimon, *Society of Friends*, p. 221.

[62] Frantzis, *op. cit.*, vol, I, pp. 380–1.

[63] Germanos, *op. cit.*, p. 51. See also Frantzis, *op. cit.*, vol. I, p. 424.

[64] Kontakis, *op. cit.*, p. 32; Deliyannis, *op. cit.*, vol. I, p. 243; Frantzis, *op. cit.*, vol. II, p. 253; Philimon, *Society of Friends*, pp. 416–7.

the work of Negris, referred to the 'coming king, whom Greece must request from Christian Europe'.[65]

The need to pursue the war without bickering and with a satisfactory use of the nation's human and material resources made the absence of a commonly accepted leader more keenly felt. As if the lack of careful preparation of the Revolution were not enough, there was also, wrote Petros Kontakis, lord of Hagios Petros, need for 'a leader to take over and direct an undertaking of such magnitude, importance and difficulty'. In 1822 Kolokotronis appeared to prefer a '*governo militare*', and the editor of the *Hellenika Chronika* wrote two years later of the need for a government with 'lordly' (*authentiki*) authority. Another newspaper, the liberal *Ephemeris ton Athenon* of Georgios Psylas, wrote in 1825 of the need for a 'dictator' or a 'dictatorial committee' to save the country, and around the same time Georgios Kountouriotis, President of the Executive, was said to have been 'considering becoming dictator of Greece'. In 1826, finally, Kolokotronis and Andreas Metaxas were thinking of asking Kapodistrias to come to the country as a 'dictator'.[66]

References like these to the need for a king or a dictator abound in the relevant sources, and although mostly the result of despair, they betrayed a growing conviction that the country wanted a strong man, preferably a crowned one, to assume all powers. Kapodistrias's name began appearing in newspapers with a frequency that leaves little doubt that public opinion was showing a preference for a ruler of this type. Kapodistrias was the '*anotatos archon*' ('highest ruler') expected by the 'patriots' of Greece, 'the one chosen by Heaven' who would arrive 'dressed in all his glory and shining bright from the divine grace'; the 'expected Messiah'. No doubt, Kolokotronis had him in mind when he said that the country needed 'a president, a kind of monarch'— an office from which, of course, he did not exclude himself; nor, it seems, did Kountouriotis or Karaïskakis.[67]

---

[65]Andreas Mamoukas, *Ta kata tin Anagennisin tis Hellados* (On the regeneration of Greece), vol. I, Athens 1839, pp. 42ff.; Dragoumis, *op. cit.*, vol. I, p. 31.

[66]Kontakis, *op. cit.*, p. 33; Deliyannis, *op. cit.*, vol. I, p. 224; vol. III, pp. 99–100; Frantzis, *op. cit.*, vol. II, p. 194; *Romas Archive*, vol. I, pp. 206–7, 325; *Hellenika Chronika*, 29 Nov. and 6 Dec. 1824; *Ephemeris ton Athenon*, 12 and 19 Dec. 1825.

[67]*Romas Archive*, vol. I, 425, 502–10, and vol. II, p. 399; *Hellenika Chronika*, 16 Jan. 1826; Kontakis, *op. cit.*, p. 66; Deliyannis, *op. cit.*, vol. III, pp. 53–4, 159, 160; *Archeia, Lazarou kai Georgiou Kountourioti* (Lazaros and Georgios Kountouriotis Archives), vol. VIII, ed. by K. A. Diamantis, Athens, 1967, p. 271.

Writing to Kapodistrias in 1825 after four years of searching for a leader, Ioannis Theotokis, one of the more outspoken liberals of the revolutionary period, said: 'No politician has yet appeared who is qualified and experienced enough to put himself above all the rest and in a sense become the centre of power, to gain the respect and confidence of all good patriots and the more mature citizens who, lacking a centre of power, are useless on these own.'[68] Smyrna's *Le Spectateur Oriental* lamented in 1826 Greece's inability, after all its suffering and sacrifices, to produce a strong man such as revolutions normally produce.[69] George Washington and Simon Bolivar came automatically to mind. Referring to the latter and his contribution to liberty, another newspaper wrote in 1827: 'How the Greeks wish they could have had such a leader! But jealous fate allowed no such man to arise. Wretched Greece! You had great resolve, your first steps to freedom were amazing, and your desperate struggle astonished the world; but you have lacked the soul of the revolution, the man of genius who would lead your steps the right way, safeguard your glory and shore up your freedom !'[70] The convenient explanation for the absence of a man of genius was the centuries-old one—the fear of 'tyranny'.

The concentration of authority, preferably in one man, was favoured by circumstances 'to bring the blessings of law and order to the wretched country'. The rule of 'one man only', of 'one head', of 'one able and virtuous man' to replace all the 'incompetent', 'dishonest' and 'bickering' men exerted an increasing attraction. 'One man in the executive, in the place of the present five, and this man to be named king', was what one of Koraes's friends wrote to him in a letter published in the *Ephemeris ton Athenon* in 1825. 'This principle', he said, 'is in accord with the constitutional institutions of most civilised nations, and will bring deliverance to our brothers who have just come out of tyranny.'[71] The following year Germanos, Kolokotronis, Andreas Zaïmis and Anagnostis Deliyannis proposed the appointment of a committee of distinguished men to 'search for a monarch' in case the candidacy of the Duc de Nemours fell flat. In 1824 a special committee of the Chamber appointed to recommend a policy to

---

[68] *Romas Archive*, vol. I, p. 325.
[69] *Geniki Ephemeris*, 21 July 1826.
[70] *Ibid.*, 12 Oct. 1826.
[71] *Ibid.*, 24 Mar. 1826, 9 Apr. and 21 Dec. 1827. See also Deliyannis, *op. cit.*, vol. III, pp. 36, 126–7, 161.

the revolutionary government of Greece, in view of the expected conference of the great European powers wrote: 'We know from the credentials of the deputies, and from news coming from all over Greece, of the disposition and will of the Greek nation to change its temporary government into a constitutional monarchy, and to elect a worthy man from a European royal family and accept him as a constitutional monarch.'[72]

Other reasons put forward besides those already mentioned were connected with particular interests or served other objectives. Two such arguments were, first, that a king from Europe would secure for Greece recognition, legitimacy, and political and financial support, and secondly, that his presence would serve as a guarantee against the schemes of the '*archons*'. Another argument used by those who saw government performing the role of a guardian for a nation of 'political minors' was the need for a king to reign over a 'tumultuous' nation. Variations of these arguments were advanced throughout the war and not only or even primarily by conservative circles.

The consent and approval of monarchical Restoration Europe was considered a vital element of the legitimacy the revolutionary government was striving to secure for the fledgling state; and monarchy, preferably constitutional but if necessary absolute, was expected to secure for the Greek state that necessary recognition and approval. The European powers, according to Metropolitan Ignatios, considered the 'system' of the Greeks a 'Carbonari movement' and did everything to misrepresent it, and why not 'since Ypsilantis declared from the very beginning that it was such'? The country needed a government 'acceptable, not only to the nation but to the foreign powers as well, since they considered all new systems a threat to the peace of their peoples.'[73] The liberal Theotokis shared the views of the wise prelate: the European powers had to be convinced that the Greek revolution posed no threat to peace, and be requested to approve the king that Greece would receive from Europe, because their approval was necessary for securing Greek liberty.[74] According to Romas, 'a royal prince, related to powerful families and descended from great heroes, can, when elected to the throne of a famous people, attract not only financial support from certain merchants but the political backing

---

[72]*Ephemeris ton Athenon,* 21 Aug. 1825.
[73]*Romas Archive,* vol. II, p. 40; *Archives of Hellenic Regeneration,* vol. II, p. 250.
[74]Philimon, *Greek Revolution,* vol. IV, p. 522. See also *Romas Archive,* vol. I, p. 214 and vol. II, pp. 116–17; 144; *Mavrocordatos Archive,* vol. IV, p. 661.

of most European governments.'[75] The prince in question was the
Duc de Nemours, whose family, according to Mavrocordatos, was
well connected in both Europe and America and more than any other
prince was expected to satisfy the liberals of Europe.[76] He was also
expected to secure 'military' back-up in the form of a frigate, which
his father had promised to send to Greece as well as the 'necessary
assistance', i.e. 'a few million francs'.[77] A declaration of the Third National
Assembly of April 1825 said that the Greeks hoped their actions and
desperate requests had proved to the kings of Christendom that
they had taken up arms 'not to build their existence on demagogic
foundations, which monarchical Europe considered unacceptable'.[78]
In 1825, according to Speliades, 'the entire nation recognised the need
to abolish the democratic system, with which it could not be governed
and which would lead it to certain ruin.'[79]

These references to the issue of governance, all from a period
that ended with Kapodistrias's arrival in Greece, were followed by
similar ones, this time, however, coming mainly from the forces opposed
to his rule. The paper *Apollon* in Hydra, the major mouthpiece of
the opposition, published a series of fiercely provocative articles against
him and his government, calling for the need to expedite the election
of a king for Greece by its European 'protectors'[80]—who, at last heeding
the wishes of all Greeks, should decide 'to deliver them from the
oppressive scourge of arbitrary government'. The paper wrote: 'Happy
the King of Greece' who was going to reign over a 'most malleable
people like the Greeks'.[81]

Following the murder of Kapodistrias and the ensuing civil strife,
the Fifth National Assembly, the obedient instrument of the government,
addressed a 'supplication' to the protecting powers to elect a king
for Greece. The president of the assembly said in a proclamation of
February 1832 that 'the future of Greece would definitely be secured
by the election of the *hegemon*'.[82] The town elders of Karytaena, in
a memorandum the same year, implored him to deliver them from the
prevailing chaos and help a country that had nowhere else to turn to

[75] *Romas Archive,* vol. I, p. 514.
[76] *Ibid.,* vol. I, p. 151.
[77] Speliades, *op. cit.,* vol. II, p. 215.
[78] *Archeia,* vol. II, p. 250.
[79] *Geniki Ephemeris,* 21 Apr. 1826; Speliades, *op. cit.,* vol. II, p. 555.
[80] Speliades, *op. cit.,* vol. II, p. 349.
[81] *Apollon,* 28 Mar. 1831.
[82] *Ibid.,* 8 July 1831.

for support but to his 'royal and fatherly providence'.[83] Identical supplications from many other districts of the Peloponnese were published in the papers of the same period. The inhabitants of the island of Poros wrote over a long list of signatures: 'The community of Poros requests the *hegemon* or his *locum tenens* to make haste and arrive, because it is convinced that the security and happiness of this land depend on his arrival.'[84]

The argument for a king to act as a guardian to a nation of political 'minors' was put forward by more than one side. Koraes, Mavrocordatos and most Moreot notables were convinced that the Revolution had started prematurely, and never tired of using this argument; so too were many of those like Dikaios who had been responsible for hostilities breaking out in 1821. All seemed to agree on the political 'immaturity' of the Greeks; for all of them a government in the role of a guardian to minors was the logical conclusion. 'A nation of men with a lust for power, tumultuous and at present definitely corrupt', as Dikaios wrote to the Moreot notables in December 1820, needed an appropriate 'system';[85] which seemingly he and the other 'Association' agents had never really explained to those who had been asked to support the break with the foreign ruler. 'Liberty in a barbaric nation is the greatest scourge,' another 'Association' agent, Epameinondas Mavrommatis, a friend of Mavrocordatos and scion of a distinguished family of Acarnania, wrote to Georgios Praïdes.[86] Mavrocordatos and Zaïmis—the learned Phanariot and the powerful Moreot notable—agreed between themselves before parting company that the Greeks 'were not yet ready to rule themselves'.[87] In an effort to explain the indifference of monarchical Europe to the nation's sufferings the editor of the *Hellenika Chronika* wondered in 1824: 'Have we shown by our conduct that we are ready for self-rule?'[88] 'A nation accustomed to be ruled for so many centuries by the will of one man is difficult to govern in any other way,' a 'man of democratic convictions' wrote later to the newspaper *Geniki Ephemeris tis Hellados*.[89] 'On passing quickly from tyranny to a radically different political system we discovered that we lack the necessary theoretical and practical knowledge

[83]*Geniki Ephemeris*, 27 Feb. 1832.
[84]*Ibid.*, 29 Jan. 1832.
[85]*Ibid.*, 29 June and 6 July 1832.
[86]Philimon, *Society of Friends*, pp. 353–4.
[87]*Mavrocordatos Archive*, vol. I, p. 173.
[88]*Ibid.*, vol. II, p. 343.
[89]*Hellenika Chronika*, 22 Nov. 1824.

to adjust ourselves to this system', the editor of *Ethniki Ephemeris* wrote in 1832.[90] The editor of another paper, *Ephemeris ton Athenon*, put it more bluntly: 'We need thrashing to perform our duties.'[91]

There were endless variations on this theme. Some felt that representative institutions should wait until the nation was 'purged of its servile habits'. Till then it should content itself with an 'appropriate' and 'suitable'—i.e. monarchical-regime. The regime in force was 'incompatible' with the nation's education and habits. 'Our brothers', wrote Polychroniades, one of Mavrocordatos' ablest associates, 'know nothing about justice, and their ideas about authority and government are mistaken.' Being 'unenlightened' and 'uneducated', the Greeks needed a political system suitable for their level of culture.[92]

In 1826 *Geniki Ephemeris* published a lengthy article summarising most of the arguments and terms used at the time against the representative institutions which some circles supported. The paper's attack was directed against those who proposed for Greece an 'uncrowned constitutional regime', a republic. The editor wrote: 'In their effort to apply foreign theories to Greece, they are making our government look like the multicoloured dress of Harlequin.' However, each people must have 'its own government, which should be in accord with its habits, its spirit, its religion, and suitable for the climate of the country.' However, some 'admirers, and justly so, of the harmonious laws of enlightened nations, seek to apply them in Greece, forgetting that the good law-giver must allow as much political freedom as the people for whom he makes the laws can make good use of. But when he allows more of that freedom than is advisable, the surplus becomes an agent of corruption in much the same way as a man who drinks more than he can hold passes from vitality to torpor because of the strength of the liquor.'[93]

In 1832, after more than ten years of discussing the basic 'features' of the 'national character' and in view of the imminent election of a monarch for Greece by the protecting powers, opinions such as 'Few in Greece have reached political maturity' and 'Happy the nation in whose constitution-building, government and administration only political adults take part' were becoming axiomatic and none dared to

[90]*Geniki Ephemeris,* 2 Feb. 1827.
[91]*Ethniki Ephemeris,* 18 Apr. 1832.
[92]*Ephemeris ton Athenon,* 23 Dec. 1825.
[93]*Ibid.,* 14 Nov. 1825; *Geniki Ephemeris,* 20 Feb. 1825; *Archives of Hellenic Regeneration,* vol. I, p. 153, and vol. IV, p. 80; Philimon, *Society of Friends,* p. 295.

question them. The indigenous élites—the local magnates, the ecclesiastical hierarchy and the captains—were only too glad that other groups were at last accepting what they themselves had shouldered all along.

Evidence of exactly how the argument for a king as a guardian of the people against the scheming indigenous élites was formulated is scarce, but its main thrusts are clear. The non-privileged Greeks of the time, even those without education, could easily understand this argument in favour of a king. No doubt they listened with interest, but not for long, to Ypsilantis's promise that his brother, the *'authentis'*, was about to come to deliver them from both the Ottomans and the *'kodjabashis'* (Turkish for local notables).[94] The archons oppressed the peoples, and a higher authority was needed to check this, as the *Ephemeris ton Athenon* wrote in 1824. The same paper wrote around this time: 'The Captain torments [our man] and his lieutenant taxes him, the Eparch thrashes him, the Gendarme puts him in gaol, the Demogeron condemns him, and the poor wretch does not know where to turn for help. People did not suffer such confusion and oppression even under the Turks.'[95]

Apollon provided the theoretical foundation for the king as protector of the people from the 'mighty': 'If Greece becomes a monarchy, as we hear it will—and should—and as its interests dictate, it will never be obliged to crown the heads of a few and dress them in the Roman toga, nor will it offer incense to a few delicate noses, while the great toiling mass is trampled underfoot. Besides, monarchy and aristocracy are not as inseparable as some of our politicians would like us to believe.'[96] The 'aristocracy' of *Apollon* did not only include the old indigenous élites—the primates, the prelates and the captains; it also included those who were acquiring power and influence after the collapse of Ottoman rule, upstarts like Dikaios who once said, concerning the prospect of Greece acquiring a king: 'And what will I be in Greece if a king comes here?'[97]

Irrespective of its hereditary or elected head, the regime had to be representative; this at least seems to have been the objective of a number of those participating in the debate in times of reduced tension. Thus, although the first constitution did not specify whether

[94] *Geniki Ephemeris,* 17 Feb. 1825.
[95] Deliyannis, *op. cit.,* vol. I, p. 239.
[96] *Ephemeris ton Athenon,* 4 and 8 Oct. 1824.
[97] *Apollon,* 16 Sep. 1831.

the head of state would be a king or an elected president, it spelt out in Article 11 that the members of the Chamber (*Vouleutikon*) were 'elected representatives of the various districts of Greece'.[98] The government would be a 'representative system' (*systema parastatikon*) or a 'parliamentary polity' (*koinovouleutiki politeia*) in which, according to Koraes, authority was 'open to all worthy men but tempered and confirmed by the votes of the citizens';[99] it would be a 'representative authority' (*parastatiki exousia*) which, according to the editor of *Ephemeris ton Athenon*, would be not 'despotic' but 'parliamentary'.[100]

This representative government, which was of course a Western import to the country, was defined and explained mostly by comparing it to forms of government with which the Greeks were familiar, such as despotism and antique forms but which their intelligentsia were assumed to be familiar, such as classical Athenian democracy. In this part of the political debate Koraes was an authoritative guide; or so he and his friends in Greece thought. The 'public assembly' (*pandemos ekklesia*) of classical Athens was vulnerable and ran the danger of being 'subjugated' by demagogues. Anyway, it was no longer possible in modern societies with large populations for all citizens to participate in an assembly; they could only elect their representatives. A citizen 'is sufficiently free when he and his property assets are secure, and when he has the right to vote for his representatives and the right to make public, orally or in writing, his opinion about public affairs.' 'I detest democracy', wrote Koraes, 'as Plato, Aristotle and all the ancient philosophers did. The more prudent Americans detest it too.' Democracy was the 'regime of fools', while oligarchy was the 'regime of the wicked'. He hoped that the Greeks would follow the 'middle road', the one that both the 'oligarchs' and the 'demagogues' hated. 'The public's authority', he recommended, 'should be limited to elections. After electing their administrators, deputies and judges, people should return to their work, the farmer to farming, the craftsman to his craft, the trader to his trade, and should no longer interfere in public affairs.'[101]

These recommendations reflected, more than the wisdom drawn from reading the ancient philosophers, the debates and practices connected with the French Revolution, British constitutional reforms

---

[98]Speliades, *op. cit.*, vol. II, p. 305.

[99]*Archives of Hellenic Regeneration*, vol. I, pp. 26, 200–201 and vol. III, p. 48; *Hellenika Chronika*, 5 Jan. 1824.

[100]Koraes, *Dialogue of two Greeks* (1831), p. 22.

[101]*Ephemeris ton Athenon*, 3 Aug. 1825.

and the 'Anglo-American polity' across the Atlantic. The latter especially exercised a strong attraction in revolutionary Greece. For most admirers of representative government, the American republic represented the best creation of man's accumulated wisdom: it was a conservative, 'prudent' regime, which appeared to favour the unhindered development of one of the most progressive societies in modern times. The wish for Greece to imitate the 'wise' laws of the 'United Districts' (*Eparchiae*)—which checked all tendencies to excess, balanced all powers, and secured independence from other countries, internal freedom and prosperity—was often expressed, perhaps because the American constitution was such a distant dream. Anastasios Polyzoïdes considered both the British and the American models of government the best that new states could ever wish to see established for their peoples. The Greeks of the time were also attracted to the Swiss and Dutch constitutions and, after the July Revolution in France, to the French constitution.[102]

The 'Anglo-American' constitution, however, was by far the most attractive: it provided for an elected president and allowed all citizens (according to Koraes) to 'ennoble their own persons', but ruled out a 'hereditary nobility'. These features, as well as the absence of a state church, distinguished the American republic from the British model, and made the former 'more accomplished'. Indeed Greece's temporary constitution resembled the American 'as its dim and very imperfect image', for the reason that the war effort did not allow the development of a 'more perfect' constitution.[103] However, others were sceptical about the prospect of Greece developing a regime substantially resembling the American. 'It would be a stroke of good fortune', wrote the editor of *Geniki Ephemeris*, 'were Greece to be ruled not temporarily but permanently under such a constitution. But to adopt America's constitution in Greece we should first have to transform the Greeks into Anglo-Americans.'[104] For the opponents of a monarchy the American model of government provided a useful point of reference, but with few exceptions they were not convinced republicans. Koraes, again, was expressing mainstream republican opinion in Greece: the situation in the country was such that, even if an 'angel' were to come down from heaven to reign, it was quite likely that, because of the

[102]Koraes, *Dialogue* (2nd), pp. 53, 55, 137–8 and *Dialogue* (1831), p. 69.

[103]*Hellenika Chronika,* 16 Feb., 17 May, 24 Sep. and 26 Nov. 1824; Koraes, *Dialogue* (1831), p. 40.

[104]Koraes, *Dialogue* (1825), pp. 56–7, 103–4, 134 and *Dialogue* (2nd), pp. 26, 34, 55.

servile habits bred in them by Ottoman rule, the Greeks would turn him into a 'devil'. The monarchy was undesirable for another reason too: a small and poor nation like the Greek was in no position to support such an expensive regime: 'I am not against this regime as such', he admitted; 'I can see that many European nations which have kings are happy states, either because they are lucky enough to be ruled by kings who look after their people's interests, or because they managed to introduce democratic principles and practices into their monarchies.'[105] Since the early phase of recommendations to the Greeks—the 'republican' phase, when he had God speak through Samuel to the Greeks against opting for a king[106]—Koraes had lost most of his initial enthusiasm for a 'democratic' government. One of his main arguments against a monarchy, in addition to the danger of the monarch being affected by indigenous corruption, was the fact that the Greeks had no royal house of their own and would thus have to invite a foreigner to be their king.[107]

Another republican, the editor of *Hellenika Chronika*, felt that the Greeks had not fought and paid such a terrible price only to provide for an extravagant regime like the monarchy. But he was ready to admit: 'Only a few, who we hope are the best patriots, want the blessings of democratic government.'[108] The convinced republican Ioannis Theotokis was willing to accept a king for the reasons already cited, but feared the negative effects of a West European one on the nation's religion. For this reason and so as not to offend the *amour propre* of the people, he proposed to accept a Greek 'archon', namely Kapodistrias.[109]

The republic was projected rather half-heartedly and unconvincingly. Those few who opted to support it did so not so much out of conviction but because they thought that the people were also not ready for a monarchy—which appeared to be the preferred option of all other political systems. However, what seemed to be generally agreed was that Greece's regime would have to be constitutional. The king wanted by most Greeks must be a constitutional one. 'All the Greeks', according to *Apollon* in 1831, 'know and admit that both the nation's wishes and the political needs of the country call for a monarchy in Greece, but it will have to be a constitutional monarchy.

---

[105] *Geniki Ephemeris*, 2 Feb. 1827.
[106] Koraes, *Dialogue* (1831), pp. 32, 47; *Ephemeris ton Athenon*, 25 Feb. 1825.
[107] Koraes, *Adelphiki didaskalia*, pp. 38–9 (see Kings I. 8: 11–18).
[108] Koraes, *Dialogue* (2nd), p. 48.
[109] *Hellenika Chronika*, 16 Feb. and 17 May 1824.

Indeed, everyone is looking forward to the time that the country is delivered from the temporary government and acquires a monarchy.'[110] According to the editor of the *Ethniki Ephemeris*, 'Everyone in Greece is of the same mind and has just one wish, to see the fate of the country, after so much suffering, built on the solid foundation of a constitutional monarchy.'[111]

Of course, the Greek newspapers of the time shaped more than they reflected public opinion in the country, or what could be described as such. They gave a mouthpiece to small political groups attached to the circles which exercised power or which aimed to acquire it; and the views they expressed were these of the editors and perhaps a very small readership. The masses—peasants, shepherds and seafarers—could not and certainly did not follow these debates. 'Nation', 'people', 'representative government' and 'republic' were abstract concepts most Greeks had never heard of. Everyone had heard of kings in some connection, but very few would risk their lives for one. Hence, to invoke popular consent for a regime suited to the 'nation' or the 'people' was somewhat presumptuous.

Koraes, whose views were sought by most of those concerned about Greece's regime, followed events in the country as best he could under the circumstances and offered his opinion freely. He too invoked the 'nation's consent', involving every 'citizen', as a prerequisite for whatever regime the nation's representatives decided to establish. So when Ypsilantis invited him to return to Greece, he replied: 'Only the nation can invite a foreign architect to construct its regime, if it decides that such an architect is necessary. And if it does so, it should invite him on terms which it will consider best for its own welfare.'[112]

The 'consent' of the nation—as elusive a notion as there ever has been in Greece—was increasingly used by the opposition to Kapodistrias, but it was invoked especially in relation to the election of a foreign prince after Kapodistrias's murder. So too was another principle, borrowed this time from the experiences of the 'Anglo-Americans': that no taxes should be collected, except with the consent of the nation's elected assembly', or spent 'without the nation being presented with a precise bill of spending'.[113]

[110]*Romas Archive*, vol. I, pp. 516–18.

[111]*Archeia*, vol. II, pp. 188, 250; *Ephemeris ton Athenon*, 21 Aug. 1825, 15 Apr. 1826; *Apollon*, 29 Apr. 1831.

[112]*Ethniki Ephemeris*, 22 June 1832.

[113]Koraes, *Correspondence*, vol. IV, p. 303.

'Agreements', 'accords' and other such terms were gaining ground in the debate about a proper and acceptable regime for the fledgling nation-state. However the range of evidence for this aspect of the search for the regime's nature is limited, no doubt because only very few of those who contributed to the debate were familiar with the theories of Hobbes, Locke, Rousseau and Montesquieu—which further weakens the argument that the demand for 'agreements' and 'accords' rested on firm ground.

Another difficulty in assessing the weight of many arguments and claims put forward during this period in Greece has to do with the actual meaning and content of terms like *genos* (stock), *ethnos* (nation) and *laos* (people), which were often used interchangeably. The terms 'people' and 'popular sovereignty', for instance, present no problem in the writings of men like Koraes who wrote that the 'people', as 'the only legitimate sovereign', bestows legitimacy on the prince it chooses, who thus becomes a 'legitimate king' and a 'servant of the law'.[114] However, difficulties are encountered in discerning the precise meaning of terms such as 'authority' (*exousia*) and 'sovereignty' (*kyriarchia*); in a translated excerpt from a speech by the President of the United States, which appeared in the Greek press in 1824, the term 'authority' is used instead of 'sovereignty',[115] and in a law proposed by a newspaper editor 'the will of the people in a union' was thought to be the 'highest law' (*hypertatos nomos*).[116] Similar difficulties arise with terms like the 'rights of man' in an organised commonwealth, which are often called the 'rights of humanity' (*anthropotes*), or the 'rights of the nation' and the 'sacred national rights', for which the Greeks had taken up arms.[117] Especially in the first two years of the Revolution, 'natural' or 'human' rights were not always distinguished from 'political' rights.[118] Thus the press, according to *Apollon*, was in duty bound to remind the ruled of their 'original rights' (*archetypa*), which did not mean their 'human rights'.[119] Similarly, in the correspondence of community councils one comes across terms and phrases

---

[114]Koraes, *Adelphiki didaskalia*, pp. 53, 54 and *Correspondence*, vol. IV, p. 293; *Apollon*, 13 and 23 May, 9 and 19 Sep. 1831; *Ethniki Ephemeris*, 18 Apr. and 11 June 1832.

[115]Koraes, *Dialogue* (1831), p. 4.

[116]*Hellenikd Chronika*, 29 Sep. 1824.

[117]*Ibid.*, 24 Sep. 1824.

[118]*Archeion Hydras, 1778–1832* (Hydra archive), ed. A. Lignos, Piraeus, 1926–30, vol. VII, pp. 21, 86 and vol. VIII, pp. 345, 615.

[119]*Ephemeris ton Athenon*, 16 Oct. 1825; *Mavrocordatos Archive*, vol. IV, pp. 1119–20.

like the 'inalienable and original rights of the citizens',[120] which meant 'political rights'. In both cases, the context was Kapodistrias's infringement of political rights.

A common feature of this and other such evidence concerning the 'human' or 'natural' rights on which the new independent and constitutional commonwealth would have to rest was their connection with the rights of man in a natural condition. This was not the same as the rights deriving form the organised state, Hobbes's commonwealth, i.e. the rights associated with the French Revolution rather than with English radicalism. These precedents, which influenced constitutional developments during the years of the War of Independence, marked a major departure from the generally prudent approach to statecraft.[121]

---

[120]*Apollon*, 11 Mar. 1831.
[121]*Ibid.*, 15 July 1831.

2
GOVERNMENT AND PEOPLE

The ancient Greeks invented democracy, but their linguistic descendants in modern times had to import representative government, a modern version of a democratic polity, from the West. Contrary to what the average Greek believes, this has not been an indigenous product, and its roots do not go back to ancient times: the intervening ages and empires swept away all traces of the ancient democracy. Representative government emerged first in Western Europe as a result of successive confrontations between the upper or middle classes and the monarchy. In the Greek lands no such confrontations occurred to produce similar results, because there were no agents to force the hand of the local monarchy, as happened in Western monarchies. Communal self-government, which in one form or another survived from Byzantine times or developed in the centuries of Frankish and Ottoman rule, was not compatible with the type of centralised government the founding fathers laboured to establish in insurgent Greece. Communal councils were not truly representative in the Western sense; they had grown not in opposition to the central government but rather as part of the latter's tax-assessment and collection apparatus. The interests they essentially represented were not those of the tax-paying subjects of the Sultan, but the central government's and their own interests. By the time of the War of Independence these councils had fallen under the control of such powerful local élites as the notables and captains, who used them to augment their own power.

This chapter deals with developments since independence, with an emphasis on constitution-making and the principle of representation. As we have already seen, representative government, irrespective of

44

whether the head of state was a hereditary monarch or an elected president, was the primary objective of constitution-making in insurgent Greece. However, not all who supported representation as the principal underpinning of government had similar motivations. Because of the general backwardness of the people, men of education assumed that their talents would naturally be in demand under a democratic system. Enlightened Phanariots such as Alexandros Mavrocordatos and the historian Spyridon Trikoupis were no doubt motivated by both considerations—by a sincere belief in democratic institutions no less than by the prospect of a political career in the new independent state. On the other hand, indigenous élites who had profited from wielding power in the name of the Sultan, and been drawn into the Revolution because they calculated that they could not afford to be left out of the new order, saw in representative government a way to entrench and reinforce their power. Their numbers in both the regional and the national assemblies of insurgent Greece were proof of their wish to control the revolutionary government. In a deeply fragmented country, the local notables and the captains were only nominally representatives of the 'nation'; what they actually represented were 'their' districts and 'their' people-their sole source of power.

These local notables in insurgent Greece found themselves in a position similar to that which the West European landed aristocracy had won from, or guarded against, the monarchy, but without a monarch. When they spoke in the name of 'their' people they did so in the sense of people attached to them by bonds other than those associated with free citizens and their chosen representatives. The representation of local notables rested on peasants tied to them by economic interests, while that of captains rested on mercenary armed irregulars. In this sense indigenous élites used representation in ways they already knew, and found themselves in a position they had never experienced in the past.

However, conflicting interests and the consequent rise of the first recognisable political factions brought the revolutionary government to a standstill. These factions were coalitions of notables and captains, which took shape when funds from the revolutionary loans raised in Western Europe became available. Representation in this sense became more politicised, but thus was only superficial because, under a veneer of claims to represent the interests of the nation, the interests of regional élites supreme. It was no coincidence that the first round of reigned vicious civil strife broke out when loan funds came on stream or were expected to do so.

Constitutional histories of modern Greece have normally treated the governments and assemblies of the revolutionary period as a promising start cut short by the arrival of Count Kapodistrias. According to this view, revolutionary governments and assemblies, though not the outcome of free elections, were representative and democratic. The liberal constitutions voted by the revolutionary national assemblies have provided the principal arguments for this assessment of government in insurgent Greece, but although these constitutions were voted and in part enacted, they were vitiated by the kind of representation of the interests of notables and captains referred to above. What Kapodistrias put an end to was not representative government deriving from the national constitution, but conflicting sets of regional bosses ruling in the name of the nation but not necessarily in its interests.[1]

The constitutions of insurgent Greece were no more than ambitious exercises by Western-educated liberals and radicals in a country deeply fragmented by regional power-brokers and lacking a tradition of representative self-government. Kapodistrias's decision to shape an enlightened and paternalistic system of government for the country was not as unexpected as his opponents maintained. After the devastation of the country by the Egyptian army of Ibrahim Pasha in 1825 and the revolutionary government's inability to pursue the war effectively and provide a measure of security for the population, most Greeks appeared prepared to welcome a strong man to impose his will on the warring groups of notables and captains. Breaking that power and

---

[1]See G.D. Dimakopoulos, *I dioikitiki organosis kata tin Hellenikin Epanastasin, 1821–1827* (Administrative organisation during the Greek Revolution, 1821–1827), Athens, 1966; 'Ai kybernitikai archai tis Hellenikis Politeias, 1827–1833' (Government principles of the Hellenic Politeia, 1827–1833), *O Eranistis,* vol. IV (1966), pp. 117–54; 'I esoteriki dioikisis tis Hellados kata tin aphixin tou Othonos' (Administration in Greece on Otto's arrival), *Mnimosyni,* vol. III (1970–1), pp. 271–327; A. B. Daskalakis, *Oi topikoi organismoi tis Epanastaseos tou 1821 kai to Politevma tis Epidavrou* (The regional statutes of the Revolution of 1821 and the Epidaurus Constitution), Athens, 1966; T. N. Pipinelis, *Politiki historia tis Hellenikis Epanastaseos* (Political history of the Greek Revolution), Paris, 1927; N. N. Saripolos, *I proti Ethnosyneleusis kai to Politevma tis Epidavrou tou 1822* (The First National Assembly and the Epidaurus Constitution of 1822), 2 vols, Athens, 1907; A. S. Svolos, *I syntagmatiki historia tis Hellados* (Constitutional history of Greece), Athens, 1972 (reprint); and N. Kaltchas, *Introduction to the Constitutional History of Modern Greece,* New York 1940. For a new and penetrating approach to the subject see Elpida Vogli, 'Politevma europaikon. Politeiakes anazitiseis kata ti diarkeia tou Agonos, 1821–1828', M. A. thesis, School of Philosophy, Aristotle University of Thessaloniki (1998).

Ioannis Kapodistrias (1776–1831)

Kapodistrias came to Greece in 1828 at the invitation of the insurgent country's last national assembly, to become its first President with extraordinary powers. The previous year the combined fleets of England, France and Russia had sunk the Turco-Egyptian fleet in Navarino bay and opened the way for Greece's independence. Kapodistrias was thought to be the only Greek of the time capable of providing the war-torn country with a government equal to the huge task awaiting it, and was welcomed as a saviour. He was assassinated three years later, in September 1831, by two members of a Maniot clan which knew no other way of showing opposition to the President's policies and measures.

Kapodistrias died before completing his task. He had given up the life of someone who had attained a very high position through his talents and integrity, to serve a people who desperately needed a leader of his credentials. His enlightened conservative outlook estranged liberals and radicals, while his drive to divest local barons of their power and confer on the central government the necessary authority to rule the country, antagonised powerful, entrenched interests. His paternalistic attitude towards the people and his tendency to withdraw from society and seek the solitude of his study did not make him popular among those whom he had offered to serve.

His involvement in the constitutional organisation of the briefly autonomous Ionian state in the last years of the eighteenth century was perhaps no more than a youthful exercise. In his mature years Kapodistrias believed that constitutional liberties, without a measure of prosperity and enlightenment in a peasant society recently freed from despotic rule, did not serve the people so much as those who spoke in their name. All that the Greeks who had been entrusted to his care needed, he believed, was honest government, reconstruction of the country's ruined infrastructure, a decent school system appropriate to a peasant society, and a defensible national frontier. The Hellas he wanted to fashion on the southeastern fringe of Europe was a European Hellas: well governed, peaceful, prosperous and enlightened. He had no illusions of a great future awaiting the fledgling nation-state, nor did he share the romantic belief in its special mission or in a manifest destiny. As a man of the Enlightenment, he believed that education, the rule of law and honest administration shape a people's future infinitely more effectively than these figments of romantic imagination.

The great European powers, which had made Kapodistrias's assumption of power in insurgent Greece possible, did not even do what little they could have done to make his task less onerous and unrewarding than it inherently was. His former link with imperial Russia proved no blessing: it always caused English and French representatives to suspect him of conspiring with the Tsar. Kapodistrias's 'Russian connection' hampered his freedom of action in pursuit of reforms, and attracted some of the less progressive lay and ecclesiastical elements constituting the Russian 'party'; at the same time it kept away from him politicians representing the so-called French and English 'parties'.

The most readable and judicious appraisal of Kapodistrias is C. M. Woodhouse's biography *Capodistria: The Founder of Greek Independence*, London, 1973. For a useful bibliography of the development of views on Kapodistrias see Christina Koulouri and Christos Loukos, *Ta prosopa tou Kapodistria. O protos Kyvernitis tis Helladas kai I neohelleniki ideologia (1831–1996)* (Kapodistrias's faces. Greece's first President and modern Greek ideology, 1831–1996), Athens, 1996.

influence and concentrating authority in the central government that were two of Kapodistrias's primary objectives. Of equal importance to the system of government he aimed to create for Greece was the establishment of a regular civil service, free from control by the regional notables and captains. Divesting regional élites of the influence they had acquired under the declining power of the Ottomans and as leaders of the Revolution was not easy, and establishing regular services was even more difficult because of their presence.

Kapodistrias had a task similar to that which faced West European monarchs in early modern times: concentrating power by breaking the dominion of regional barons. However, in contrast to European monarchs, he had no class opposed to the interests of the powerful barons on which he could depend. Westernised liberals and radicals, when they did not oppose his rule, could not be counted on as a countervailing force against the barons—who, as might be expected, dressed their opposition to Kapodistrias's concentration of authority in the central government's hands as a fight for constitutional rule. Kapodistrias could only appeal to the people directly, but he had no means of reaching them. Besides, he did not believe in such methods of winning support for his rule; he was strongly convinced that it served the people better than any other form of government then available, and wished it to be in the name of the nation and on behalf of the people, as a protection against their petty tyrants, until they had enough political maturity to consent to being governed by their freely elected representatives.

By the time he was assassinated in 1831 by a clan of Maniot captains, Kapodistrias was an isolated leader, disowned by most of those who were in a position to reach the people. Even foreign representatives, with the exception of the Russians, were not disturbed by his death, perhaps because he was less open to foreign intrigue than those who opposed him had been. Hard-working, profoundly devoted to the reconstruction and regeneration of a devastated Greece, and deeply convinced that his paternalistic rule was what the modern Greeks needed to heal the wounds of war against the Turks and vicious civil strife, Kapodistrias was cut down by assassins who knew that he was a far greater threat to their interests than the Turks had ever been.

Kapodistrias's successor, the youthful Bavarian prince who became King Otto of Greece, had a much better chance of succeeding where his predecessor had failed; he had brought with him, in addition to competent advisers from Bavaria, a Bavarian army, guaranteed great European power support, and a foreign loan. Moreover, he could not have been associated with any of the three protecting powers. One more round of civil strife in Greece following the assassination of Kapodistrias had made the feuding factions willing to accept high-handed treatment without serious opposition. Local insurrections of disgruntled Maniot clans in 1834 and of irregulars dismissed from paid service to make room for a regular army the following year did not seriously threaten the new regime.

The Bavarian regency ruled Greece in Otto's name until he came of age, and used the initial and most critical period to establish regular and competent services. However, it refused even to consider granting a constitution. Like Kapodistrias, its members were convinced that Otto's regime was as good and efficient as any that the Greek people could have hoped for—a government for, if not of, the people. As for a government *by* the people, this was ruled out altogether. Representation was also ruled out for the reason given by Kapodistrias: to prevent a return of the local notables and captains to the scene. It was considered that this would be calamitous for the future of the reforms the regency pushed through. To circumscribe their influence in the countryside still further, the Bavarians made what was described as 'communal self-government' an integral part of the administration. Communal councils, elected from government-nominated candidates, essentially constituted the lower ranks of an administration fashioned after the French administrative system of provinces, districts and clusters of villages: the *demes*.

Exclusion from government office and its spoils caused discontent among the notables and captains since it dangerously weakened their control over their clienteles. Mounting opposition from this quarter took the form of calls for a constitutional charter, and disappointed liberals were quick to join the opposition to Otto's absolutism thus providing the necessary arguments in favour of a constitution. The convergence of groups so disparate and with such different interests and objectives was made possible by the operation of three loose political coalitions, each identifying with one of the three protecting great powers: France, England and Russia. Discontent among philorthodox circles over the church question and disaffection among the unemployed irregulars, especially those from Thessaly, Epirus and Macedonia, contributed to the opposition to Otto and the Bavarians.

However, according to all reliable accounts, Otto and the monarchical institution he represented remained popular in spite of opposition from all these circles: they secured a semblance of national unity in a country still fragmented and not yet recovered from the destruction of property and the divisions of the ten years of war and attendant civil strife. A conspiracy of representatives from the three parties, which was able to enlist the backing of the Athens garrison, succeeded in issuing a *pronunciamento* on September 1843 that obliged Otto to convene a constitutional assembly—this came as no surprise to anyone except the King. The representatives of Greece's protecting powers, though not privy to the conspiracy and far from believing that a liberal constitution was a pressing need for the country, did nothing to prevent the King's humiliation, perhaps because there was little they could legitimately do. A compromise between Otto and the conspirators, which was made possible by the fear of bloody civil strife and the knowledge that the governments of France and England favoured such a compromise, allowed the King to preserve his royal prerogatives under a monarchical constitution.[2]

The Constitution of 1844 provided for a bicameral parliament and practically universal suffrage; it also brought back on the scene the forces that both Kapodistrias and Otto had done everything to

[2]J. A. Petropulos, *Politics and Statecraft in the Kingdom of Greece, 1833–1843*, Princeton, 1968; G. P. Nakos, *To politeiakon kathestos tis Hellados epi Othonos mechri tou Syntagmatos tou 1844* (The government of Greece under Otto until the 1844 Constitution), Thessaloniki, 1972; T. N. Pipinelis, *I monarchia en Helladi, 1833–1843* (The monarchy in Greece, 1833–1843), Athens, 1932.

keep at a distance. Even before the Constitution was promulgated in March 1844 and while the assembly debated its provisions, the local notables and the captains of the revolutionary war—some fifteen years older now and mostly comfortably settled, yet anxious to move back and run the show again—gave the country a taste of what was to come: unstable and changing alignments and alliances of politicians around a set of leaders of the same generation, which provided the country with governments whose main preoccupation was survival in office. A master of this art was Ioannis Kolettis, the recognised patron of the Roumeliot *pallikars* (former warlords) and leader of the 'French party'. Kolletis outmanoeuvred his political opponents, particularly Mavrocordatos and Andreas Metaxas, leaders respectively of the English and Russian parties, who were no match for him in winning electoral contests. Kolettis kept himself in power by promising them portfolios as well as encouraging a potentially dangerous element, the brigands of central Greece, to exercise its talents across the frontier with the Ottoman domains in the Greek *'irredenta'*, thus exporting lawlessness and presenting their predatory forays as the work of liberators. Above all, Kolettis managed to survive by following a 'centrist' policy, a course calculated not to offend powerful vested interests by pushing through radical changes. The price of this governmental stability was social and economic stagnation.

Kolettis's government of *pallikars* was followed, after his death in 1847, by short-lived governments held to ransom by the *pallikars*. The wave of revolutionary events in most West and Central European countries in 1848 barely touched Greece, which witnessed instead a surge of banditry under ageing and not so ageing warlords. Opposition newspapers in the capital—and subsequent writers looking for parallels to contemporary events in Western Europe—tried in vain to discern radical influences in this surge of brigandage. Greece in the 1840s and subsequent decades simply did not have a working class or a class of peasant serfs to provide the manpower for a radical revolution, or a middle class independent of the state to lead one. The country produced scores of brigands, who robbed with impunity in the name of the unredeemed brethren to the north, whom ostensibly they planned to liberate.

Widespread illiteracy, primitive communications, violence by brigands or gendarmes and victimisation made popular representation problematic: universal suffrage in a situation of backwardness and insecurity made peasants unwilling accomplices in a political game, which the Constitution had initiated and which had strengthened the position of the local bosses in their effort to seize the government and the public purse. It was therefore far from being a blessing.

The parliamentary records of this period present a dismal picture of parliamentary life. In particular, debates in the chamber did not rise above a low level of exchanges between the deputies. Discussions of the electoral results in fiercely contested seats betray the means used by the candidates to defeat their opponents—ranging from outright slander to the use of brigands to keep voters away from the polls or tamper with the votes in the ballot boxes. The incorporation of the seven Ionian Islands in 1863, in addition to other welcome changes it brought in its wake, upgraded Parliament somewhat; 'Septinsular' deputies infused into the debates a more refined style of discourse than what had previously been customary for the Moreot and Rumeliot deputies.

Perhaps more striking was the predominance of debates on external events and foreign policy over ones dealing with domestic matters and therefore of more immediate importance to the people. Deputies competed in displaying their concern for the future of the nation. The everyday grievances of the peasantry seldom found their way to Parliament, while events connected with the Eastern Question were given prominence, sometimes out of all proportion to their significance for the country.

Deputies were representatives not only of their districts but of the entire nation, and the latter included the part lying outside the state boundaries no less than that to which they owed their election. Ever since elections for the national assemblies of the War of Independence, the 'Greeks abroad' had raised the question of their representation and exercised a dominant influence over the minds of parliamentarians. How could deputies to Greece's Parliament possibly represent the interests of the Greeks who were still subjects of the Ottoman sultan (and in the twentieth century would become citizens of foreign countries)? A broad definition of Greek citizenship, combining both *jus soli* and *jus sanguinis*, has permitted Greek deputies ever since to maintain that they could do so. And if the principle of no taxation without representation has been one of the principal underpinnings of the demand for representative government, representation without taxation infringed upon the principles of democracy by making deputies represent tax-paying citizens of another country.

Conversely, this approach to citizenship, which allowed the inclusion within the Greek body politic of subjects or citizens of foreign countries claiming Greek 'descent', permitted the exclusion from this body politic of all those who, though residents of Greece, did not meet the requirement of 'national consciousness'. This allowed the state to deny such people-for reasons of national security- the rights of citizenship, including the right of representation. Gypsies or nomadic shepherds were easily denied the right of representation, and Communists who were considered a danger to public security were denied the right to vote.

Even more inimical to the growth of truly representative government than economic and social backwardness was the painfully slow development of stable political parties. Up till the rise to power of Harilaos Trikoupis in the 1870s and the King's acceptance of the principle that the leader of the majority party in Parliament should be given the mandate to form a government, the formation of political groupings around a leader who could only govern if it so pleased the King was really at the monarch's discretion too. Political leaders till then vied with each other for the monarch's favours rather than to build reasonably stable parties aiming to win power through as broad a consensus as possible.

The sudden and meteoric rise to power of Eleftherios Venizelos in the second decade of the twentieth century marked a new departure in representative government. In addition to supervising Greece's expansion in Epirus and Macedonia and the incorporation of Crete and the Eastern Aegean islands—for which he is mostly remembered and admired—Venizelos was responsible for a series of constitutional and administrative reforms and for creating the first truly modern political party in Greece. In the space of less than five years, the Cretan statesman totally restructured political life. Following the 1909 Goudi *pronunciamento* and with the backing of army officers who blamed the political parties for the nation's failures, Venizelos was able in 1911 to carry through a new constitution that was to become a powerful instrument in the hands of a parliamentary majority, as well as a set of important and long overdue administrative changes. More important, perhaps, he created a new party, the Liberal Party, and recruited under its banner a group of ambitious leaders willing to implement his vision of reforming the governance of the country. The emergence and the practices of Venizelos's Liberal Party, in addition to providing the country with a stable government at a most critical phase of its history, worked as a catalyst in another direction as well: it forced its political opponents to coalesce into a conservative alignment, out of which emerged the future royalist party when Venizelos clashed with King Constantine over Greece's stance in the First World War.

This clash—the so called National Schism (*Dichasmos*)—revealed how fragile representative institutions had always been in Greece: a disagreement over foreign policy and a division at the top, without any deeper social roots, destabilised the whole structure and turned elected governments into quasi-dictatorships. If respect for the rights of the minority is the ultimate measure of a democratic regime, then the governments of this tumultous period of the First World War were not governments of all the Greeks. Parliamentary majorities, even when democratically elected, became parliamentary dictatorships, pushing minorities down the slippery slope into unconstitutional activities. Such developments almost made the unstable majorities and shifting allegiances of the nineteenth century appear less dangerous to good parliamentary practice and the rights of political minorities.

Arrogant majority rule has been one of the main arguments ever since in favour of an electoral system other than the majority system, which favours the growth of two large parties alternating in office. Small parties have consistently and vocally argued that simple proportional representation, in addition to securing a voice in Parliament for all political currents and shades of opinion, would prevent governments from ruling essentially as parliamentary dictatorships. According to this view, consensual governments resting on alliances of parties formed inside Parliament are preferable to single-party ones.

Venizelos's parliamentary record is a case in point. He ended his second and perhaps most dramatic period in office by accepting defeat in 1920, at the height of his achievements for Greece which were contested by his opponents, However, he bowed before the people's sorereign decision to entrust the government to his opponents, showing by this act that he valued that form of government itself more than the achievements he had secured through it. However, fifteen years later when out of office he chose to encourage a conspiracy of army officers who tried to overthrow a democratically-elected representative government run by his political opponents. What is ironic about this failure to sustain faith in representative institutions to the bitter end is that he had encouraged unconstitutional activities not to overthrow but to protect representative institutions.

The great statesman's final act sealed the fate of the Republic, which his former Liberal associates had seriously undermined during his absence abroad; so much so that the anti-Venizelists, who were essentially former royalists, became its only true champions as it disintegrated. The restored monarchy in 1935 was not given a chance to re-identify itself with representative government: King George II followed the advice of his prime minister Ioannis Metaxas, who was no friend to parliamentary institutions. Moreover, events in Europe and in the eastern Mediterranean, as interpreted by the governments of both Greece and Britain, left little room or time for the Greek parliamentarians to clean up their act and stop their antics. It is not perhaps without significance that a new Parliament in 1936 handed over power, by its own free will, to Greece's future dictator, Metaxas, a sworn enemy of liberal democracy.

Authoritarian rule in the country was not new; the element of novelty consisted in the institutional form which its ambitious leader tried to give it. However what must have disturbed dedicated parliamentarians more than the fascist façade of the Metaxas dictatorship was the ease with which political parties were pushed aside the moment they practically abdicated their role of running the country. After 1936 and for the next ten years, they were in limbo. Dictatorship, war against the Axis, foreign occupation and the first stages of civil strife made parties and representative government a distant memory. In the years of Axis occupation in particular, and in the light of what was presented as an impressive increase in the Left's influence in the country, a return of the pre-war parties seemed unlikely. However their leaders—or at least most of them—had survived to claim their institutional role when the Communists made their bid for power in 1944. This resuscitated the old parties. Contemporary observers marvelled at the resilience with which the men of the '*Politikos Kosmos*' (politicians in general), though deprived of the means to keep their clienteles dependent on them and without access to means of communication with the public, managed their comeback.[3]

It now seems surprising that they fought the Communist insurgency after 1946 with Parliament in session the whole time. The same old parties that had abdicated power and been so easily swept aside in 1936 by a former army officer turned politician managed now to serve and protect the representative institutions against an avowed enemy far more dangerous to them than the Greek fascists of the 1930s. The politicians of pre-war times received a new lease of life

---

[3]See Reginald Leeper, *When Greek Meets Greek,* London, 1950, pp. 211ff. Leeper was British ambassador to the Greek government-in-exile during the Axis occupation and the first stages of the Civil War when it returned to Greece.

from the new consensus that emerged in the common effort to fight and defeat the Communist insurgency with the very means provided by representative government.

The post-war reconstruction strained representative institutions in other ways. Cold War anti-Communism, the American involvement, a powerful army and the Cyprus question troubled political life but did not derail it. A strong conservative figure in the person of Constantine Karamanlis kept right-wing forces on a reformist course and rebuilt the country's shattered economy. Karamanlis's dynamic lead forced the remnants of the defeated Left and the old Venizelist parties that opposed his National Radical Union to form respectively the United Democratic Left and the Centre Union. The Communist Party, outlawed in the final stage of the civil war, withdrew its party machine from Greece, finding refuge in the Communist countries of the Warsaw Pact.

It was a flawed democracy, but the best that a wounded Greece could produce: a government of most of the people and for nearly all the people. Friction with Britain over the future of Cyprus limited the scope of Karamanlis's foreign policy. A negotiated settlement of the issue in 1959–60 brought some relief to his government but little satisfaction to a public whom his predecessors had led to believe in *Enosis*, i.e. union of Cyprus with Greece, as an undertaking that was not impossible. On the home front the Centre Union led a strong protest movement both inside and outside Parliament against the 'fraud and violence' by means of which the right-wing establishment and a politicised army rigged the elections of October 1961. The Left's unexpectedly strong showing in the previous elections (1958) no doubt tempted right-wing agents of the ruling party to justify strong-arm methods in the name of national security. However, it is very doubtful that Karamanlis himself was privy to the use of such methods.

The 'relentless struggle' of the ageing leader of the Centre, George Papandreou, led to a radicalisation of slogans and forms of action against conservative rule. He and his radicalised Centre Union youth section took to the streets, thus causing violent clashes with the police amid daily rumour of conspiracies. A quarrel with the King in 1963 over a state visit to Britain precipitated Karamanlis's resignation and seeming withdrawal from political life. This brought to an end the first part of this statesman's hitherto successful political career.

Karamanlis's departure from the political scene in 1963 was not only the result of his clash with the monarchy. Papandreou's rhetoric, the sinister attack by right-hing thugs in league with police officers on a popular deputy of the Left in Thessaloniki in May 1963, resulting in his death, and the vociferous writings of the Centre Union press created an atmosphere of crisis in which the conservative leader was unable to keep his party together, short of taking extraordinary measures or availing himself of the services of right-wing military conspirators. He chose to withdraw from the scene, perhaps loath to witness the unmaking of the political stability which he had so painstakingly created during the previous eight years.

The year 1963 marked the 1,000th anniversary of the Mount Athos monastic community, the 100th anniversary of Greece's royal dynasty—and the end of post-civil-war stability. A crowd-pulling and experienced political leader like George Papandreou and an immature and badly-counselled monarch in the person of the youthful Constantine II allowed themselves to be led into positions from which they and their advisers felt that they could not withdraw. The outcome of this confrontation in 1965 was political instability, charges and counter-charges of conspiring against the state, and the eventual suspension of the Constitution and representative institutions by right-wing army conspirators.

Democracy was undermined and eventually suspended due to the ruthless determination of the conservatives to remain in office and the Centre's equally ruthless determination to gain power at any cost. Both camps spoke in the name of the Constitution and representative institutions, and both displayed a lack of moderation and sober judgement with few parallels in the country's turbulent political history, with the possible exception of the confrontation of 1935–6.

The fall of the military dictatorship in 1974 brought back from deportation or self-exile abroad most of the old hands in politics and some new ones; it also brought a change of regime and a new constitution, as well as the legalisation of the Communist Party—all three the work of Karamanlis, who returned from self-imposed exile more liberal than he had been in the past. The fall of the dictators also brought back a new leader, Andreas Papandreou, who created a new party out of the old Centre Union, markedly more radical than its predecessor. The two men dominated the post-dictatorship scene and set their seal on representative institutions, Karamanlis until 1980 and Papandreou thereafter. The Constitution of 1975, as amended in 1985, produced representative institutions which have survived the two men who shaped them, as Greek society gradually grew to accept the principles that gave them birth.

Politics and the public domain

Writing in 1875 on the parties of his time and their role in the country's life, Emmanuel Roïdes left the following definition of a Greek political party: 'A group of people able to read and to mis-spell, sound of limb but hating all work, who will serve under any leader and seek to make him prime minister by any means, so that he may grant them the wherewithal to live without having to dig.' A year later the same keen observer of Greek politics drew on his knowledge of medieval history to comment on the dispensing of favours by the political parties: 'Our politicians are very similar to the Byzantine emperors, who allied themselves with the Franks, the Turks or the Bulgars to secure their throne and as a result were obliged, both themselves and their subjects, to become their tributaries. Like them, our politicians, in order to create or strengthen a party, recruited mercenaries off the streets, and rewarded them with appointments to redundant public positions. In time these mercenaries became so numerous and impudent that they constitute in Greece today a most fearsome power, before which king, government, parliament and indeed the entire nation fall trembling to their knees.'[4]

The author of *Pope Joan* was not alone in presenting Greek politics in such a negative light. Most accounts before and after Roïdes by both Greek and foreign observers have agreed on at least one aspect: that people join political parties in Greece in the hope of securing a post in the administration, which would otherwise be inaccessible to them. A news item, lost in the roar of Turkish aircraft flying over the Aegean, confirms Roïdes's assessment of Greek political parties: more that 15,000 hopefuls were listed as members of *both* the major parties.

This aspect of Greek politics, which falls into the category of the spoils system characteristic of all parliamentary regimes, has been explained by the imperfect operation of the country's public appointment system and by the state having been, in the absence of attractive and secure employment in the private sector, the major employer since Independence. However, this explanation leaves unexplained the lure of state employment even when this is precarious and far from lucrative, and why this practice persists even after the state has ceased being the principal employer.

It appears that the continuing attraction of state employment is to be explained by the modern Greek's deeply-felt insecurity; though rarely touched upon by social scientists, this never fails to stare the

---

[4]Emmanuel Roïdes, *Apanta* (Works), ed. by Alkis Angelou, Athens, 1978, vol. II, p. 138, from the satirical paper *Asmodaeos*, 8 June 1975, and p. 198 from the same paper, 11 July 1876.

student of modern Greek history in the face. Difficult as this admittedly is to prove with what is considered acceptable historical evidence, the relentless drive of most modern Greeks to bond with the state must certainly betray their sense of insecurity with regard to life, property and honour, and their equally strong feeling of living in a world where resources are scarce.

Both these features—insecurity no less than awareness of a world of scarce resources, which developed through the centuries of arbitrary rule and institutionalised dispossession of the weak by the mighty—motivated the drive to seek public office not only for its material rewards but, even more, for the sense it conveys of entering the circle of the powerful few and leaving behind the world of the impotent and vulnerable. In this light, politics for the modern Greeks after Independence represented a convenient way into the public domain, a world of privilege and power. It was a way open to all; and although it did not always secure the coveted position among the select few, no one would have accepted that it was not a precondition for attaining that position.

Thus politics was the means of entry to the public domain; however, limited space made it no more than a temporary haven for those who enjoyed the favour of the ruling party. Such favours were much in demand, and privileges were often withdrawn to satisfy other claimants. More important, these privileged positions passed with each change of government to a new set of office-seekers, as new political patrons were obliged to look after the interests of their clients.

Until the advent of parliamentarians and reformers with a vision like Harilaos Trikoupis and Eleftherios Venizelos, who instituted security of tenure in the civil service to free it from the ravages wrought by government changes, public office did not provide the security which might have made it attractive as a career. The privileged individuals who occupied public positions did all they could to feather their own nests. Eventually they would be ousted to make room for a new set of clients, who acted in the same fashion. Only the most adaptable survived long enough to give the state service something in return for what they gained from it.

The public sector—first penetrated, then exploited for a while, and finally abandoned—has never been for the average Greek an area which could seriously claim his loyalty and with which he could identify. Corporate loyalty outside the family has been as rare as a sense of security outside the same social unit. Modern Greeks entered the civil service as marauding invaders in enemy territory: to plunder, pillage and bring the spoils back to the haven of the family. The accumulated humiliations and disappointments of the political hireling, finally rewarded by his patron with a cherished position in the civil service, turned this humble client into a petty tyrant who held hostage those who could not avoid obtaining his signature and rubber stamps on official documents. Thus he controlled the destinies of his ephemeral subjects, until the time when he would return to the fold of the family, and again become the loyal brother and son or the loving father.

Politics in this sense helped to create and develop a public sector reminiscent of the attitudes and practices inherited from the pre-Independence past but not adaptable to the cultivation of corporate loyalties outside the family, from which a civil society could have grown. As in other areas, the past shaped and ruled the present under a veneer of impersonal and orderly regularity. Behind a façade of order, justice and continuity lurked the arbitrary but predictable decisions of the political client acting the part of a civil servant. The civil service thus acquired a life of its own, independent from and essentially inimical to the society it had been established to serve. Eventually, when security of tenure was secured, it grew and expanded, not only beyond society's needs but beyond society's capacity to support it. In other words, the civil service acquired not only a life of its own but a purpose of its own: to look after the interests of its members, even when they did not perform as expected.

Authoritarian regimes or governments ruling with emergency powers have occasionally threatened to remove public office tenure in order to get rid of unnecessary employees. Some actually did remove it, but as a rule such purges drove away not the expendable public servants as such, but the politically undesirable opponents of these governments or merely those unwilling to cheer the new leaders. Parliamentary governments brought back into the public service all the purged officials along with a new intake of political conscripts.

Like authoritarian rule, inflation has been a scourge for civil servants, but apparently not harsh enough to drive them out of the service. The runaway inflation and famine of the occupation years in the early 1940s tried their endurance, but no more than that of other city-dwellers who enjoyed none of the small benefits accruing to state employment. Many died in the famine of 1941–2 and many more suffered privations and humiliations in the years that followed. Although the civil service was badly shaken by the war and civil strife, it survived to see its ranks swell again in the years of reconstruction and recovery.

Successive governments, parliamentary as well as absolutist, have enacted a huge corpus of laws regulating various aspects of the civil service, such as selection and appointment procedures, promotion, tenure and remuneration. Each ministry, as well as administering one sector of public life, has had to deal with the problems of the staff under its jurisdiction, a task that has taxed the abilities of many talented ministers. Governments have been held to ransom by the country's public employees, and even the most powerful head of government has had to take account of the needs and whims of this 'workforce' and its leaders.

European Union membership obliged successive Greek governments to face, among other problems, the bloated civil service in the light of the progressively unmanageable deficit in the public sector. It has thus finally been realised by politicians and the public that, short of a drastic reduction in the size of the civil service and notwithstanding respectable achievements in all other sectors, the country faces the real danger not only of falling behind its European partners in many ways, but of being brought to a standstill by the very body that was established to oversee and regulate its creative forces.

Political leadership

In Greece political parties—as organisations playing a vital role in creating the consensus necessary to govern in a liberal democracy and as conduits for the wishes of the people—have seldom outlived their founders. Large issues, both internal and external, have contributed to the founding of parties and influenced their programmes and practices, but the personality and talents of their founders have always been decisive in their success or failure. From the first loose collections of personal groupings during the War of Independence to the political entities created and shaped by statesmen such as Harilaos Trikoupis, Eleftherios Venizelos and Constantine Karamanlis, political parties in modern Greece have mainly been products of their founders whose names they bore with pride .[5] The Communist Party is the exception.

Like all legitimate political formations, Greek parties have aspired to govern the country by mobilising support and electing deputies

[5]The best study of the subject is Gunnar Hering's, *Die politischen Parteien in Griechenland, 1821–1936*, Munich, 1992, 2 vols. See also Gregorios Daphnis, *Tà hellenika politika kommata* (The Greek political parties), Athens: Galaxias, 1961, the work of a keen observer of Greek politics.

to Parliament. The drive for political mobilisation has allowed them to penetrate regions and social strata of the country which had never before been involved in procedures associated with the election of civil authorities. In this sense they have played a highly important role in incorporating into the Greek polity large, formerly inactive sections of the population, such as the peasants.

Parties thus contributed to the transformation of an inert citizenry into a modern nation. Like school attendance or service in the national army, though on a smaller scale, involvement in party politics contributed to involving modern Greeks citizens speaking a variety of dialects and coming from a variety of regions in the interests and objectives of the nation-state as such. Eager to increase their political support and expand their bases, parties took their message to the smallest villages and the most inaccessible shepherd communities, where previously the representatives of the state in the person of the gendarme or the tax-collector had been rare and unwelcome visitors. By contrast, politicians offered peasants and shepherds for a fleeting moment the prospect of a less precarious life—indeed, a life of plenty and fulfilment. The recipients of these promises knew that only a handful among them could be accommodated in the world opened up by the politicians, but nonetheless hoped that they too might be among the elect few. The fact that some did manage to obtain satisfaction was proof to all and sundry that the system could work. Such interaction was not just about mundane benefits like jobs or loans; for a few days before elections people who lived on the margins of Greek society were made to feel like important players in the life of the nation: parliamentary candidates and local party bosses addressed them by name and took pains to explain important national issues.

Greek political parties have been conservative, liberal or radical on some issues, and studying them from this angle can be a useful exercise in political theory and practice. However, a different approach is also needed; the parties should also be seen as companies set up to meet a crisis, or sometimes to cause a crisis with a view to capturing power and running the country in the way a company would do— aiming primarily to maximise shareholder value, but for the benefit, if possible, of the general public as well.

Seen in this light, the party leader in Greece has often functioned like the chairman of a board of directors—which has almost invariably been selected by the leader, just as general staffs are selected by commanders-in-chief and ministers were appointed in the past by absolute monarchs. Party machineries and membership have been extensions of their leaders—their ambition, vision, moral position and fantasies. Ioannis Kolettis, the first elected prime minister of Greece, was such a leader: he set up a party from among his war associates and friends as an instrument for the realisation of his ambitions, and ran the country for three years until his death in 1847. In addition he exhibited at least two features common to most Greek party leaders in office: first, the pursuit of a course intended to antagonise as few interests as possible so as to stay in power as long as possible, and secondly, the diversion of public attention away from the real issues, or their presentation in ways expected to win public support. Highlighting the situation of the unredeemed Greeks and the prospects for their liberation was such a device. Governments had frequent recourse to it and never failed to get the desired results. The practice proved irresistible to most governments: the Turks or the Bulgars were often 'mobilised' by Greek governments under pressure to divert public attention away from intractable domestic issues.

The March 1844 electoral law provided for the election of deputies by absolute majority and universal male suffrage in two rounds in eight days, but it did not provide that elections would be held within the *same* eight days or in two rounds throughout the country. This allowed Kolettis and the 'Constitutionalists' to outmanoeuvre Mavrocordatos who, in spite of being in office, was no match for the Epirot politician in the art of manipulating public opinion, in both the capital and the provinces. The first parliamentary elections in Greece lasted for most of the spring and summer of 1844 and gave Kolettis a comfortable majority.

Kolettis's 'Constitutionalist' or 'French' party and the other two loose collections of followers of leading personalities (dubbed the 'English' and the 'Russian' parties), which had come into being in the years of the War of Independence, survived till the Crimean War (1853–6), when another set of politicians entered the field. A new electoral law in November 1864, following the promulgation of a new constitution that same year, did not appreciably change the character and *modus operandi* of the political parties. The small electoral districts of the previous law were maintained, but plurality was introduced in place of the absolute majority required under the old law for the election of deputies. The new law reduced the election period from the previously fixed eight days to four and introduced an innovation expected to facilitate voting by those unable to read: instead of a ballot, voters cast a small lead ball into one of the ballot boxes allocated to each of the district candidates standing for election.

Alexandros Koumoundouros (1815–1883)

Born in the Mani peninsula in the Peloponnese, Koumoundouros was elected to Parliament for the first time in 1851 and became Minister of Finance in 1856. He first became Prime Minister in 1865, and held that position ten times. He was a political opponent of Harilaos Trikoupis and was credited with the extension of Greece's territory in 1881 to include Thessaly and parts of Epirus. He was also responsible for distributing land to landless peasants and title deeds to long-standing squatters on state-owned land.

Harilaos Trikoupis (1832–96)

Harilaos Trikoupis was the most important Greek reformer of the 19th century. His contribution was multifaceted: he was responsible for ensuring that the royal head of state would refrain from granting a mandate to governments that lacked the confidence of parliament; he introduced legislation securing the tenure of civil servants; he created a modern political party based on liberal democratic principles as well as on party discipline; and he improved the training and standing of the armed forces. Most important of all, he created the necessary infrastructure for the take-off of the Greek economy. However, his efforts were obstructed by unfavourable international circumstances, and his foreign loans were instrumental in bankrupting the state. Although he did not live to witness the fruits of his long-term growth strategy, subsequent generations of politicians reaped where the had sown.

Born in Nauplion, the son of Spyridon Trikoupis (historian and prime minister), he studied law in Athens and Paris and entered the diplomatic service in 1856. While serving in London he was elected representative of the city's Greek community in the Hellenic Parliament. As a parliamentarian he made good use of his diplomatic skill during the negotiations which resultd in the accession of the Ionian islands to Greece in 1864. In 1866, after resigning from the diplomatic service and being elected representative of Missolonghi, his family's home town, he became foreign minister in a government headed by his future political opponent, Alexandros Koumoundouros and signed a treaty with Serbia. During the 1874 constitutional crisis his famous article 'Who is to blame ?', criticising royal interventions in parliamentary politics, earned him a brief prison sentence, but his position was vindicated. He was foreign minister again in the 1877 grand coalition under Constantine Kanaris, and in 1880, after the fall of a Koumoundouros government, he became prime minister. His defeat in 1885 by his chief political opponent, the populist Theodore Deliyannis, reflected public discontent with his austerity programme. The see-saw of victory and defeat between Trikoupis and Deliyannis continued during the decade 1886–96, but with the default of 1893 the popularity of Trikoupis waned until his abject electoral defeat in 1895. He died a year later in a Paris hotel while Greece was hosting the first modern Olympic Games.

Trikoupis's times mark a transition between two eras of modern history. As steam was replaced by electricity, so the more developed Western economies entered a protracted recession, with a concomitant dearth of domestic demand for capital. In their quest for customers, many Western banks turned to the states of the developing periphery of Europe and Trikoupis was quick to avail himself of the credit available to stimulate his country's economy. His substantial investment in the construction of railway networks was aimed at integrating disparate agricultural regions into a unified expanding market. His venture however yielded fewer economic results than anticipated, in the short term at least. Domestic markets were still in their infancy and could not be spurred by technology to reach a state of development that would have required decades of constant growth and social change. Although this and other public works laid down the infrastructure of a transport system that proved invaluable for the economy's future take-off, railways were seen in Trikoupis's time as a premature and costly undertaking that benefited speculators, financiers and international middlemen. Such people became a familiar spectacle in Athens and the object of vituperative attacks by Deliyannis. The latter championed a form of splendid isolation from international financial influences, believing in the virtues of an agrarian economy that aspired to self-sufficiency rather than economic growth. Deliyannis's major flaw was his predilection for irredentist adventures that proved inconsistent with his utopia of independence from foreign creditors and great power influence. His policies in fact caused more foreign intervention in Greek affairs than Trikoupis' own policy for growth.

At about the same time, Russia's return to Balkan affairs after a long period of absence following its Crimean misadventure revived the slumbering Eastern Question. The Russo-Turkish war that ended in 1878 with the San Stefano treaty encouraged the irredentist debate in the Balkans. The Greek electorate was faced with the dilemma of choosing between Trikoupis giving priority to domestic development and Deliyannis's agenda of territonal aggrandisement. Trikoupis had visited Serbia, Bulgaria and Romania in 1891 in an abortive attempt to forge a Balkan alliance, but was soon disappointed and thereafter pursued a policy of abstaining from confrontations with Turkey. During the Cretan uprising of 1889 he went so far as to discourage the insurgents and was for that reason defeated in the elections.

The Greco-Turkish war of 1897 was largely created by the political camp that considered irredentist priorities more pressing than development and growth. Its disastrous outcome vindicated Trikoupis's moderation.

Bibliography

G. Tsokopoulos, *Harilaos Trikoupis. Viographia*. Athens: Fexis, 1896; K. Gardika Alexandropoulou, 'I helleniki koinonia tin epochi tou H. Trikoupi' in D. Tsaousis ed. *Opsis tis hellenikis koinonias tou l9ou aiona* (Facets of Greek society in the 19th century), Athens: I. Kollaros, 1984. pp. 177–91; A.L. Andreadis, *Ta dimosia oikonomika tis Ellados*, (Greece's public finances), Athens, 1924; E.Stassinopoulos, *O Stratos tis protis ekatontaetias* (The army in the first 100 years), Athens, 1935, pp. 55–60; C.M. Woodhouse, *The Story of Modern Greece*, London: Faber & Faber, 1968, pp. 172–82; *Peri Harilaou Trikoupi, ek dimosievmaton* (About H. Trikoupi from publications), vols 1–16, Athens: Sakellariou, 1907–12; Lefteris Papayannakis, *Oi hellenikoi sidirodromoi, 1881–1910* (The Greek railways), Athens : MIET, 1982.

Ballot boxes were divided into two compartments, one painted black and the other white; this allowed voters to vote either for (white) or against (black) any one of the candidates by casting the ball into the appropriate compartment. (Ever since, to say that someone was 'blackened' in an election has meant that he lost.) Demetrios Voulgaris, Epameinondas Deligiorgis, Alexandros Koumoundouros and Harilaos Trikoupis dominated politics at the head of parties consisting of their personal followers which, with the sole exception of Trikoupis's party, did not survive their founders' demise. Neither the lead ballot-ball nor Trikoupis's successful struggle in the mid-1870s to oblige the King to give the mandate to the party with a parliamentary majority (*dedilomeni*) was enough to move political parties into a new stage.

The majority system, instead of favouring the growth of two large parties as instruments for shaping a broad consensus outside Parliament, turned the effort to win parliamentary seats into vicious battles between local bosses, who in turn had a firm hold over the leaders under whose name and party they were elected. Electoral contests were so many local battles to capture and hold parliamentary seats. By the end of Greece's involvement in the First World War this system was perfected by highly ingenious ministers for internal affairs. The anti-monarchical regime that emerged from the 1922 army revolt against King Constantine passed a law in September 1923 whereby the 'narrow' electoral districts were kept in 'Old Greece', while 'broad' (large) districts were established in 'New [northern] Greece', and

Muslims and Jews voted separately. This aimed to deprive the opposition parties of seats which they would have won under a more equitable system. A new law in September 1926 marked a radical departure from previous electoral practices by introducing proportional representation throughout the country. However, the old systems were not abandoned but were occasionally brought back for reasons already explained, as in the general election of 1928 which secured a landslide victory for Eleftherios Venizelos, and that of 1935 which favoured his opponents. What all major parties have so far steadfastly refused to adopt as part of their objectives has been the incorporation of the electoral law into the country's constitutional charter to protect it from manipulation by ruling party majorities to help channel politics in predictable directions. The argument that flexibility in setting the rules for the next electoral engagement can prevent political deadlocks is another way of saying that a parliamentary majority is justified in manipulating these rules in order to prevent the minority from unseating it.

Although society was mostly agrarian and fragmented by familial loyalties and patronage, institutions representing urban liberal principles were strengthened throughout the second half of the nineteenth century. The constitution of 1864, extending universal male suffrage, was the most advanced in Europe. Furthermore, it would be fair to say that not all politicians submitted to the rules of the political game; some deserved the distinction of being considered reformers.[6]

Given that Greek political parties were not class-based (at least not until the appearance of the Communists) but rather groupings of notables, they tend to fall in two categories according to their leader's performance. There were those who tried to emulate Western parliamentary models, and others who placed their faith in national ingenuity to solve the idiosyncratic problems of the country. Alexandros Mavrocordatos, Trikoupis and Venizelos belong in the former category, while Kolettis, Voulgaris and Theodoros Deliyannis in the latter. Be that as it may, the most significant indigenous challenge to political patronage came not from the moderniser Trikoupis but, ironically, from the populist traditionalist Deliyannis, who believed in an insular, agrarian Greece, self-sufficient in foodstuffs. Through his populism Deliyannis recruited mass support and undermined the one-to-one

[6]For a concise analysis of party politics in the nineteenth century see Gregorios Daphnis, 'I politiki katastasi tis horas, 1865–1881' (The political condition of the country, 1865–1881) in *Istoria tou ellinikou ethnous* (History of the Hellenic world), vol. 13, Athens: Ekdotike Athinon, 1977, pp. 237–53, 277–98.

clientelistic relationships that had existed before. Similarly, Andreas Papandreou's populism in the 1980s undermined traditional clientelistic networks. His personal appeal to a public disfranchised by the Civil War, as well as to the newcomers from rural Greece who lacked connections in the urban centres, established a populist route of mass recruitment that circumvented the patron-client networks of his political opponents.[7] One would be tempted to classify Constantine Karamanlis with the modernisers, and Andreas Papandreou with the traditionalists, yet after the Civil War the innovative content of westernisation was replaced by a conservative backlash. Westernisation between the 1950s and the 1970s was associated with the rigid official creed of the victors in the fratricidal struggle of the 1940s. The conservatives were certainly the unquestioning champions of all that was Western.

Karamanlis was no doubt a conservative committed to the economic reconstruction of a war-ravaged Greece. In his successive incarnations of the 1970s he took it upon himself to bring the country into Europe, although this required its deep and total transformation. Andreas Papandreou, who emerged as a radical challenger of the conservative order in the 1960s, promoted a Third World creed and a populist discourse when he took power which addressed his public's emotions rather than its rational faculties.

Revolution and defeat: the Civil War, 1943–9

Wars are tragic events and civil wars doubly so. Because they involve mortal combat between opposing sets of the same people, they hurt more and their wounds take longer to heal than is the case with wars against foreign peoples. The English Civil War of the seventeenth century was fought to reaffirm parliamentary control over monarchical rule by divine right, the American Civil War to secure the Union against secession, and the Spanish Civil War to defend a republican regime against the forces of the *ancien régime*. The Greek Civil War of the 1940s was not fought over great social issues by different classes or over irreconcilable political differences; indeed, the country was allowed to slip into uncontrolled violence unleashed by right-wing and left-wing extremists whom the leaders of the government camp and the KKE were often unable or unwilling to rein in until too late. The KKE fought and lost a war with ill-defined objectives; the

---

[7]On this subject see Nicos P. Mouzelis's 'Theoretical Implications: Clientelism and Populism as Modes of Political Incorporation' in his *Politics of the Semi-Periphery*, London: Macmillan, 1986, pp. 73–94.

government fought and won the war for which it possessed, in addition to clearly defined objectives, a mandate from the great majority of the people.

Writings on the Civil War have reflected the political battles of the post-war period and the internecine war within the Left for supremacy in charting the right course for the KKE. The former clash, between apologists for the 'victors' and the 'defeated', involves a passionate and politically-charged debate over who was responsible for the outbreak of Civil War. The latter clash, between opposing sets of the 'defeated' and their apologists, involves a no less passionate and ideologically-charged debate over who was responsible for losing the war. In this sense—and until what really happened is elucidated— these wars of words over the Civil War will go on, because they serve ends other than those of Clio.[8]

Events and developments connected with the Civil War can be divided into four main periods. The first ran from the autumn of

---

[8]C. M. Woodhouse's *The Struggle for Greece, 1941–1949*, London, 1976 (repr. 2002), remains the best account of the war so far. See also his *Apple of Discord*, London, 1948. See also the following: Stefan Troebst, 'Yugoslav Macedonia, 1944– 1953: Building the Party, the State and the Nation', *Berliner Jahrbuch für osteuropäische Geshichte*, 1994/2, pp. 103–39; Ratislav Terzioski, 'IMRO – Mihailovist Collaborators and the German Occupation, 1941–1944' in Pero Moracaled, ed., *The Third Reich and Yugoslavia, 1933–1945*, Belgrade, 1977, pp. 541–603; O. L. Smith, 'The Boycott of the Elections, 1946: A Decisive Mistake?', *Scandinavian Studies in Modern Greek*, 6 (1982), pp. 69–88, and 'A Turning Point in the Greek Civil War, 1945–1949: The Meeting Between Zachariadis and Markos, July 1946', *Scandinavian Studies in Modern Greek*, 3 (1978), pp. 35–46; Heinz Richter, *British Intervention in Greece: From Varkiza to Civil War, February 1946 to August 1946*, London, 1985; Mark Mazower, *Inside Hitler's Greece: The Experience of Occupation, 1941–1944*, London, 1993; Evangelos Kofos, *Nationalism and Communism in Macedonia*, Thessaloniki, 1964, and *The Impact of the Macedonian Question on Civil Conflict in Greece*, Athens, 1989; John S. Koliopoulos, *Plundered Loyalties: Axis Occupation and Civil Strife in Greek West Macedonia, 1941– 1949*, London, 1999; John O. Iatrides, 'Perceptions of Soviet Involvement in the Greek Civil War, 1945–1949', *Studies in the History of the Greek Civil War*, ed. by L. Baerentzen *et al.*, Copenhagen, 1987, pp. 225–48; N. G. L. Hammond, 'The Allied Military Mission in N.W. Macedonia, 1943–44', *Balkan Studies*, 32 (1991), no. 1, pp. 107–44, and *The Allied Military Mission and the Resistance in West Macedonia*, Thessaloniki, 1993; D. H. Close, ed., *The Greek Civil War, 1943–1950: Studies of Polarization*, London, 1993; R. V. Burks, *The Dynamics of Communism in Eastern Europe*, Princeton, 1961; Elisabeth Barker, *Macedonia: Its Place in Balkan Power Politics*, London, 1950, and 'Yugoslav Policy towards Greece, 1947–1949', *Studies in the History of the Greek Civil War*, pp. 263–95; Lars Baerentzen, 'The Paidomazoma and the Queen's Camps' in *Studies in the History of Policy towards Wartime Resistance in Yugoslavia and Greece*, London, 1975; and G. M. Alexander, *The Prelude to the Truman Doctrine: British Policy in Greece, 1944–1947*, Oxford, 1982.

1943, when the left-wing resistance organisation EAM (*Ethniko Apeleftherotiko Metopo* or National Liberation Front) and its military arm ELAS (*Ellinikos Laïkos Apeleftherotikos Stratos* or Greek People's Liberation Army), sponsored and controlled by the KKE, made a spirited bid either to co-opt or to suppress all other organisations active in the resistance against the Axis occupying forces. A truce was arranged in January 1944 with a view to pursuing more active resistance against the Axis with British support and guidance. The second ran from the 1944 truce until the Varkiza accord of February 1945, which officially ended the battle for the control of Athens between ELAS and the government forces, supported by British units sent from Italy. The third ran from the Varkiza accord till the resumption of large-scale hostilities in the autumn of 1946 between the Communist rebels and government forces, and the fourth from the resumption of fighting in 1946 till the final suppression of the rebels in August 1949.

Earlier interpretations of the Civil War focused on the last of these periods and regarded the preceding developments as distinct 'rounds' in the war. The main reason for this approach was its connection with the Cold War, officially launched in 1946 as a relentless drive by the US-led West to stem the tide of Soviet-sponsored expansion of Communist regimes in Eastern Europe and the Near East. However, it is now increasingly evident that domestic factors played a much more important part in the outbreak the Civil War's if not also for its outcome. Such factors were the intense struggle between the parties for position and power; the destruction of life and property caused by the Axis occupation and the ensuing suffering; the intense passions and deep rifts the occupation had caused; and the question of the future of Macedonia, which at the time was more than an academic exercise in semantics.

The first bout of clashes between Communist-sponsored resistance to the Axis forces and other organisations resisting those forces had all the characteristics of the subsequent conflict. Three of those organisations which ELAS attacked were EDES (*Ellinikos Dimokratikos kai Ethnikos Syndesmos* or Greek Democratic and National League); EKKA (*Ethinki kai Koinoniki Apeleutherosi* or National and Social Liberation); and PAO (*Panellinios Apeleutherotiki Organosis* or Panhellenic Liberation Organisation). EDES was a league of republican army officers and politicians under Napoleon Zervas, an officer who had been active in the interwar military coups. The organisation survived the ELAS attack but limited its area of operation to Epirus, which became an anti-ELAS stronghold with British assistance. Zervas gradually agreed to embrace the cause of the monarchy in the person of King George II, who had the full support of the British government. EKKA was a small organisation of army officers and politicians under the republican officer Demetrios Psaros, whose death at the hands of ELAS in 1944 led to EKKA's dissolution. PAO started as an organisation of army officers from Greek Macedonia, whose main concern was Bulgaria's designs in the region. A number of its bands which took the field in the central Macedonian highlands were also attacked by ELAS in the autumn of 1943 and dissolved. Some of its officers sought refuge in the Greek army units operating in the Middle East under Allied command, others joined ELAS, and still others supported various right-wing bands or militias in northern Greece operating with the tacit support of the German occupying forces.

The purpose of these attacks as explained by KKE and ELAS was to eliminate elements opposed to placing all resistance organisations under a single command, as well as organisations and individuals collaborating with the Axis occupying forces. Placing all resistance organisations under a single command essentially meant incorporating them into the common structure of ELAS, which was by far the largest organisation in terms of numbers, and under the control of Communist political commissars. Moreover, the leaders of these organisations, particularly army officers, were unwilling to place themselves under the command of Communist warlords. Many of these officers had fought with distinction against the Axis invaders and were not prepared to take orders from those who had seen little or no action in 1940–1 (most Communists has been imprisoned before and during the war). As for the charge of collaboration with the occupying forces, it was a useful pretext for ELAS to get rid of all those who refused to serve with it; collaboration was impossible to disprove before guerrilla tribunals manned and controlled by the KKE. It is now established beyond reasonable doubt that many of the charges of collaboration against opponents of KKE and ELAS were fabricated by commissars and guerrilla tribunals answering to those authorities.

Civil strife during this initial period took the form of ELAS attacks against EDES bands in Epirus and PAO bands in central Macedonia. In addition to knocking out the resistance organisations and individuals refusing to fall into line, the ELAS drive aimed at removing obstacles to a possible link up with Communist-controlled resistance in neighbouring Yugoslavia and Albania. Similar drives by Enver Hoxha in Albania against the nationalist 'Balli Kombetar' and by Tito against the Serb nationalist movement of Draga Mihailovich, though not concerted due to the lack of effective contacts between the two Communist parties, and the lack of confidence in each other's designs, reflected the dominant Communist objective in the region: to prepare the way for seizing power.

The British liaison officers attached to the various resistance organisations were unable to save non-left resistance groups even where they tried to do so. Only EDES was saved after a truce arranged by the British liaison officers in January, separating its domain in Epirus from that of ELAS to the east and south. However, this proved a fragile arrangement; EDES was knocked out a year later when ELAS was making its bid to seize Athens.

British policy with regard to Greek resistance to the Axis occupying forces aimed at increasing pressure on these forces to make their occupation as costly as possible; that at least is what the Middle East general headquarters suggested. British liaison officers attached to the Greek resistance organisations were supposed to further this end, and make sure at the same time that the Communist-sponsored resistance, namely ELAS, did not secure undisputed control of the country and thus impose a regime that would be difficult to dislodge after the war. The British Foreign Office in particular was concerned over the fate of King George II, Britain's man in Greece and a loyal ally. The issue that worried the British was the KKE's opposition to his return to Greece before a plebiscite on the question of the monarchy was held. Political precedent left little doubt that the outcome of such a plebiscite depended on the aims of those holding power at the time. If the KKE had been allowed to win, through ELAS, a position of dominance in the country before liberation, the question of the regime in Greece would have been decided according to Communist party policy. The British government considered the King's return a guarantee that normal political life would be restored and that British interests in Greece would be safeguarded.

The KKE was one of the principal actors in the events described here, having had at its disposal a network more extensive and effective than any other political party in occupied Greece. Persecution of Communists during the Metaxas dictatorship and the consequent need to operate underground proved a great asset during the occupation. Unlike all the other political parties incapacitated by foreign occupation, the KKE was able to operate because of its skill in establishing and operating an extensive underground network. This enabled the KKE to win control of the first armed bands that took to the mountains;

these consisted of Communists and leftists in general who had fled the cities to avoid arrest by the occupying authorities. These first bands grew in strength as young peasants were driven to the mountains by the harsh Axis rule, which included brutal reprisals, and eventually by the KKE, whose policy was to build a strong military arm. The EAM's patriotic slogans proved irresistible, as did the legitimacy derived from recognition of ELAS by GHQ Middle East as a section of the military machine fighting against the Axis. Eventually ELAS developed into a powerful instrument in the hands of the KKE and had a twofold aim: resistance to the Axis occupying forces and concentration of its own power in order to secure an unassailable position at the liberation. However, to maintain and develop the effectiveness of this army, the KKE needed military and other supplies including financial assistance, legitimacy and acceptance by a large section of the population until it was in a position to impose its will. All three requirements were integrally connected with Britain's needs and objectives in the region. The British provided, or promised to provide, military and financial assistance for specific operations against the Axis forces; and they regulated its flow in such a way as to steer the KKE and ELAS in the desired direction. The British were also instrumental in providing the required recognition of ELAS operations as part of the Allied effort. Finally, they were in a position, through BBC broadcasts to occupied Greece, to influence public opinion over ELAS.

Thus the KKE, though increasingly powerful, was not a completely free agent, but its freedom increased to the extent that its dependence on British military and political objectives decreased. This became glaringly evident in 1944, when ELAS launched a large-scale conscription campaign and pressed into its ranks, along with reluctant peasants, former collaborators such as the Slav Macedonian militias who had fought under the Italians and the Germans in northen Greece. With their Axis sponsors evidently about to withdraw from the country, these militias promised to serve their new masters.

By the summer of 1944 divided counsels in the KKE leadership and the pursuit of the twofold aim mentioned earlier had created a deceptive lull both in occupied Greece and in Cairo, where the Greek government-in-exile had moved from London. Following a Communist-inspired mutiny in the Greek army and navy units in the Middle East under British command, the KKE and the left-wing parties under its influence agreed to participate in a conference of politicians purporting to represent Greece's parties. The outcome of the conference of May 1944 was a 'National Government' resting on a 'National Contract' and headed by the Venizelist politician George Papandreou. The KKE and the small left-wing parties waiting upon it agreed to enter the 'National Government' with reservations and claims for ministerial portfolios which no Greek prime minister at that time would have been prepared to satisfy. Liberals were ready to interpret the KKE's ambivalence as the product of divided counsels in the Communist leadership, while conservatives interpreted it as signalling its lack of confidence in democratic government. Indeed, everything the KKE did in this period tended to justify conservative reservations and fears. ELAS hunted down its opponents in Greece who refused to fall into line, while certain collaborators were tacitly absolved of their sin and allowed to join the resistance. This was the case of the Slav Macedonian militia mentioned earlier. Past grievances of locals against the authorities, quarrels with the Asia Minor and Pontus refugees over land ownership, and surviving Bulgarophilia had allowed Bulgarian, Italian and German officers to win over a number of Slav Macedonians and turn them against the rest of the Greeks. Access to foodstuffs and animal feed, as well as sheer opportunism, sent some 15,000 Slav Macedonians of west and central Greek Macedonia across to the other side of the barricade.[9]

Over one-third of those who were compromised in this way in the eyes of their neighbours received arms from their Axis patrons and formed village garrisons to prevent ELAS from obtaining supplies and intelligence. These Slav Macedonian militiamen, who came to be known as *Komitadji* (men of the Komitato or Committee), first appeared in the district of Kastoria in March 1943, and their Italian and German patrons—Bulgaria's occupation zone was limited to Western Thrace and eastern Greek Macedonia—used them as auxiliaries to guard bridges and road checkpoints and carry firewood for their needs. These militiamen did all the things that peasants do to each other under authorities who do not consider the well being of those they rule their primary concern.

The autumn and winter campaign against EDES and PAO left the *Komitadji* unscathed, which raised questions about the real motives behind the ELAS attacks against its opponents. It soon became clear that of the Slav Macedonian marauders operating under Axis protec-

---

[9]The subject is discussed in John S. Koliopoulos, *Plundered Loyalties: Axis Occupation and Civil War in Greek West Macedonia, 1941–1949*, London, 1999, pp. 57 ff.

tion were receiving this preferential treatment because other Slav Macedonians, perhaps as many as had gone over to the Axis, had crossed the northern border to Yugoslavia and were now doing everything they could to attract the 'misguided' to the 'right' side of the struggle.

The situation was much more complicated than ELAS and the KKE were willing to admit at the time. The Slav Macedonians of the region were becoming increasingly responsive to calls from Yugoslav Macedonia to join in a struggle to establish a 'free Macedonia'. To win the Slavs of Yugoslav Macedonia away from Bulgarian influence and attract them to the resistance movement against the Axis, the Yugoslav resistance leader, a Croat by the name of Josip Broz, or Tito, offered them the status of separate nationhood in a future Communist and federal Yugoslavia. As expected, the first to heed the call for separate Macedonian nationhood were the Slav Macedonians who had been compromised by collaboration and, with an Allied victory over the Axis likely, were now eager to join the winning side. The formerly Bulgarophile Slav Macedonians went through a timely mutation and were transformed into fanatical Macedonians. The medium for this was the Communist-sponsored resistance to the Axis in Greece and Yugoslavia. However, the KKE leadership of the time pretended not to see that ELAS was flirting with secession: Macedonian nationhood in a federal Yugoslavia meant that eventually Greek Macedonia would have to be ceded too—KKE leaders disavowed this, or chose to say as little as possible. A fundamental objective of the founders of Macedonian nationhood in the summer of 1944 when ELAS opened its door to the 'misguided' Slav Macedonians of Greece, was the 'liberation' of Greek Macedonia—and Bulgarian Macedonia—and their union with the fledgling People's Republic of Macedonia.

Conscription of these Slav Macedonians was presented as a drive to 'disarm' all those whom the Axis had armed against ELAS. The only plausible explanation must be sought in their value as mercenaries in the KKE's drive to build as massive a revolutionary army as possible in preparation for their seizure of power. Slav Macedonians tainted by collaboration and compromised in the eyes of other Greeks were no doubt expected to be obedient revolutionaries. They had acquired additional value to the KKE with their promise to act as a link to the Yugoslav Partisans, who were expected to assist the KKE in its drive to seize power.

Whatever the motives behind the 'disarming' of the Slav Macedonian Axis collaborators might have been, by the time the Axis occupying forces withdrew from Greece in October 1944 there were no such collaborators to bring to justice: all had vanished into the ranks of ELAS or across the frontier. As will be seen later, they were tried for collaboration with the Axis occupying forces in the last years of the Civil War by military tribunals and *in absentia*, since they were now rebels against the government of the country. The ELAS patrons of the 'misled' Slav Macedonians of Greece were in for a surprise, as the last German troops were abandoning the country: some 1,000 of them, all now fervent Macedonians, abandoned their ELAS units and crossed over to their Yugoslav Macedonian '*metropolis*'. The ELAS leaders professed their shock and revealed the pro-Axis past of the fugitives, but by this time, in the autumn of 1944, they had other concerns and could not give this incident their full attention.

The Greek government, escorted by a British military force, had just arrived. It carried with it an agreement signed in September, at Caserta in southern Italy, by representatives of the Greek government and all resistance organisations, providing for a British commander to head all armed units in liberated Greece and for their eventual disarmament and the formation of the new Greek national army. Most people hoped that another round of civil strife would be averted, but everything conspired against a peaceful liberation of the country.

The experience of harsh Axis rule and a Communist-sponsored resistance as much concerned over post-liberation political developments as over fighting the occupying forces—in conjunction with Britain's interests and objectives, explained earlier in this chapter—produced an explosive situation in newly-liberated Greece. There had been two governments recognised outside the country: the émigré government, headed by the King and recognised by the Allies, and that in Greece which received its mandate from the Axis occupiers. There was also a 'shadow' government, its authority exercised by the EAM and its network of appointed committees, which claimed to rule in the name of the Greek people. At the liberation ELAS moved out of its highland strongholds and took control of the entire country, except for Athens, which became the seat of the émigré Greek government—without the King, but with a British military contingent at its disposal. Those who had been associated in one way or another with the Axis occupying forces and their hirelings were either arrested and imprisoned or showed their faces in public as little as possible in the hope that their activities during the occupation would be forgotten. The dramatic events that followed made their case an issue of no-one's primary concern.

There were now two loosely defined camps, a left-wing one headed by the KKE and represented by the EAM, and a pro-government one. The latter drew on the forces that had opposed EAM rule and suffered for this opposition, as well as on the forces that had arrived in Athens from the battlefields of Italy and the Middle East. Conservatives in general identified with the government camp, while liberals, even when not sympathetic to the EAM, were ready to see it as a promising political force and willing to allow it an increased role in government. The EAM had been projected during the Axis occupation as a staunch and uncompromised defender of freedom and democracy, a broad political front that had sprung from the people to wage a relentless struggle against tyranny, whether foreign or indigenous. This was at least how many people living in cities and unused to EAM rule viewed this organisation. Although the government had fought for the same objectives, it was burdened with a king who was inextricably associated with the arbitrary rule of the Metaxas dictatorship he had helped to create. The government was also thoroughly discredited by the EAM for having abandoned the country to the foreign invaders and sought refuge in distant lands. In the immediate aftermath of the liberation, centre or moderate public opinion in Greece was not unsympathetic to the EAM, and also not entirely sympathetic to the government.

The extension of EAM rule over most of the country from October 1944 until some time after the suppression of the December rebellion in Athens, but above all the rebellion itself, drastically changed political sympathies and affiliations. Moderate opinion was swept away, and there was no longer a centre to count upon as a viable political force; old and new liberals went over to the government camp. The contest after December 1944 was not between Right and Left, as is sometimes suggested; it was a desperate and senseless fight by the Communist Left against all other political forces.

The Communist uprising in Athens in December 1944 was neither desperate nor senseless; nor did it result from the deadly shots fired at the EAM-sponsored demonstration at Syntagma Square on December. Gregoris Farakos, at one time secretary-general of the KKE who was expelled from the party in the late 1980s, refuted the widely-held view that the 3 December uprising was triggered by these particular killings. Farakos presented credible evidence that the party's decision to rise predated the incident.[10]

---

[10]Gregoris Farakos, *Ares Velouhiotes, to Hameno Archeio. Agnosta Keimena* (Areas Velouhiotes, the lost archive: unknown documents), Athens: Ellinika Grammata, 1997). See also *Dekemvris tou 1944* (December 1944), Athens: Filistor, 1996, pp. 79–95.

The KKE leadership, not as divided as was once believed, pushed ELAS on to a risky but calculated venture. It possessed overwhelming superiority over its opponents, but did not make proper use of the forces at its disposal. ELAS did not lack either able commanders or seasoned troops, but it had not developed systematic plans for seizing and holding the capital, and appeared not to know what to do with power. Even while fighting raged in Athens, battle-hardened units of the north were sent to suppress EDES in Epirus. This was used in support of the argument that the Athens rising was no more than a show of muscle to force the government to accept EAM as an equal partner.

Supported by the KKE leadership, ELAS entered the battle for Athens with the intention of overthrowing the government. It did not expect the resistance put up by the British to keep Athens in government hands. British troops were hurriedly dispatched to fight for Athens, not from secondary fronts but from Italy, where they were engaged in a serious campaign against the Germans. Moreover, KKE leaders could not possibly have known of the Moscow agreement the previous October between Churchill and Stalin, which accorded Britain a predominant position in Greece in exchange for a similar Soviet position in the other Balkan and East European countries. Nor could they possibly have been expected to change course on the basis of the meagre advice that reached them from Stalin and other Communist leaders. This advice, even when it was forthcoming, was cryptic and not sufficiently discouraging. Finally, all Communist-sponsored resistance movements in the region were doing what ELAS was trying to do: seize power. The assault that ELAS launched in December 1944 with the object of seizing power was not extraordinary, but the stiff British resistance to it was extraordinary and unexpected.

The KKE was not provoked into an all-or-nothing war for control of Athens. In 1944 it did not have its back to the wall: it had reached the height of its trajectory and its influence, and the seizure of power was not its only option. By opting for a violent seizure of power, because it lacked confidence in democracy, it followed the course of the other Communist parties of Eastern and South-Eastern Europe, and not that of the Communist parties of France and Italy. In this sense the December 1944 rebellion was the last and most violent stage of the drive by the KKE in the autumn of 1943 to knock out its political opponents.

The KKE was not dragged down the slippery slope of violent actions by its resistance heroes, as it was to be in 1945–6. Its organs were in full control of both the EAM and ELAS and of the party membership. The Politburo exercised undisputed control over policy and strategy as they were articulated in the Central Committee meetings. Social revolution was the ultimate objective, and the Communist-sponsored and -controlled resistance movement was the means of attaining that end. The KKE had built its formidable machine, ELAS, precisely to that end, and not simply to stage a show of force to scare its political enemies into a partnership for democracy. The party was united, deservedly proud of its achievements during the Axis occupation, and scornful of its political enemies. Greek Communists felt morally and politically superior to their opponents. This was not an unwarranted attitude, but it proved calamitous for both the party and the country.

The KKE plunged with all its strength into open rebellion in December 1944, and was defeated because it had no well-formed plan for usurping power. However, no other Communist party of the region had such a blueprint either. Internal and external factors, as well as management of military power, decided the contest both in Greece and in neighbouring countries with similar resistance movements.

The forces the British and the Greek government threw into the fight proved superior to ELAS: they were better led and supplied, but they also had a better plan of action and a clear objective. ELAS, though superior to its opponents in overall numbers, was dispersed throughout mainland Greece and lacked the means required for their quick concentration in the capital. Finally, ELAS troops, even seasoned ones, had been trained for guerrilla terrorist attacks on Axis-armed villages, brief clashes with the occupying forces and sabotage, not for regular warfare. An early victory in March 1943, when several bands of armed peasants ambushed and overwhelmed an Italian battalion at Siatista, West Macedonia, was a rare occurrence. More than a year later, in July 1944, an entire ELAS division (the once proud 9 Division) in the same region, did not stand to give battle against German units that swept across north-western Greece like wildfire, and dissolved in the space of less than ten days. The re-assembled regiments of this division were subsequently engaged in local operations, such as the assault on EDES in Epirus and the senseless attack in November 1944 on the Axis-armed Pontian refugees of Kozani, West Macedonia, in which several hundred of the Pontians were killed.

ELAS was good for overwhelming such opponents but not for standing against regular troops who had seen serious military action. The guerrilla army did not lack good commanders. Several hundred regular officers, mostly cashiered Venizelists whom the Metaxas dictatorship had denied the honour of fighting in the 1940–1 war against the Italians and the Germans, were given commands in the ELAS units. However, they squandered their skills and expertise in endless punitive attacks against the KKE's political opponents, following decisions taken by ELAS's political commissars. Such were the attacks on the Kozani Pontians, on the German-armed 'Security Battalions' in the Peloponnese in June 1944, and on local armed men throughout northern Greece.

The Varkiza accord of February 1945, in addition to officially terminating hostilities, provided for the dissolution and disarming of ELAS. The rebels surrendered arms, but only in part, and they did not all go home to assist in rebuilding the ruined country. It seems that most of the weapons, certainly the automatic and more sophisticated ones, were hidden away for future use. Not long after the Varkiza accord several thousand former ELAS guerrillas were sent across the border to special camps in Bulgaria, Yugoslavia and Albania. Eventually, more than 5,000 of the former resistance fighters and recent rebels concentrated in the special camp of Bulkes, Voivodina. This town, which had been abandoned by its long-term German inhabitants who followed in the wake of the retreating German troops, was placed by the Yugoslav Communists at the disposal of the KKE for quartering and training a rebel reserve for future use.

Caches of hidden ELAS arms began to be discovered by the Greek authorities, in most cases aided by those who had been instrumental in hiding them. Soon, also, news of the rebel camps outside Greece started reaching the authorities and the public. The right-wing press used both issues to warn of an imminent resumption of attacks from the ELAS bands, which had not laid down their arms and had taken to the mountains once again. One such band of ELAS diehards was headed by Aris Velouchiotis, captain of the three-man leadership of ELAS and one of those who had persuaded a reluctant KKE leadership in 1942 to support the development of armed resistance in the Greek highlands. Aris and his men were hunted down in June 1945 by the local 'National Guard' in central Greece, having been disowned and condemned by the KKE leadership for refusing to abide by the Varkiza accord and surrender their arms.

It was not easy then, nor is it now, to explain KKE policy in the aftermath of Varkiza. The interim Communist Secretary-General, George Siantos, was eased out of his post in May by Nikos Zachariadis, the youthful leader who had returned as a hero from Dachau, where he had been kept throughout the war. KKE pronouncements were mixed: there were frequent warnings that unless the authorities reined in right-wing bands terrorising EAM supporters and left-wing sympathisers in general, ELAS would be brought back to life. There were also frequent assurances that the KKE was sincerely working for the restoration of normal political life. The recourse to violence was also condemned, but 'self-defence' was allowed; right-wing terrorism in the countryside was condemned, while left-wing bands operating in the mountains were simply referred to as 'armed bands'.

There is little doubt now that KKE leaders wished to avoid a new round of civil strife before the party was ready for it. The KKE and ELAS had suffered a humiliating defeat and, even more important, the party had forfeited all sympathy beyond its members and was politically isolated. Moreover, ELAS had fought alone without any assistance from the Communist resistance movements beyond Greece's northern border. Moderate counsels prevailed over those who, like Aris Velouchiotis, pushed the party in the direction of meeting right-wing violence with left-wing violence.

Moderate counsels also prevailed in the government camp, despite strong pressure from right-wing elements for total war against the Communists. Charges against left-wing criminals who had committed atrocities during the December fighting, such as the abduction and execution of various Athenians, were not as extensive as right-wing public opinion expected. On the other hand, those who had held high office under the Axis occupying forces, as well as black marketeers, faced stiff charges in the special tribunal established to try crimes of that kind, and stiff sentences were handed out.

It is now becoming increasingly clear that the leaderships of both camps, the government no less than the KKE leadership, actually wished to end the confrontation begun by ELAS in 1943. Both, perhaps for different reasons, needed peace. Admittedly the government had prevailed over the rebels, but it had only done so with heavy British support. Normal political life was difficult enough to restore, and the KKE could not be persuaded that the government was really working for such a restoration while a strong foreign military contingent operated in the country. Moreover the Gendarmerie, the National Guard and two army units (one division and one company) were either unreliable or inadequate.

The Gendarmerie had been newly restructured, and it had not really been purged of elements compromised by collaboration with the Axis occupying forces; could not be counted upon to fight against organised military units. Even more unreliable was the National Guard, which had been formed during the December fighting by enlisting any able-bodied man who hated the Communists. The National Guard at first, and the Gendarmerie later, tolerated the arming of right-wing men and their unauthorised use as auxiliaries even if they did not openly encourage it. The number of those coming out as staunch supporters of the government increased dramatically after the suppression of the December rebellion. The times favoured right-wing opportunists.

Violence in the countryside increased soon after the Varkiza accord because it had been left unchecked. Repression or persecution of Communists and other left-wing sympathisers by the authorities of the Metaxas dictatorship and the succeeding occupation regime, and of right-wing sympathisers by the EAM and ELAS in the areas under their control during the occupation, did not favour reconciliation. Too many had been injured in some way and thought the time opportune to seek satisfaction for their grievances. Old and new feuds raged, fanning passions and violence, which conditions in the countryside also favoured. Destroyed bridges and roads seriously hindered the movement of vehicles, thus further reducing the land's low yield. The fact that animals had been killed or taken away from their rightful owners made matters worse. Beasts of burden and draught animals had been commandeered by the Axis occupying forces or by the resistance bands, and many of them had died. After the liberation animal theft soared, further undermining husbandry; so did the slaughtering of animals in winter for lack of feed or to save their starving owners.

The chronic undernourishment of the upland peasantry appeared to worsen after liberation instead of improving. Food was scarcer and more expensive in villages than in towns. The shipments of food and clothing distributed by ML (Military Liaison), UNRRA (United Nations Relief and Rehabilitation Agency) and the International Red Cross, could meet only a fraction of the requirements of all who, even by the low living standards of Greece at that time, were considered in need (i.e. the vast majority of the population). Distribution by local committees of such food, as well as of equally scarce and costly clothing, was bound to produce recriminations and charges of misappropriation. What mattered was not whether the charges were well founded or not, but their volume and frequency. Competition for scarce food and clothing and abuses in their distribution further aroused passions and led to violence.

News of the appearance of armed men outside the villages increased insecurity in the countryside and calls to arm against them. These were the uncompromising or insecure former ELAS guerrillas—the 'persecuted' ELAS fighters, according to official KKE and EAM pronouncements—who on the one hand provided the authorities with the arguments they needed to build the repressive machinery against the Left and, on the other, took the KKE and EAM leadership hostage on the slippery road to civil war. The number of these 'persecuted' former ELAS guerrillas must have been small at first, because after Varkiza most of them had crossed the northern border for sanctuary in the camps already mentioned. The authorities on the Greek side of the border appeared satisfied with the exodus of Communists and Slav Macedonians of all political hues, expecting that their departure would facilitate the establishment of law and order by denying their right-wing opponents the opportunity to settle old accounts.

The Greek authorities could not possibly have known that this departure of 'undesirable' men across the border was part of an operation planned and executed by the KKE leadership to build up a reserve for a future conflict at a safe distance. Nor could they have imagined that these very men would return a year later as dangerous avengers. In 1945 it appeared as if former ELAS commanders and their men were fleeing persecution by their opponents—or justice—across the frontier or in the hills.

The long tradition of banditry and the employment of self-styled defenders of law and order to suppress those on the wrong side of the law was given new life by the inability of the authorities to have loyal and effective regular armed forces at their disposal. Had such forces been available, they would have been able to get rid of the self-styled 'vigilantes' and of the equally self-styled 'people's fighters' and folk heroes. This tradition of lawlessness was sustained equally by the reluctance of the KKE leadership to rein in all these rogue fighters and prevent them from providing the right-wing *condottieri* with all the justification they needed to pursue their activities and make their services indispensable to the authorities. This reluctance of the KKE leadership to prevent the ELAS resistance heroes from creating the impression that the 'people's struggle' was not dead is difficult to explain, especially in view of the need to rebuild the shattered party. This notion of a 'continuing struggle' was, of course, useful to the KKE as long as those who kept it alive could be effectively controlled and were not allowed to become more popular than the fragile truce allowed: it had its uses as a counterweight against right-wing terror and as a bargaining chip in the KKE's effort to persuade the government to treat the Left more seriously that it was doing. Moreover, news of the activities of left-wing bands in operation and of the punishment of right-wing terrorists was no doubt expected to shore up declining morale among the KKE and EAM grassroots and sympathisers.

The KKE appeared not to have renounced the aim of seizing power by force; at least this was the impression of those in the government camp who were convinced that the KKE's pledges that the party was prepared to co-operate with its opponents in the establishment of law and order should not the trusted. The caches of ELAS weapons, which included mountain artillery and mortars and which were being discovered with disturbing frequency, could not really be explained away as being intended for use by the 'persecuted' ELAS fighters in self-defence against right-wing armed bands. Similarly, the policy of pacification was not really served by news about the growing numbers of 'persecuted' former ELAS fighters operating in the highlands of Greece or concentrating in the Bulkes camp in Yugoslavia. Even if the ELAS weapons had remained hidden and the Bulkes camp had been set up solely to protect insecure and persecuted ELAS fighters, it is hard to believe that the KKE leaders were oblivious to the danger of being diverted from their initial moderate positions by all these revolutionaries, who were being sent to Bulkes or allowed to take to the mountains.

In 1945 it appeared that events in the countryside were no longer dependent on political developments in the capital, where the government issued laws which did not bring peace because people in the countryside ignored them with impunity. The government of George Papandreou was replaced by that of Nikolaos Plastiras, which in its turn gave way to that of Petros Voulgaris, and this was followed by the government of Themistocles Sophoulis. These short-lived governments resorted to widespread arrests and deportations of armed left-wingers and of all those suspected of giving them shelter. The authorities made use of a law of 1971, a powerful instrument against brigands and their collaborators. The number of those who could be charged with assisting or simply sympathising with armed left-wingers was staggering. As a result, the number of imprisoned or detained left-wing sympathisers increased dramatically. The country's courts of law were simply swamped by a deluge of suits brought against thousands of individuals. Criminal courts were seriously understaffed, following the government's drive to purge the justice system and dismiss members of the judiciary who had compromised themselves during the period of Axis or EAM rule. On the other hand, summoning thousands of witnesses from inaccessible villages caused delays and prolonged indefinitely the detention of those against whom suits had been brought.

In 1945 the government in Athens, which was in a position of power *vis-à-vis* the defeated Left, had two choices: to destroy both right-wing and left-wing bands and effectively seal the northern frontier with the Communist countries, or to take no such action and allow the already bleeding countryside to drag the country into a fully-scale civil war. It later became clear that, short of effectively suppressing all who defied law and order and sealing the northern frontier, and short of disregarding KKE tears for the 'persecuted' fighters, civil war would have been unavoidable, as it finally was when mounting violence in the countryside reached the point at which it could no longer be controlled using routine methods.

It appears that Greece slipped into civil war because the national government, no less than the KKE leaders, was not so much unwilling as powerless to keep its own extremists in check. The traditional KKE position that Greece was thrown into civil war by the governments of Britain and the United States and their puppets in Greece with a view to destroying the Left as a political force rests primarily on Cold War rhetoric, and is impossible either to prove or to disprove. The equally traditional position of the Right that those responsible for the civil war were the Soviet Union and the Balkan Communist countries, as well as the Greek Communists, although more credible, essentially rests on a similar basis. It has by now become clear that the role which the Soviet Union and the Communist countries bordering on Greece played in the Greek Civil War was decisive. However, the 'Communist conspiracy' theory leaves out the scarcely concealed differences and antagonisms between Stalin and Tito, between Tito and Dimitrov, between the Slav Macedonian Communists and the other Communists in Greece, and among the Slav Macedonian Communists themselves. Neither the Greek nor the Yugoslav Communists were ordered or even advised by Stalin to become involved in the Civil War because neither Tito nor Stalin ever imposed that war on Greece. Although both supported the Greek Communist rebels, they did this less out of solidarity towards their Greek comrades, than because they wanted to keep Greece's Western allies busy and allow the Soviet Union to consolidate its position in Eastern Europe. It is true that Tito never missed an opportunity to attack the Greek government for its alleged persecution of the Slav Macedonians, but this was done primarily to satisfy public opinion in the 'People's Republic of Macedonia'. For Greece the main problem with these Yugoslav attacks was that both the KKE and the Greek government appeared to give them more attention than they warranted, and to attribute to them intentions and motives which did not correspond to the reality.[11]

One aspect of Yugoslavia's role in the outbreak of renewed civil war in Greece which has curiously been overlooked in both contemporary and subsequent studies of the war's causes was the role of the uncompromised and persecuted heroes of the Greek resistance. Yugoslav Partisan leaders, though dismissive of the Greek Communists as a revolutionary force and resenting their 'nationalist' bias on the question of Greece's Slav Macedonians as well as their apparent willingness to work for the establishment of a stable political situation, viewed with sympathy resistance leaders and subsequent rebels such as Markos Vapheiadis and considered them the only hope for a Communist take-over in Greece. The predominantly anti-Zachariadist post-Civil War trend in Greek and foreign left-wing writing, and its emphasis on the heroic and tragic aspects of the Communist guerrilla fighting in the Civil War, left no room for dispassionate analysis of the role of these heroes in the events that led to open confrontation. Zachariadis's opportunism in the last stages of the war has diverted attention from the dangerous opportunism of Aris, Markos and the other resistance heroes and subsequent 'uncompromised' fighters of the 'people's' struggle in Greece. This treatment has generally overlooked or underestimated the undeclared war of armed bands in 1946, which resulted in acts of vengeance against former ELAS fighters or EAM sympathisers which the government authorities could not prevent, and from similar acts of vengeance against right-wing armed men or sympathisers, which the KKE leadership was equally unable or unwilling to control.[12] However, the government failed the country in not being able to raise an effective and reliable regular armed force and equally effective and reliable security forces to

---

[11]Woodhouse, *The Struggle for Greece*, pp. 181 ff.

[12]For some well-deserved and directed blows against 'revisionist' left-wing writing see Ole Smith, 'The Greek Communists, 1941–1949', review article in *Epsilon*, 2(1988), pp. 77–101. See also Woodhouse, *The Struggle for Greece*, pp. 183, 188–9 and Richter, *British Intervention in Greece*, pp. 261, 276–7, 486–91, 513.

suppress armed bands in the countryside when this would still have been possible.

In the situation brought about by Axis and EAM rule as well as by the December 1944 uprising, acts of violence committed by armed men on both sides were unavoidable; so too was some form of warfare between armed bands. However, the development of this kind of warfare into a full-blown civil war was not unavoidable; nor was the full-scale Communist rebellion aimed at seizing power in the part of the country bordering on Yugoslavia and Albania.

Another aspect of the civil conflict, underestimated in left-wing revisionist studies, was the role of the Greek Slav Macedonian autonomists in both the outbreak and general direction of that war. The KKE and EAM journals referred to them as 'persecuted Slav Macedonian ELAS fighters', while Greek Slav Macedonians called themselves '*Makedontsi*', the name used at the time in the People's Republic of Macedonia to identify those belonging to the new nation. As already seen, they had served, in quick succession and even simultaneously, more than one master and cause until the time when Tito gave them a new identity and a new cause to fight for. These *Makedontsi* began intruding in the spring of 1945 into the Greek frontier highlands in small bands to avenge past or current wrongs. Their numbers increased as more and more Slav Macedonians were prosecuted in Greece, nominally for collaboration with the Axis occupying forces but in essence for having eventually opted for the KKE or the People's Republic of Macedonia. Of some 8,000 Slav Macedonians estimated to have crossed between 1944 and 1945 into the Republic, the *Makedontsi* raiders perhaps did not exceed 1,000. Later, in 1947, the Yugoslav government maintained that as many as 24,000 Slav Macedonians from Greece had sought refuge in Yugoslavia in the post-Varkiza period, but this number almost certainly included Slav Macedonians who had fled before the December 1944 rebellion.

Of these initial *Makedontsi* raiders, whom the KKE party journals represented as being 'persecuted ELAS fighters', perhaps not more than one-third had really served with ELAS. They had generally led a precarious existence in refugee camps which the government of the People's Republic of Macedonia had set up for the purpose. Their leaders, men like Paschalis Mitropoulos, Michael Keramitzis and Naum Peïos, were doing odd jobs for the government of the Republic, and most of them were members of the KKE and, at the same time, of the Republic's ruling Communist Party. These refugee raiders projected

Macedonianism among Greece's Slav Macedonians and heralded the imminent 'liberation' of '*Egejska Makedonia*' (Macedonia of the Aegean), i.e. Greek Macedonia. It soon became clear that avenging past or current wrongs was not their primary objective; what these *Makedontsi* really did was promote the People's Republic of Macedonia as the only hope for Greece's Slav Macedonians. The motive behind these raids was to make the Republic attractive to them and, strange as it may seem, to facilitate their crossing over into it. Right-wing reprisals for such raids achieved exactly that end by driving an increasing number of otherwise peaceful and reluctant peasants across the frontier.

There is no official evidence from the Republic's government to suggest that attracting as many as possible of Greece's Slav Macedonians over to the Republic was indeed official policy. Their presence there as refugees was no doubt a powerful propaganda asset for the Communist regime in the campaign to win support for its national aim to 'liberate' Greek Macedonia. However, one would think that their value as 'persecuted brethren' was not negligible. Moreover, although the departure of Greece's Slav Macedonians was a short-term propaganda asset in the Republic's war of words with Greece, it was self-defeating in the long run because it amounted to an irredentist claim on a Greek Macedonia depleted of its *Makedontsi*. Those who undoubtedly wished to attract them over to the Republic to serve their own political ends were their leaders, who needed a political clientele of their own.

Whatever were the motives and objectives of those who were behind the *Makedontsi* raids in northern Greece, the impact of these raids on the situation in the country was calamitous. In addition to being blamed by the government for fomenting band warfare, the KKE was charged with conspiring with a foreign power to cede Greek territory. As mentioned elsewhere, the KKE had distanced itself in 1935, with Comintern encouragement, from the interwar policy for the establishment of a 'united and independent Macedonia', and had adopted instead a policy which favoured the 'equal treatment of minorities'. This was still the official policy of the KKE. The projection of Macedonianism from across the frontier, however, put the party in an unenviable position. Reiteration of this policy did not silence criticism, because it satisfied no one. The *Makedontsi* of Greece had been, or continued to be, members of the KKE and, like the resistance heroes, they held the party hostage. The KKE resented *Makedontsi* propaganda in Greek Macedonia, but was never able to put an end to it, partly because *Makedontsi* propagandists had the full backing of the Republic's ruling Communist regime, and also because *Makedontsi* rebel numbers increased as band warfare intensified in the northern Greek provinces.

In the autumn of 1946 the KKE leadership made an effort to control *Makedontsi* activities in Greek Macedonia and succeeded in persuading their leaders to place these activities in the Slav-speaking villages of Mt Bernon (Vitsi) under a unified rebel command. The KKE leaders used on this occasion the services of one of its ablest commanders in the region, George Giannoulis, whom they were to execute two years later for losing an important battle on Mt Grammos. The agreement provided for unhindered co-operation and joint operations of the bands on the two adjacent border mountains, but it remained a dead letter until the rebel army moved its headquarters into the *Makedontsi* preserve, in the autumn of 1948, and placed their activities under its command. But by then the KKE leaders depended on their hosts for practically all their needs, particularly the need for reserves. In early 1949 the *Makedontsi* made up more than half of the rebel army, a fact which explains their final exodus following the defeat of the rebel army in August the same year.

In the mean time the rebels had established in 1946 the Democratic Army of Greece or DAG (*Demokratikos Stratos Elladas*) to wage a total war against the government. It was their second blunder-after a political one, when the KKE decided to boycott the general elections held on 31 March the same year. This gave all the arguments they needed to those who presented the KKE as an absolutely unreliable political force bent on revolution. The reasons given by the KKE for abstaining, such as intimidation of left-wing sympathisers and the fact that the electoral rolls had not been revised to reflect the changes since the elections of 1936, were not unfounded; however, these irregularities, it was suggested, constituted one more reason for the KKE and the EAM to take part in the elections and secure as strong a position in Parliament as possible.

In the summer of 1946 former ELAS commanders who had sought refuge across the border began entering Greece and forming large bands. Throughout the mainland, but primarily in the northern districts, these returning avengers unleashed an impressive hunt for right-wing sympathisers, mostly government appointees in the village councils, as well as gendarmes. One such avenger was Giannoulis, mentioned earlier, who roamed the Grammos mountain range leaving a bloody trail behind him.[13]

This impressive show of force thinly disguised the main rebel objective in the Greek north: to win and hold territory. The raids, ostensibly undertaken to punish right-wing terrorists and other 'monarcho-fascists', were essentially directed against gendarmerie posts and other government representatives in the countryside, such as village councillors. Right-wing terrorists and predators had cautiously withdrawn to the safety of the towns as soon as rebels began raiding villages. At the same time, guerrilla demolition squads blew up viaducts on mountain passes, thus attempting to seal off the north from the rest of the country. A series of attacks against villages like Deskati on Mt Chassia in September 1946 left behind hundreds of dead and wounded. This operation was undertaken to press-gang into the rebel army some 200 'volunteers' from Deskati and the neighbouring villages, but it was becoming ever more evident that the rebels were building an army, not to punish right-wing predators but to win and hold territory adjacent to the countries where 'people's rule' had already been established.[14]

This was the 'free territory' in which the guerrilla chiefs established their headquarters, where they also kept the necessary 'guerrilla courts' for dressing up the execution of 'monarchofascist traitors' with some kind of judicial legitimacy. Each guerrilla-held village had its own garrison and 'democratic' council appointed by the chiefs themselves. They also collected taxes, confiscated articles they needed, requisitioned animals and food, and forced peasants to perform various duties. Mobile presses produced the printed material required for the needs of the guerrillas: orders, certificates, identity cards and propaganda leaflets.

It was evident that the former ELAS persecuted fighters and returning avengers were in the process of replacing the authority of the government with their own authority in the name of the KKE and 'people's rule'. Towards the end of 1946 the KKE party organs started a well-orchestrated campaign of reporting clashes between 'armed men' and 'monarchofascist forces' in Thessaly, mainland Greece and the Peloponnese, but refrained from reporting developments in the northwest. After December 1946, when it was announced that

---

[13]See his diary in Achilleas Papaioannou, *Giorgis Giannoulis* (in Greek), Athens, 1990. Papaioannou was one of Giannoulis's Lieutenants.

[14]Koliopoulos, *Plundered Loyalties*, pp. 244 ff.

the United Nations had decided to send a special commission to examine charges by the Greek government that the guerrillas were being assisted by the country's northern neighbours, reports on guerrilla activity in the northwest vanished totally from the KKE party newspapers.

In the mean time the March 1946 elections had produced the first parliamentary government in Greece after ten years of arbitrary rule, both indigenous and foreign, but had not solved the country's serious political problem. Following the elections, however, the rebel activity described above amounted to a revolution against the legitimate government of the country—which the KKE leaders denied, to no great avail. By the autumn of 1946 the KKE-sponsored armed bands of former ELAS fighters and subsequent conscripts, organised into units and under the unified command of the Democratic Army of Greece, had irrevocably crossed the line from haphazard violent actions against right-wing bands to organised military operations to wrest territory and establish their own authority.

The composition of the Democratic Army of Greece and the motives of those who joined it were the subjects of a lively debate between the government and the KKE. Were the guerrillas 'volunteer fighters for people's rule', as the KKE maintained, or young peasants pressed into the rebel army by its political commissars, as the government seemed to believe? Evidence from both sides leaves no room for doubt that the majority of the DAG's guerrillas were conscripts, not volunteers, from the areas where the guerrillas had entrenched themselves, which were primarily in northern Greece. This was a measure dictated by the need of the DAG to avoid defeat, because of the long duration of the war, the rebel army's failure to gain permanent control of any extensive tract of country, including major towns, and the government's slow but relentless drive from the south which restricted the rebel army's 'free territory' to a belt along the north-western frontier. Another decisive factor which differentiated the DAG from its predecessor, ELAS, was patriotism. Volunteer service with ELAS had been inspired by a higher motive than such service with DAG. In the period of Axis occupation there was never any question as to which cause was the righteous one. Following liberation and the December 1944 rebellion, the KKE made a desperate effort to present the government as being kept in place not by the people but by foreign powers, and to portray the DAG as the direct offspring of ELAS. However, the issues of right and wrong and one's patriotic duty to fight for the fatherland were no longer as clear as they had been during the occupation. Although most of the rebels were press-ganged into the DAG by political commissars, they fought with no less devotion to the cause their leaders had imposed on them than the men of the National Army. Indeed, in the initial stages of the conflict and before it became apparent that the KKE and its army were heading for massive defeat, the armed forces at the government's disposal were no match for the rebels, who indisputably had the edge over them. This was also the case before it became obvious to all but the KKE's most fanatical or naive adherents that the left-wing guerrillas were no longer 'persecuted' former ELAS fighters or EAM sympathisers, but a revolutionary army aiming to establish 'people's rule', as in Greece's northern neighbours and with their political and military support.

Another aspect of the rebel army was the very small proportion of Communists in its rank and file, even at the high point of its development and apparent power. This, it was suggested, was proof of its 'democratic character'.[15] The DAG was as 'democratic' as any army, whether revolutionary or regular, Communist or liberal, as much in its 'bandit' phase—i.e. till early 1948, when former ELAS fighters with heroic and ostentatious war names appeared to be its dominant element—as in its second and final phase, when it was controlled by high-ranking KKE cadres. This undisputed control left little room for democratic decisions on who were to be admitted or allowed to leave its ranks. Peasants joined the DAG because they could not avoid doing so; they were likely to be recruited into the rebel army up till 1948 and into the National Army thereafter, because the rebels in the first period and the government authorities in the second were in a position of power and thus in control of peasant destinies.

The attempt to distinguish volunteer service with the DAG from forced recruitment rests on the implicit but equally mistaken assumption that a guerrilla was free to leave that army when he realised that its leadership's practices were contrary to his expectations. Returning to civil life was not allowed for two reasons: first because it deprived the rebel army of indispensable manpower, and secondly because the rebel army's loss would be the government's gain, since guerrilla deserters were normally conscripted into the national army. Returning to civil life was also impossible because many guerrillas were essentially seeking refuge in the rebel army to avoid being held to account on real or fabricated charges or, more likely, to avoid victimisation by right-wing terrorists.

[15]Woodhouse, *The Struggle for Greece*, p. 233.

Thus volunteer service with the DAG was the exception rather than the rule. Needless to say, it was more common with the DAG than with the National Army—which, again, does not mean that service with the rebels was more appealing than with the government forces. It simply meant that many young peasants were persecuted after 1945 by the government authorities and sought refuge with the rebels. Hatred and fear, more than the conscious espousal of one cause or the other, were the determining factors whenever a peasant decided to go over to the rebels or let himself be drafted into the government army. When they joined the rebels, as in the early period, it was mainly out of hatred or fear of the government; and when they opted for service with the National Army rather than with the rebels, as in the second period, it was because they hated or feared the rebels more than the government. An additional motive, normally ignored, was peasant shrewdness. The embarrassingly large number of deserters from the National Army to the DAG in 1945–6, and the equally large number who deserted from the guerrillas to the government forces after 1947, were not the result of a change in the political sympathies of the peasants but reflected their calculation of which camp had the better prospects of beating the other.

It seems that guerrilla army leaders had no difficulty enlisting men into their army; indeed, they brought in more than the KKE leadership had expected. However, by 1948 the rebel army had exhausted all the reserves to which it had access: all those who had not been recruited into that army were beyond its reach, having been either drafted into the national army or deported to the Aegean islands—or, like most able-bodied Slav Macedonians, having crossed into the People's Republic of Macedonia.

The drastic limitation of the rebel army's recruitment base coincided with the quarrel between Tito's Yugoslavia and the Soviet Union and the eventual public condemnation of Yugoslavia by the Comintern. This caused a serious crisis in the KKE's relations with Greece's Slav Macedonians at a time when the DAG was forced to withdraw into the Slav-speaking region of northwest Greece. Conscription of Slav Macedonians was now more difficult than before, because most of them identified with the Yugoslav Communists in their quarrel with the Comintern.

Decay had set in, and defeat one year later saved the leadership of the DAG from the humiliation of witnessing the collapse of the 'people's revolutionary army' which the KKE had been busy building up since 1946. Mass desertions were one sign of its advanced stage of disarray; another was increasing surveillance of guerrillas to detect declining morale or 'anti-patriotic' behaviour. The number of political commissars and 'assistants', attached to military commanders increased; so did 'spontaneous' requests from guerrillas for assistance in re-establishing close 'contact' with the party. Party 'nuclei' and 'assemblies' proliferated at all levels. The number of generals in the people's liberation army increased, while fewer of yesterday's heroes were now in responsible positions. Giannoulis was shot without a trial.

In 1948 the rebels carried out an operation which ever since has been one of the most debated aspects of the civil war: they carried away into the Communist countries of the Balkans and Eastern Europe more than 25,000 Greek children aged between three and fourteen. The KKE and DAG propaganda machines referred to the operation as 'evacuation' to save the children from the sufferings of war and from being turned by the government into 'monarchofascists'. The Greek government maintained that the children were abducted and carried off to be brought up as Communists and used eventually by international Communism against their own country.

The nature and outcome of this operation, as well as the issues it raised, have not encouraged dispassionate discussion of either the operation itself or those issues. Even serious scholarship has not always been unbiased in assessing the motives of those responsible. The only 'moral' justification the operation's guarded apologists could put forward, in addition to the undeniable humanitarian reasons, has been found in the government's efforts at the time to concentrate poor peasant children from the war zone in special schools in southern Greece, sponsored by Queen Frederica, for the duration of the war.[16]

Both positions—the government's no less than the KKE's—had some justification, and were no doubt taken into account by those who decided to carry out the operation. Concern for the safety and wellbeing of children exposed to total warfare certainly cannot be ruled out as a rationale for their evacuation. On the other hand, the KKE was fighting to carve out a foothold in northwestern Greece as an extension of the Communist Balkans, and in early 1948 the prospect of securing it did not seem unrealistic. For the KKE leaders, cut off from the rest of Greece and cornered in the northwest, the idea of garnering all available human resources for immediate or future

---

[16]See Lars Baerentzen, 'The "Paidomazoma" and the Queen's Camps' in *Studies in the History of the Greek Civil War*, pp. 127–57.

use in the war against the government, was not as extraordinary as it might seem with hindsight. Moreover, the transfer of children to places of safety away from Greece satisfied another and more immediate consideration: it freed their parents serving with the DAG from caring for them so that they could devote all their energies to waging war.

Most of the removed children, it seems, were of Slav Macedonian origin. This further complicated the question and appeared to justify the Greek government's worst fears, belying the KKE's assurances that the children would not be de-hellenised. With the assistance of its Western allies, the Greek government waged an international campaign for the repatriation of the children in the first few years after their removal, but it was soon realised that their return to Greece was uncertain, and when it became clear that Slav Macedonian children were indeed being de-hellenised and turned into fanatical *Makedontsi*, the issue of their repatriation was quietly dropped. Western philanthropy helped some of the children to go to Australia, Canada and the United States, where they played an important role in the growth and radicalisation of the *Makedontsi* irredentist movement directed by the People's Republic of Macedonia against Greece. These children and the other Slav Macedonian political refugees who assumed *Makedontsi* nationality were denied repatriation as having forfeited Greek nationality.[17]

Another contentious issue of the war was the removal of the village populations to the cities in the last and most dramatic stage of the conflict. Peasants began to flee from the countryside to the nearest towns in the autumn of 1946, as soon as the left-wing bands raised the banner of revolution against the government authorities; some of them had barely settled back into their villages after liberation from EAM rule before they were forced to leave once again. The first to take this route to safety were the appointed officials of the government: schoolmasters and rural guards, as well as the chairmen of village councils, also government appointees. They were followed by relatives of young men who had joined the Gendarmerie, the National Guard or the National Army. Peasants left their villages *en masse* in the early months of 1948, when the government decided to relocate them in the towns in order to deny the Communist insurgents their sources of manpower, supplies and intelligence.

[17]See Eirene Lagani, *To 'Paidomazoma' kai oi hellenogiougoslavikes scheseis, 1949–1953* (The 'children's abduction' and Greek-Yugoslav relations, 1949–1953), Athens, 1996, pp. 105 ff.

The allocation of responsibility for the mass movement of peasants away from their homes and into the towns and cities was disputed at the time, as it has been ever since, between the government and the rebels and their apologists. It is now clear that the evacuation of the peasant population became government policy in 1947, but it is equally clear that not all the displaced peasants, indeed not even a majority of them, were evacuated by government decision. The rebels wanted to keep the peasants in the villages for the same reason that the government wanted them evacuated. They needed them to defeat their opponent and thus gain exclusive control of the countryside. If the rebels regretted the displacement of the peasants, they did so because they were losing their main source of manpower and supplies.[18]

The displaced peasants caused problems to both contestants, the government no less than the rebels. Sheltering, funding and providing medical care for them, as well as cleansing the towns of human and animal refuse, proved beyond the capacity of the government authorities. Housing in particular was an enormous problem, only solved when peasants were sent home in 1949 and 1950. Pressure on the authorities to send the peasants home increased in late 1948 as conditions in the towns deteriorated in yet another sector: the provision of food. The countryside had ceased to produce enough food to satisfy demand and depended largely on what was brought in from outside. The return of the displaced peasants was now the declared policy of both sides, but in practice it proved impossible because each side—the government even more than the rebels—was convinced that keeping the peasants in the towns hurt its opponent more than the opponent would publicly admit.

Another much debated aspect of the civil war was the fate of the arrested rebels and collaborators. The lists of rebels with prices on their heads, the records of mass trials and convictions of captured rebels and, after 1947, the frequent executions raised questions as to whether the government was still pursuing a policy of combating the rebels and their sympathisers or was engaged in an all-out war against the KKE. It has become evident since that after the general election of 1946, and particularly after the formation of a provisional rebel government in December 1947, the government decided to use all necessary means and an all-out effort to suppress the KKE insurgents by force. The KKE was already waging an ideological war against the right and the centre, and after 1946 supported an insurrection aiming

---

[18]Koliopoulos, *Plundered Loyalties*, pp. 267 ff.

to bring down the government or at least to carve out for itself a Communist domain in the northwest. The government responded by waging total war against the Communist insurgents and their bases in the country.[19]

Statistics have revealed that a large number of those sentenced to death were Slav Macedonians, because on top of the usual charge of armed rebellion they were also convicted as members of a separatist political organisation. Additional reasons for this high proportion were no doubt the high number of Slav Macedonians in the rebel army after 1948, the fact that many of them also faced charges of collaboration with the Axis occupying forces, and the simple fear that this seditious movement inspired in the Greek authorities.

The government was out to crush Communist rebellion, and the military tribunals were ready to oblige. In contrast to those charged with crimes committed in the years of Axis rule, which involved a lengthy judicial process, rebels and their collaborators were as a rule dealt with summarily. The charges of bearing arms illegally, formation of an armed band and defection from the National Army were difficult ones to refute, as was the charge of conspiring to sever part of the national territory. Death sentences were usually carried out one week after conviction.

By the last year of the war the Communist insurgents had been pushed north to their last redoubt, and their defeat in the field, after they had been defeated politically, seemed only a matter of time. Anti-Communism was rife in the country, especially in the beleaguered towns, and all those suspected of harbouring pro-Communist sympathies, including the Slav Macedonians of the northern districts, risked imprisonment or deportation. Although the war was waged with Parliament in session and the Constitution in force, government authorities were not always acting according to the letter of the law to suppress the insurrection.

Another victim of the protracted Civil War was the Slav Macedonian population of Greece's northern districts bordering the Balkan Communist countries. Association with the Axis powers during the years of occupation, as well as with the People's Republic of Macedonia and later with the Communist insurgents, irreparably undermined their position and turned them into an easy target. Their villages lost a sizeable part of their population, who crossed over to the People's Republic of Macedonia as refugees. Many more were

[19] *Ibid*, pp. 276 ff.

executed along with other Greek Communists, victims of a war that
could have been avoided.

The Civil War heritage and post-war politics

The Civil War constitutes the single most important factor in Greek
political developments after the liberation from the Axis occupation.
It is impossible to understand post-war tensions between different
sectors of Greek society without considering the significance of
this catalytic event and the legacy it left behind. The transition from
coalition governments in the 1940s to single-party conservative governments in the 1950s, the return of the liberal centre to power after
eleven years of a conservative monopoly (1952–63), the brief interlude of the Centre Union relaxation policies (1964–5), the clash of
a popular prime minister with the crown and the royal intervention
in parliamentary politics, the military regime of 1967 and its collapse
seven years later due to the Cyprus disaster, the return and establishment of the most orderly parliamentary regime in post-war history,
and finally PASOK's advent to power in the elections of 1981—all
were directly or indirectly influenced by the deep cleft bequeathed
by the Civil War.

The nature of the division which culminated in war is discussed
above. In this chapter we point out some of the reasons which led to
it: the role of the pre-war dictatorship (under the aegis of the crown)
in lowering the prestige of parliamentary politics, the emergence of
the Communist Party during the occupation as a major resistance
force, the relative ineffectiveness and apathy of most prominent
politicians during the same period, the unpopularity of a king who
was widely associated with foreign power tutelage, and above all the
devastation of the economy by the occupation forces and the
incalculable suffering it brought to the population, radicalising the
poorer sections and bringing them into contact with left-wing
resistance. If resistance fighters who sought to establish social justice
made up the moral backbone of the leftist camp, devotees to Stalinist
orthodoxy formed its leadership. The nationalist camp included smaller
resistance movements, a number of credible liberal politicians of the
pre-war period, and a multitude of conservatives who rallied around
the King and foreign support. Collaborationists, eager to secure
absolution for themselves, became the most intransigent enemies of
Communism. However, it was the Soviets who unwittingly provided
the threat that lent cohesion to the nationalist camp and stiffened its

resolve. Stalin had honoured his agreement with Churchill to allow Britain a free hand in Greece in 1944, but in 1947 demanded a withdrawal of foreign troops. He also demanded the demilitarisation of the Dodecanese islands, which Italy had ceded to Greece in that year. Finally Communist Yugoslavia and Bulgaria, with their claims on Greek territory, gave the nationalists a credible cause to fight for.

The Greek Civil War, like others of its kind, created a political, ideological and institutional polarisation that permeated all facets of social activity. This polarisation, however, was implemented not by a dictatorial regime but by a state which, despite various constitutional irregularities and extraordinary measures, observed the strictures of parliamentary democracy.[20] The Communist Party, which abstained from the 1946 election and instructed its followers to deny its legitimacy, was outlawed a year later, not without reservations on the part of those who took that decision. However, most of the Greek parties continued to operate freely during the Civil War. The ideological polarisation left little margin for the leadership and the middle-class intelligentsia to deal with issues other than on lines compatible with the nationalist creed and with a West European identity. The Left was either muzzled or fled the country after its defeat. Consequently Greece completely missed out on the constructive dialogue between liberal and socialist principles which was occurring elsewhere in Europe at this time.

The state had a considerably enhanced role in the post-war era. By assuming the entire burden of reconstruction and the allocation of massive foreign aid on the one hand, and the promotion of nationalist orthodoxy on the other, it increased its role in society. With unemployment rife and an economy which managed to reach its pre-war level only in the 1950s, it became the chief employer and persisted as the chief agent of patronage even after reconstruction was completed and the economic boom had set in. From 1940 to 1970 the Greek population increased by 19% while the number of civil servants increased by 140%. State planning, involving regulation of prices, the exchange rate and investment, and the extension of credit to the private sector, made the state the motor of the much-sought-after economic growth.

An all-pervasive state ideology legitimised by democracy and passed on through the channels of education and the state-controlled

---

[20]Constantine Tsoucalas, 'The Ideological Impact of the Civil War' in John Iatrides, ed., *Greece in the 1940s,* University Press of New England, 1981, pp. 319, 328.

radio confronted its Socialist or Communist adversaries—not with principled liberal arguments but with the concept of a threatened nation pitted against enemies bent on its destruction. The Civil War of the 1940s was given the derogatory term 'bandit war', and for many years after it was over, this term, signifying the baseness of the rebels' motives, continued to be used. Thus a nationalist anti-Communist fundamentalism emerged which, unlike nineteenth-century irredentism, was defensive, exclusive and parochial.

Within the state apparatus a cluster of agencies appeared consisting of police, the military and other guarantors of public order and the official credo, and their functionaries operated relatively free of parliamentary scrutiny. Liberal attempts in 1964–5 to dislodge these functionaries from their power-base provoked the wrath of the Crown. Yet, a redeeming feature of the state's all-pervasive role was its own scrupulous attachment to a legalism which often became a sanctuary for its citizens and even the victims of persecution.

No institution had a greater stake in the prolongation of the Civil War heritage and the anomalies that emanated from it than the Crown. In this the King owed much to the Communists insurrection and continued the incantation of the 'threat from within' for years after it had lost all meaning. Throughout the war the future of the monarchy remained an outstanding issue between the Greeks and their allies, and the royal family returned to Greece in 1946 only after a plebiscite. King George's death in 1947 brought his brother Paul to the throne, and the interventions of his dynamic wife Queen Frederica in affairs of the state became a permanent feature of his reign; she simply exercised in an indiscreet manner the extra-constitutional powers that the political anomalies of the time had granted to the Crown. Both she and later her son Constantine, who succeeded his father in 1964, failed to understand that the power of the institution they represented was far from permanent. Although the monarchy at first secured the unity of the victorious camp, it gradually became a divisive element even arming loyalists. Frederica's rivalry with Marshal Papagos, who had been head of the government armed forces in the Civil War, split the officer corps into two. Her fear that the renowned general would have an influence in the army that would rival that of the King became a self-fulfilling prophesy. Long after Papagos's death, his military followers nurtured their hostility to the Crown until they made it impotent in 1967 and finally abolished it altogether in 1973.

With socialist parties isolated from the political debate (though not from representation in Parliament) the only political force capable of breaching an archaic system that favoured growth but not modernisation was that of the centrist liberals under George Papandreou. The general aim of the centre forces was to put an end to political polarisation, reform the educational system, clearly define and secure civil liberties, and further the democratisation of the political process. The Centre Union party, the result of a merger of forces ranging from moderate right to socialist, found its following in the growing urban areas, where anonymity weakened the power of clientelism, and collective grievances could easily be voiced. Communists and socialists had formed the United Democratic Left (EDA) which, in the elections of 1958 before the creation of the Centre Union, became the second largest party in Parliament with over 25 per cent of the vote, benefiting from popular resentment against Karamanlis's rule and the disarray of the centrist parties which were at daggers drawn with each other.

Papandreou's determination to challenge the Crown's influence in the armed forces placed him on a collision course with King Constantine in the summer of 1965. In the wake of his forced resignation, forty deputies decamped from the party and supported a government appointed by the King to prevent elections that would have brought the popular Papandreou back to power. The clash between the head of state and the head of government created a crisis and a power gap which the military were to fill two years later.

The failure of the Centre Union, in spite of its popularity, to consolidate itself in power and survive the attack from the monarch, betrayed the fragility of post-war democracy in Greece and the resolution of army and police diehards to resist change. In no other profession was allegiance to the Crown or to members of the conservative cabinets more important for promotion than among the military—a dependence which eventually caused friction within its ranks. Officers formed clandestine organisations to 'purify' the army from leftist deviation, and at the same time secure their own corporate interests, and waited for the opportunity to assert their independence. The weakening of parliamentary institutions in 1965–7 encouraged certain officers who had come of age in the Civil War period to intervene in politics, while professional grievances and their sense of isolation from the rest of society undermined their loyalty to the state.

The coup of 1967 was caused by a variety of factors. One was that international détente had reduced the significance of the armed forces as guardians of the country against external threats. The justification for the take-over was to avert a Communist uprising, but in fact it was meant to prevent George Papandreou from winning the forthcoming election. Furthermore, the junta hoped to exert control over networks that had begun to lose their cohesion by reviving the spectre of the Civil War and thus rejuvenating the sense of national mission—which, according to them, should always imbue the armed forces of the nation. Finally, some colonels sought to emancipate the military from its dependence on a conservative political camp which had failed to retain power. Thus a great number of them took part in the coup, hoping to further their own prospects of promotion in view of the impending mass dismissals.

The Junta Constitution of 1968 was indicative of the mentality of those in power. Civil rights were excluded from the charter and the emasculated legislature that emerged from it would have no authority over issues of defence and foreign policy. In 1973, following an abortive coup against the junta by navy units, the military regime deposed the King who had fled the country after his own abortive attempt against them in 1967. Although brutal and amateurish in administering the state, the regime had the good fortune to ride the crest of a sustained economic boom, and therefore secured prolonged acquiescence from the people.

With the coup against Makarios on 15 July 1974 and the ensuing Turkish invasion of Cyprus, the military regime in Greece collapsed. On 23 July members of the Junta, handed over power to politicians, who summoned Karamanlis, who had been self-exiled in France since 1963, to assume the leadership of a civilian government and hold elections. The landslide in his favour at the 1974 election signified a deep change, without provoking the stunned but still dangerous forces of the military regime into action. The outcome of a referendum the same year that sealed the fate of the monarchy was a reflection of the public mood in favour of change. Although Karamanlis maintained a neutral stance on the issue, his silence was widely interpreted as a condemnation of the institution which had failed to guarantee the stability of the parliamentary regime. The vote in the referendum was 69% against the monarchy.

Having gained 220 out of the 300 seats in Parliament in the 1974 elections, Karamanlis' New Democracy party was scarcely impeded by the opposition, consisting of the Centre Union with its sixty seats, Andreas Papandreou's PASOK with twelve and the United Left with eight. However, the outcome of the 1977 elections, held at a safe distance in time from the military's intervention in Greek politics, betrayed a growing leftward shift in the electorate which was best

Constantine Karamanlis (1907–98)

Greece's leading postwar politician, Karamanlis was born in Serres, Macedonia. In 1936 he was first elected deputy with the Populist Party and was re-elected after the war (1946) under the same banner. He joined the Greek Rally Party in 1951 and served in several cabinets before assuming his most successful post as Minister of Public Works. He became Prime Minister following the death of Alexander Papagos in 1955, and founded his own Greek Radical Union soon after. This party under his leadership won the elections of 1956, 1958 and 1961. In 1961 he was faced with the formidable opposition of the Centre Union forces under George Papandreou, who accused him of having won the election by electoral fraud and violence. The assassination of the left-wing deputy Gregoris Lambrakis by extreme rightist thugs contributed to his electoral defeat in 1963.

Between 1963 and 1974 he lived in Paris and made his triumphant return to Greece when the seven-year regime of the Colonels collapsed. He reconstituted his party under the name New Democracy and won the elections of 1974 and 1977. He was elected President of the Republic in 1980, but chose not to be a candidate in 1985 following the reluctance of Prime Minister Andreas Papandreou to support him. He was elected to his final term as President in 1990.

Karamanlis made his mark as the driving force behind postwar reconstruction, the statesman who engineered Greece's orderly return to democracy in 1974, and the architect of Greece's entry into the European Community. As an individual he personified all the virtues of the paternal society of the 1950s and '60s: hard work, austerity, avoidance of rhetoric, dedication to the public good and a degree of authoritarianism to bring about the needed results. Although scarcely democratic in sharing decision-making with the members of his cabinets, Karamanlis possessed good sense which prevented him from rushing into foolhardy ventures.

His lifelong friend and collaborator, Constantine Tsatsos, believed that Karamanlis could not be classified along the left-right political spectrum but constituted a *sui generis* type of politician who maintained an uncompromisingly steady course throughout his career. This and other such characteristics were precisely what made him the epitome of a conservative leader. His Hobbesian view of human nature and war of all against all, as well as his fear of disorder, were combined with a predilection for a strong executive branch in government.

He often assumed the role of the collective superego, lecturing the people for submitting to demagogues and the easy life. However, imposing his own harsh standards on the electorate and asking them to emulate his own restraint, he allowed the pendulum of public preferences to swing eventually to Andreas Papandreou. The latter proved the living antithesis of Karamanlis. Besides appealing to the ego and the instincts of the voters, he made political capital by dismantling his predecessor's legacy.

Karamanlis rarely betrayed his bitterness against the saboteur of his life's work. He withdrew from his presidential duties with dignity and in course of time was acknowledged as one of Greece's foremost statesmen.

Bibliography

Archio, Konstantinos Karamanlis. 50 years of Political History, vols 1–12, Athens: Ekdotiki Athenon, 1997; T.A. Couloumbis, 'Karamanlis and Papandreou: Style and Substance of Leadership', *Yearbook 1988*, Athens: ELIAMEP 1989; Maurice Génévoix, *La Grèce de Caramanlis. Ou la démocratie difficile?*, Paris: Plon, 1972; Constantine Tsatsos, *O agnostos Karamanlis* (The unknown Karamanlis), Athens: Ekdotiki Athenon, 1984; C.M. Woodhouse, *Karamanlis: The Restorer of Greek Democracy*, Oxford: Clarendon Press, 1982.

illustrated by PASOK's rise from 13.6 to 25.3 per cent and the decline of New Democracy from 54.5 to 41.8 per cent.[21] After almost five years as head of government, Karamanlis was elected President of the Republic by Parliament in 1980. His term in government was marked by a cautious purge of Junta personnel from the state mechanism, the recognition and legalisation of the Communist Party, the withdrawal of Greece from the military arm of NATO in protest at its inaction over the Cyprus invasion, the liberalisation of the state, and the negotiations that led to Greece acceding to the European Community in 1981. Karamanlis's own political transformation since his earlier departure from politics in 1963 reflected the change of mood of his conservative constituency and his new party's more liberal position, which deprived the Centre of the potent platform it had enjoyed the 1960s. However, the demise of the Centre Union significantly enhanced the following of PASOK, leading to its 1981 victory.[22]

PASOK's constituency was made up of inherited Centre Union

[21]For details on the elections of 1974 and 1977 see the volume on Greek elections edited by Howard Penniman, *Greece at the Polls: The National Elections of 1974 and 1977*, Washington, DC: American Enterprise Institution, 1981.

[22]For more details on the rise of PASOK see Christos Lyrintzis, 'Political Parties in Post-Junta Greece: a Case of "Bureaucratic Clientelism"?', *West European Politics*, vol. 7, no. 2 (April 1984), pp. 109–14.

Andreas Papandreou (1919–96)

Born in Chios at the time when his father George Papandreou was Prefect of the island, he studied at Athens University and got his Ph.D. from Harvard where he worked as a graduate assistant. He became Professor of Economics at the University of Minnesota in 1951 and at the University of California, Berkeley, in 1955. In the United States he was associated with the Stevenson liberals. Karamanlis brought him back to Greece with his American wife and his children in 1961 as head of the Centre for Economic Studies in Athens. He was elected deputy of Achaia in 1964 and served as Minister of Coordination in his father's Centre Union government in 1964–5. He was briefly detained during the 1967 dictatorship and allowed to leave the country, after pressure on the Colonels from President Lyndon Johnson. He founded the Panhellenic Liberation Movement (PAK) abroad and returned to Greece two months after the collapse of the military regime to head his creation, the Panhellenic Socialist Movement (PASOK). He was in Parliament in 1974–96 and Prime Minister in 1981–89 and 1993–6.

Andreas Papandreou was the most accomplished 'changeling' in Greek politics. A person of some personal charm and with a level of intelligence that made him contemptuous of most of his own generation of politicians, he performed about-face turns in policy without alienating his supporters. When the ratification of Greece's treaty of accession to the European Community was brought before Parliament for discussion in 1980, Papandreou and his PASOK deputies walked out, declaring their unyielding opposition to the EC. Once in power (a year and half later), this negative attitude was dropped as $800 million from EC funds was channelled to Greece's rural areas. In his second term he became the champion of the EC in Greece.

Papandreou's most significant action *vis-à-vis* the EC was the Greek Memorandum which set conditions to future enlargement, demanding the implementation of the 'Integrated Mediterranean Programmes' designed to finance and assist Mediterranean countries of the EC with structural impediments to development. At the December 1985 summit in Luxembourg, he withdrew his reservations concerning the amendment of the Rome Treaty which would facilitate the decision-making process in the EC by limiting the use of the veto. The measure was advantageous to big countries in the Community, and Papandreou's cooperative attitude was rewarded with the formal recognition of the 'convergence' between the economic structures of member countries—a principle which favoured the weaker states, including Greece.

While in opposition (1974–81), Papandreou vowed that his future government would withdraw Greece from NATO and remove American bases from Greek soil. However, his defence policy after his October 1981 electoral victory did not deviate substantially from that of his predecessors. In 1983 he signed an agreement with the United States renewing the tenure of its 'facilities', as they were called, and the next day unabashedly celebrated with his followers the beginning of the process of dismantling the US bases in Greece.

Papandreou's foreign policy, stripped of its more flamboyant rhetoric, was not very different from that of many other Western states in spite of the impression he liked to give. Yet he insisted on portraying himself as a far greater maverick than his actions implied. In doing so he was addressing a Greek public thrilled at the prospect of attracting European attention after years of docile agreement on basic Western tenets of foreign and security policy. Furthermore, his tactics of appearing as an uncompromising champion of Greek interests, combined with promises of social benefits for all 'non-privileged' Greeks, was the binding tissue that kept the wide spectrum of his followers together. Very few Greeks would ever admit to being 'privileged'.

During Papandreou's terms in power, the lower-paid saw their incomes rise, but this was not due to any redistribution policy since it was mostly financed by loans. The implication of this social policy was that he bought favours with the electorate by shifting the cost to future taxpayers. He bequeathed a sky-rocketing public debt that has been the most serious obstacle Greece has had to face in joining the Eurozone.

As a politician who improvised from day to day, Papandreou postponed confronting the mounting problem of Greece's debts until his final term in office. Well known for his nonchalant decision-making at the best of times, he could later invoke his poor health for working only a few hours a day. Nonetheless, this last term proved to be his most constructive. After a bumpy start, Greece improved relations with Albania and FYROM (Former Yugoslav Republic of Macedonia), while the economic ministers imposed an austerity programme in line with European Union convergence requirements which survived Papandreou's leadership. Observers have pointed out that not having to bother about his own re-election freed him in his last years from the shackles of wooing the electorate with promises he knew were impossible to keep.

Bibliography

Eleftherotypia, special supplement on A. Papandreou, 19 June 2001. T. A. Couloumbis, 'Karamanlis and Papandreou: Style and Substance of Leadership', *Yearbook 1988*, ELIAMEP, 1989, pp. 129–49; V. Keramas, *To aporrito imerologio sto Kastri* (The secret diary of Kastri),

Athens: Papazissis, 1989; S. Kouloglou, *Sta ichni tou tritou dromou*. *PASOK 1974–1986* (In the traces of the Third Way: PASOK 1974–86), Athens: Odysseas, 1986; Michalis Macrakis, *To xekinima*. *Andreas Papandreou 1933–43* (The Beginning: A.G. Papandreou), Athens: Katoptro, 2000. A. Papandreou, *Democracy at Gunpoint: The Greek Front*, London: Pelican, 1973. A. Papandreou, *I Ellada ston kosmo*. *Exoteriki politiki* (Greece in the world: foreign policy), Athens: Livanis, 1994; Nick Papandreou, *Father Dancing*, London: Penguin, 1996; Potis Paraskevopoulos, *Andreas Papandreou*. *I politiki poria tou 1960–95* (His political route 1960–95), Athens: Sinchroni Elliniki Istoria, 1995.

support,[23] a generation that came of age in the Junta period and the left-wingers of the Civil War who had been living on the margins of political life. Papandreou enfranchised the latter and capitalised on the guilt feelings of certain conservatives who had supported right-wing governments of all kinds. His appeal to nationalists across the whole political spectrum deprived the right wing of its most effective rallying point and the Communist Party of its less servile followers. The PASOK psychodrama of the first half of the 1980s assisted most Greeks to act out their frustrations and inhibitions, though at considerable cost to the economy.[24]

The New Democracy party, faced with an identity crisis after its founder Karamanlis opted for the Presidency of the Republic, changed leadership twice before the post was offered to Constantine Mitsotakis in August 1984. A onetime Centre Union deputy who had clashed with his leader George Papandreou in 1965, Mitsotakis was faced with the double task of consolidating his leadership in New Democracy and warding off attacks from Andreas Papandreou.

The election of June 1985 gave PASOK a comfortable margin (45.82 per cent and 172 deputies in Parliament), and it then continued to pursue its programme unhindered by leftist or rightist opposition. There was a clearer correlation of income level and electoral behaviour in 1985 than in 1981. Business people, managers, well-to-do professionals and the legal and medical associations opted for New Democracy. The latter party, with 40.84 per cent (126 deputies) of the vote, added 4.98 per cent to its 1981 percentage, while the Communist Party (KKE) with 9.89 per cent (twelve deputies) lost 1.4 per cent. The

[23]View expounded by George Mavrogordatos, *Rise of the Green Sun: The Greek Elections of 1981*, Athens, 1983, p.3.

[24]In his important book *The rise of the Greek Socialist Party* (London: Routledge, 1988) Michalis Spourdalakis argues that PASOK's development was the product of social and political contradictions in postwar Greece.

Eurocommunists, with 1.84 per cent, elected one deputy. Throughout his campaign Mitsotakis criticised the ever-increasing dependence of Greece on foreign loans in order to finance a bloated and expensive state machine.[25]

Seven years of PASOK in power precipitated certain social and economic changes in Greece. The public sector predictably became more cumbersome and the private sector refrained from new investment, lacking confidence in a government that paraded its hostility to business. Some measured social modernisation was introduced and legalised: civil marriage was allowed, divorce was simplified and the institution of the dowry was abolished. An important feature of developments in Greece after 1981 was that the country's European vocation was reinforced by the upgrading of its democratic institutions and its full membership in the European Union. Despite PASOK's Third World affiliations, Greece became more entrenched in the Western camp than before 1974. There was nevertheless an element of anachronism in PASOK's overall concept of world politics. Since much of the movement's appeal was based on redressing the grievances of those on the losing side in the Greek Civil War, Papandreou verbally reconstituted the Cold War climate. His constant evocation of the oppressive tactics of the conservatives in the 1950s, his Third World orientation and his unrelenting attacks on the United States prevented his followers from coming to grips with contemporary reality. His belated decision to fall into line with the other members of NATO and the EU did not come in time to alter his reputation as the maverick of the Western world.

Papandreou's illness during the summer of 1988 and some serious scandals that erupted in the winter of 1988–9 marked a turning-point in the fortunes of PASOK. Although the elections of June 1989 took a toll on the party, with its electoral share falling to 38 per cent, New Democracy with 43 per cent was unable to form a government because of an electoral law introduced by PASOK to meet this very eventuality, and entered a coalition of limited mandate with the Communists. This extraordinary electoral partnership between the Civil War adversaries put an absolute end to the last remnants of the fratricidal heritage in Greece. The elections of November 1989 gave New Democracy 46 per cent of the vote-still not enough to allow it to govern. The three parties—ND, PASOK and the KKE—

[25]T. Veremis and M. Dragoumis, *Historical Dictionary of Greece*, Metuchen, NJ: Scarecrow Press, 1995, pp. 11–15.

then entered a National Union coalition under the octogenarian former banker, Xenophon Zolotas, as a way out of the impasse. Several months later the declining economy brought about the fall of the government and new elections in April 1990. New Democracy managed to teach the necessary margin with a majority of only one deputy.

The Mitsotakis government was caught in crossfire between domestic and external developments. The difficulties of balancing the budget and trimming the public sector in face of the fierce opposition of PASOK and the unions it controlled, and Foreign Minister Antonis Samaras's handling of the issue of the Former Yugoslav Republic of Macedonia and its appellation, brought the New Democracy government down prematurely. The elections of 10 December 1993 returned PASOK to power with 47 per cent of the vote under the ailing Papandreou, while Mitsotakis was replaced as leader of his party by Miltiades Evert.

Papandreou's last term of office was marked by a worsening of Greece's isolation from its European partners over the Macedonian issue and the absence of the ailing Prime Minister from active politics. Papandreou was hospitalised in November 1995, and the protracted saga of his replacement while the country remained practically leaderless ended in January 1996 when PASOK deputies chose Kostas Simitis as prime minister.

Simitis proved to be cool and predictable where Papandreou had been impulsive and unfathomable. For a decade those who had elected PASOK had an opportunity to act out their fantasies by identifying with someone who promised everything, asked for nothing and did very little. Unlike the stern Karamanlis, who demanded continuous sacrifices from the Greeks, Papandreou appealed to their appetites and their insouciance. Paying lip-service to the redistributive rhetoric of socialist parties, he avoided taking from the rich to give to the poor, preferring to borrow from abroad to satisfy his followers. However, the accumulation of huge deficits made the economy more dependent on the EU and therefore progressively restricted PASOK's waywardness.

The elections of 1996 gave PASOK, led by Simitis, a mandate restoring Greece to its westward course. Three and a half years later the country was enjoying improved relations with all its neighbours, the economy had met most of the criteria for entering the Economic and Monetary Union (EMU) of the EU, and Simitis secured yet another mandate by the electorate (see table).

PARLIAMENTARY ELECTIONS, 1996 AND 2000

	1996		*2000*		
	%	Seats	Votes	%	Seats
PASOK	41.49	162	3,008,081	43.798	158
New Democracy	38.12	108	2,934,948	42.733	125
					(incl. 2 Liberals)
Communists (KKE)	5.61	11	379,280	5.22	11
Coalition of the Left	5.12	10	219,988	3.203	6
Dikki	4.43	9	184,648	2.688	–

The KKE, a party like no other

Greek Communism grew out of the country's first purely Marxist socialist party, the Socialist Workers' Party of Greece (*Socialistikon Ergatikon Komma Ellados*—SEKE). It was founded in Piraeus in November 1918 by the General Confederation of Greek Workers, then in its, early stage with a programme of action which drew heavily on the 1891 Erfurt Programme of the German Social Democratic Party. SEKE applied first for membership of the Second International, and when the Third International (Communist International or Comintern) was created, SEKE became a member in 1919. Eventually it became the Communist Party of Greece (*Kommunistikon Komma Ellados*-KKE).

The Communist Party of Greece (KKE) bore the mark of the troubled times in which it was born, and especially that of the Moscow-inspired and -controlled Comintern. The KKE opposed the legacy of the World War that had just ended, and particularly the Greco-Turkish war that broke out not long after it joined the Comintern. This opposition was expected and unavoidable for a socialist party with its clearly Bolshevik orientation. However, in Greece this opposition placed the party on a collision course, not only with the ruling parties of the time but with the entire state system, which was locked in mortal combat with the nation's oldest enemies, the Turks. More than anything else, the new party became associated with across-the-board rejection of accepted policy and was presented by its opponents as an agent of external subversion—which in a sense it was and continued to be for most of its life.

The principal difference from the other political parties at that crucial juncture of its history was that while they derived legitimacy from identification with the country's national aspirations in war, the Communist Party sought its legitimacy through association with a foreign power fiercely opposed to the war. The Greek party of socialist revolution identified the nation's interests not with the triumph of national aspirations in the ongoing war, but in the defeat and humbling of those who pursued these aspirations by means of the war.

Triumphant nationalism was not the only enemy of the new political party; indeed, triumphant Greece was soon to be humbled by the resurgent Turkish nationalism. At first the party had very limited access to the traditional networks of mobilising political support; initially it had fewer than 100 cadres and no more than 1,000 members. Greece then lacked a working class homogeneous and sizeable enough to respond to the call for socialist revolution against the capitalist state. In fact, it lacked a capitalist class as well, at least in the Marxist sense of the term. It did not lack a peasant class, which made up the great majority of the population, but relatively few peasants were landless. With the exception of those in lowland Thessaly, where ownership of large landed estates had not been affected by the province's cession to Greece in 1881, peasants of Old Greece and, to a large extent, those of Epirus and Macedonia had managed to acquire most of the land which, as was the case elsewhere, the state considered national land by right of conquest.

Also, Greece did not possess a radical tradition. The War of Independence had lacked the social dimension which early Greek Marxist historians tried to discern: insurgency, to the extent that it was not motivated by the prospect of legitimate plunder, was kept alive by a leadership set on a course to secure liberty and independence from foreign and arbitrary government. Radicalism never touched Old Greece, perhaps because the only section of the population which saw its fortunes constantly declining, the transhumant shepherds, never 'looked back in anger' but indulged in brigandage and irredentism. Septinsular radicalism, which was real enough, could not possibly have affected a sedentary Greek continental population.

The First World War and its subsequent peace treaties offered the Communists in Greece an unexpected support base: among the groups of Asia Minor and Pontus refugees as well as the substantial minorities of Slav Macedonians and Muslims. Shortly after entering the Greek political scene, the Communist Party was presented with an unprecedented political challenge: to move forward as a champion of the radical reform of Greek society and its state services. However, its near-absolute dependence on international Communism and the lack of an indigenous radical tradition decisively limited its appeal as a political party and confined its role to that of a subversive movement.

Greek Communism was driven to positions which could easily be represented by its opponents as treasonable. The questions of Macedonia and the refugees were interconnected and required imagination and political flexibility, both of which have always been in short supply in the KKE. Almost two-thirds of the destitute refugees were settled in the part of Macedonia which had been won by the Greek army in the Balkan Wars. They were settled next to a multilingual population, of which as many as 250,000 were Slav Macedonians before the wars. They and the Vlachs, as well as the Albanians and the Greeks, both indigenous and refugees, became a fertile ground for Communist propaganda. However, the Comintern had somewhat different priorities. Soviet-controlled by 1924, it imposed on its Balkan subsidiaries a common policy on the Macedonian question. It recognised Macedonia as 'a geographic and economic entity', and emphasised the need to opt for its political unity and independence. The Slavs, the Greeks, the Vlachs, the Albanians and the Muslims were recognised as so many 'peoples'. The Slavs, eventually, became in Communist terminology the 'Macedonians', while 'Greeks' were only the Christian refugees in Greek Macedonia. These were thought to be insignificant details in view of the immense revolutionary potential of the Communist approach to the Macedonian question.[26]

The ultimate objective of Communist policy on a question that had vexed the Balkan countries and the European powers for the previous fifty years was the creation of a sizeable Macedonian state out of lands that now formed integral parts of Greece, Bulgaria, Yugoslavia and Albania. In such a putative state, all its peoples were expected to live in peace for ever after, while enjoying harmonious relations with all the neighbouring countries. The outcome of this proposed change in the political map of the southern Balkans would have created for Greece's recently settled refugees new trials and tribulations, perhaps including a new uprooting since they were not 'Macedonians'.

This line on Macedonia created for the KKE a twofold dilemma. At the political level the Greek Communists faced the real danger, if they were to fall in to line with the Comintern over Macedonia, of alienating the refugees of Greek Macedonia, one of their most obvious bases of support. At the national level they faced an even more serious problem: this was that accepting the Comintern policy on Macedonia

---

[26]See Alekos Papanagiotou, *To Makedoniko Zitima kai to valkaniko kommounistiko kinima, 1919–1939* (The Macedonian Question and the Balkan communist movement, 1919–1939), Athens, 1992, for a thorough analysis of the question.

essentially meant working for the cession of national territory, by definition an act of high treason. The KKE leadership chose to accept the internationalist line of a 'united and independent Macedonia' and by so doing paid a heavy price: the KKE's political appeal was drastically reduced and, at the same time, the party placed itself outside mainstream policy on the future of Greek Macedonia, thus assuming the role of a foreign agent of subversion.

The question of the future of Macedonia caused the first major crisis in the party of revolution and created its first splinter groups and outcasts. Much more serious and no less damaging to its impact on Greek politics were the profound differences of opinion during the same period over the correct interpretation of the situation in the country following the arrival of the refugees, and over the elaboration of the right course for the party. In general, the party leadership appeared to be counting on an imminent breakdown of the state system and a socialist revolution. Political instability and the consequent change of regime in 1924 as a result of army intervention in 1922 and 1923, in conjunction with the acute social and economic problems associated with the settlement of the refugees, convinced the party leadership that Greece was ripe for a Communist takeover. Perhaps even more important for the future of the party, this conviction was also fed to the Comintern, which in turn did everything to force it down the throats of those who doubted this assessment of the situation in Greece.

Human rights activists, Social Democrats and proponents of a more realistic assessment of social and political development in the country were condemned as 'opportunists' who had 'sold out' to capitalism. Meanwhile *Rizospastis*, the official party newspaper, was being abandoned by its readers who were disillusioned by the party's apparent inability to come to grips with the actual situation in Greece, and the disunity in its ranks. High-ranking cadres were expelled for 'anti-party behaviour', while others chose to leave the party in the summer of 1923, as the leadership tried to purge itself of 'ideological deviants' and make the party fit the Bolshevik model. Socialist revolution had succeeded in Russia; therefore it would have to succeed in Greece too.

At its Third Extraordinary Congress, in November-December 1924, the KKE further defined its identity and orientation. It dropped its original name and assumed the one by which it has since been known; it became an organic part of the Comintern, adding to its official title 'Greek Section of the Communist International'; it 'bolshevised' its ideology, programme and apparatus; and adopted the Comintern line on the need to work for a 'united and independent Macedonia and Thrace', already mentioned.

The decision on Macedonia and Thrace reflected the party's position on what was described as the 'national question', i.e. the question of the various minorities acquired by Greece in the period 1912–22. The position rested on the liberal principles of national self-definition (*autokathorismos*) and self-determination (*autodiathesis*), as decided in the same congress and published in *Rizospastis* in February 1925. These principles were adopted by the Comintern and its Balkan branch, the Balkan Communist Federation, because of their revolutionary potential in the region. The KKE condemned Greek official efforts to 'nationalise' the Greek parts of Macedonia and Thrace by settling Asia Minor and Pontic refugees in these parts and denying the indigenous 'peoples' the right to have their own schools and use their own languages. It spoke of the 'Macedonian people' and the 'Thracian people', in the sense of the population of Macedonia and Thrace. These 'peoples' were recognised, *inter alia,* as having the right—which the Communists vowed to fight for—to unite their dismembered lands into 'independent' states, parts of a soviet Balkan federation.[27]

Volatile Balkan ethnic semantics trapped the KKE, then as well as later, in politically dangerous territory. As might have been expected, the 'peoples'/'populations' soon became in Communist terminology the 'nationalities' of these lands dismembered by the Turks, the Bulgars, the Greeks and the Serbs. The states of these nations were engaged in breach of their international obligations—in 'nationalising' these lands either by getting rid of those who did not meet all the criteria of their nationals (language and/or religion principally), through forced eviction or voluntary migration, or by trying to assimilate them using both stick and carrot. Greece had pursued both courses in the past and was pursuing them most vigorously at the time. The KKE opposed this policy in the name of the liberal principles already mentioned, and in its place proposed an unrealistic solution to the question: the 'unification' and 'independence' of lands whose 'unity' and 'independence' rested on no intrinsic factor but solely on the expected destabilising effect they would have on the 'bourgeois' governments of the existing nation-states in the region. Few Greek Communists were prepared, either then or later, to question the wisdom of this expedient; even though few if any would have been prepared to agree with the 'principle' put

---

[27]Giorgis D. Katsoulis, *Istoria tou Kommounistikou Kommatos Elladas* (History of the Greek Communist Party), vol. II, Athens, 1976, pp. 120–32.

forward by the Comintern at its Fifth Congress in 1924, namely that the inhabitants of Macedonia and Thrace were 'neither Greeks, Turks, Bulgars, Albanians nor Serbs, but Macedonians and Thracians with a Macedonian and Thracian consciousness respectively'.[28]

Doctrine prevailed over objective truth and reality because the Communist revolutionary line created its own truth and reality. This doctrine not only gave rise to continued dissension over the KKE's role in society, but caused a major rupture in its relations with the Workers' Confederation in 1925–6, even as the party faced widespread persecution by the Pangalos dictatorship. The party leadership was not prepared to tolerate dissenting voices at a time when a modicum of ideological flexibility would have allowed it to increase its support among Greek workers. Imprisonment and deportation reinforced the centrifugal forces within the party. Would it not have been preferable for the party to draw wisdom from a journal called *Marxist Archive*? Was it not better for it and the country to follow a thoroughly 'legal' course? Was it not even better, in view of past blunders, to 'liquidate' the existing party and found a new one on a sound basis? These dissenting voices produced many splinter groups, which questioned the Bolshevik orientation of the party: they were symptoms of the endless ideological struggle waged among groups with very different political ancestry and without a homegrown radical tradition to bind them together. Imported Bolshevism proved inadequate as a binding force in the first and crucial decade of the party's life.

Dissension, which was more pronounced in Athens and Piraeus, restricted the party's electoral basis to 3.8 per cent of the vote in the elections of November 1926 in these two cities. In the same elections the party polled 11 per cent in Thessaloniki, 14.8 per cent in Larissa, 15 per cent in Rodope and more than 16 per cent in the district of Evros. It secured ten seats in the Chamber of Deputies. This was an unexpected showing, even under a favourable electoral system (proportional representation). One of the reasons for this success was perhaps the conspicuous silence of the party on the question of Macedonia during the election campaign, later condemned by the March 1927 Third Party Congress.[29]

Dissension, like Bolshevism, was more than anything else a reflection of the bitter ideological battles that were being fought, following the eclipse of Lenin, within the Communist Party of the Soviet Union.

[28] *Ibid.*, II, pp. 140–1.
[29] *Ibid.*, II, pp. 209–10.

This was a feature of which the KKE would never be able to rid itself. As a result of the legitimacy the party derived from its association with the maternal party, the impact that Soviet Communism (whether in crisis or not) had on its Greek 'chapter' was more important than any local development. It was the very reason for Greek Communism's existence.

The KKE defined itself and Greece through the eyes of the Soviet Communist Party: Greece was a backward, semi-feudal and semi-colonial country, dependent on Anglo-American capital. Its working class was the only class that could lead the oppressed masses, and the KKE was the only power that could lead the workers in a struggle to overthrow the bourgeoisie and seize power in the name of the proletariat.

This was the assessment of the situation in Greece by the Fourth Party Congress in December 1928, four months after the party hit rock-bottom in the general elections; these brought Venizelos back to power with new ideas for coping with activities amounting to insurgency against the existing regime. Under the notorious special Law 4229 of 1929 to combat the spread of ideas aiming to overthrow the existing regime, many Communist cadres were imprisoned or deported for attempts to proselytise. It was the response of the liberal state to radical acts and language on the part of the party of revolution in Greece, especially regarding the adoption of the general strike as the decisive step in a Communist seizure of power.

New elections in April 1929, this time for the upper chamber, whittled away the party's electoral base still further to 1.7 per cent. Low electoral returns and repressive state measures, as well as Soviet-made ideological issues, exacerbated conflict within the KKE leadership. Finally, in November 1931, the Comintern stepped in to rescue its Greek 'chapter' with an appeal to put an end to dissension, 'bolshevise' the party fully, impose 'iron discipline', and 'liquidate' cadres who deviated from the party line. The Comintern also reminded its Greek section of the need to remain active in the direction of the 'oppressed nationalities, the Macedonians, Turks, Albanians and Jews', and to give active support to their right to national self-determination and separation. To make its point clear, the Comintern dismissed the old party Politburo and appointed a new one in its place. Among the newly-appointed cadres was one destined to dominate the party for the next quarter-century: Nikos Zachariadis. However, what really saved the KKE from continued internecine friction and possible complete collapse as a political organisation was a growing radicalisation of tobacco and other workers.

The deepening economic crisis, which hit workers more than other sections of the Greek population, heightened the KKE's attraction to the unemployed. An increasing number of refugees also appeared to be heeding the call of the Greek Communists, following their disappointment when Venizelos abandoned Greek refugee claims against Turkey in 1930 by bringing about a Greco-Turkish understanding. On the other hand, the state's repressive measures against the Communists, as well as the rise of fascism abroad and in Greece, gave the KKE the unexpected role of a martyr of freedom and a defender of human and political rights. In the general elections of March 1933 it increased its share of the vote to 4.6 per cent.

A crucial year in the history of KKE was 1935, when political upheavals led to the restoration of the monarchy in Greece by force and fraud, and the adoption by the Comintern of the 'popular front' as the principal weapon in the struggle against fascism. In this situation the KKE was projected as a serious political factor in Greek politics. Repressive measures and persecution of Communists and all who expressed sympathy for different aspects of Communist policy distracted public attention from the KKE's primary aim, which was to overthrow liberal democracy and impose Communist dictatoriat rule, as well as such secondary concerns of Communist policy as support for human and political rights. Increasingly the KKE represented itself as a consistent opponent of fascism and authoritarian rule. This new image, and increasing political support from the refugees, helped it to broaden its electoral appeal, and the Communists' base of support was further broadened as a result of the 1935 Comintern directive to drop the divisive 1924 line on Macedonia and Thrace and adopt in its place a new line, 'equality for the minorities', which was expected to facilitate cooperation of the Balkan Communist parties with all the political forces opposed to fascism. The party's Sixth Congress in December 1935 promoted the image of the KKE as a serious political player by adopting the 'people's democracy' as its principal electoral objective.[30] All the above and an electoral law favouring small parties gave the KKE and its junior partners in the general elections of January 1936 a respectable 5.75 per cent of the votes and fourteen deputies in the lower chamber.

This electoral contest, the last of interwar Greece, projected KKE on to the Greek political scene as holding the balance, on account

[30] *To Kommounistiko Komma tis Elladas. Episima Keimena* (The Communist Party of Greece. Official Documents), vol. IV, Athens 1975, pp. 296–7, vol. VI, Athens, 1987, pp. 337–9.

of a split vote in a hung parliament where neither of the two large political parties, the Liberals and the Conservatives, had enough votes to form a government without additional parliamentary support. Behind-the-scenes negotiations led to an agreement in February 1936 between the Communists and the Liberals who, in exchange for Communist support in the chamber for the election of a Liberal as Speaker and of a Liberal cabinet, pledged to repeal all anti-Communist legislation, including Law 4229, grant an amnesty to all those condemned for political offences, and dissolve all fascist organisations.

This Liberal–Communist agreement was a crucial test for Greece's liberal democracy. Was the agreement to be interpreted as a bold step by the Communists to enter political life as a responsible parliamentary party, respecting parliamentary government for its own sake? Or was it a step on the way to seizing power and imposing the dictatorship of the proletariat, which incidentally the Greek Communists had not renounced as their long-term objective? Equally, was the agreement to be seen by the Liberals as an opportunity to co-opt the Communists into parliamentary life and turn them into responsible participants in the country's liberal democratic system? Or was it an instrument to force the Conservatives to come to terms with them on the crucial issue of shared influence in the armed forces?

The agreement proved stillborn, and the two strange bedfellows did not have the chance to prove that they were not motivated primarily by the pursuit of short-term party gains in signing it. Their previous attitude towards each other held few prospects for the success of this agreement, while their subsequent attitude and policies leave little room for doubt that they were motivated by narrow party calculations and objectives. The Communists scorned their opponents more than the situation warranted, while the Liberals were too engrossed in their quarrel with the Conservatives over control of the armed forces to see that this agreement could not have been implemented without an effort to dismantle the authoritarian state they themselves had set up.

The savage reaction to the agreement from the Conservatives, and the Liberals' unwillingness to defend it as a legitimate effort to end the political deadlock, eased the establishment of authoritarian rule by reactionary forces in August 1936. The KKE did all it could during that troubled summer to create a situation similar to that in Spain before the outbreak of civil war there. Widespread strikes and street clashes with the police were exploited by the enemies of liberal democracy to pretend that civil strife and a Communist bid for power were imminent. The KKE proved General Metaxas's best, though unintended, accomplice in his own bid for power.

The KKE was left with the satisfaction that it had seen authoritarian rule coming and had warned its political opponents of this well in advance. Metaxas did not need to try very hard to convince King George that the country desperately needed a dictatorship to prevent it from slipping into civil war and a Communist takeover. Both knew that the Communists were not in a position to pose a serious threat to the Greek social and political fabric, but they had little difficulty in convincing the KKE's political opponents to let them deal with the Communists as if they actually posed a serious threat to the regime. The major political parties appear to have been eager to abdicate their responsibility for dealing with the political crisis and allow a dictator to do the job for them. Fear of Communism thus became a credible bogey for the major political parties, thus opening the door to unconstitutional government.

Even more ironic, is the fact that the Greek Communists did all in their power to make this bogey appear real. They gave the impression that they were seriously preparing to seize power, and that they genuinely believed such a bid to be realistic. Their opponents were only too glad to take them at their word, not only to strengthen their case against Communism, but also to elaborate a credible ideology opposed to it. The Metaxas dictatorship of the latter half of the 1930s was first and foremost anti-Communist, and its contribution to Greek politics was the attempt to turn anti-Communism into a crusade.

The Metaxas dictatorship attacked the KKE with a viciousness unparalleled in modern Greek political history and plunged the party into utter confusion. Its political leaders were rounded up and jailed or exiled to barren Aegean islands, its organisation was infiltrated by government spies, and a fake party newspaper was published to mislead the ignorant and sow discord. Thus the party working for the socialist revolution in Greece was driven to near-extinction. Many of its cadres weakened under pressure and renounced Communism; they and all those suspected of colluding with the dictatorship carried the stigma of collaboration, and some went out of their way afterwards to prove to the party leadership that they had renewed their commitment to Communism and regained their faith in the socialist revolution. One of those who renounced Communism was Athanasios Klaras, the future brutal guerrilla leader, known as 'Aris', who dominated the Communist-controlled Greek resistance to the Axis occupation forces in the Second World War.

The party leadership subsequently recognised that although its line during the years of dictatorial rule was correct, it was not equipped to protect its organisation from the dictatorship. The party had faced persecution before and known how to go underground to pursue its subversive operations. The Pangalos dictatorship had persecuted Communists for their activities, and subsequent governments, both authoritarian and democratic, had done the same, but the party had never before been attacked so brutally, systematically and efficiently. Its entire leadership—the Central Committee elected by the party's Sixth Congress in 1935—and almost all the middle-rank cadres, numbering some 2,000, were arrested and imprisoned or exiled for the duration of the dictatorship.

The party did not really go underground during the dictatorship; for years it survived inside the country's prisons and places of deportation, especially in the Corfu high-security prison and the Acronauplia camp, where the Communist leadership maintained a semblance of party unity and operation. The Acronauplia section of the leadership in particular played a vital role guiding the remnants of the party machine outside. Once they left prison, they became the most respected and admired élite, an undisputed revolutionary 'aristocracy' destined to play an important role in party affairs during the 1940s.

The outbreak of the Second World War in September 1939 increased the confusion in the ranks of the KKE on account of the Nazi-Soviet pact of August 1939. With most of its leaders detained and its internal cohesion smashed by the dictatorship's security services, the party was thoroughly isolated. The members of the 1935 Central Committee who had avoided arrest constituted what became known as the 'Old' Central Committee, which remained attached to Comintern policy. The Nazi-Soviet Pact thoroughly confused them over the question of the war's character. For nearly two years, until the German attack on the Soviet Union in June 1941, this section of the KKE leadership considered the British and French 'imperialists' responsible for the war. Not even the Italian attack on Greece in October 1940 changed their assessment of the war's 'imperialist' character, and they kept to this line even after Zachariadis wrote his famous letter from prison shortly after the Italian attack, describing Greece's war against Italy as a war of 'national liberation' and calling on all Greeks, including Communists, to join and fight in the war.

The 'Old' Central Committee questioned the authenticity of the letter; indeed, a few months later Zachariadis himself questioned the wisdom of Greece continuing to fight Italy after repelling its forces from Greek soil and called for an end to participation in the 'imperialist' war. However, the Zachariadis letter calling for a peace treaty to be negotiated between the belligerents with the mediation of the Soviet Union became the principal guideline for most Greek Communists for the Greek war effort against Italy and Germany in April 1941. The German attack on the Soviet Union in June 1941 ended the confusion within the KKE over the 'character' of the war and initiated a new period in the party's history. It would not be an overstatement to say that 'Operation Barbarossa' saved the KKE from utterly discrediting itself in the eyes of the Greek people and gave it a new lease of life.

The Axis occupation of the country gave the KKE the opportunity to emerge as a major political force: the party unreservedly supported mass resistance against the Axis forces and even gained a taste of power for the first time. By promoting its image as an uncompromising enemy of Axis rule, and calling for the formation of a patriotic front against it, the KKE became one of the principal political players in the country. However, this new role tempted the KKE leadership to consider seizing power by force or by the threat of force. This is how the KKE's political opponents interpreted the party's attempt to expel all who refused to put themselves under its command from the ranks of the resistance to the Axis.

The 1940s witnessed the impressive growth in the appeal of the KKE and its equally impressive decline. Divided counsels—in the absence of Zachariadis, the Party's Secretary-General, who was in the Dachau prison camp—and lack of experience in handling serious national issues led the party leadership into positions from which it was difficult to draw back. What was thought to have been staged by the leadership—or the majority of it—as a show of force to oblige the Greek government to accept the KKE as an equal partner in December 1944, led to a bloody civil war and not only the destruction of the formidable guerrilla army it had built up over the previous two years, but also the loss of its credibility as a reliable political player. It also cost the party most of its hard-won support gained during the years of resistance to the Axis.

Politically defeated in 1944 and increasingly isolated by a series of decisions that further undermined its credibility as a parliamentary political party, the KKE leadership was unable to resist all those, including its war resistance heroes, who pushed it into making one more attempt to gain power. In 1949 it had to face a crushing defeat. The emerging Cold War and great power involvement could barely disguise one of the basic features of the Greek Civil War: the KKE's desperate effort to seize power by force and exert influence as it had done during the Axis occupation by fighting a foreign enemy. It was an unprecedented failure of leadership, which led to an unprecedented political and military defeat.

The principal failure of the Greek Communist leadership, besides its underestimation of their political opponents, was their inability to digest a simple truth: that the position the party had won leading the wartime resistance could not be retained without the army it had built up to force all opponents into submission. They missed the chance to lead the Greek Communists in the manner of their Italian and French counterparts and give Greek Communism a European orientation; trapped by their own rhetoric and unrealistic assessments based on shaky premises and faulty assumptions, they did not allow the party to come of age and outgrow its heroic phase. They also denied Greece the benefits of a left-wing opposition not traumatised by the bitter taste of defeat. Their dependence on the Soviet Union differed in kind from the Greek government's reliance on Western support; whereas the government could move its allegiances according to the prevailing wind, the KKE had no such margin of choice.

Another legacy of the party's role in the resistance to the Axis occupying forces had been its discovery of revolutionary messages in the utterances of the Greek War of Independence heroes. Communist resistance fighters drew heavily on the established national pantheon, the Klephts and the Armatoles, and in many cases assumed their names as *noms de guerre*. To reach the Greek people, the party promoting socialist revolution in general 'nationalised' its discourse and dressed it up in the colours sanctioned by the dominant state ideology. The Nazis and the Italian Fascists were assimilated to the Turks of Ottoman times, the fight against them to the War of Independence, and the resistance heroes to so many Klephts and Armatoles. Identifying the collaborators and all who were unwilling to answer the KKE's call to arms with the Greek élites under Ottoman rule who were reluctant to revolt against it was perhaps unavoidable, but it was unfortunate since it blocked the party's cooperation with its opponents after liberation from Axis rule. Mounting contempt for those opponents, combined with incorrect assessments of the situation and possibly hidden designs, isolated the KKE ideologically and politically and precipitated its demise.

Allowing the party to slide into revolt against the government in 1946 was not unavoidable, although it was predictable in view of all the above; however, defeat *was* unavoidable and probably predictable, though not on the scale the KKE actually suffered in 1949. Persecution of resistance fighters by right-wing bands in 1945–6 goaded the party to reply in kind, sanctioning it as 'self-defence'; it did not justify seizing land in the north and trying to establish 'people's rule' in the seized territories. Military and political assistance from Greece's northern neighbours, notably the Yugoslav Communist regime, fanned the flames of Slav Macedonian separatism in Greek Macedonia, i.e. in the very region where the KKE guerrilla army appeared to concentrate its power and activities, and cast serious doubt on the KKE's assurances that it would not accept the dismemberment of Greek Macedonia. It is very doubtful whether the KKE leadership of the time would ever have acquiesced in the loss of Greek territory, as the Greek government accused them of doing, in order to satisfy their supporters and allies across the border. It is equally doubtful whether the KKE and its guerrilla army would have been able to protect northern Greece from their Communist allies, but for the British and American refusal to allow the spoliation of the part of Greece coveted by its northern neighbours. In 1949 the KKE leadership reversed their position on the Macedonian question and returned to the old Comintern line of favouring Slav Macedonian separatism, thus confirming the worst fears of its political opponents. This reversal of policy on Macedonia appears to have been the result not only of the effort to attract Greece's Slav Macedonians to the guerrilla army but also of the leadership's decision to place the party on the 'correct', i.e. anti-Yugoslav, side of the Soviet-Yugoslav (Stalin-Tito) dispute raging at the time.

The party leader and their guerrilla army withdrew after their defeat to the Communist countries of Eastern Europe and to the Soviet Union. In bitter exile and cut off from the realities of postwar Greece, the KKE settled in for what proved an endless debate over who was responsible for causing and then losing the Civil War in Greece. For nearly half a century the KKE leaders have been trying, in a futile exercise of self-deception by sticking to half-truths and untruths, to avoid giving a convincing explanation of who was to blame for the senseless slaughter and defeat of 1946–9.

The one person who was perhaps most responsible for causing, if not also for losing, the Communist guerrilla war, namely the guerrilla commander Markos Vapheiadis, had already been relieved of his duties in 1948 before the final collapse, but when defeat was imminent he was the first of a growing number of high-ranking cadres who mounted a relentless attack against the party head, Nikos Zachariadis, darling of the party rank-and-file. Zachariadis had survived the Metaxas dictatorship, the Axis occupation and the Civil War, but was finally defeated when his own cronies in high office turned against him after the death of Stalin. It was a fitting end for a man who had risen to high office by manoeuvring behind the scenes and had kept that office by getting rid of all those who at one time or another questioned the wisdom of his decisions. Having been deposed in 1956, he tasted bitter exile in Siberia, and finally committed suicide there having spent his last years isolated, humiliated and forgotten.

Banned in Greece till the fall of the army Junta in 1974, with its leaders in exile and racked by fierce quarrels, the Greek Communists were represented in the country's political life by the United Democratic Left (EDA), which fared significantly better than the KKE ever did as a parliamentary party. The EDA was thought by many to be operating as the agent of the banned Communists, but it managed to appeal to a much wider public than the KKE ever did before the war. This was because it operated much more effectively as a party of protest against the excesses of the Right than against the Centre parties. While in exile in February 1968, a moderate wing of high-ranking Communists and members of the Central Committee split off from the KKE, and the split soon reached Greece where most of the leading Communists were imprisoned by the Junta. After the Soviet invasion of Czechoslovakia in August the same year, the 'dissidents' increased in number and influence, creating what they called the 'KKE of the Interior' to distinguish themselves from the orthodox KKE known for its subservience to the Soviets and its agreement with their action in Czechoslovakia.

The army Junta gave Greek Communists a new lease of life. Persecution turned them once more into martyrs of freedom. Communist insurgency in the late 1940s had by then faded from the public memory, as attention was diverted to stories of arrest, imprisonment and torture of Communists by the Junta's military police and security police. The KKE was once again portrayed as the party of uncompromising resistance to authoritarian military rule, although neither its appeal, its policies nor circumstances had favoured the growth of armed resistance as in the years of Axis rule. Besides, political resistance to the military Junta was not limited to the Greek Communists; much more effective abroad was the anti-Junta rhetoric of organisations such as Andreas Papandreou's Panhellenic Resistance Movement (PAK), which made inroads into the KKE's traditional arsenal of slogans. Other 'bourgeois' organisations also tried to fight the Junta as best they could while the opposition of respected person-alities such as Karamanlis to its brutal regime deprived it of any kind of legitimacy. While during the Nazi occupation the Communists came to be respected and feared, under the Colonels they were mostly pitied for being persecuted for what they were, and not for the little that they did.

When the collapse of the military Junta terminated the ban against the KKE, the party came out of the shadows and exile after twenty-five years. As its ageing cadres and heroes of the 1940s started returning to the country, the party braced itself in an effort to reclaim the political territory on the left of the political spectrum which it considered to be its own preserve. The 1974 and 1977 general elections secured it respectable electoral returns, but not the position of influence its leaders were hoping for. Much had changed since its last appearance in a political contest, and this tended to limit its appeal. However, what seems to have restricted the KKE's appeal more than anything else was the emergence of a serious rival for the support of left-wing voters in the form of Papandreou's PASOK, which encroached on the KKE's traditional electorate. While in opposition during the second half of the 1970s, PASOK, in addition to gradually undermining the credibility of Karamanlis's reformist conservative rule, robbed the traditional Left of most of its slogans and heroes. Recruiting Manolis Glezos, Markos Vapheadis and countless other personalities of the Left was Papandreou's astute move to co-opt the traditional Communist following into his own camp.

Papandreou made new incursions into the KKE's ideological and political territory when he came to power in the 1980s. The recognition of left-wing resistance to Axis rule as part of the 'National Resistance' in the same period was welcome to the Left in general, particularly to the political refugees and former Communist guerrillas who had returned to Greece in the same period and become active in politics, for once, in favour of party in government. Equally welcome were the pensions awarded to a large number of old men and women who claimed to have taken part in the resistance to the Axis. It was obvious that the PASOK government sought to win over to its side not only the surviving resistance fighters, but also the aged and poor peasants in the mountain regions where Communist-controlled resistance had entrenched itself during the years of Axis occupation. Such measures won over to PASOK a section of the population which till then the KKE had regarded as its own preserve. This was a successful strategy to deprive the KKE of part of its political support and buy off its resistance heroes at a relatively small cost. Defeated in the Civil War, swept away by the currents of the Cold War, and living as political refugees for more than a quarter of a century in distant lands, the KKE's heroes of the 1940s were in a sense defeated for a second time on returning to Greece by the offer of paltry medals and meagre pensions that severed them totally and finally from the party of their youthful allegiance.

The collapse of Communist regimes in the Soviet Union and Eastern Europe that shook the world in the late 1980s further reduced the KKE's appeal. A new generation of leaders, who had come of age in the years of military rule, found great difficulty adjusting Communist Party ideology to a rapidly changing world and employing new means and a new language for reaching prospective supporters. Meanwhile radical protest was monopolised by the Socialists. Anti-American and anti-European, the KKE seems at the start of the new millennium to be hopelessly anchored in the past and unable to play a serious role in Greek politics—destined perhaps to shrink first into a political curiosity and then into final oblivion, as happened to most Communist parties in Western Europe.

Homo politicus

The year 1922 is the true divide between the old and the new century in Greece. The period preceding it witnessed Greek preoccupation with irredentist claims and territorial expansion, the consolidation of parliamentary power and the construction of a liberal democratic state according to the designs of a visionary Western-oriented élite. By 1922 Greece's expansion had reached its limit. Eleftherios Venizelos had already put the finishing touches to the liberal state, and the large estates of Thessaly were being expropriated and parcelled out to landless peasants.[31]

No one realised that most but not all of the era's themes were culminating in the tragic finale of 1922. The political cleavage between Venizelos's and the Crown's adherents persisted as a sinister theme connecting the two eras. The *Dichasmos* (national schism), with all the

---

[31]Costas Costis, *Economie rurale et Banque Agraire. Les documents,* Athens: Fondation Culturelle de la Banque Nationale de Grèce, 1990, p.40 (table of expropriations of estates).

Eleftherios Venizelos (1864–1936)

Born in Chania, Crete, Venizelos studied law in Athens. He entered Cretan politics in 1889 and became a leading figure in the revolutionary movement for the unification of his island with Greece. From the moment of his arrival in Athens in 1910 at the invitation of the Military League (an organisation of officers bent on rejuvenating politics) until his death in exile in 1936 he dominated Greek politics. Founder and leader of the Liberal Party, which became a rallying point and springboard for many distinguished politicians (George Kafandaris, Alexander Papanastasiou, Andreas Michalakopoulos, George Papandreou), he tried to endow it with principles rather than patronage networks.

During his first term as Prime Minister (1910–15), Venizelos reformed the administration of the state, public education and the national economy. Through a timely network of foreign alliances he achieved Greece's territorial expansion during the Balkan Wars and the First World War. His commitment to Greece's involvement in the latter on the side of the Triple Entente caused a cleavage between his followers and the supporters of King Constantine I, that bedevilled Greek politics throughout the interwar period.

His defeat in the crucial elections of 1920 and his failure to control his military followers in 1923–4 caused him to withdraw from politics till 1928. During his last term as Prime Minister in 1928–32, he extricated Greece from its isolation by reviving and improving its bilateral relations with Romania, Italy, Turkey and Yugoslavia, but was also faced with the repercussions of the international economic crisis.

Venizelos was less devoted than Harilaos Trikoupis to the principle of the superiority of parliamentary government over all other forms of governance. His own preference was for the Aristotelian division of polities into pure and corrupt versions. He was therefore less concerned with the system as such than with its actual operation. However, the success of this view wholly depended on the virtues of the personalities that were placed by choice or station in life in the key positions of power. When Venizelos salvaged the monarchy after the officers of 1909 had challenged its authority, and made King George I the arbiter of parliamentary politics in 1910, he had not anticipated the rapid succession of events that brought Constantine to the throne in 1913.

Before 1915 Venizelos had encouraged a bipolar system of governance in which the head of state and the head of government shared substantial authority. In doing so he hoped that a grateful monarch would always offer his consent on vital decisions of reform and foreign policy. When the clash between the Crown and the Prime Minister occurred in 1915 over Venizelos's decision to enter the war on the side of the

Triple Entente, Constantine was prepared to defy the writ of Parliament. Not only had he become popular as commander-in-chief in the successful Balkan campaigns (an office given to him by Venizelos) but he was also in harmony with his Prime Minister's theory that the King should partake in important political decisions. Under such circumstances the national schism became inevitable.

Venizelos's view of the state was a synthesis of Trikoupis's intention to make it the motor of growth by creating a mighty infrastructure, and Deliyannis' vision of agricultural self-sufficiency and welfare considerations. Although he inherited Deliyannis' orphaned constituency, mainly because Tricoupis' party had been preserved by his rival Georgios Theotokis, his reformist promise won him the overwhelming support of those in the middle class that had not declared their political preference before.

Bibliography

Doros Alastos, *Venizelos*, London: Lund Humphries, 1942; Grigorios Daphnis, *Ta Ellinika Politika Kommata, 1821–1961* (The Greek political parties, 1821–1961), Athens: Galaxias, 1961; George T. Mavrogordatos, *Stillborn Republic: Social Coalitions and Party Strategies in Greece, 1922–36*, Berkeley: University of California Press, 1983; George Ventiris, *I Ellas tou 1910–1920* (Greece of 1910–20), vols I-II, Athens: Ikaros, 1970; Thanos Veremis and Youla Goulimis (eds), *Eleftherios Venizelos. Kinonia, economia, politiki stin epochi tou* (Eleftherios Venizelos: society, economy and politics in his times), Athens: Gnosi, 1989.

trappings of a clash between conservatives and liberals, appeared strange in a country without an *ancien régime* and a landed aristocracy who would look to the royal house for inspiration. King Constantine's belated popularity after the Balkan Wars of 1912–13 was largely due to his role as commander-in-chief in military campaigns that were the natural outcome of Venizelos's irredentist agenda. By a twist of fate Constantine became the rallying point of the war-weary population of Old Greece (as opposed to the newly-acquired territories) and of the traditional parties that had joined forces against a ground-breaking Venizelos in the elections of 1912.

The irony about the 1915 pro-royalist coalition against Venizelos was that it included more or less the same parties that had been overruled by King George I in 1910 in favour of the Cretan newcomer. The King had then made use of his prerogative to appoint the Prime Minister, and by choosing Venizelos had changed the course of history. Five years later King Constantine reversed his father's choice; he rejuvenated the old political parties that were already past their prime in 1910 and became their actual if not institutional leader.

The schism was consummated after the catastrophe in 1922 with the blood of five anti-Venizelist politicians and the commander of the Greek Asia Minor forces. Accused of high treason, they were in fact executed for their alleged responsibility for what had occurred. The misguided presence of the Greek forces in Turkey had been opposed by the royalist parties in 1919, but Venizelos's power and his conviction that Britain backed his decision carried the day. The anti-Venizelist royalist coalition that won the 1920 elections lacked the courage to reverse a campaign already in progress, although it had promised to 'bring the boys back home'. Despite the admonitions of one of their own, General Ioannis Metaxas, they pursued a disastrous course that led to the catastrophe and paid for a decision that had not been theirs. It took the anti-Venizelists a decade to regroup and win an election. During that time various Venizelist factions competed for power virtually unopposed.

The role of the 1922 refugees was catalytic to all subsequent developments in Greece. They posed a social challenge that strained the tolerance of the natives, introduced new perceptions in the closed society of the urban and rural centres, changed the face of party politics beyond recognition, gave the economy a vital transfusion of skills and labour, and affected the views of the intelligentsia as no other single source of influence had ever done before.

The refugee phenomenon was not altogether new in the Greek state. From its very foundation, as is seen elsewhere, the inhabitants of Roumeli (mainland Greece) and the Morea (southern Greece) began to acquaint themselves with the communities of their Cretan, Epirot and Macedonian brethren who sought their support in their irredentist struggles. These latter joined the rebellion, first as volunteer warriors and then often as refugees after every failed uprising. The spectacle of makeshift camps was common. Although mostly of the Orthodox persuasion, not all of these refugees spoke the language of the New Testament. This was nothing new. Albanians, Vlachs and Slavs had added spice and variety to the traditional Greek representatives who met in Epidaurus in 1821 to forge a constitution that would unify politically a fragmented communal pattern of existence. Whereas the Ottoman administration was based on a network of communities and local notables designated for the collection of taxes, the French blueprint of centralized administration and a unitary state became the ideal of the Greek insurgents.

The process of convergence was not without reversals. In 1844, when the Ottonian constitution was being drafted, the parochial

The Asia Minor Catastrophe

The 'catastrophe' of 1922 ranks among national disasters second only to the Civil War of 1946–9 in Greek perceptions. It marked the end of Greek expansionist policy (the 'Great Idea') and brought more than 1 million destitute refugees to a country of barely 5 million inhabitants. Providing food and shelter and ultimately incorporating the displaced people into society has been one of the most successful projects undertaken by the Greek state.

The factors that led to the catastrophe were multi-faceted. Although the First World War was over for most belligerents in 1918, the Greek army was still at war. With a mandate by its victorious allies to maintain order in the coastal city of Smyrna and the Aidin province, the Greeks landed in 1919 and began a mop-up operation against the remnants of Turkish resistance in the region. Eleftherios Venizelos's electoral defeat in November 1920 was the outcome of war fatigue suffered by a population whose young men had been under arms since 1912. The new government, made up of anti-Entente and royalist politicians, weakened Greece's credibility among its allies. Furthermore the pernicious legacy of the national division that began in 1916 had taken its toll in the armed forces.

King Constantine, brought back to the throne by plebiscite, ordered a campaign against the stronghold of the Turkish forces under Mustapha Kemal in Ankara. Despite the dire warnings of such military experts of the royalist camp as Ioannis Metaxas, the government plunged ahead with little awareness of the logistics that such an undertaking required. As the army made slow progress towards its objective facing stiff resistance from the retreating Turks, Constantine installed himself in Smyrna with Prime Minister Demetrios Gounaris to supervise the operation. However, the Greek advance foundered on the last obstacle to Ankara, the fortified banks of the river Sakaria. Kemal counter-attacked in August and repelled the Greeks. Given Italian rivalry with Greece over the control of Asia Minor and France's change of position after agreeing to supply Kemal with arms and ammunition, British support alone could not arrest the impending collapse. The Turkish offensive a year later split the Greek defences and commenced the wholesale eviction of the entire Greek presence from Anatolia.

attitude of the 'autochthonous' Greeks (those born within the realm of the free state) carried the day.[32] The 'heterochthonous' Greeks (born outside the realm) were denied the right to vote and those who

---

[32]E. Kyriakides, *Istoria tou synchronou Ellinismou 1832–1892* (History of contemporary Hellenism), vol. I, Athens, 1892, pp. 487–505. Minutes of the parliamentary debate on the issue of Autochthons versus Heterochthons.

held posts in the civil service lost them, but before long the measure fell into disuse. A similar cleavage was generated by the Balkan Wars of 1912–13 as new territories, with their populations, entered the kingdom. On the eve of the national schism, Greece had increased its territory from 25,014 to 41,993 square miles and its population from 2,700,000 to 4,800,000.[33] Naturally, the members of the political establishment of Old Greece refused to share its privileges with the newcomers and resisted the continuation of the irredentist process itself when their grip on the control of the state began to appear precarious. The national division between a neutral stance and a pro-Entente commitment of the Greek forces was another symptom of the growing pains of a small culturally homogeneous state. The royalist slogan 'A small but honourable Greece' was a synonym for the *status quo* of an 'autochthonous' Greece. The task of unifying the new territorial acquisitions under a single authority was not the over-riding concern of the old establishment, which feared the loss of its power and privileges. The same was true with the much-increased scale of the 1922 refugee phenomenon. The threat, real or imaginary, that the dispossessed newcomers from Asia Minor posed to shopkeepers and small property-owners all over Greece was coupled with the ominous contagion of the Bolshevik revolution that disturbed the sleep of bourgeois Europe.

Greek political parties were certainly unprepared for the symptoms presented by interwar radicalism, and much more alarmed than the true extent of the threat to the social order really warranted. Industrial unrest, general strikes, agitation and corporatism were perceived as signs of impending doom.[34] However, the schism had produced a parliament dominated by the liberal camp, and precluded a coalition of bourgeois political forces to face the crisis. By 1925 most liberal politicians were unwilling to assume the cost of harsh economic measures that would benefit the anti-Venizelist opposition whether inside or outside Parliament. They were even prepared to abdicate their own responsibilities and allow a 'caretaker' military figure like Theodore Pangalos to do the dirty work for them. It was under these circumstances that military corporatism reached its brief heyday and became an operatic feature of mid-1920s Greece.[35] In a traditional society where clientelism reigned supreme, the attempt by the military to introduce

---

[33]D. Dakin, *The Unification of Greece, 1770–1923,* London: Benn, 1972, p. 202.
[34]T. Veremis, *Ikonomia kai diktatoria* (Economy and dictatorship), Athens: MIET, 1982, pp. 23–25.
[35]T. Veremis, *The Military in Greek Politics: From Independence to Democracy,* London: Hurst, 1997, pp. 70–89.

the element of professional corporatism in their interventions was ultimately condemned to failure. The ponderous coup of 1935, masterminded by the only military organisation set up to achieve corporatist aims (*Elliniki Stratiotiki Organosis*—ESO), failed miserably, but posed yet another challenge to the parliamentary system as the only source of legitimacy.[36] Although patron–client relationships destroyed all attempts at horizontal organisation of claimants, the social isolation of the refugees and their lack of connections, other than their dependence on specific politicians, encouraged the development of a corporatist identity, as well as a form of class identity within their ranks that profoundly affected Greek politics.

The influx of about 300,000 men of voting age, ranked almost solidly with the liberal camp, determined the pattern of elections, at least until 1932. Furthermore the anti-monarchical stance of the refugees, as opposed to the anti-Constantinist sentiments of the mainstream Venizelists, was another novelty with a special impact on the 1924 change of regime. The native liberals opposed King Constantine as a person rather than the institution he represented. His father King George I, though hardly a popular monarch, had steered the Crown clear of dangerous reefs during his long reign and had acquired a reputation for wisdom by striking compromises with his parliamentary adversaries. If Constantine had not challenged Venizelos's authority as the elected prime minister, he would have been remembered for his presence at the front line in the Balkan Wars. The refugees had no such recollections but harboured the bitter memories of forcible expulsion from their homeland, which they associated with the anti-Venizelist government then in power and its leader King Constantine. Their loss of property and status had the effect of inspiring them with revolutionary ideals, with which the cautious radicalism of the natives could not be compared.

Local conferences of refugees that convened through 1923 to determine a common position in Greek politics concluded that they owed unqualified allegiance to Eleftherios Venizelos.[37] True to their commitment, the refugees backed the Liberals in the elections of 1923, 1926 and 1928. Some observers believe that without this support the Venizelist camp could not have dominated the polls through-

---

[36]M. Janowitz, *The Military in the Political Development of New Nations,* University of Chicago Press, 1965, p.68.

[37]Dimitris Pentzopoulos, *The Balkan Exchange of Minorities and its Impact upon Greece,* London: Hurst, 2002 (prev. publ. 1962), p. 176

out this period.[38] Yet in spite of their decisive electoral impact the refugees were under-represented as a group in Parliament. Although they formed 20 per cent of the total population, their deputies amounted on average to only 12 -13 per cent in the House (the most they ever gained was thirty-eight seats out of 300 in the elections of 1932).[39] This was due to their geographical dispersal, which gave them a 'dominant voice in determining the victory or defeat of the old political parties of Greece, but prevented them from forming an independent political force'.[40]

The Ankara Convention of 1930 between Greece and Turkey, which cancelled the claims of the refugees to their abandoned properties in Anatolia, constituted a watershed for refugee political behaviour. The widespread disillusionment with parliamentary politics felt by the refugees as a result led to a significant swing to the left and the development of a class consciousness. It was a way of 'sublimating their alienation by struggling for an envisioned international order in which ethnic minorities would not constitute political problems'.[41] In the 1931 by-elections in Thessaloniki, where the refugees formed 48 per cent of the population, the Liberal candidate received only 38 per cent of the vote (compared to 69 per cent three years earlier) while the Communists doubled their share.[42]

However, the flight of refugee votes to the anti-Venizelist camp was caused by false promises of compensation for their lost property and was only temporary. Given its history, the Populist Party could never aspire to reconciliation with the refugees. During the Venizelist coup of 1935 the refugees unanimously backed the Venizelist rebels against the Populist government.[43] The majority of refugee defectors from Venizelism went to the Communist camp, but this transition was not easy. In 1924 the Comintern decided that the Greek, Serbian and Bulgarian parts of Macedonia ought to form a united and autonomous state within a Balkan Confederation. For the Greek Communists (KKE) the implications of this decision, which amounted

---

[38]Gregorios Dapnnes, *Ta Ellinika Politika Kommata, 1821–1961* (The Greek political parties), Athens: Galaxias, 1961, p.146.

[39]Pentzopoulos, p. 187.

[40]*Ibid.*, p. 188.

[41]John A. Petropulos, 'The Compulsory Exchange of Populations: Greek-Turkish Peacemaking 1922–30', *Byzantine and Modern Greek Studies,* vol. 2, 1976, pp. 158–9.

[42]Pentzopoulos, op. cit, p.192.

[43]George Th. Mavrogordatos, *Stillborn Republic: Social Conditions and Party Strategies in Greece, 1922–36,* Berkeley: University of California Press, 1983, pp. 211–13.

to a surrender of newly-acquired territory, were grave. Such party luminaries as Ioannis Kordatos and Seraphim Maximos warned their comrades of the consequences that this would have for the refugees in particular and the masses in general, but they were ignored and resigned in despair. The decision to fall in line with the Comintern split the Greek Communists, but the damage could not be undone: the refugees settled in Macedonia refrained from joining the KKE's ranks. The fear of again becoming an ethnic minority in a united Macedonia with a hostile Slavic majority determined the political choices of the rural settlers for years to come.

Refugees who did become members of the KKE soon realised that they would have to give up their allegiance to their special refugee cause and bow to their party's priorities, which often clashed with their own corporate interests. The party's opposition to Venizelist 'imperialism' during the Asia Minor campaign, its subsequent support of the native workers against the newcomers, and its condemnation of the massive settlement of refugees in Macedonia and Thrace 'as part of a sinister plan of the Greek bourgeoisie for a forcible alteration of the ethnic composition of these regions',[44] highlighted the predicament of the Communist refugees.[45]

In 1934 the adoption of the 'Popular Front' strategy against fascism allowed the KKE to relax its ideological rigour and revise its position regarding the refugees. The policy for an 'independent Macedonia and Thrace' was replaced by 'full national and political equality for all national minorities', and an extra effort was made to win over republicans who were disappointed with the Venizelist camp. By 1935 about half of the Central Committee and most of the Politburo members were refugees, including the party's Secretary-General Nikos Zachariadis.[46] The refugees as a distinct group began to lose their cohesion but offered their radical zeal to the Communist movement.

One of the most important new developments of the post-1922 era was the end of the territorial expansion of Greece. The country had at long last acquired permanent borders. The transition from the twentieth century's second decade of glory and expansion to

[44]Mavrogoradatos, p. 219.
[45]Mavrogordatos's point that, although the KKE sought to infiltrate the refugees, its own aims were often incompatible with their interests is well substantiated. See Mavrogordatos, pp. 218–20, and his use of KKE sources, footnotes 109–19 (pp. 218–21).
[46]Maovrogordatos, pp. 222–3.

the third of defeat and retrenchment was not easy for the Greeks to accomplish. Some felt trapped within the claustrophobic confines of a problematic state, others sought to rationalise Greece's predicament and exchange the loss of the Great Idea with a new concentration on westernisation and development. George Theotokas's book *Elefthero Pneuma* (Free Spirit),[47] published in 1929, was a timely attempt to rid his generation of the wreckage of past illusions and stem the tide of pessimism or mystical escapism represented by the poet Karyotakis and Sikelianos respectively.[48] The poet Karyotakis, who took his own life, became a symbol of the post-war lost generation, while Sikelianas attempted to revive the pagan glory of antiquity. Theotokas praised the symbiosis of the worthy and contradictory elements that comprise Greek tradition, the legacy of folk and scholarly achievement, of the self-taught warrior Ioannis Makriyannis and the sophisticated bard Cavafis alike. But his main preoccupation was to steer Greece back into the mainstream of European tradition of which it had always been part.[49] A general turned politician and dictator also tried to establish a cultural continuum that would bring Greece into what he perceived as the European mainstream. Ioannis Metaxas's 'Third Greek Civilisation' was akin to Mussolini's visions and was as opposed to pessimism, escapism and Communism as was Theotokas. Yet his scheme was exclusive and in fact insular, while the vision of Theotokas was inclusive and cosmopolitan. Although some intellectuals sought to counter Greece's psychological self-isolation, a kind of parochialism was already setting in.

The 'autochthonous' interpretation of the nation in 1844 was doomed by an expanding kingdom. As the historian Constantinos Paparrigopoulos well understood, a cultural concept of unity could provide a bond that would facilitate the acculturation of Albanians, Vlachs and Slavs inhabiting the Hellenic state. Thus Isocrates's dictum 'We consider Greeks those who partake of our culture' became the basis of nineteenth-century Greek irredentism. The present cultural homogeneity of the Greeks owes much to the open and flexible notion of what constituted 'Greekness' in the era of the Great Idea.

[47]George Theotokas, *Elefthero Pneuma,* Athens: Hermes, 1929, 1973.

[48]Mario Vitti, *Istoria tis neoellinikis logotechnias* (History of modern Greek literature) Athens: Odysseas, 1978, pp. 293–341.

[49]K. Th. Dimaras, 'O telesphoros syngerasmos' (The effective conversion) in *Istoria tou Ellinikou Etnous* (History of the Hellenic world), vol. 15, Athens: Ekdotiki Athinon, 1978, pp. 487–9.

The content of Greek nationalism was transformed during the interwar period. Besides the Asia Minor catastrophe and the sealing of Greek borders, the Comintern's stance—adopted by a dutiful KKE—proved a formidable challenge to Greece's territorial integrity. Thus the danger 'from within' became an entirely new threat to a state which hitherto had only known external enemies.

The new content of Greek nationalism was a denial of the Communist creed. It was also connected with the insecurity that prevailed after the First World War, which had to do primarily with the threat from the 'north'. Class analysis and 'historical materialism' that cut across national distinctions, in conjuction with claims to Greek territory from Bulgaria, Yugoslavia and Albania, indirectly determined the state's ideological orientation. Whereas during the irredentist years state ideology reflected a generosity towards potential converts to Hellenism and tolerance for ethnic idiosyncrasies, the interwar state strove for Hellenic authenticity as something conferred by history. An exclusive and privileged relationship with antiquity became one of the two legitimising elements of Greekness. The other was ideological purity.

Metaxas, not unlike other theorists of the Right such as Pericles Yannopoulos and Demosthenis Daniilides, relegated religion in his state to a secondary role.[50] Ancient Greece was his primary source of reference and the ideal that differentiated Greeks from their Slavic neighbours and by implication from the Communists. His anti-Communism and anti-parliamentarianism brought him close to the contemporary Fascists, but his racism was muted. In his 27 October 1936 speech in Serres he spoke of the Greek race and its vocation as a 'chosen stock'.[51] Although the concept had been aired previously, it nevertheless marked a departure from the cultural nationalism of the past and set a precedent that would find imitators in the post-war future. His least successful novelty was the cult of the state as a living organism with a mission to unify the nation. In their time-honoured tradition the Greeks made fun of grandiloquent nonsense and remained distinctly unimpressed.

The nation-state was no doubt the culprit responsible for most

[50]The most systematic study of the Metaxist ideology was produced by Constantine Sarandis, 'The Ideology and Character of the Metaxas Regime' in *The Metaxas Dictatorship: Aspects of Greece, 1936–40,* Athens: ELIAMEP, Vryonis Center, 1993, p. 159.

[51]Sarandis, op.cit., p. 150.

of the misdeeds of an otherwise creative European era. In Greece the nation was viewed as the spiritual side of the system and the state as its reincarnation, and the latter could never mobilise the allegiance of its world-weary citizens to justify its failures. On 28 October 1940 the Greeks closed ranks behind Metaxas because the fascist challenge was perceived as a threat to the nation (*ethnos*) and the fatherland (*patris*). The post-1922 decline of Liberal Democracy and its demise over the decade following 1936 nevertheless weighed heavily in the calamities that befell Greece later.

In the mean time the displacement and relocation of people, as with the Asia Minor refugees, undermined patron-client relationships and facilitated the advent of ideologies. The arrival of the refugee newcomers in the rural and urban centres destroyed the fabric of traditional political relations and helped to recreate the network of political camps and confrontations. This, however, was a long-drawn-out process.

The attitude of political parties towards the 'other', whether the refugees or ethnic groups, depended entirely on their point of entry into Greek politics. It was not because of ideological inclination that the Venizelist Liberals favoured their refugee clients, nor did the Conservative Populists draw Jewish and Muslim support because of their party platform. As long as the Venizelist/anti-Venizelist divide prevailed, the refugees gave their allegiance to their political patrons, whereas the old-established Jews and the Arvanites (descendants of the Albanians) voted unanimously for the anti-Venizelists.

Even under the Metaxas regime, state relations with the 'others' on the basis of their party allegiances did not change. Metaxas was thus more friendly towards the Jews, the Arvanites and the Muslims, than the liberal Venizelists had ever been, and certainly less friendly towards the refugees of the urban (as opposed to the rural) centres and the Slav Macedonians.

The Anatolian refugees established in rural Macedonia were mostly Turkish-speaking or speakers of Pontic Greek (equally unintelligible to the natives) and for that reason could not have exerted a Hellenising influence in the region. Their identity conformed to the Christian Orthodox culture of their 'Rum' communities, but their inevitable affinity with the Greek state as their most important source of support and security would eventually transform most of them into ardent patriots. In the mean time they unwittingly became the cause of a significant cleavage among the natives of Macedonia. The antagonism of the Turkish-speaking refugees towards the Slavic- and Greek-speaking natives over the abandoned properties of the departed Turks had far-reaching consequences for the society of northern Greece. Many Slav-speakers opted for the Communist party and some joined the Democratic Army of the 1946–9 Civil War with a secessionist agenda, while the rural refugees became right-wing nationalists supporting the cause of the Hellenic state.[52] There were of course significant exceptions, such as the 'red town' of Kilkis, but on the whole the rural refugees sided with the authorities against the left-wing rebels.

The war years and foreign occupation (Italian, German and Bulgarian) became the most important factor in the reconstruction of the networks of loyalties. As the liberal-conservative divide was overtaken by that between Right and Left, a new shift of loyalties began to develop. Existing differences among the refugees and native groups in Macedonia, as well as in the clash between loyalists and secessionists, certainly played their part in the subsequent position of each in the Right–Left spectrum. However, it should not be presumed that Right-Left positions coincided with those of loyalists-secessionists. The Chams of Epirus, certain Vlachs of Thessaly and many Slav Macedonians collaborated with the occupation forces (who can be characterised as extreme right-wingers), mostly out of opportunism and to settle old accounts with their opponents in the region. Nor should the pattern of behaviour of the secessionists in the Democratic Army be equated with that of all the members of the KKE, as was often claimed by right-wing propaganda.[53]

Even though the 1941–9 period recast the entire issue of refugees by practically eradicating their corporate position in Greek politics, those who did not escape the shanty neighborhoods of Athens and the poor urban quarters on the city's periphery reminded the Greek state of their existence by casting their vote for EDA (United Democratic Left) and for the KKE once it was legalised.[54]

The entire transformation of political discourse in Greece from liberal-royalist to Left-Right was greatly influenced by the refugee factor. In the urban centres the refugees became associated with the Communist 'enemy from within', while in rural Greece they impeded the acculturation process of bringing the Slav-speakers into the Hellenic tradition and diverted their loyalties into other directions.

---

[52]John S. Koliopoulos, *Leilasia phronimation* (A pillage of convictions), Thessaloniki: Vanias, 1994; *Plundered Loyalties, op. cit.*

[53]Koliopoulos, *op. cit.*

[54]Renée Hirschon, *Heirs of the Greek Catastrophe: The Social Life of Asia Minor Refugees in Piraeus,* Oxford: Clarendon Press, 1989.

Civil strife healed the political cleavages of the interwar period and created new ones. Venizelists and royalists slowly closed ranks against the left-wing threat, and the new cleavage transformed the nationalism of the past into the 'national-mindedress' (*ethnikophrosyne*) of the postwar anti-Communist state.[55]

The Civil War cleavage divided the Greeks into roughly two categories: a large one of anti-Communist liberals, conservatives and right-wingers and a smaller one of trapped socialists, left-wingers and avowed Communists. The ruling intelligentsia represented a neo-Kantian school of thought and experimented with an aristocratic form of democracy, expounded by a close associate of Prime Minister Karamanlis, Constantine Tsatsos. A Venizelist of the pre-war period, Tsatsos believed that freedom was a private achievement, not a benefit that could be distributed to the public. His contemporary at Heidelberg University, Panayotis Kanellopoulos, another prominent member of Karamanlis's cabinets, savoured a concept of freedom that would spring from an ideal polity, not unlike the Platonic Republic. In a period preoccupied with considerations of rapid reconstruction and economic growth, these scholars in politics offered an occasional recognition of excellence that propelled architects such as Dimitris Pikionis (1887–1968) and Aris Constantinides (1913–97) to prominence.

However, post-war modernisation was mostly centred on the economy. When Greece entered an association agreement with the European Economic Community in the early 1960s, it did not then occur to the able Greek negotiators to address the philosophical roots which made Greek society so different from the core of the European Community. Collectivism as opposed to individualism was a subject that had appeared mainly in debates between left and liberal exponents throughout the interwar period.

The absence of the individual from the Greek philosophical tradition, and indeed from society itself, had been remarked on by George Theotokas in his *Elefthero Pneuma* (Free spirit) in 1929.[56] His views generated a storm of opposition on both left and the right.[57]

[55]George Mavrogordatos, '*The 1940s between Past and Future*' in John Iatrides and Linda Wringley (eds), *Greece at the Crossroads: The Civil War and its Legacy*, University Park, PA: Pennsylvania State University Press, 1995, pp. 31–47.

[56]The book was reprinted in 1973 during the days of the junta, and was edited by another member of the generation of the 1930s, Constantine Dimaras.

[57]Takis Papatsonis, a poet with religious inclinations, attacked Theotokas' views in 1932. His essay was included in his collection *Tetraperatos Cosmos* (Whole Wide World), vol. A, Athens: Ikaros, 1966, pp. 541–7.

Although the coherence of his message was lessened by his youthful enthusiasm, Theotokas identified individualism as a vital element of Western achievement and noted its absence in Greece's past. Left-wing adherents naturally reacted to a clarion call that undermined their appeal for a mass struggle, but even political liberals refused to recognise a view that praised individuality. No less a liberal than George Seferis revelled in the collective psyche of Greece's traditional society. In his 1943 lecture on Makriyannis in Cairo he referred to the warrior-writer of 1821 in order to develop his views on the Greek collectivity. 'The Greeks in the old times believed in "we" and not "I". Because whenever the ego sought to override the collectivity, Ati, the implacable fate that preserves balance in the world, strikes it down.'[58]

The polarisation in politics and society caused by the Civil War created a formidable obstacle to the development of a social democracy of the kind that flourished in post-war Europe, and delayed the return of the liberal centre for a decade. When the Centre Union party came to power in 1963 as an umbrella movement covering a wide political spectrum, its message was not conciliatory, but it offered a reformist mission in opposition to the oppressive institutions of a right-wing state.

The subsequent regime of 1967–74 precipitated a unique reconciliation between the left-centre and the right, as all united in opposition to the dictatorship. The consensus against the Junta constituted the solid ground on which democracy was re-established after its seven-year eclipse. The populism of the 1980s and the ideological charade of the Left aping the nationalism of the Right, while the Right espoused the statism of the Left, with the Centre impersonating both Left and Right according to circumstances, delayed the return of a liberal Centre. The elections of April 2000 confirmed that centrism in its liberal form had become dominant in Greek politics. Yet the Simitis era of Centre politics provoked little discussion among politicians on the nature of the liberal polity. Even accomplished liberals such as the former minister and (at the time of writing) leader of a small party in parliament, Stephanos Manos, are preoccupied more with the economic than with the political side of liberalism. In Greece, as in all other member states of the European Union, '*homo politicus*' has been largely displaced by '*homo economicus*'.

[58]Seferis, *Dokimes*, p. 197.

Part II. INSTITUTIONS

3

THE CHURCH OF GREECE

The Church of Greece came into being in 1833 when the Bavarian regency unilaterally proclaimed, in the name of King Otto, its independence from the Patriarchate of Constantinople. By the same royal decree of July 1833—the work of Georg von Maurer and two prominent supporters of a Greek national church, Theokletos Pharmakidis and Spyridon Trikoupis—it became autocephalous, acquired its own synod, and recognised King Otto as its head.

The expected and understandable negative reaction from a number of prelates was never strong enough to endanger the newly-established order in the country, while the equally expected and understandable opposition from the Ecumenical Patriarchate was treated with the respect and understanding due to the sensibilities of the 'mother church'. In 1850, after tortuous and protracted negotiations, the Patriarchate of Constantinople finally recognised the independence of the new institution.[1]

The settlement of this vital question of the fledgling kingdom represented the triumph of the lay state over ecclesiastical authority, and was a reflection of the ideas and principles on which the kingdom was being founded. The newly-established Church of Greece was

---

[1]The subject is discussed in Charles A. Frazee, *The Orthodox Church and Independence, 1821–1852*, Cambridge, 1969. In his excellent summary of the Orthodox Church, Philip Sherrard, a devout Orthodox scholar, wrote: 'The Orthodox Church is very much a communion of local churches, whose universal nature is testified by the unity of its faith; and the guardian of the unity of the faith is ultimately the whole congregation of the faithful.' John Campbell and Philip Sherrard, *Modern Greece*, London: Ernest Benn, 1968, p. 199.

not only made independent of the Ecumenical Patriarchate; by the same token it was made subservient to the state. Although granted a privileged position in relation to other religious establishments, it was essentially turned into a state entity under the supervision of a ministry; and although the initial Bavarian settlement of the church question was later relaxed to allow it a measure of freedom within the secular state, the head of the Church always had to understand that the Minister of Education and Creeds was his superior. The blow to the authority and prestige of the Ecumenical Patriarchate was severe, but in the light of the requirements of the sovereign nation-state it was unavoidable.

Driven by Western principles and ideas about the position and role of religious establishments and confronted with an uncomfortably large and potentially destabilising religious component, Bavarian and Greek state-builders like Pharmakides and Spyridon Trikoupis took considerable pains to place the Greek Church under close watch and use it to promote such secular objectives as education and, somewhat later, Greek national aspirations among Orthodox Christians. Eventually the Church of Greece was made to identify so thoroughly with the modern Greek state's hellenising drive, inside and outside the state borders, that it would not be an overstatement to speak of a modern Hellenic church very much at odds with its own history.

One of the pious views of modern Greece concerns the role of the Orthodox Church in the establishment of the modern Greek nation-state. According to this view, the Church, in the role of a latter-day Noah's Ark, saved the Greek nation in the centuries of the Turkish and Western 'deluge' following the fall of the eastern Roman empire in 1453. The Orthodox Church, by protecting the true faith against both Muslim and Latin temporal princes in the centuries of foreign rule, preserved Greek identity and kept the Greek nation from being assimilated by the nations of its foreign rulers. According to the same view, the Orthodox Church welcomed the Greek Revolution in 1821 and blessed the arms of the Greek insurgents. Indeed, many Orthodox prelates assumed a leading role in insurgent Greece and played an important part not only in ecclasiastical but also in political and military matters. Following Independence, a Latin prince and his Western advisers severed the links that had united the Church of Greece with the Ecumenical Patriarchate and placed the Church under the authority of his temporal power.[2]

[2] See Chrysostomos Papadopoulos, *He Ekklesia tes Hellados* (The Church of Greece), Athens 1951. The author was Archbishop of Athens in 1923–38.

Efforts to see the Orthodox Church and its role in modern Greece in a proper historical perspective, on the basis of evidence from both lay and church sources, have foundered on the hard rock of embedded suspicion of the motives behind any such endeavours. As in the case of the mythical Greek 'hidden school' (*krypho scholio*) under Ottoman rule, the notion of the Orthodox Church playing the role of an active and enthusiastic agent in the establishment of the independent Greek nation-state seemed unassailable. Revisionist historians questioning it have always been portrayed as so many Western agents conspiring to rob the Greeks of their faith and identity.

In presenting the massacres of Turks by insurgent Greeks as irrefutable proof of a religious war of Christians against Muslims, contemporary Western observers and subsequent commentators unintentionally supported the view of the Orthodox Church playing a leading role in the War of Independence. It is now established that Church leaders were not more—indeed they were much less—enthusiastic freedom fighters than most other representatives of Greek élite groups with a vested interest in preserving the Ottoman Sultan's decrepit but still formidable empire. The truth is that the hand of the Orthodox hierarchy was forced by the reprisals of the Ottomans against the Church's prelates at the outbreak of the 1821 uprising; by the burden of its accumulated debts that might be written off in the expectation of a clean slate under a new regime; and by the real fear of Orthodox prelates that they might have to pay with their lives for outrages committed in order to compromise a rather reluctant leadership. Orthodox prelates took part in the War of Independence, not only as religious leaders leading the faithful against the temporal power ruling the Greeks, but also in the expectation of preserving a position in the new regime as dominant as what they had enjoyed under the old one. When they fought against the Turks, like the rest of the Greeks, they did so not as Christians against Muslims but as Greeks against Turks.

The idea of the Orthodox Church hierarchy welcoming the opportunity to establish a Greek nation-state by carving territory out of the Ottoman empire in the way shown by the leaders of the French Revolution, flies in the face of both common sense and all available evidence. Concepts such as popular sovereignty and the temporal state, which were central to the Greek insurgency, were anathema to the Orthodox Church of the time. So too was the prospect of breaking up the institution into as many national churches as there were nascent nation-states in the Ecumenical Patriarch's spiritual domain. The self-same Patriarch Gregory V, who was hanged on the Sultan's order for the disloyalty of his Greek flock, had condemned in so many words the leader of the Greek insurrection in the Principalities, Alexander Ypsilantis. Although there can be little doubt that Gregory V would have felt awkward about issuing this condemnation, he was certainly in line with the time-honoured Orthodox Church policy on such matters, of serving the interests of the Orthodox Ecumene as interpreted by its leadership.

Orthodox Church apologists have tried in vain ever since to explain Gregory's act in terms other than traditional Orthodox obedience to the Turkish ruler. The 'Paternal Instruction' of 1798 (published under the name of Anthimos VI, Patriarch of Jerusalem, but possibly written by Gregory V), which condemned the Greek stirrings for freedom, did not represent a departure from traditional Church relations with the Sultan and from the equally traditional attitude towards most things associated with the West. Blind obedience to the Muslim legitimate monarch, as a formal chastisement for the sins of the Eastern Roman emperors, was an article of faith for the Orthodox Church and an integral part of the doctrinal foundation on which its relations with both the Sultan and the West rested.[3]

Thus the movement for Greek national independence, and the consequent launching of the Greek nation-state, could not possibly have been welcome to Church leaders in the way that it has subsequently been portrayed. The turning-point in the attitude of the prelates to the War of Independence was the summary execution of all the metropolitans and bishops whom the Ottoman authorities could lay their haunds on. The survivors understandably threw in their lot with the revolutionaries, raised the flag of insurrection and blessed their arms. However, the Orthodox Church was subsequently presented not only as having actively participated in the movement for Greek independence but as having worked for it ever since the fall of Constantinople in 1453. Church leaders and lay apologists set about constructing for the Church a history that would make it fit into the Greek nation-state. According to this construct, the Church created in 1833 by royal decree had in fact existed since St Paul's time and had come eventually to be associated with the Roman empire's 'Illyricum', i.e. the Greek peninsula and the adjacent islands; it had been free of

---

[3]For a probing analysis see Paschalis M. Kitromilides, 'Imagined Communities and the Origins of the National Question in the Balkan's Modern Greece' in M. Blinkhorn and T. Veremis (eds), *Nationalism and Nationality*, Athens, 1990, pp. 23–66.

Latin control and influence well before the Schism of 1054—indeed, ever since it had been detached from papal jurisdiction by the Eastern Emperor in 733. The Crusades and Latin and Ottoman rule turned it into a truly Greek institution, a repository of traditional Greek values and a vehicle of Greek identity immune to Western incursions.[4] At the same time the Church of Greece, which identified with the modern state's ever-expanding domain, was limiting the Ecumenical Patriarchate's spiritual domain to a mere shadow of what it had been before Greek independence. The young Germanos Karavangelis, Metropolitan of Kastoria in the early twentieth century, was a typical representative of this Hellenic church: impatient with Patriarchal sensibilities, this fiery prelate expanded the aspirations of the Greek nation deep into Slav-speaking western Macedonia as no Greek lay national agenda had dared to do up till then.

Before being nationalised, the Church of Greece had first to be brought into existence as an institution. Vacant sees, resulting from the murder of metropolitans by the Turks, together with an increasing number of refugee prelates from northern districts where the insurrection had been put down, in conjunction with the *de facto* termination of Patriarchal control over southern Greek ecclesiastical affairs, all facilitated the objectives of the westernised state-builders. Old metropolitan sees, and new ones carved out of the old to satisfy refugee or upstart prelates, formed the new church—the launching of which, as already indicated, met some opposition.

Opposition increased as a result of the government's decision to regulate monastic affairs and property. Empowered by two special decrees of October 1833 and March 1834, the government closed down almost two-thirds of the 524 monasteries and convents in the kingdom, seizing their assets to finance the programme of state education. Centuries of peasant piety and insecurity of lay property had created a situation which confronted Bavarian and Greek state-builders with both a problem and a tempting prize: hundreds of religious houses, most of them with only a small number of monks or nuns each, controlled considerable tracts of land and other property, which the state and the peasant tenants of monastic estates were eager to seize. State officials were never short of convincing arguments, nor was the Church's reaction or public discontent strong enough to force

[4]Gerasimos I. Konidaris, *Symbole eis ten eisagogen tes ekklesiastikes historias tes Hellados* (A contribution to the introduction to the ecclesiastical history of Greece), Athens, 1938, pp. 56.

the government to retreat on the monastic question. Scandals and serious and credible charges of mismanagement, and equally credible arguments for the need to raise the funds for state education, weakened the appeal of conservative reaction against the dispossession and closing down of monasteries and convents with dwindling populations.

Opposition to the settlement of the Church question of 1833–4 flared up in the next few decades in the form of peasant uprisings in the Peloponnese incited by Orthodox fanatics like Kosmas Flamiatos of Cephalonia. Flamiatos lived in Patras and conspired with other like-minded opponents of the settlement to fight against the Western-oriented government of the country with the support of Russian representatives in Greece. Another such firebrand was the self-styled monk and 'saintly father' Christophoros, also known as 'Papoulakos', who incited peasants in the early 1850s in collusion with Flamiatos's Philorthodox conspirators, to oppose everything coming from the 'heretical' West, including public education. Serious opponents of the new order like Konstantinos Oikonomos, a firebrand of Orthodox tradition, should not be associated with mavericks such as Flamiatos and Papoulakos. It was perhaps one of the main and lasting weaknesses of the old ecclesiastical order that opposition to the new order was channelled to and voiced by charlatans, and dissipated itself in inconsequential peasant unrest which as a rule alienated the educated Philorthodox thinkers.[5]

The settlement was finalised in 1852, when the Greek Parliament approved the 'Synodical Tome', which the Ecumenical Patriarchate had issued two years earlier: this proclaimed the 'canonical union' of the Church of Greece with the 'Mother Church' while accepting the former's autocephalous status. The final settlement did not change the national character of the Church or of Greece, and was made possible by the need of the Patriarchate to re-establish relations with the only Orthodox church that promised to keep the 'Great Church' in touch with the West and prevent it from falling under Russian tutelage; and because of the need of Greece's government not to let the Greeks cut themselves loose from this religious attachment. Even more decisive was perhaps the Greek Church's pressing need to ordain new metropolitans: the old ones were disappearing one after another, and the Greek Holy Synod could not—short of a rupture

---

[5]For more information on Flamiatos and Christoforos Panagiotopoulos, better known as 'Papoulakos', see S.M. Sophocles, *The Religion of Modern Greece*, Thessaloniki: Institute for Balkan Studies, 1961, pp. 48–50.

amounting to schism—ordain new ones before its canonical recognition by the Ecumenical Patriatch.

In the second half of the nineteenth century, the Church of Greece's hellenisation and subservience to the state proceeded without serious opposition from either the Church hierarchy or Philorthodox circles. This was because the country was launched on its irredentist phase which allowed no internal distractions such as those it had gone through in the 1830s and '40s. Greek state pressure to mobilise all efforts in the drive to push the nation's frontier into the Balkans, while reclaiming lands and peoples that had come under Slavic influence in previous centuries, was also felt by the Church establishment, which was called upon not only to bless the national effort but also to contribute to the drive to reinforce the educational and ecclesiastical status of Greeks in the contested lands. The pressure was also felt by the Ecumenical Patriarchate, whose metropolitans in these lands were coerced into supporting the Greek national effort. The last vestiges of the Patriarchate's reluctances to deviate from its traditional determination to steer clear of disputes like the Greek–Bulgarian clash over Macedonia were swept away in the long and fierce conflict between Greece and Bulgaria for control of churches and schools in the contested territories. The challenge from Bulgaria's national Church, which threatened to limit drastically the Patriarchate's spiritual jurisdiction in the Sultan's European domains, obliged the Patriarchate to allow its metropolitans in the region to be guided by Greece's consuls, pretending all the time that the fierce struggle against the Bulgarian Exarchate was a religious one. The stormy career of one of the most independent-minded patriarchs, Joachim III, who ascended the patriarchal throne twice, reflects the protracted nature the Patriarchate's conflict with Greek national interests.[6]

The Ecumenical Patriarchate's loss was the Greek Church's gain. While the Patriarch's spiritual domain shrank and he progressively became a revered relic of the past, the influence and prestige of the Archbishop of 'Athens and all Greece' increased proportionately. The Greek national state protected its Church from being trapped in a position similar to the dilemma that faced the Great Church of

---

[6]See Evangelos Kofos, 'Patriarch Ioachim III (1878–1884) and the Irredentism Policy of the Greek state', *Journal of Modern Greek Studies*, 4 no., 2, (1986), pp. 107–20. See also Paschalís M. Kitromilides, 'To telos tis ethnarchikis paradosis' (The end of the ethnarchical Tradition), *Amitos sti Mnimi Photi Apostolopoulou*, Athens, 1984, pp. 486–507.

Constantinople in its effort to adjust Ecumenical Orthodoxy to the pressures of Western Enlightenment in the eighteenth century and Greek nationalism in the nineteenth. The Church of Greece, despite the anguish of our contemporary Neo-Orthodox[7] over the loss of 'our Orthodox East', was spared the utter confusion which the Great Church experienced as it tried to combine religion with nationalism and Orthodoxy with Hellenism.[8]

Religious societies that appeared in Greece between the latter part of the nineteenth century and the post-1945 period included such influential groups as *Anaplasis* in 1887; the *Apostolic Mission* of the Greek Church (1930), supervised by the Holy Synod; the 'Orthodox Christian Corner'; a society of intellectuals called *Aktines*; and the Union of Cooperating Christian Corporations, better known as *Zoe*. Following in the steps of Protestant activism, *Zoe* became the most conspicuous of the lot. Its many publications expounded religious and ethical principles as guidelines for the life of a good Christian, and its membership penetrated all levels of society. In its heyday *Zoe* ran more than 2,260 Sunday schools with up to 200,000 students. In the lean 1950s it provided solace to the war-ravaged country, but development and prosperity proved its most formidable opponent.[9]

In order to win over its hierarchy, the Greek state made its Church an integral part of the country's national development: it associated the institution with the War of Independence and its formative myth, made its members state employees and, perhaps more important, not only made Orthodoxy the country's dominant religion but, by forbidding proselytism, also gave it protected status. These privileges, the last two of which are incompatible with some of the principles on which the modern liberal state is based, have made the Church of Greece a more conservative institution than was originally intended and certainly an obstacle to the necessary periodic adjustments by the

---

[7]The 'Neo-Orthodox', according to V. Xydias, challenge the Church's 'secularized conservatism'. See 'Notation: *new* or *old* Orthodoxy in the Limelight', *Journal of Hellenic Diaspora*, XI, 2 (summer 1984), pp. 69–72.

[8]See Kitromilides, 'To telos tis ethnarchikis paradosis', pp. 486–507. Also Christos Kardaras, *Ioakeim III–Char. Trikoupis I antiparathesi* (Ioakeim III–Char. Trikoupis: the confrontation), Athens, 1998, for a collection of letters between the two.

[9]A revealing document on *Zoe* was produced by a one-time follower, Christos Yannaras: *Kataphygio Ideon* (Refuge of Ideas), Athens: Domos, 1987. The author castigates *Zoe* for being an oppressive institution of zealots. For a description of religious societies see Sophocles, *op.cit.*, pp. 52–60. The subject nevertheless calls for a thorough researcher.

country stemming from its European Union membership. It is doubtful whether the Church leadership would ever dare to demand from the government a new role for itself, despite signs that it tries to expand its role as originally defined. References to the Byzantine and Balkan aspects of modern Greek identity, which some prelates are fond of making, should not be seen as expressions of a deeper doctrinal opposition to the country's European orientation, but as reflections of a certain Orthodox fundamentalism, with roots in the Philorthodox reaction to the settlement of the Church question in the nineteenth century. As for relations with the Ecumenical Patriarchate, it is no longer the country's Church which is pressing for closer relations with the 'Mother Church' in Constantinople, but the Greek government. This reversal of roles can be explained in the context of the government's policy directed at opening new channels of communication with the other Balkan countries. According to the view which provides the basic arguments favouring such a policy, the Ecumenical Patriarchate is better suited than the Church of Greece to facilitating the implementation of this policy. However, re-establishing the Ecumenical Patriarchate as a credible agent would require regional rearrangement no less ambitious in scope than the reconstruction of the Ottoman empire or the establishment of a new political unit with similar preoccupations.

Although the government of the Church is entrusted to a Holy Synod presided over by the Archbishop of Athens, decisions of the Synod are validated by the commissioner (procurator) of the Greek government. According to the charter of 1852, Eastern Orthodoxy is the religion of the state and it is the state that appoints bishops and priests, pays their salaries and administers church property. Subsequent charters (1923, 1925, 1931, 1939, 1943) amended the original without changing the dependence of the church on the state. In this extreme form of dependence the prelates of the church had to pay the price for their political views. At the time of the schism between royalists and liberals, in 1917, the Archbishop of Athens and several bishops were deposed and replaced.[10]

The 21 April 1967 military regime added an element of comic relief to the institutional control of the Church by the state. By advertising the relationships on every possible public occasion, the Colonels heaped more discredit on the Church than it had suffered throughout all the previous decades. After the coup of 1967 the

[10]Campbell and Sherrard, *Modern Greece*, p.197.

Archbishop of Athens was obliged to retire and another favoured by the Junta was 'elected'. When the dictatorship collapsed in 1974, separation of the Church from the state was considered in earnest by all sides in the new Parliament. The discussion of the 1975 Constitution gave Karamanlis's New Democracy party a chance to make a clean break with its conservative antecedents and dissociate itself from the right wing in postwar politics. In the draft constitution the status of the Church of Greece was changed from a state institution (*nomokratousa ekklesia*) to an established church (*epikratousa ekklesia*), and Orthodox doctrine was renamed 'the creed of the majority' rather than the official religion of the state. While in the opposition PASOK insisted on full separation of Church and state, demanding that the former become 'completely free beyond any official state input',[11] the defence of the existing relationship was taken up by the Church's highest authority, the Holy Synod. Although prelates invoked history and tradition to defend the *status quo*, they were in fact reluctant to give up the benefit to them of being civil servants and their monopoly on the nation's official faith. With the advent of PASOK to power in 1981, its leader Andreas Papandreou reiterated his party's resolution to separate Church from state but added a cryptic statement that allowed space for manoeuvre: 'The separation will deal with administrative matters, not with the Church's ties to the nation.'[12]

The saga of Bill 1700, concerning the future status of the Church, summarised the reformist position of a socialist government whose appetite for church property proved stronger than its urge to modernise the institution itself. In 1986 Papandreou sacked his Minister of Education and Creeds, Apostolos Kaklamanis, who had incurred the wrath of the Holy Synod by introducing a first draft of Bill 1700 that highlighted the expropriation of monastic property. The new minister, Antonis Tritsis, made a more genuine effort to recast the new bill in a reformist mould. 'The crux of the bill was article 8 (paragraph 8) which proposed to revise the Constitution Charter of the Church by reintroducing the conciliar principles of Orthodox theology at

[11]See *PASOK: Syntagma ya mia Ellada dimokratiki. Eisigiseis tis omadas epistimonon.* Athens: Kedros 1975. Mentioned in Elisabeth Prodromou, 'Democratization and Religions Transformation in Greece' in P. Kitromilides and T. Veremis (eds), *The Orthodox Church in a Changing World*, Athens: ELIAMEP–CAMS, 1998, p. 146.
[12]Quoted in I.M. Konidaris, *O Nomos 1700/1987 kai I prosfati krisi stis skheseis ekklesias kai politeias* (Law 1700/1987 and the recent crisis in Church-state relations), Athens: Sakkoulas 1988.

all levels of the ecclesiastical organisational structure.'[13] The application of the conciliar principle involved elections for clerical and lay representatives at parish, diocesan and metropolitan level. The power of the Archbishop of Athens would be curtailed by this innovation, and the participatory principle would decentralise the flow of authority.[14] Papandreou's meeting with Archbishop Seraphim, without the minister being present, resulted in a compromise that sealed the fate of Bill 1700: Article 8, referring to the elected committee structures, was abrogated. Tritsis resigned from the Ministry and from the party on 9 May 1988, and Parliament passed a revised version of Bill 1700 in August that year, which in essence maintained the *status quo*.[15]

The Church of Greece bears the marks of its long subservience to the state. As a mere government agency whose affairs are determined by the Ministry of Education and Creeds, it has ceased to attract prelates of the calibre of Theokletos Pharmakides in the nineteenth century or Chrysostomos Papadopoulos in the twentieth. Although the memory of reactionary upheavals may still occasionally stir priests into populist oratory, their credibility has suffered.

The decision of the Simitis government to strike religious affiliation off future identity cards sparked a bitter controversy between the Church's prelates and state officials. Archbishop Christodoulos of Athens, with an eye on the media, disregarded the wisdom of his predecessors who had deliberately shunned the limelight. His frequent appearances before the TV cameras heightened his popularity with churchgoers, but earned him the suspicion of intellectuals and the ruling Liberal Left. The identity card issue made the Church confront its predicament: either to carry its campaign against the government to its ultimate conclusion—the separation of Church and state—or to back off and lose face. Its representatives will probably follow the more prudent course, as they have always done in the past.

---

[13]Prodromou, *op.cit.*, p. 123.
[14]*Ibid.*, p. 124.
[15]*Ibid.*, pp. 131–2.

4

THE MILITARY

The initial mission of the nineteenth-century regular army and its professional officer corps was to consolidate the authority of the centralised state. Having accomplished that, officers became preoccupied with Greece's irredentist aspirations. While pursuing this double mission of propping up the state and promoting its expansionist goals, they rarely questioned civilian supremacy or parliamentary rule. When they did become involved in politics following the outbreak of the First World War, officers were recruited by liberals and royalists to serve their ends rather than to serve their own corporate interests.

The interwar period is a watershed in modern Greek history. The Asia Minor debacle of 1922 and the influx of more than 1 million refugees into a country of barely 5 million transformed Greece. The few developed urban centres received the bulk of the destitute newcomers and among their ranks the Greek Communist Party (KKE) found willing recruits. This new party was a threat to the established order and was accused of conspiring to alienate recently acquired national territory. Compelled by its loyalty to the Comintern, the KKE subscribed to the slogan of the sixth Balkan Communist Conference in 1924 for a 'United and Independent Macedonia and Thrace'.

Such developments not only increased the insecurity of the state in relation to its internal enemies; it also changed the entire content of Greek nationalism. From an ideology open to all the Christian inhabitants of the unredeemed territories, it became the exclusive preserve of those Greeks who were thought to harbour true Greek national 'consciousness'.

The military embraced the new creed with some delay but with a vengeance. Fragmented into patron–client networks throughout the interwar period, they strove to promote their professional aims within the larger liberal-royalist confrontation. The only organised assault upon the authorities that conformed to the pattern of a corporate military conspiracy, namely the coup of 1935, was eroded by the antagonisms between rival networks and failed miserably. This coup was the first and last of its kind to involve so many different actors and the first to nurture visions of removing civilians from the management of the state. Its failure taught the officer protagonists that the state would not replace its civilian arbiters with the military unless the latter could show evidence of a much greater threat to the social order.

War and occupation reshuffled the military pack and rekindled rivalries between liberals and royalists. The political upheavals in the Greek forces in exile, and attempts to influence the Greek government in Cairo and London, were encouraged by the KKE's dominance over the resistance forces in occupied Greece. The plan to incapacitate the regular army so as to exclude it from the liberation of Greece succeeded, but the Communist guerrilla forces nonetheless failed to usurp power. The Civil War of 1946–9 made the officer corps the homogeneous preserve of conservative nationalist values. Furthermore, the influence of British and American military missions, in conjunction with special training, encouraged among the military a sense of autonomy and power to take political decisions on its own. Between 1952 and 1963 clandestine rightist organisations, which influenced promotions and vital appointments, sought to create a network in the army's leadership that shared anti-Communist fervour and strong views on the running of the state.

The 1967 coup that launched the seven-year military dictatorship was sparked by a crisis between the monarchy and Parliament. The most important cause of this backlash from an extremist military group was the emergence of international détente, which threatened to reduce the army's significance as the guardian of the state against both internal and external enemies. Although, in this and every other way, the regime of '21 April' was an anachronism, it maintained power for seven years through its use of repression and with the help of an unprecedented economic boom that came to Greece in the late 1960s.

In the past, patron–client relationships between politicians and the military had guaranteed civilian supremacy as well as causing resentment among officers who did not enjoy effective political connections. The most ardent exponents of an autonomous vocation for the officer corps were usually products of a peasant background who resented their more fortunate and better-connected colleagues. The report by General P. Panourgias on the events leading to the 1967 coup, presented to Karamanlis and later published in the newspaper *Acropolis* (20 August 1974), noted the social gulf between high- and low-ranking officers in the army. This was largely due to the fact that the Civil War, heightened by the need for an expanded officer corps, lowered the Military Academy's standards of admission. The fact that tuition was free attracted members of peasant and lower-middle-class background[1].

The transformation of civil-military relations in Greece during the latter part of the twentieth century cannot be explained by political factors alone. From the 1970s the social fabric changed rapidly. The rise of *per capita* income, the widening of professional options, the incorporation of the military academies into the system of university entrance examinations, and finally the prodigious growth of urban centres, changed the social background and the value system of the military. The core values and ideas that determined the behaviour of officers ever since they became politicised were derived from practices that pervaded rural Greece. For example, the patronage that corrupted urban institutions was affected by the rapid urbanisation of the post-war period. In 1896 Athens had a population of 80,000 out of the country's total population of 2,400,000; in 1951 it was 1,379,000 out of 8,500,000; and today the population of greater Athens is over 4,000,000 out of 10,000,000.[2] Much of the recruitment to the Greek forces between 1916 and 1967 was from the rural areas, but since the 1960s cadets have increasingly been products of the major urban centres that are home to more than half of Greece's population. During PASOK's second term, universities were grouped according to their subject specialisations for the purpose of entrance examinations, and students who failed to enter the institution of their first choice could still find a place in their second or third choice. The military schools trailed behind institutions of technology and natural sciences in the same category.

There is no way of measuring the persistence of traditional 'heroic' values among officers, but one questions whether the observation of W.H. McNeill is still true: 'During the twentieth century, a pro-

[1]Nicos P. Mouzelis, *Politics in the Semi-Periphery: Early Parliamentarism and Late Industrialization in the Balkans and Latin America*, London: Macmillan, 1986. pp. 144–5, 259.

[2]See the analysis of William H. McNeill, *The Metamorphosis of Greece since World War II*, Oxford: Basil Blackwell, 1978, p. 4.

fessional corps of officers (since 1949 about fifteen thousand strong) has become the special guardian of this [heroic] aspect of Hellenism. Its members stand in selfconscious opposition to the commercial spirit that informs so much of the rest of Greek life.'[3] Since the aristocratic tradition which dominated West European armies and differentiated military from civilian behaviour has no place in Greece, the urbanisation of the officer corps has made it more compatible with middle-class values. Does the demise of the 'heroic tradition' of the mountains mean that city education nurtures respect for democratic institutions and parliamentary politics among officers? If the current officer corps adheres to the values of the rest of society, this alone would indicate a return to normality.

Patronage, though far from extinct in Greek politics, is less apparent than before in the modern depersonalised urban environment. In the new setting an additional form of political recruitment emerged after PASOK became an important political force: populism.[4] This spontaneous communication, and indeed identification of the populace with the populist leadership of Andreas Papandreou, undermined the representative nature of parliamentary politics by reintroducing a nebulous concept of direct democracy. Populism, unlike patronage, favours rapid mass cooptation into the political process and a break with traditional mores and the political establishment. However, since it offers a blueprint for vertical social action and therefore appeals to all classes, it could prove a pole of attraction to the urbanised military.

We have come full circle to the original predicament of the nineteenth-century state-builders who sought to establish Western institutions and imbue Greek society with Western values. Although the military never acted as an agent for modernisation in Greece, it has nevertheless been an important component in the institutional framework created by a modernising elite. The military no doubt fullfilled their irredentist mission but subsequently became an impediment to the proper functioning of parliamentary institutions. Throughout the authoritarian phase of Greek democracy, the officer corps that emerged from the war and Civil War experience had totally identified with the right-wing values of the political elite who won the conflict. Like sorcerers' apprentices, the officers of 1967 succeeded only in uniting the political world against their dictatorship

---

[3] *Ibid.*, p. 24.

[4] For more about populism in Greek politics, see Mouzelis, *Politics in the Semi-Periphery*, pp. 42, 44, 234, 249.

and thus unwittingly served the unifying policy they had aspired to usurp.

The term 'metamorphosis' was used by W.H. McNeill to describe the transformation of the geographic distribution of Greece's population between the late 1940s and the mid-'70s. However, the prodigious movement of peasants into the cities was not accompanied by the formation of ghettoes or a spectacular rise in crime and political violence. Internal migration from the villages to urban centres was completed 'with very little adjustment of family behaviour'.[5] McNeill attributed this orderly 'metastasis' to the market orientation of peasant life and the tight-knit organisation of Greek nuclear family units. Wide acquaintance with the workings of the market and the firm structure of the family are two immutable elements in Greek society that appear to have merged in a creative though at times tense coexistence. It is perhaps this binary phenomenon of market forces, spurring people to movement while anchored on the familial bedrock of traditional values, that can explain the idiosyncrasies of Greece. It may also explain the ease with which Greeks of the diaspora adjust to their host-countries while clinging tenaciously to their own identity, or the enthusiasm of Greek citizens for a wider European citizenship while paradoxically they impede the progress of a civil society within their own state.

[5]McNeill, p. 248.

5

EDUCATION: THE MIGHTY
GREEK SCHOOL

One of the most enduring inventions of nineteenth-century Greek thought was the idea that the Greeks had been deprived of proper education throughout the centuries of Turkish rule. The Turks, according to Greek national lore, forbade the operation of Greek schools, thus denying the Greeks the opportunity to develop arts and sciences as the free peoples of Europe did in the same period. The only schools in subjugated Greece were the 'hidden' or 'secret' schools operating at night in churches and monasteries, where a priest or a monk taught reading and writing to a handful of students. A painting by the nineteenth-century painter Nikolaos Ghyzis, entitled 'Hidden School' and depicting a priest teaching a few children to read by candlelight, gave the myth visual 'evidence' and an easy point of reference. Generation after generation of Greek pupils were taught that the 'hidden school' in the dark centuries of Turkish rule preserved a semblance of learning among the subject people, and have seen Ghyzis's black-robed schoolmaster tutoring his humble students. Evidence that lay schools of high quality operated in seventeenth- and eighteenth-century Greece, catering also for the needs of clerics, and the argument that these were not greatly inferior to educational establishments in most other European countries have not been enough to demolish the 'hidden school' myth.[1]

---

[1]Manuel I. Gedeon's *I pneumatiki kinesis tou genous kata ton 18. kai 19. aiona* (The intellectual movement of the nation in the eighteenth and nineteenth centuries), ed. by Alkis Angelou and Philippos Eliou, Athens, 1976, is a classic of great value to the student of modern Greek education. For a recent examination of the question of the

Such myths are not laid to rest when attacked, if they die at all; indeed, revered national lore has proved extremely resistant to scholarship and is better left to die a natural death. 'Hidden' or not, education in Greek lands before Independence flourished in commercial and administrative centres, as Greek élite groups entrenched themselves in the administrative machine of the Sultan and in the new diaspora. Prelates also became involved in lay education; indeed, some of the most eminent representatives of the Greek Enlightenment were clerics who either established schools themselves or were invited to teach in them. Greek education had never ceased to exercise its appeal to the Sultan's subjects. The Patriarchate of Constantinople, despite its ecumenical character, never questioned the use of Greek as its official language and always expected its hierarchy to have a good Greek education. The languages of the other Balkan peoples were considered inferior and inadequate for the needs of an Orthodox prelate. The Serbian Ecumenical Patriarch of the fifteenth century, Raphael I (1475–6), was contemptuously described by his Greek contemporaries as a 'Bulgar', 'Serb' and 'barbarian' because he spoke no Greek; indeed, he was denigrated by the Church establishment for speaking only Serbian as his '*alloglottia*' (foreign speech).[2]

Greek schools-few at first but increasing in number as a growing Greek commercial class established itself in the economy of the Ottoman empire in the eighteenth century, and growing numerous towards the end of that century-gradually became a dominant feature of the Greek lands. Wealthy Greek merchants in Western Europe and in the Habsburg and Romanov empires built schools in their home towns in northern Greece, where most of them came from, and endowed them with sufficient funds to operate. Mainly in the first few decades of the nineteenth century, priests who had graduated from these schools subsequently staffed them, and they provided for the needs of all the Sultan's Orthodox subjects.

Two subsequent cases are indicative of the Church's attachment to Greek and dedication to its diffusion among non-Greek-speaking Orthodox. The first concerns the drive to reclaim northern lands lost

---

'Hidden School', see Achilleas A. Mandrikas, '*Krypho Scholeio': Mythos i pragmaticoteta?* ('Hidden School': myth or reality?), Athens, 1992.

[2]Elisavet A. Zachariadou, *Deka tourkika engrapha gia tin Megale Ekklesia, 1483–1567* (Ten Turkish documents on the Great Church, 1483–1567), Athens, 1996, p. 74.

to the Greek language in the centuries of foreign rule, and the second a similar drive to extirpate non-Greek-speaking enclaves in central Greek lands. In the 1770s a fiery Orthodox preacher, the monk Kosmas of Aetolia, tried to stem the tide of mass conversions to Islam in the northern Greek lands by founding Greek schools in a score of villages in Thessaly, Epirus and Macedonia, where the language had long been abandoned for Albanian, Vlach or Slav, and obliged peasants to speak only Greek. 'You must make your children learn Greek', he told his audience, 'because Greek is the language of our church, and our nation is Greek.' He went on to throw out this challenge: 'Let those who will promise not to use Albanian at home rise and say so, and I shall absolve from all of their sins.' He exclaimed on another occasion: 'Do you not see that our nation has grown savage from ignorance and we are no better than wild beasts?'[3]

A century later another cleric, Metropolitan Dorotheos Scholarios of Demetrias, faced a similar situation in the mountainous western region of Thessaly, where the Vlachs remained attached to their own language, which Dorotheos, himself of Vlach descent, considered 'degenerate and useless'. To assist in the drive to extend the domain of Greek in what the contemporary German geographer Heinrich Kiepert described as 'unexplored regions', Dorotheos founded and endowed in 1866 a Greek school in the Vlach village of Ventista (now Amarantos) high up on Mt Pindus where the Vlach shepherds, 'poor and absolutely indifferent to the benefits of education and ignorant of the Greek language', took better care of their sheep than of their children.[4]

What can be said about schools and education under the foreign rule of both the Ottomans and the Venetians is that both were associated with the Orthodox Church—which, as the only recognised authority of the Orthodox Christians, required schools for the education of its upper clergy. The Patriarchal Academy in Constantinople was such a school; as were later establishments in a number of towns, islands and monasteries. Indeed, the lay schools of later years grew

---

[3]Phanis Michalopoulos, *Kosmas o Aitolos* (in Greek), Athens, 1940, pp. 12, 46, 47, 97 ff.

[4]Photios Ar. Demetrakopoulos, 'Dorotheos Scholarios. O poiesas kai didaxas' (Dorotheos Scholarios: the creator and the teacher), *Trikalina*, 9 (1989), pp. 107–20. See also Theodoros A. Nimas, *I Ekpaideusi sti Dytiki Makedonia kata tin periodo tes Tourkokratias* (Education in western Macedonia in the period of Turkish rule), Thessaloniki 1995, pp. 131–2, 159, 160, 161.

out of these early church schools. When additional Greek élite groups, such as the Phanariots and the merchants, were added to the clergy, Greek schools and education acquired new patrons with their own educational needs.

The curricula of the early schools were designed largely for the needs of future upper clergy, but these were also schools for the perpetuation of the Greek élites—the more talented children of well-off laymen. The employment of church funds and concern for their proper operation explain the fact that many schools were attached to churches or monasteries, but funds from enlightened members of the Phanariot aristocracy and the growing mercantile class contributed to the increase in these schools and the expansion of their curricula to include the sciences. However, there was not a corresponding change in their staff or their location, and the teachers continued to be drawn mainly from the Church hierarchy and the monasteries. The first textbooks produced by the Church were not replaced even when more appropriate primers became available.[5]

Greek Independence naturally gave a great impetus to Greek schools, both in the newly liberated lands and in the rest of the Balkans. State primary and secondary schools were gradually set up in all cities and towns of independent Greece, and eventually in all major villages. A couple of private schools in Athens were primary schools—especially the Arsakeion school for girls, established by the Philepaideutiki Hetairia and funded by the diaspora magnate Apostolos Arsakis—achieved the highest educational standards of the time. However, more than any other educational establishment of the fledgling nation-state, the founding in 1837 of the National and Kapodistrian University of Athens opened a new era in Greek education. The University of Athens not only produced the first indigenous Greek intelligentsia and professional class but was also instrumental in creating an intelligentsia for the unredeemed Greeks and, to a considerable extent, professionals and intellectuals for the other Balkan peoples. Perhaps more than any other Balkan educational institution, the first Greek university contributed, without specifically intending to do so, to the growth of Balkan educated élites, who in their turn supported the claims of the Balkan peoples to nationhood. During the same period and more deliberately, the University of Athens penetrated the Greek irredenta ideologically through its graduates, 560 or one-fifth of whom

[5]Gedeon, *op.cit.*, 8, 9–10, 150ff.

in the first forty years of its existence were from lands outside the Greek kingdom. Around this time the Greeks of those lands possessed as many as 2,000 schools, built up over a century and attended by as many as 150,000 pupils of all ages.[6]

In the last quarter of the nineteenth century, when Bulgarian and other competing Balkan national schools were appearing in the southern Balkans, a great effort was undertaken to reclaim for the Greek language lands which had long been lost to Greek culture. Under state auspices, scores of teachers educated in the kingdom or in local schools and many thousands of books published mainly in Athens were sent each year to the Greek schools outside the realm. In this drive to plant the national language where it had been uprooted or indeed had never taken root, the Greek government competed with other state agencies in the Balkans. No small town or village and indeed no poor hamlet was overlooked in the effort to bring regions long abandoned to non-Greek tongues within the embrace of modern Greek culture.

Greek schools in the contested northern lands, primarily Macedonia and Thrace, increased until by the turn of the century Bulgaria's efforts to shore up its own national language there began to produce results, and Bulgarian schools and pupils increased faster than those of their competitors. Bulgarian national schools appeared to have had a stronger appeal since they offered a language close to the vernacular spoken by most of the peasants in these regions. Romanian schools, on the other hand, seemed unable to squeeze the Greek schools out of the Vlach communities because, by the time of Romania's entry into the national school contest in the last decades of the nineteenth century, Vlachs had long been hellenised in sentiment if not in speech—or so it was believed in Athens.[7]

There can be no clearer evidence of the attraction exerted by the Greek schools among the non-Greek-speaking communities in the contested lands than the complaints from representatives of the Greek national state in those lands that 'Hellenism' there was restricted to

---

[6]K. Xanthopoulos, *Synoptiki ekthesis tis pneumatikis anaptyxeos ton neoteron Hellenon apo tis anagenniseos auton mechri toude* (A brief report on the intellectual development of the modern Greeks from their rebirth until today), Constantinople, 1880, pp. 57,58, 62ff.

[7]Sophia Vouri, *Ekpaideusi kai ethnikismos sta Valkania. I periptosi tis voreiodytikis Makedonias, 1870–1904* (Education and nationalism in Northwestern Macedonia, 1870–1904), Athens, 1992, pp. 32–3, 52–3.

the Greek schools, and the primary motive of those attending them was not Greek national sentiment but the social and economic advancement expected from knowledge of the Greek language. 'In Krushevo [Macedonia]', wrote the Greek consul at Monastir in 1890, 'Hellenism is concentrated mainly in the Greek schools. What primarily motivates both pupils and parents is self-interest, since Greek schools are far superior to Romanian ones and the Greek language is necessary to make a living, which the Krushevites are clever enough to realise. I have no doubt that we would find instead German or French schools if they were better than the Greek ones.' 'The national aspect of education', wrote the same consul elsewhere, 'is of no concern to the Monasteriots whatsoever; they support Greek education and letters solely for the sake of their children's future.'[8]

Greek- and non-Greek-speaking pupils, in the contested lands more than in the kingdom of Greece, struggled with Greek primers in the purified national vernacular to gain the benefits which a Greek education was expected to secure. Greek national sentiment, the assumed motive behind Greek school attendance and its expected outcome, was never more elusive. What everyone concerned could easily discover and pursue was the practical value of Greek education. In addition to being the language of the mighty Church structure, Greek was the only time-honoured means—in the contested lands no less than in the kingdom—of escaping from the squalor of Balkan peasant life. But for this practical value, neither compulsory school attendance nor the assumed national sentiment in the Greek irredenta would have convinced parents that they should let their children attend school and thus forgo the immediate proceeds of their labour. Needless to say, it was the same expectation and not prohibition of their use by the authorities that undermined attachment to the non-Greek spoken languages of the contested lands after their eventual incorporation into the Greek national state.

Thus in the space of two centuries the Greek school—the Church or communal school initially and the national school after Greek Independence—transformed modern Greece in a profound way; indeed, the Greek school brought modernity to areas that had remained outside recorded civilised life since time immemorial. In references to the condition of Greek education under Turkish rule, the role of the Orthodox Church in preserving a semblance of education has

---

[8] *Ibid.*, pp. 66,82.

always been stressed and praised by students of modern Greece. The standard argument has been that the Church preserved the Greek nation by halting the abandonment of the Orthodox faith and preserving the Greek language. There is ample evidence to support this argument, but the two premises on which it rests—prevention of apostasy and the preservation of the language—cannot withstand less pious probings. Conversions to Islam never ceased in Turkish-ruled Greek lands, but conversions to Catholicism in lands ruled by Venice or Genoa, such as Crete, the Ionian Islands, Cyprus and certain Aegean islands never assumed similar proportions; indeed, conversions to Islam in Cyprus and Crete increased after their conquest by the Turks in the sixteenth and the seventeenth centuries respectively. The Greek language fared no better than the Orthodox faith under the auspices of the Church, since large sections of the subject population abandoned Greek for the language of the masters, and the languages of other subject peoples, such as Albanian, Vlach or South Slav, were never seriously threatened before the advent of the Greek Enlightenment and the Greek national state. What brought the Greek language back to areas previously lost to it and hellenised large sections of the population was not the Church but national education after Independence.

The language had receded to a perilous extent in the spiritual domain of the Orthodox Church in the early centuries of Turkish rule; so had Greek education, for reasons associated with the general decline of the Orthodox political leadership, but also because education for the laity had never been among the Church's objectives. Kosmas of Aitolia and Dorotheos Scholarios were representatives of a new breed of Orthodox cleric: they operated in an intellectual climate unknown to their predecessors and indeed to their successors as well. The Greece of the eighteenth and nineteenth centuries, home to the fiery monk of Aetolia and the metropolitan from the Vlach mountain village, was very different from that of Eugenios Giannoulis, another monk of Aetolia, who condemned the ignorance and barbarism of Greek peasant life in the seventeenth century, albeit with a fine sense of humour.[9]

---

[9]Evgenios Giannoulis of Aitolia, *Epistoles. Kritiki ekdosi* (Letters: a critical edition), ed. by I. E. Stephanis and Niki Papatriantaphyllou-Theodoridi, Thessaloniki, 1992, pp. 185, 268–9, 270, 282, 292–3.

University of Athens (1837–)

This, the first institution of higher learning in the independent kingdom of the Hellenes, was founded by King Otto on the German model. The University was endowed through private and public donations, and since 1882 its council has submitted its annual budget to the Ministry of Education for approval.

Following Otto´s abdication in 1862 the institution was renamed after the first President of Greece, Ioannis Kapodistrias, and temporarily housed in the stately home of Kleanthis before moving in 1841 to the splendid neo-classical structure designed by the Danish architect Christian Hansen, which overlooks what has become the busiest street in Athens that bears the University's name (Panepistimiou).

Today the University has five schools (Theology, Law, Arts, Health Sciences, and Natural Sciences) divided into twenty-nine departments. With 70,000 undergraduate and graduate students, more than 1,500 teaching staff, and its administrative personnel, it is the largest university in Greece.

The University's academic year begins on 15 September and ends on 15 June, and is divided in two semesters consisting of thirteen weeks of teaching and two weeks of examinations. Eight semesters is the minimum attendance required for all degrees, except Medicine which requires twelve.

Part III. THE ECONOMY

6

THE ECONOMY

During the first decade of the independent Greek state, between 60 and 64 per cent of the population were employed in agriculture, 12.2 per cent in animal husbandry, 12 per cent in commerce, and 6.8 per cent as 'technicians'. The rest included professionals and civil servants. 70.7 per cent of all arable land belonged to the state, and around 83 per cent of the 120,000 peasant families were landless and worked as share-croppers. The Peloponnesian currant ('raisin of Corinth'), intensively cultivated on family plots, was the major Greek export item. Although Patras, Nauplion, Kalamata and Navarino were the chief ports for the currant trade, the island of Syros was the centre of international commerce in the Aegean.[1] Independence changed the structure of land ownership and therefore the nature of agricultural production; before, the large Ottoman estates had produced wheat for export and it was only state ownership of the land afterwards and the cultivation of small plots by families of share-cropper tenants that caused the rise of the currant.[2] The elusive promise of land distribution and the eventual formation of small landholdings through squatting on public property attracted a section of the mountain-dwellers back again into the plains.

Ioannis Kapodistrias, the first President of Greece and the pioneer in dealing with land issues, believed that the peasantry would be

---

[1]For a comprehensive study of the Greek economy in 1833–43 see John A. Petropulos, 'The Greek Economy during the first Decade of Othonian Rule', *Deltion tis Istorikis kai Ethnologikis Etairias tis Ellados,* vol. 24 (1981), pp. 142–228.

[2]For a comprehensive analysis of land tenure in Greece see William W. McGrew, *Land and Revolution in Modern Greece, 1800–1881,* Kent, OH: State University Press, 1985.

integrated into the new order through land grants. His untimely death postponed land distribution for several decades. King Otto and his Bavarian regency were confronted in 1833 with empty coffers and accumulated debts, and their anxiety to satisfy foreign creditors and meet rising expenses led them to 'grasp at the national property as a fiscal panacea'.[3] In other words, the sale of public land would provide funds with which to pay off foreign debts. Armansberg, the most influential of the regents who managed public affairs while Otto was still a minor, intended to raise income 'for the endownment of Greek families'.[4] The regency also had high hopes of land-leases of varying length, but the results were disappointing. Few families responded to the endowment scheme, the property leased was mismanaged, and the public domain was constantly depleted through usurpation and encroachment.

The National Assembly that met after Otto's deposition included in the 1864 Constitution a mandate to future governments to legislate for a new distribution programme. Sotirios Sotiropoulos, Minister of Finance in several cabinets between 1864 and 1888, became the chief architect of the distribution laws of 1871. These consisted of two related measures, one to distribute arable land, and the other to legalise the arbitrary planting of vines and trees on national land. As a result, the government of Alexandros Koumoundouros recognised illegal holdings, and granted titles to nearly 50,000 peasant families—a process facilitated by conversion from Ottoman to Roman-Byzantine principles of tenure. The rule of usurpation in Roman law reversed the Ottoman inalienability of public land and made possible the recognition of squatters' rights after thirty years of occupation and use. The absence of a land registry and official tolerance allowed squatters to present their holdings as a freehold. Kapodistrias's vision of a society of small holders was thus vindicated forty years after his death. However, the Greek state missed the opportunity to enhance its credibility by distributing the land itself rather than merely recognising a *fait accompli*.

The Koumoundouros distribution of titles and the ensuing proliferation of small family plots further encouraged Greek agriculture to specialise in a few export items. Thus the production of currants dominated the Peloponnese at the expense of cereals. During the 1870s currant exports made up more than half of the value of all

[3]*Ibid.*, p. 157.
[4]*Ibid.*, p. 158.

The Lavrion Bubble

The dispute over the exploitation of the silver and lead mines of Lavrion attracted wide attention in the early 1870s and took the Greek public on a spree of speculation.

In 1864 a Franco-Italian firm (Roux-Serpieri) purchased mining rights from the Greek state, but it was soon discovered that the agreement did not clarify whether the company's rights included the surface remnants of previous extractions or were confined to mining ore from the pits. The dispute between the company and the Greek state raged for two years (1871–3) until a magnate from Constantinople, Andreas Syngros, bought the entire concern. This caused a buying spree of the company's shares which made their price sky-rocket. The subsequent crash wiped out the savings of many small and middle-ranking investors and introduced the Greeks to the workings of European stock exchange bubbles and their tendency to burst when over blown.

---

exports. Cereals declined from 41 per cent in 1845–6 to 38 per cent in 1860, and plummeted to 23.7 per cent in 1880–1. The domestic demand for wheat imports allowed Piraeus to overtake Ermoupolis on the island of Syros as the state's busiest port.[5]

The Greek balance of payments deficit was exacerbated by the irredentist adventures of the last quarter of the nineteenth century. Outstanding external debts precluded the issue of new loans, gave rise to a series of domestic loans to finance the uprisings in Crete, and created a vicious circle of servicing old debts by contracting new ones. The servicing of the War of Independence debt was discontinued during the reign of King Otto—to the detriment of Greece's creditworthiness. The Greek Minister in London, Ioannis Gennadios, eventually reached a settlement with creditors in 1873–8, which restored the country's credibility in the international markets.[6]

The acquition of the Thessaly breadbasket in 1881 increased Greek territory by 26.7 per cent and its population by 18 per cent, but added a new problem to the existing ones. Many large Ottoman land-holdings were bought by Greek diaspora magnates before Thessaly became part of Greece, and the peasant population ceased under the new legal regime to be attached to the land their fathers had

---

[5] E. Kofos, 'I Ethniki Ikonomia' (The national economy) in *Istoria tou Ellinikou Ethnous*, vol. 13, Athens: Ekdotiki Athinon, 1977, pp. 310–11.
[6] *Ibid.*, p. 314.

cultivated and were driven to seek employment elsewhere. The waves of displaced share-croppers in search of their promised land created a radical movement that kept the government awake at nights.

Peloponnesian currants were the major Greek export item throughout the second part of the nineteenth century, and price fluctuations had an immediate effect on the livelihood of the small farmland cultivators who were at the mercy of moneylenders till harvest time. Single-crop cultivation in southern Greece was mainly induced by the blight that devastated French vineyards in the 1870s and spurred Greek farmers into attempting to fill the vacuum of the market. Currant production increased from 43,000 tons in 1861 to 100,700 tons in 1878. Improvements in transport and later, in 1880, the abolition of the tithe (one-tenth of production withheld by taxation) encouraged farmers to increase their production.

However, when the French vineyards recovered, the effect on Greece's agrarian economy and indeed its society was long-lasting. As French production returned to normal in the 1890s, the demand for Peloponnesian currants contracted, generating ever-increasing unsaleable surpluses. When France imposed a high tariff on imports from Greece in 1892, the price of currants plunged by 70 per cent in the London market. Despite efforts by the Greek government to relieve the plight of bankrupt peasants, thousands migrated to the United States.[7] However, the plight of Peloponnesian currant-growers was not the only factor influencing this exodus, and between 1906 and 1914 more than 250,000 people left Greece.

On the eve of the First World War, agriculture was the occupation of 65 per cent of the Greek population. Nevertheless one-third of grain and other basic foodstuffs was imported because of this sector's low productivity.[8] In the Peloponnese small producers smarted from the chronic currant crisis, while the large landholdings of Thessaly, representing around 35 per cent of Greece's cultivated land in 1914, proved even less helpful to the national economy. The absentee landlord-enterpreneurs who had purchased most of this land from its Ottoman owners (known by their Turkish name, '*chiftlik*'), refused to plough in capital to improve productivity, preferring instead to rent out the land for grazing or tenant farming. Furthermore, the well-

---

[7]John Campbell and Philip Sherrard, *Modern Greece,* London: Ernest Benn, 1968, pp. 97–8.

[8]George Leontaritis, 'Ikonomia kai koinonia apo to 1914 os to 1918', *Istoria tou Ellinikou Ethnous*, vol. 15, Athens, 1978, p. 74.

connected *chiftlik* owners were in a position to convince their political protégés to maintain high tariffs on imported grain in order to protect their own low-grade production from foreign competition. The end-result was that the addition of Thessaly to Greece caused the price of bread to rise, rather than fall as had been expected.[9]

The rise of grain prices generated a political alliance between the landless peasants and the urban middle class, both demanding the parcelling out of the large landholdings. Although the Liberals had championed redistribution from their advent to power in 1910–11, it was the arrival of the first Anatolian refugees in 1914–17 that compelled them to take action. The drafting of laws for the expropriation of the large landed estates was begun in 1917 by the revolutionary government in Thessaloniki, but was actually put into effect after 1922, when the influx of refugees from Turkey became the overriding national issue. The expropriation of estates for distribution rose from only one in 1918 to sixty-three in 1920 and 1,203 in 1923–5.[10]

The Entente embargo on enemy goods and trade during the war caused a state of imposed protectionism for Greek products. Also, the Anglo-French demand for food supplies generated by the Macedonian front encouraged Greek producers to rise to the challenge and reap the consequent economic benefits. After 1923 the price of agricultural products declined, but farmers increased their production to make up for their loss of income.

The fragmentation of large landholdings diminished moneylending as the main source for farming loans. The National Bank of Greece moved in to fill the credit gap, and cooperatives handling agricultural credit proliferated. Between 1923 and 1927 credits to farmers increased from 220 million to 1,144 million drachmas.[11]

Greek industry, with its sluggish growth throughout the nineteenth century, was never a match for commercial enterprises in attracting credit. The war brought commerce to a halt and created the artificial circumstances that protected Greek industry from foreign competition, but the end of the war revived all the adverse factors that had impeded industrial growth in Greece. Post-war industry survived in the food sector and in consumer goods that did not require technological

[9]N. Economou, 'I elliniki koinonia kai ikonomia stin proti dekaetia tou 20ou aiona' (Greek society and economy in the early 20th century), *op.cit.*, vol. 14, Athens, 1977, pp. 195, 196.

[10]The expropriation of land and distribution is described in a basic reader on the history of Greek agriculture in A. Sideris, *I georgiki politiki tis Elladas, 1833–1933* (Agricultural Policy in Greece), Athens, 1934, pp. 176–81.

[11]Sideris, *op.cit.*, p. 184.

sophistication and depended on domestic raw material. According to 1920 statistics, workshops of between one and five workers made up 91.7 per cent of the industrial sector, and those employing over twenty-five workers only 1.4 per cent.[12]

Between 1923 and the early 1930s, the social and economic structure of Greece went through a rapid transformation. The more than 1 million refugees who had descended upon a country of slightly over 5 million acted as the catalyst of profound change. The implementation of the land reform and the task of financing the rehabilitation of refugees increased the range of state authority and the importance of such institutions as the National Bank of Greece.[13] Public activities generated a prodigious increase in expenditure (between 1915 and 1925 the number of public employees doubled) and a corresponding rise in the volume of taxes. The external national debt had more than trebled from 1914 to 1926. Outstanding debts to foreign creditors had become an obstacle to contracting new loans, and André Andreadis, a distinguished professor of economics, warned the government that the servicing of loans in 1927 would require 40 per cent of the country's annual income.[14]

The various stages of interwar economic development may be described as follows. First, from 1923 to 1927 the economy faltered under the pressure of insuperable odds as governments strove to buttress the value of the drachma. Second, from 1927 to 1932 the drachma was stabilised by George Kafandaris's economic policy and growth was resumed, but it foundered on international economic adversity. And third, in 1932 Greece was obliged to suspend interest and amortisation payments on its foreign debt. The subsequent years were dedicated to the management of the crisis caused by the default.[15]

---

[12]X. Zolotas, *I Ellas is to stadion tis ekviomichaniseos* (Greece in the stage of industrialisation), Athens 1964 (2nd edn), p. 32.

[13]For an account of banks in operation in 1919–28, see table 68 in Costas Costis, *Economie rurale et la Banque Agraire. Aspects de l'économie de la Grèce pendant l'entre-deux-guerres (1919–1928). Les documents,* Athens: Cultural Foundation of the National Bank of Greece, 1990, pp. 148–51.

[14]André Andreadis, *Mathimata Demosias Iconomias* (Lectures on public finance), vol. IV, Athens 1927, pp. 74–80.

[15]For a brief appraisal of the Greek economy in the interwar period see M. Mazower and T. Veremis, 'The Greek Economy, 1922–41' in R. Higham and T. Veremis, eds, *The Metaxas Dictatorship: Aspects of Greece,* Athens: ELIAMEP, 1993, pp. 111–30. For a comprehensive analysis in English see Mazower, *Greece and the Inter-War Economic Crisis,* Oxford: Clarendon Press, 1991.

From the early 1930s state intervention succeeded in generating an unprecedented growth of wheat production. Anticipating war in Europe, the dictator Ioannis Metaxas embarked on an effort to secure self-sufficiency, and furthered price-support supervised by the Central Committee for the Protection of Domestic Wheat Production (KEPES). He also declared a moratorium on certain agricultural debts and facilitated the repayment of others. Between 1928 and 1937, KEPES maintained the domestic price of wheat at a consistently higher level than international market prices, and in the last three years before the war handled a quarter of Greece's total wheat crop. This output rose from 30 per cent of domestic consumption in 1927 to 60 per cent in 1935–9. Cotton production rose fourfold throughout the 1930s and tobacco became the leading export item. Over 80 per cent of Greece's visible exports were agricultural products, of which tobacco accounted for nearly half and currants for a quarter. In the mid-1930s Britain, Germany, the United States and Italy absorbed 64 per cent of these exports, but in the later 1930s Germany emerged as Greece's major customer and supplier.[16]

By the end of 1939, war in Europe had obliged the Greek government to allocate an additional 1,167 million drachmas to military appropriations. Between July 1939 and October 1940, banknote circulation increased from 7,000 million to 11,600 million drachmas and the wholesale price index rose by 20 per cent. Mussolini's attack on Greece upset the tentative balance of the economy. Land and sea transport was disrupted and the mobilisation of most able-bodied men affected production. The financial burden of the war was met by increased taxation, a war lottery and British loans without specific repayment terms. An increase in note circulation was accompanied by a scarcity of consumer goods. By the spring of 1941 commodity prices had risen by between 50 and 150 per cent above prewar levels.[17]

The Nazi occupation dealt the economy a mortal blow and destroyed the very basis of Greece's productive capacity for years to come. 'The low level of industrialization and the predominance of small-scale production would point toward the enforcement of a mostly extractive rather than "reproductive" economic policy on the part of the occupation authorities. Such a policy would use the Greek area as a source of

---

[16]A. F. Freris, *The Greek Economy in the Twentieth Century*, London: Croom Helm, 1986, pp. 77–99.

[17]Naval Intelligence Division, *Greece*, vol. 2, Geographical Handbook Series, Norwich: HMSO, October 1944, pp. 191–2.

non-reproducible resources, a form of plunder as it were, rather than maintain its organised forms and integrate them into the global system of the Axis production.'[18]

The great famine during the winter of 1941–2, which claimed more lives than the Albanian front, was the gruesome outcome of the pillaging of the Greek economy by the Axis. The requisition of foodstuffs and fuel, and especially the appropriation of means of transportation, cut off the urban economy from its rural sources of supply. Occupation expenses and their rate of growth indicated the cruelty of the occupation regime. In November 1941 these expenses were 25 billion drachmas and by August 1943 they had reached 850 billion. 'The then director general of the Ministry of Finance estimated that the burden ... was five times higher per capita in occupied Greece than in occupied France.'[19]

The occupation expenses were met with unbridled issues of new currency. The effect of such a practice on the value of occupation drachmas can easily be seen in the steadily increasing number of zeroes with every new issue. When money had lost all its value and transaction required loads of paper, the economy reverted to simple every bartering of goods.

The hardships visited on the population, occupation and civil war (1946–9), combined with Western fears of a Communist take-over, made Greece a major recipient of aid under the Marshall Plan. Initiated by the US Secretary of State George Marshall in 1947, the Plan, administered by the Organization for European Economic Cooperation (later renamed OECD), at first targeted Austria, Greece and Italy, but was soon extended to all the war-stricken countries of Western Europe. Between 1945 and 1950 Greece received US$ 2.1 billion in all forms of aid, a sum greater than the total of all foreign loans contracted between 1821 and 1930.

The dwindling of foreign aid after the end of the Civil War made economic growth an imperative of the 1950s. The most pertinent input in the debate over the nature of this growth was provided by the 'Varvaresos Report', submitted to the government of Nicolaos Plastiras in 1952. The Governor of the Bank of Greece, Kyriakos Varvaresos, who wrote the Report, warned the government against

---

[18]Stavros Thomadakis, 'Black Markets, Inflation and Force in the Economy of Occupied Greece' in John Iatrides, ed., *Greece in the 1940s,* University Press of New England, 1981, p. 63.

[19]*Ibid.,* pp. 65–7.

investing public funds in heavy industry and favoured an economic development based on agriculture, light industry, tourism and shipping. Although the Varvaresos Report emphasised the role of the private sector, the political consensus in post-war European reconstruction favoured substantial state involvement in the economy.[20]

The mixed economy model prevailing at that time was championed by most prominent economists and politicians in Greece, regardless of their party affiliation. The public sector was deemed to be the motor of the economy during the first two decades, only to become later the millstone round its neck. In 1950 the national product finally attained its pre-war level, but Greece was by European standards still an underdeveloped, agrarian (34 per cent of GNP) country with its industrial sector (25 per cent of GNP) fragmented into small family units.

An important landmark in post-war development was the 9 April 1953 devaluation of the drachma and the lifting of most controls, which impeded exports. Spyros Markezinis, the Minister of Coordination in the 'Greek Rally' government under Alexandros Papagos, was the architect of a stabilization policy that restored public faith in the economy. Prices remained relatively stable in the following decade, and private savings increased.[21]

The monetary reform of the conservatives was followed by a policy to attract foreign investment through such incentives as cheap electric power, tax breaks and repatriation of profits. The policy began to bear fruit in the late 1950s, and foreign capital as a percentage of overall investment rose from 3.4 per cent in 1955 to 8 (1958), 24 (1963) and 31.8 (1965), from which point it started to decline.

At the same time the state encouraged government-controlled financial institutions such as the National Bank of Greece to merge with other banks, while new ones were set up to finance industrial growth. The National Bank of Industrial Development (ETBA) was the largest stockholder in many thriving firms in the late 1960s, but in the 1980s it became the dumping ground of moribund companies nationalised only in order to save their workforces from dismissal. The expansion of the public sector from utilities (telecommunications and electric power) to other fields, initially had a benign effect on growth, but it would soon trap the economy in the inertia of the

[20]Zacharias Demathas, 'Anikodomisi kai anaptixi' (Reconstruction and growth) *Greece in the Twentieth Century, Epta Imeres-Kathimerini*, 28 November 1999, pp. 24–5
[21]Campbell and Sherrard, *op. cit.*, pp. 299–301.

civil service mentality and the corrupt priorities of party politics. Public expenditure rose from 28.4 per cent of GNP in 1974, to 31.8 per cent in 1980 and 48.2 per cent in 1990.[22]

The period 1952–72, with a yearly average of 7–8 per cent per capita growth of GNP, witnessed a restructuring of Greek society.[23] Despite the improvement in farming and living conditions in the countryside, large numbers of the agrarian population migrated to the bustling urban centres or went abroad (mostly to Germany) as emigrants or 'guest workers'.[24] The remittances that flowed into the Greek economy as a result helped to improve the chronic deficit in the balance of payments.

After a period of sustained growth and low inflation, the crisis of 1973–4 introduced a pernicious and lasting factor in the economy. The inflation rate, which had run at 3 per cent for a decade, jumped to 15.5 per cent in 1973 and 26.9 in 1974. The culprits were to a certain extent the first oil crisis and the crisis of the dollar, but the incompetence of the Greek dictatorship exacerbated the problem. By policing prices and curtailing credit, the Colonels succeeded in causing an economic recession. Since the process of accession to the European Economic Community had been frozen because of the dictatorship, the Greek government was isolated from its natural habitat.

The Karamanlis government that picked up the pieces after the collapse of the Colonels' regime embarked on a statist rather than a free market course to lower inflation and resume growth. It was this time-honoured prescription, which had proved successful in the 1950s and 1960s, that the Finance Minister, Panaghis Papaligouras, applied once again. Throughout New Democracy's two terms in power, major nationalisations of Greek businesses went into effect: Olympic Airways, Esso and the Commercial and Ionian Banks were made to join the white elephants of the public sector, while the conservatives were accused by liberals of suffering from 'socialmania'. By the end of the 1970s public expenditure had overtaken public revenue, forcing the state into a new spiral of contracting loans.[25]

[22]Panos Kazakos, 'Post-War Economic History' (unpublished), 1999, pp. 14–21, 34. See also his contribution to the collective, *Istoria tou Ellinikou Ethnous*, vol. 16, Athens: Ekdotiki Athnon, 2000. pp. 227–36

[23]In 1963–5 the annual growth rate was 9–11%.

[24]Kazakos, *Istoria ...*, p.233

[25]*Archion Karamanli* (The Karamanlis Archive), Athens: Ekdotiki Athinon, 1996, vol. 8, p. 260

If Karamanlis and Papaligouras failed to tackle the structural flaws of the Greek economy, they made one vital contribution to the country's modernisation by achieving Greece's accession to the European Community as its tenth member in 1980. However, this new era for Greece started on the wrong foot because it coincided with the advent to power of PASOK. Yet in spite of twists and turns, the journey has proved a salutary experience for Greece. EC membership imposed strict rules and disciplines on the economic behaviour of the political parties, and introduced long-term structural changes that no politician would have dared to undertake on his own initiative.[26]

The electoral victory of the Socialists in 1981 reflected the frustration of those in the middle and lower-middle classes who felt that they had missed out on the boom of the 1960s and 1970s. Between 1968 and 1978 the annual growth rate had averaged 6.6 per cent. Foreign capital inflows represented a decreasing percentage of total investment, and some economists argued that Greece was becoming less dependent on foreign capital. However, economic growth was import-based, constantly widening the foreign trade deficit. By 1981 this deficit, which was partly covered by immigrant and merchant marine remittances, tourism and foreign loans, became unmanageable. At the beginning of the 1980s inflation rose steadily to reach 20–26 per cent while the economy stagnated. The public sector continued to expand, placing an ever-larger burden on the strained economy.[27] PASOK added to this burden by involving the state in making good the losses of the private sector. Firms indebted to state banks were kept artificially afloat because of the government's concern to prevent the growth of unemployment. In certain cases loans to large businesses were simply converted into equity while the firms were taken over by the state. Although after his re-election in June 1985 Andreas Papandreou sought to attract private investment by declaring his faith in a vigorous private sector, businessmen failed to

[26]Panayotis Ioakimidis, 'Measuring Incorporation: The Case of Greece in the European Union', *ELIAMEP Southeast European Yearbook, 1994–95*, pp. 105–33; Iacovos S. Tsalicoglou, *Negotiating for Entry: The Accession of Greece to the European Community*, Aldershot: Dartmouth, 1995, pp. 166–71. See also P. Kazakos, 'Socialist Altitudes towards European Integration in the Eighties' in Thedore C. Kastriotis, ed., *The Greek Socialist Experiment*, New York: Pella, 1992, pp. 257–78.

[27]A rosy picture of PASOK's performance was painted by Constantine C. Vaitsos, then Deputy Minister of Finance, in his article 'Problems and Policies of Industrialization' in Zafiris Tzanatos, ed., *Socialism in Greece: The First Four Years*, Aldershot: Gower, 1986, pp. 76–86.

respond. His second term began with a 15 per cent devaluation of the drachma and anti-inflationary measures which brought the inflation rate down to 18 per cent but produced little sign of improvement in productivity.[28]

After decades of sustained growth it fell to the Socialists to witness the beginning of a decline. In the 1980s the rate of growth of the GNP fell to 1.6 per cent, and in 1987 Greece was overtaken by its EC partner Portugal. The main reason for this was the failure of the Greek socialist governments to restructure the economy after the second oil price shock, when most developed countries moved away from labour-intensive industries towards those based on higher technology. However, such readjustments inevitably caused a rise in unemployment, which PASOK could not face. Instead of taking measures that would make the economy more competitive, Papandreou sought to cushion the impact of decline on the average citizen by spending on welfare programmes. The entire economic philosophy of PASOK throughout its first term was focused on day-to-day survival at the expense of the future.[29]

Although EC membership revived foreign investment, the end of protectionism hit indigenous firms hard. High consumer demand had always outstripped domestic supply, increasing imports and inflation. PASOK's lax incomes policy further fueled private demand and worsened the chronic trade imbalance. Transfers from the Community cushioned the current account deficit up to a point, but at the same time stimulated demand and thus worsened the trade deficit. The persistent trade imbalance was also exacerbated by the high cost of labour and its consequence, low productivity. Although the incomes policy under the 1985 stabilisation programme reduced unit labour cost below that of the EC, the problem returned with a vengeance when the stabilisation policy was suspended by Papandreou. The lax incomes policy of PASOK and the disastrous involvement of the state in the economy (nationalisations, aid to cooperatives etc.) were once again financed through domestic and external debt accumulation. Regular tax revenues never kept pace under Papandreou with regular expenditure.

The factor which made formal Greek statistics somewhat unreliable in the bleak picture they painted was a vigorous parallel economy

[28]T. Veremis, 'Greece and NATO. Continuity and Change' in John Chipman, ed., *NATO's Southern Allies*, London: Routledge, 1988, pp. 250–55.

[29]Theodore C. Kariotis, ed., *The Greek Socialist Experiment. Papandreou's Greece 1981–89*, New York: Pella, 1992, pp. 203–55.

which defied fiscal control. As Robert McDonald noted, 'monitoring the self-employed—particularly tradesmen, professionals and landlords—is notoriously difficult and the large numbers of small industrial and retail establishments makes inspection of books difficult.'[30] It is suggested that this factor makes the true GDP much higher than the official record shows.[31]

Remedies to the ailing Greek economy, applied only during the brief successful term of Kostas Simitis at the Ministry of the Economy (1986–7), were adopted several years later during the New Democracy interlude (1990–3). The Mitsotakis government was faced with the task of balancing the budget, liquidating problem firms under state management, and trimming the public sector.[32] Minister Stephanos Manos, one of the few genuine economic liberals in the conservative camp, pursued austerity and the deregulation of public enterprises with single-minded zeal, but his policy began two years too late. Although inflation fell within a year from 15 per cent in 1992 to 12.3 per cent, Manos's stringent and unpopular measures contributed to the defeat of New Democracy in the October 1993 elections.

The Maastricht treaty and the collapse of Communism in Eastern Europe had a profound effect on Greek policies. The treaty established standards of performance among the EU members that wished to join the Economic and Monetary Union and abandon their national currencies in favour of the euro. Since Greece was an aspiring candidate for the Eurozone, its government came to grips with the real structural flaws that held the country back. The end of Communism reduced the appeal of the command economy and deprived both socialists and conservatives of the utopia of a benign powerful state that would deliver society from economic hardship. Henceforth the two big parties in Parliament began to move to a more liberal economic outlook, which had never been popular in the cocooned social structure of Greece.[33] In 2000 Greece became a member of the Economic and Monetary Union of the EU.

[30]Robert McDonald, *Greece in the 1990s: Taking its Place in Europe*, EIU (Economist Intelligence Unit) Economic Prospects Series, Special Report no. 2099, February 1991, p. 75.

[31]*Ibid.*, pp. 19, 39, 53, 64, 68, 75. Also Panayotis Pavlopoulos, *The Paraeconomy in Greece*, Athens: IOBE, 1987.

[32]Robert McDonald, 'Prospects for the Greek Economy', *ELIAMEP Yearbook 1990*, Athens: Hellenic Foundation for European and Foreign Policy, 1991, pp. 240–52.

[33]See the contributions on the economy by Papademos, Alogoskoufis, Giannitsis and Thomadakis, in Harry J. Psomiades and Stavros B. Thomadakis, eds, *Greece, the New Europe and a Changing International Order*, New York: Pella Publishing, 1993.

After his electoral victory in 1993 Andreas Papandreou declared his intention to bring Greece into the EMU and left the policy of converging with EU criteria to his ministers. When Kostas Simitis became Prime Minister in 1996, a new era in the country's economic policy was already under way. Four years later the liberalisation he set in motion secured accession to the EMU.

The difficult road to convergence included the lowering of inflation from 14.2 per cent in 1994 to 2 per cent in 1999 and the public deficit from 14 percent of GNP in 1993 to 3 per cent in 1999. The public sector began to contract after 1990, but some of the indebted public companies, such as Olympic Airways, had still not been privatised by 2000 and continued to drain resources from the taxpayer to finance its inefficiency.

Despite the austerity measures, the rates of growth in 1998–9 at 3 per cent had overtaken the EU average. The fact that the process of convergence did not lead to recession may be explained by a variety of factors, all of which contributed to Greece's upward swing. The EU windfalls provided valuable support to the economy, the lowering of interest rates afforded cheaper money to business, the international decline in raw material prices kept inflation in check, and finally there was the new-found bias of the socialist government in favour of the private sector. The 12.3 per cent devaluation of the drachma in 1998 did not detract from this trend.

It is fair to say that if Greece had not been admitted to the European Community in 1981 it would have had trouble entering later. In the 1980s it was a bastion of Western defence in a Communist environment and, though among the poorest of the West European states, it was the most developed in its own region. If we suppose, for the sake of argument, that the socialist government of Andreas Papandreou, with its Third World populism and anti-Western rhetoric, had disqualified Greece from entry, it is entirely possible that a very different scenario would have unfolded. The absence of EU windfalls would have compelled Papandreou to move further into nationalising private companies and therefore inflating the non-productive public sector; also that the trade balance would have gone further into the red and the private sector would have failed to produce the generation of competitive businessmen who came of age in a climate shaped by EU rules. Thus, the effect of the EU on Greece's political leadership was salutary. If the Papandreou phenomenon can be seen as a legacy of the Civil War, Costas Simitis and some of his ministers are certainly offspring of the EU.

EU membership can be debated by the Danes and refused by the Norwegians, but the Greeks cannot afford such a luxury, living as they do in their problem environment. The acculturation into the ways of the EU is probably Greece's most valuable asset in dealing with its neighbours within the Balkan habitat. However, even with this trump card up its sleeve Greece managed to get sucked into the Balkan imbroglio for almost three years (1992–5) before disentangling itself from regional conflicts such as the 'Macedonian' issue and joining the EU mainstream. If Greece had remained outside the EU it would have missed a role-model for its own civil society and would not have benefited from the privatisation drive generated by its membership of this supranational organisation.

Part IV. SOCIETY

7

A LAND OF PEASANTS

Following the destruction of the medieval Greek aristocracy when it became prey to Latin princes and Muslim beys, and before the rise of such groups as the local Moreot and Hydriot chieftaincies, the continental mountain captains or Armatoles and the merchants, the land was essentially inhabited by people who, though recorded for taxation purposes, left few traces of their existence. History passed them by. Their religious leaders did not exactly constitute a distinct social class: priests shared the life and status of common peasants, while bishops and metropolitans were essentially Christian administrators, whose tenure of office depended on the whims of the foreign ruler. On the other hand, the Phanariots (the Greek-speaking élite living near the Ecumenical Patriarchate's seat in the Phanar district of Constantinople) constituted a world that had little connection with the peasants.

Foreign visitors and those rare local men who managed to acquire an overall view of their community life gave useful accounts of peasant life. As in the unwalled city-states of inland continental Greece described by Thucydides, entering pre-nineteenth century Greece from the surrounding sea amounted to a time travel into past centuries. The happy and carefree men and women who figure in the works of foreign and Greek romantic writers of the nineteenth century led a life that barely differed from that of their beasts of burden: they normally lived under the same roof, and their and life-chances were similiar. Nationalist historians and folklorists of the same and subsequent times held up the Greek peasantry as the backbone of the nation, a solid element left unchanged since antiquity, while Marxist writers endowed them with dormant or primitive revolutionary tendencies.[1]

Greece entered modern times as a land of peasants, but its peasants joined modernity at a very slow pace. The first to be exposed to habits, attitudes, modes of production and exchange, products and ways of life associated with modern times were the peasants of island and coastal Greece. Contact with Western visitors or merchants and travel to other Mediterranean ports made those Greeks more receptive to Western ideas and life-styles than their inland compatriots. Eventually the latter too, especially the ones who lived near major routes, came into contact with the Western way of life when land communications became relatively safe and opened up Central Europe to Greek and other Balkan merchants. For a long time, however, the system of government did not favour the introduction of change in the mode of production and in everyday life.

A very conservative regime, arbitrary rule and administration of justice, insecurity of property and heavy taxation favoured stagnation rather than change, and kept the peasants in a state of backwardness and perpetual poverty. The abandoned villages and deserted churches that were observed by Western travellers in the last decades of Ottoman rule signified a reduction of the agricultural population. This was the result of the land's advanced decline and inability to sustain human life, due to utter neglect of the country's agricultural infrastructure. The Turkish administration aimed at extracting revenue for the imperial government or for the holders of privileged posts, while Ottoman landowners pocketed the agricultural surplus from agricultural production through taxes, and had no incentive to increase productivity. Most at the few native Greeks who were landowners owned smallholdings on mountain slopes. Greeks who tilled the lowlands normally enjoyed the right to cultivate the land, while ownership and taxation rights remained with the state, religious foundations or Muslim proprietors.

---

[1] The best study of rural Greece is William W. McGrew's *Land and Revolution in Modern Greece, 1800–1881,* Kent, OH: Kent State University Press, 1985, in which the student can also find an excellent bibliography on the subject. The influx of refugees in the 1920s and the pressing need to settle them produced the first substantial interest of the state in rural Greece. Some representative studies of the period are Chrysos Evelpidis's *La réforme agraire en Grèce,* Athens, 1924; Konstantinos Karavidas *Agrotica* (Agrarian matters), Athens, 1931; Demetrios Loukopoulos, *Georgika tis Roumelis* (Agricultural matters of Rumelia), Athens, 1938; and A.D. Sideris. *I georgiki politiki tis Hellados kata tin lixasan ekatontaetian* (Greece's agricultural policy during the past hundred years), Athens, 1934.

Neglect of the agricultural infrastructure was evident in ubiqui-tous ruins of bridges, roads, watercourses, cisterns and mills. Marshes and swamps were the results of environmental neglect and a sign of serious deterioration. Without any forest conservation and drainage control, the land's steep slopes and narrow valleys became vulnerable to torrential drainage, soil erosion and silting. Runoff from heavy rains transformed plains into marshes, and no river valley had escaped this process. In addition to the loss of fertile land, stagnating bodies of water made malaria endemic, which made life in the lowlands hazardous.

Dispelling myths and disposing of old and pious fallacies always entails the danger of being trapped by other myths. In the case of Greek peasants this danger is considerable, because reliable evidence is rare: information about them normally comes from people who either despised or idealised them. Both biases have endowed their subjects with features which had less to do with real peasants than with their own prejudices and agendas.

One misconception comes from the unspoken assumption that peasants in Greece led identical or similar lives. It is now becoming increasingly clear that peasant lives in Greece varied significantly from place to place on account of infinitely varied conditions. Climate and available resources, as well as proximity and access to administrative or urban centres, were major determining factors. Southern Greek peasants differed from northern ones, islanders from inlanders, lowland and coastal peasants from mountain-dwellers. Differences in political or administrative conditions were also responsible for differences in the way life was organised. Venetian rule in the Ionian Islands had left its mark on the life of the local people; so too had a measure of autonomy and certain immunities granted by the Ottoman overlords to mainland communities or regions like the Mt Pelion villages in Thessaly, the Mt Zagori villages in Epirus, and the Mani peninsula in the Peloponnese.

Another misconceived assumption is that the Orthodox Church had imbued the Greek peasants with uniform values and therefore uniform lives. It is true that Orthodoxy was a unifying factor, but it is no less true that language was not the insignificant factor it is often assumed to be, even the language of the pre-national peasant world. The Orthodox Albanians of southern Albania, Epirus and Attica, the Vlachs of Thessaly, Epirus and Macedonia, and the Bulgars (the later Slav Macedonians) of Macedonia and Thrace did not always see eye to eye with the Greek-speaking Orthodox of the lands that were eventually incorporated into the Greek state.

Another such assumption is that identical or similar occupations and means of livelihood generated contact and common ways of life and values. The world of peasants that confronted King Otto's regime in 1833 was one of bewildering variety. Administrators and army officers were exasperated by the multitude of cultural or ethnic groups scattered across the Greek kingdom, leading a life apart and viewing themselves, and viewed by others, as separate and self-contained. The wandering and elusive Gypsies differed from one another as much as they did from sedentary peasants. Transhumant Albanian shepherds, on the other hand, were fragmented into as many separate and secluded groups or clans as there were mountain slopes in Achaea, the Argolid, Attica, Boiotia, Phthiotis and other districts of central and northern Greece. Their Albanian and/or Vlach languages and their common means of livelihood did not obliterate distinct features, customs and values which merited separate names. Forest-dwellers of the Mt Agrapha slopes, who did not have permanent homes but lived in huts and could be spotted from a distance only by the smoke rising from their fires, taxed the linguistic ability of Greek officials to give them commonly recognisable group names; like the Albanian transhumant shepherds, they eluded efforts not only to record them but also to give them group names within such broad categories as 'hut-' or 'tent-dwellers' (*kalyvites* or *skenites*), 'nomads', 'wandering shepherds' (*metavatikoi voskoi*) or 'Vlach shepherds' (*vlachopoimenes*), which were mostly misleading or conveyed very little that distinguished these groups. Distant clan origin, customs anchored in past ages, surviving memories of feuds with neighbours, and features of speech, dress or habits not always apparent to outsiders were what made these groups self-contained communities and separated them from each other as much as from the sedentary peasants.

What really unified the disparate ethnic and cultural elements was the Greek national school and eventually the movement for Greek national independence. That those non-Greek linguistic pockets in the predominantly Greek-speaking southern Ottoman Balkans survived for so many centuries is testimony to their resistance to assimilation into a commonly recognised superior culture. Orthodox and partly hellenised Albanian tribes, like the Suliots of Epirus, constituted a confederacy which practised institutionalised plunder and lived on the backs of the Christian peasants of the same province. Bulgarians in the Greek north did not exactly welcome the abolition of the Bulgarian archbishopric of Achris in the eighteenth century. Finally, the Vlachs of the same area, before becoming involved in the carrying trade and in commerce, and before their rapid hellenisation around the same time, were perpetually at daggers drawn as transhumant pastoralists, with the sedentary and no less Orthodox agriculturists. Unity and uniformity were attained by the nation-state through assimilation.

Until the advent of the Greek state in the region one can legitimately speak of many varieties of peasant life in a fragmented land, not of peasants with the preocupations and pursuits normally associated with the citizens of a unified modern state. These differences must be kept in mind in any attempt to examine peasant life in pre-national Greece.

Agriculturist peasants tilled the land with very rudimentary implements. Tools were made of wood from a nearby or distant forest, the ploughshare normally tipped with iron. Shallow ploughing failed to clear the weeds but retained more of the moisture in the dry hot summer than occurs with the modern equivalent. Peasants customarily raised their crops without animal manure, other than what little was obtained from cattle, sheep and goats. Harvesting was done with a sickle, manufactured locally to suit local needs which varied from place to place. Threshing was done mostly by the hooves of animals and sometimes with a heavy spiked wooden plank drawn by an animal on a stone floor which might be covered with a thin layer of clay mixed with cattle dung. Winnowing involved throwing the grain in the air with a wooden shovel for the evening breeze to blow the husks away.

The cropping system in use involved growing grain on a given field every two years alternating with fallow. But as suitable land became scarce, this was replaced by rotation. Thus wheat was followed by barley, but preferably by a summer crop or pulse or tobacco when the soil permitted. Poorer soil was normally sown with rye. Rudimentary terraces were built on mountain slopes, especially in the more arid south usually and in the islands. Where peasants did own land, landholdings were usually small and barely adequate to sustain even a small family. Wheat did not satisfy the needs of all households and was customarily supplemented by rye and maize, especially in upland villages. Some grain, notably wheat, reached the uplands from the lowlands, where communications and lowland surpluses allowed. Otherwise highlanders supplemented their frugal diet from the chestnut forests around them. Upland peasants also produced some walnuts for their own needs and for sale to lowland peasants in exchange for grain or winter vegetables, like cabbages and leeks, that could be stored.

Tending vineyards was an inherited tradition, which claimed many of the working days in the year for a typical grower, and was well suited to a region of smallholdings. Vines were grown on the sunny slopes of hills primarily for winemaking but also to supply grapes for the table. The quality and consumption of wine increased as one moved from north to south and from the islands and the coasts to the interior uplands. Wine supplemented the peasant's diet, and in addition provided the spirits required for special occasions. Its alcohol content was increased in some places by adding during fermentation a home-made sweetener called *pekmez*, a thick liquid made from boiling grape juice, in order to prevent it turning sour in the summer. In the south resin was added as a preservative. A spirit called *raki* was distilled from grape skins and, like wine, was consumed by peasants in most places.

Tobacco cultivation, which like vine-growing required many working days in the year and was suited to smallholders, increased in the second half of the nineteenth century. However, it became an important export product only after the First World War and the arrival of the Anatolian and Pontic Greeks. Soil, skill and the dryness of the summer determined its quality and price. The mulberry tree was grown in well-watered parts mainly for the leaves which are host to the silkworm, and the silk cocoons were exported due to the lack of a local silk industry. Opium poppies were cultivated in Macedonia for sale but also for use in the home, mainly to relieve pain and put crying babies to sleep. Its production and sale became a monopoly in 1925; cultivation thereafter was allowed only by special government permit and virtually came to an end. Beans of various kinds were grown wherever water was available. South of Thessaly and throughout the islands and the coastal areas the olive tree was grown for its oil and fruit, which formed a large part of the peasant diet.

Peasants kept small and resilient hill ponies, which were used chiefly as pack animals. Mules were bred to be used in rougher country, while donkeys were mostly ridden for short journeys to nearby market towns, particularly to and from the fields. The cattle were small and rather lean, and kept primarily as draught animals, not for milk or meat. A powerful but slow draught animal, the buffalo, was more widely used in the plains. Peasants kept a pig or two, and the meat helped to sustain their families in winter. Poultry were kept for meat and eggs. The peasants also kept bees, since for most of them honey and *pekmez* were the basic sweetening agents.

Sheep and goat breeding was an important sector of the land's economy. Each peasant family kept a small number of those animals where the environment allowed, but the transhumant Vlachs and Sarakatsan shepherds were the country's traditional pastoralists. From spring to autumn Mt Pindus and the mountains of Macedonia provided grazing for large flocks of sheep and goats from the lowlands of Sterea Hellas, Thessaly, Epirus and Macedonia. The Vlachs and Sarakatsans practised transhumance, raising sheep and goats for milk which was made into several kinds of cheese. Large flocks, accompanied by herding families with their horses, mules and possessions, moved in late April from the lowlands to the highland pastures and returned in November to winter on the snow-free plains and coasts. Some pastoral groups moved their flocks over longer distances, but the majority practised a migratory cycle following the turn of the seasons and exploiting more or less the same mountain grasslands and lowland winter grounds. Migratory herdsmen followed pre-arranged and relatively safe routes, usually along rivers, on both their spring and autumn journeys. The dates for these migratory movements were not altogether uniform, but they usually coincided with two important festivals of the Orthodox Church: those of St George in the spring and St Demetrius in the autumn. In general, departure from the lowlands was possible when the lambs and kids born in December and January had been weaned, the snows had melted on the mountain slopes, and the first grass of summer permitted the move. Throughout the summer the shepherds were busy making cheese, shearing and getting their produce to market. The descent from the mountains began soon after the first snowfalls, usually in October.

The steady expansion of arable land, especially in the twentieth century, radically changed the appearance of the uplands. Indigenous or refugee agriculturists cleared extensive tracts of bush around their villages. This reduced the pasturage available for flocks of sheep and goats belonging to local and visiting shepherds, while the more intensive cultivation of the plains and valleys greatly reduced the areas of winter grazing and at the same time seriously hindered the movement of migratory flocks. Thus, with the expansion of arable land at the expense of grassland, the traditional complementary relationship between highlands and lowlands was broken and with it the old system of stockbreeding. Already hostility on the part of the state towards a way of life and economic activity that were difficult or impossible to incorporate into the predominant system of political, social and economic relations had been undermining the fortunes of transhumant pastoralism. Rising rents for pastureland made the maintenance of large flocks a growing burden. To halt the decline, the state intervened after the First World War to protect the rights of those leasing pastureland and set a limit to grazing rents. But intervention came too late to save the migratory shepherd—if he could be saved at all, short of a totally different attitude towards a way of life that was considered inimical to the national interest and the prestige of the state. This was in contrast to the attitude to the sedentary peasant, who was seen as solid and reliable and deserving all possible encouragement to remain attached to the soil.

The country's pastoral communities were losing men to the bands of brigands operating in the highlands from spring to autumn. Impoverished and demoralised shepherd families allowed a young male member to attach himself to a band of brigands, while another male might find employment with peasant sheep-owners. Other young mountain-dwellers entered the gendarmerie or attached themselves as guides to flying columns of gendarmes and soldiers pursuing brigands. The pastoral community was losing its attraction for shepherd families, as its capacity to provide a measure of prosperity and security was progressively undermined. Brigands, herdsmen in the service of sedentary peasants who kept sheep and goats, and a fair number of gendarmes were essentially drifting members of a traditional world in a state of dissolution at a time when the towns and the plains could not absorb them because they could not provide employment suited to their skills and agricultural capital.[2]

The decline of transhumant pastoralism has been one of the major social and economic developments associated with the country's peasants. Land ownership has been an even more important development than declining pastoralism. In the space of one century, from the War of Independence in the 1820s till the settlement of the refugees from the Asia Minor Catastrophe in the 1920s, Greece was transformed from a land of shepherds and landless peasants into one of landed peasants who also owned a sizeable portion of their stock. The transformation was perhaps unavoidable, in view of state policy to turn peasants into a class of land proprietors and in the absence of a distinct class of large estate-owners. However, it was no less significant for Greek society than other developments and policies, and it reveals certain features of Greek state policy which are worth examining.

One aspect of this transformation was the reversal of a demographic pattern, which had been established since early modern times if not earlier: the relocation of a remarkably large part of the population

<hr/>

[2]Koliopoulos, *Brigands with a Cause*, pp. 277 ff.

on mountain slopes. This relocation was both a result and a cause of the physical deterioration of the plains and river valleys and not so much a consequence, as was once thought, of a flight to higher ground to avoid Turkish exactions and misrule.[3] As a result the population of the highlands increased while prolonging this remarkable demographic pattern well into the twentieth century. It contributed to transhumant pastoralism by allowing pastureland to expand in the lowlands and thus favouring a complementary relationship between lowlands and highlands. Owners of large estates in the plains and on the coasts earned profits by leasing land as winter pasture to transhumant shepherd communities and thus prolonging this medieval pattern of social and economic relations.

As has already been noted, the modern state founded in the 1820s steadily modernised these relations by favouring the sedentary peasant as against the migratory shepherd, who eluded taxation and service in the national army and was easily associated with brigandage and plunder in general. For nearly a century and using every possible measure and type of action, Greek governments restricted the freedom of movement of migratory shepherds while at the same time catering for the needs of the settled peasants. For nearly half a century the highlands sent their demographic surpluses to the lowlands or to foreign lands. Transhumant pastoralists generally settled in communities near their former winter pastures, while other mountain-dwellers who lacked such ties with the lowlands emigrated in search of a more promising life. Highland population surpluses had been on the move to augment precarious family fortunes throughout the latter period of foreign rule. However, this early movement was practically limited to the dominions of the Ottoman Sultan and of the neighbouring Habsburgs and Romanovs. Post-Independence emigration—particularly the wave, amounting to a great exodus, that took place in the last decade of the nineteenth century and the first two of the twentieth—was not unrelated to the decline of the Greek highland communities.

Migration to the provincial towns and the major urban centres of the country was slow at first for the reasons explained elsewhere, but it increased dramatically after the Second World War. The Civil War of the late 1940s sent to the towns and cities a great wave of

---

[3]Apostolos Vakalopoulos, 'La retraite des populations grecques vers des régions éloignées et montagneuses pendant la domination turque', *Balkan Studies,* IV (1963), pp. 265–76.

destitute mountain-dwellers, fleeing a world in rapid decline and brutalised by civil strife. The organised return of peasants to the countryside after the Civil War to relieve the congested towns and cities and start food production anew was a desperate effort to bring the mountain communities back to life.

The typical peasant settlement was the nucleated village, a compact cluster of houses standing alone in a wide stretch of open land. It was the product of history no less than of the use of resources, and had begun in most cases as a settlement of serfs cultivating the lands of Byzantine, Frankish or Turkish masters. Villages on mountain slopes or plateaux tended to develop in the vicinity of, respectively, passes or converging roads. Water supply was a determining factor in their emergence.

Peasant dwellings were of different types. Climate, the availability of building material such as timber and stones, and the needs of the occupants determined the house type in a region. Generally, the houses were rough constructions of readily available material, which have survived only in the accounts of those who visited and recorded their visits. Thatched walls as well as roofs for the migratory shepherds, sun-dried brick walls and thatched roofs for the peasants of the plains and valleys, stone walls and roofs for sedentary mountain-dwellers, and small stone houses for the islanders were the dominant types. The only village buildings that have survived are the churches and the houses of the local landlord or the merchant, who had chosen to built for posterity a place that distinguished him from the rest of the inhabitants but not ostentatious enough to catch the eye of the local Turkish master.

These houses were not places of leisure but shelters, protecting families and their stock from the elements and wild animals. Peasants normally lived under the same roof as their pack and draught animals, which provided them with some of the warmth needed to brave the cold of the winter nights. An upper floor for the family, leaving the basement for the animals, distinguished the better-off peasants from the rest. A fireplace provided the necessary heat for cooking and some warmth for the senior members of the family sitting next to it, while women and children sat at some distance and received little or no warmth. Olive oil lamps and pinewood splinters provided all the light the peasant family needed. The introduction of kerosene lamps amounted to a revolution: they lit the dark interior of the peasant house and allowed its occupants to do indoor work in winter, such as carding, spinning and weaving. Kerosene lamps and iron plate stoves burning wood not only increased the amount of light and heat in the peasant house interior, but distributed them throughout the room for the benefit of all the family.

For dress and footwear peasants used materials which were easily acquired locally. Coarse and heavy woolen garments for the winter cold and lighter clothing for the summer heat were made at home by the women of the family or by an itinerant tailor whose services were hired in winter. The peasant feared the winter cold, but feared the spring and summer sun no less: he protected himself from both with woollen or knitted clothes. These garments were simple and made to last, because they could only be replaced at considerable cost. Nothing was discarded unless no member of the family could any longer make use of it. Functional value was the primary consideration; ornaments were reserved for special occasions and mainly for members of marrying age. Black—the black of bereavement—was the cloth colour of most family elders in a world where death was omnipresent.

Climate, *mores* and scarcity of resources ruled the appearance of the peasant. Elaborate national costumes preserved in folklore museums and described in old travellers' accounts were reserved for the more prosperous members of the community. Common peasant dress was simple and unattractive and was no more than what people with the most basic means of livelihood and in precarious or forbidding circumstances could afford. For mainland peasants a long shirt fastened at the waist with a belt and baggy trousers, and for islanders a shirt, with a coarse woollen capote for both, were the standard Greek peasant dress. Foreign and local romantic imagination embellished this dress with gold and silver, which were simply beyond the means of the local peasants; besides, in a world of utter insecurity of life and property the prudent peasant avoided ostentation. What often seems to elude the modern student of peasants of past ages is their avoidance of whatever could catch the eye of the mighty of the land. As in the case of the folk ballads and heroes, elaborate folk dress has been created for the peasants by imaginative people who had never shared the rigours of their lives.

To cover their feet peasants again used whatever was locally available and what they could afford. Makeshift sandals of untreated pigskin satisfied their needs in the summer, but afforded no protection against the tangled and thorny plants covering much of the ground, and had to be guarded against hungry dogs. Sheepskins wrapped around the feet and legs were normal protective coverings against the winter cold. Proper leather shoes were only worn by the few who could afford them and for special occasions like weddings and major saints' days. One acquired such shoes only on reaching adulthood; younger members of the family used whatever their elders could spare, or one simply did without. The introduction of cheap rubber shoes—long-lasting, firm and water-resistant—was another revolutionary change in the lives of peasants.

Poorly sheltered and modestly clad and fed, the Greek peasant kept body and soul together by the good use he made of available resources. It was the very insecurity of life and property, and scarcity of resources, that sharpened his intellect and steeled his resolve to survive. A benign climate and equally benign religion made life less intolerable than elsewhere under comparable circumstances by providing frequent occasion for relaxation and moments of mirth and festivity. Reserve was a deeply ingrained and prized quality, and want was borne with dignity. The peasants of Greece were not exactly the noble descendants of the classical sages and heroes whom foreign and Greek romantics hoped to see, but nor were they brutes either. Long years of servitude and a harsh environment had not divested them of their humanity.

Freedom from foreign bondage did not exactly turn the peasants of Greece into regenerated Hellenes, as the Western and Greek romantics believed it would. However, it increased their freedom to improve their lot, gave them the opportunity to obtain from the state most of the lands it had won in the War of Independence: they fell on these national lands without delay and with greater enthusiasm than they had initially shown in shaking off their former masters. Party clientelism and alternation in power of sets of politicians open to pressure from their political clients, in conjunction with the lack of cadastral registers and title deeds or fixed lines of demarcation between private holdings and community or state property, made state-owned land an easy prey to the peasants in the various districts. A land distribution programme enacted in 1871 during the prime ministerial term of Alexandros Koumoundouros secured for peasants legal titles to the holdings they had already occupied and cultivated.

The acquisition of Thessaly ten years later added a new stock of landless peasants, who this time did not have the opportunity to seize the land they occupied. This was because Thessaly was ceded and not conquered; by the treaty of cession the Greek state recognised all property rights in the acquired province, and therefore the former serfs and cultivators of the land joined Greece as peasants without any right to the land or what it could produce. The landlords possessed all rights over it, including that of evicting their former serfs. Pressure to acquire land increased, but remained a local issue. It eventually subsided when the 1911 constitution opened the way for the expropriation of landed estates and their distribution to the former serfs.

The arrival of the refugees from Asia Minor in the early 1920s and the need to settle a sizeable part of them in the newly-acquired areas of Macedonia and Thrace presented the authorities with a task of staggering proportions. The land abandoned by the departed Muslims or Bulgars, as well as communal or monastic land, could only satisfy part of the needs of the destitute newcomers, who settled in the midst of an indigenous peasant population no more prosperous than themselves, for a life of want unrelieved by any hope of improvement.

8

THE SEARCH FOR A MIDDLE CLASS

Capitalism and liberal government have been associated with the entrenchment in public life of the West European middle classes:, who are credited with establishing market economies and the institutions of constitutional and representative government. Modernity itself has been thought to be organically connected to the rise of this agent of profound change in the world. Whether lauded for their role in ushering in modernity or vilified for modernity's less attractive and benign aspects, the middle classes have never been denied a dominant role in restructuring the world they lived in make it conform to their interests and vision of life.

Greece too has been 'modernised' by its middle class; at least, this is the generally prevailing view. The Greek mercantile class produced what could be described as a Western-oriented Balkan Enlightenment, and sustained a movement for national independence which led to the establishment of a Greek nation-state in the southern Balkans. In more than one sense, that class has operated as a mediator of Western ideas and practices.[1]

However, defining this class has been an intractable problem.

---

[1] This issue has not been satisfactorily studied. Neo-Marxist studies of the 1970s have added little in terms of serious research. Instead, they have provided impressionistic pictures of Greece, with the use of selective material to verify what was already established and known: that the country was part of a world market economy and that, as such, its economy and society developed under the influence of this world system. For such representative studies see Kostas Vergopoulos, *Kratos kai oikonomiki politiki ston 19° aiona* (State and economic policy in the 19th century), Athens, 1978, and Konstantinos Tsoukalas, *Exartisi kai anaparagogi. O koinonikos*

Which social elements of pre-Independence Greece constituted the country's middle class and which its upper class? The problem is that a group of people can be considered in social terms only in relation to another such group, or as distinct from it. In this sense, to define Greece's middle class one has first to search for and locate its social neighbours.

Greek society under foreign rule—Ottoman rather than Venetian—consisted of a large class of land-owning or landless peasants and shepherds, artisans organised in guilds, and an upper class of functionaries in the service of the foreign overlord. The rise of commerce, especially in the last three decades before the outbreak of the War of Independence and in the context of the Napoleonic wars, produced a group of merchants exploiting a considerable portion of the trade, by both sea and land, in the Eastern Mediterranean and the Balkans. Eventually, wealthy merchant communities grew up in a number of port cities and major centres, such as Trieste, Smyrna, Constantinople, Odessa and Vienna. A few Greek islands—most notably Chios, Hydra, Spetsae and Psara—also benefited from this commercial activity, but their merchant communities were seriously damaged by hostile acts by the Turks during the Greek War of Independence.

The independent Greek kingdom inherited very little from the pre-Independence merchant class; its members, as might be expected, chose to remain abroad to pursue their interests in more prosperous lands rather than return to the devastated and impoverished motherland. Local commerce and manufacturers took some time to recover from the heavy blows they had received in the war. But local or professional pre-war élites, such as the district notables, the captains of Armatoles and the Phanariots, did not have the kinds of pursuits or ways of life normally associated with a middle class. Early post-Independence Greece lacked even major commercial centres; Patras and Nauplion were minor port cities, while Athens, the country's capital after 1834, was for a long time primarily an administrative centre.

Eventually, in the context of the expanding Greek kingdom, Greek

---

rolos ton ekpaideutikon mechanismon stin Ellada, 1830–1932 (Dependence and reproduction: The social role of the educational mechanisms in Greece, 1830–1932), Athens 1977. Real representatives of the Greek upper strata can be found in the memories of Andreas Syngros, *Apomnimonevmata* (Memoirs), ed. by Alkis Angelou and Maria Christina Chatzeioannou, 3 vols, Athens 1998, and Demetrios G. Kambouroglou, *Apomnimonevmata mias makras zois, 1852–1932* (Memoirs of a long life, 1852–1932), ed. by A. N. Karavias, 2 vols, Athens, 1985. See also McGrew, *op.cit.*, pp. 9 ff.

society did produce a class with most of the features of the middle classes of modern times. Merchants, manufacturers, bankers and, most of all, state functionaries were its constituents and in the absence of a traditional upper class, this class projected itself to the top rank of Greek society and acquired most of the trappings of an upper class. Its representatives have normally been referred to as *astoi* (meaning both city-dwellers and bourgeois) and the class itself as *astiki taxi* (bourgeoisie). These and other similar terms, which have been adopted to assimilate this class with its supposed equivalents in the rest of Europe, can easily mislead the student of Greece. This is because, in spite of all the obvious and undeniable similarities between this Greek 'middle' class and its Western prototypes who brought about the greatest changes in the West, there has been at least one fundamental difference between the two. While the Western middle classes developed in opposition to state authority that restricted the free operation of market economies, the Greek equivalent developed as a state appendage and thrived on state revenue. In this sense the totality of such diverse elements as bankers and army officers, merchants and university professors, manufacturers and lawyers shaped its world outlook always in the context of the state's authority, interests and objectives. It favoured liberal democracy to the extent that the state embraced that regime.

The search for differences in such constructs as modern social classes can be as misleading as the search for similarities in them; and, as with all historical generalisations, the arguments put forward to question neat analogies like the ones mentioned above are of limited value. However, breaking down such constructs as classes into their component parts and searching for their boundaries helps the student of Greece to locate groups of people with relatively similar concerns, objectives and life-styles.

The first such groups that can be distinguished from the mass of peasants, shepherds and seamen by a life-style resembling that of Western middle-class groups were various categories of upper state functionaries. Moreot notables, Rumeliot captains and their sons, who had survived the shocks of war without sinking into poverty, enlisted themselves in state service in various capacities. The local élites manned the communal councils and—after the promulgation of the first constitution in 1844—Parliament; the regular army, especially after the departure of the Bavarian military contingent; and the gendarmerie. Paid service with the government secured for this group a prominent place in the country's upper social strata.

Educated Greeks from other European countries, including those from the Danubian principalities, Russia and Constantinople who had managed to survive politically, likewise sought and secured paid service of this kind. Although lacking in power and influence compared with the old local élites, they surpassed them in education and in the prestige that this secured for them among a people who, while illiterate, admired the educated. The University and the educational establishment in general, as well as the Ministries of Foreign Affairs and Justice, remained their exclusive preserve until the country's educational system was able to produce a new local intelligentsia. In this the University of Athens and the new universities established in the twentieth century played an important role. They turned out not only educated members of society, but individuals educated to serve the state first and foremost. This further increased the size and special weight of this state-subsidised 'middle' class.

This aspect of Greece's upper social strata has not received the attention it deserves: free state education up to and including university, a prized feature of the egalitarian state, has created a state-subsidised Leviathan, a ruling class that has grown on public revenue and replenished its ranks though the state educational system. Thus university education at the expense of the state and with a view to modernising society developed into the principal medium for the reproduction and steady expansion of a class of state mandarins with little inherent desire for change.

The incorporation of the Ionian Islands in 1864 and of Thessaly in 1881 enriched the country's upper strata with, in the first case, a petty and impoverished aristocracy dating from the time of Venetian rule but proud of its titles and heritage, and, in the second, wealthy Diaspora Greeks who had acquired landed estates from the departing Turks. The slow but steady commercial expansion in the second half of the nineteenth century and the first decade of the twentieth produced a number of rich Greeks and powerful merchants like Andreas Syngros and Emmanouil Benakis.

Trikoupis's administrative and economic reforms of the 1880s and the sweeping reforms of Venizelos in the 1910s further strengthened the mercantile element of the country's upper strata, while the timid industrialisation of the interwar period added an industrial-financial element to the class structure. Postwar reconstruction opened the way to the top for a number of building contractors who had provided apartment houses for the expanding populations of the Greek cities. Last but not least, the expansion of international shipping added a touch of lustre and glamour to the Greek upper strata.

After Greece joined the European Community, Brussels became a new source of revenue for the government-subsidised middle class. This 'hybrid' middle class, brought to life and sustained by the state to modernise an underdeveloped society and economy, has always been open to new blood, perhaps because it never had—and never cultivated—an identity different from that of the rest of the people. Most of its members were (or their fathers had been) former peasants, shepherds and seamen: talent, the right connections or sheer good luck would secure a place at the top table, especially in the last quarter of the twentieth century. However, positions and fortunes have always been precarious, and lost as quickly as they were won.

Members of the securely established second-generation or older middle class have always taken pride in their humble origins while the 'new poor' have correspondingly liked to exaggerate their exalted origins. Descendants of the old Ionian aristocracy, bearers of names made famous in the country's wars of national liberation or in politics but since fallen from grace, have always tried to retain what little they could secure from 'departed worth' or to claim rewards for past family services, but with little success, in a society recognising no such debts and rewarding those currently with the right connections or with obvious talent.

Academy of Athens (1926–)

This establishment of scholarly excellence founded through an Act of Parliament and set up by the astronomer Demetrios Aiginitis, Education Minister in 1926, was originally endowed with public and private donations and its charter was modelled on the Belgian example.

There are sixty-five seats in the Academy divided into three 'orders': twenty-five for the Natural Sciences, twenty-five for Literature and the Fine Arts and fifteen for the Moral and Political Sciences. When a seat is vacated, aspiring members submit applications and are judged by the appropriate order for their life membership.

The Academy is housed in a splendid Neo-Classical mansion in Panepistimiou street, and finances a research centre dealing mainly with History and Social Anthropology. Academy prizes are given out in an annual ceremony attended by state dignitaries.

Although such important figures as Leonidas Zervas (Chemistry), Vassos Krimbas (Agriculture), Demetris Trichopoulos (Medicine), Dionisios Zakithinos (History), Constantine Tsatsos (Philosophy), Panayotis Kanellopoulos (Sociology), Andre Andreadis (Economics),

Dimitrios Pikionis (Architecture), Constantine Karatheodori (Mathematics) and Nikos Hatzikyriakos-Ghikas (Art) have been Academicians, the institution has on the whole been conservative in its choices.

Athens College (1925–)

This distinguished private institution of secondary education was founded in 1925 on the model of the British 'public school'. It was officially named 'Greek-American Educational Institution', and was at first backed financially by the Greek tycoons and benefactors Emmanouil Benakis and his son-in-law Stephanos Deltas. Since 1929 an American Board of Trustees based in New York has conducted drives for funds which proved vital for the development of the school.

Although Athens College provides solid education in the English language, the basic courses were taught in Greek and the school operates with a Greek administration and board and under the laws that govern Greek state schools. Academic excellence as well as extra-curricular activities, sports, theatre and student government have made entry to the school a highly desirable goal for many Greeks. Tuition fees are high but, thanks to fund-raising among the alumni, scholarship programs have allowed children from remote areas of Greece to attend. Politicians such as Andreas Papandreou, Miltiades Evert, Andreas Andrianopoulos, Stephanos Manos and Antonis Samaras were among those who have graduated from Athens College.

The school has also produced a generation of prominent Greek businessmen but it has never become a school for 'rich boys'. Many young people of limited means found their way to success through Athens College and to the best universities in the United States and Britain. In the 1970s the school became coeducational. It now operates in two campuses, in Kanza and in Psychico.

9

MIGRANTS, REFUGEES AND
THE DIASPORA

People have been moving in and out of Greece since the beginning of recorded time. A benign climate has always attracted migrants from less inviting lands to the north, while till recently scarce resources have driven surpluses away. From the invasions and settlements of late medieval and early modern times right up till the late-twentieth-century wave of illegal immigrants from neighbouring and other poorer countries, Greece has been a land exporting more people than it receives. The refugees from the Asia Minor Catastrophe, who exceeded in number all other previous or subsequent waves of immigrants, were the exception to the rule. In the centuries of foreign domination, Greeks from mainland Greece and the islands replenished the Greek stock of western Anatolia, re-settled old colonies round the Black Sea, and established new colonies in the northern Balkans and the north Mediterranean littoral. Greek merchant communities were established in many major West European cities like Paris, Amsterdam and London. This was the modern Greek diaspora, one of the most striking aspects of the nation's history, which has consistently fascinated students of Greece. The even more striking capacity of the land to produce population surpluses in times of great adversity seems to have attracted little attention.

People are driven to leave their homes for other lands not so much by poverty as by the expectation of a better life than what they are leaving behind. They are also driven away by war. In post-Independence Greece and until the 1940s, people generally left Greece as emigrants and came into it as refugees. Generally, however, people left of their own volition and moved to lands promising a better life, while most of those who came to Greece were forced by adverse circumstances.

The extensive destruction of human life, stock, olive groves and buildings during the War of Independence left the fledgling new kingdom in the southern Greek peninsula devastated and under-populated. Various incentives, such as promises of land grants and a rather lenient citizenship law (1835), did not succeed in making Greece more attractive to new settlers. Instead of immigrants, Greece received crowds of destitute refugees from across the frontier with Turkey or from Crete after each irredentist insurrection and its savage suppression. The suppression of insurrections in 1821–2 in Thessaly, Epirus and Macedonia sent the first wave of refugees to the southern Greek insurgents. They were former Armatoles in Turkish service who had been replaced by Muslim Albanians. Unused to any employment other than paid armed service and unable to secure work outside the irregular bands that made cross-frontier sorties when Greece's relations with Turkey were in crisis, these first refugees were a burden even when they did not practise brigandage, as many of them did.

The first refugees from the irredenta were precariously settled not far from the northern frontier, in towns like Lamia, Atalanti, Missolonghi and Amphilochia. Some found refuge on northern islands like Skyros and Skopelos, which formed one of the points of a triangle infested by amphibious pirates operating on small and swift boats from their lairs on barren islets. Northern Euboea, the northern Sporades, the prongs of the Chalcidice peninsula and the sea route to and from the port of Thessaloniki were never free from their depredations. Irredentist Athens journals presented their exploits as operations to liberate the unredeemed brethren across the frontier and so perpetuated their existence. New refugees from Epirus, Thessaly, Macedonia and Crete replenished the stock of refugees living on or outside the margin of legality.

The only newcomers in this initial period who could be described as immigrants were Germans who followed King Otto to his kingdom as military officers or soldiers and experts in many fields. However, all military men and most civil officials left Greece well before King Otto was obliged to abdicate and depart. Affluent Greek merchants of the diaspora generally refrained from settling in the newly-independent kingdom, whose capital Athens promised little of what the great cities of Europe offered to their more privileged citizens, which they undoubtedly were. These Greeks were attracted to Athens only in the later nineteenth century when it acquired some of the characteristics of a major European city.

Instead of immigrants, refugees flocked to Greece in increasing numbers. To those coming from the Sultan's dominions others were added from the newly-independent Balkan states like Romania and Bulgaria—countries antagonistic to Greece. The national movements in both these countries were directed not only against their Turkish rulers but also against the Greeks who had occupied positions of power there. As a result Greeks were forced to leave these countries, especially at times of strain in the relations between their governments and Athens. Friction over the influence—and control—of the pockets of Vlach- or Bulgarian-speakers in Epirus, Macedonia and Thrace throughout the period between the Congress of Berlin in 1878 and the Balkan Wars of 1912–13, left the Greeks in Romania and Bulgaria vulnerable to harassment by hostile authorities or mobs. Greeks who resisted assimilation had no choice in times of tension but to depart as emigrants or as refugees when hostility towards them filtered down to the local authorities. No useful distinction can be made between emigrants and refugees in this period of aggressive nationalism, when no international organisation existed to monitor the treatment of people by their governments.

The incorporation of Eastern Rumelia into the Bulgarian principality in 1885 opened the way for the gradual expulsion of the province's Greek population. Greek-Bulgarian friction over the future of Macedonia and Thrace sent to Greece periodic waves of ethnic Greek refugees from Eastern Rumelia, the largest of which happened in the middle of the first decade of the twentieth century. The number of refugees from Bulgaria increased during the Second Balkan War and particularly during the First World War and the 1920s. The Greek-Bulgarian convention of Neuilly (1919), which provided for the reciprocal and voluntary 'emigration' of Greeks from Bulgaria and Bulgars from Greece, regulated from then on the ethnic cleansing in both countries, placing it on the basis of a bilateral convention and under the auspices of the League of Nations.

Exact figures for people who left one country as nationals of another in this period are hard to come by. Those leaving a country as emigrants or refugees were unwanted people and thus not recorded; this was also the case with those coming in. There was no government service responsible for either category, whether incoming or outgoing. Both were given in round figures, the result of rough estimates, often to meet the transient requirements of national propaganda. A working estimate would have more than 100,000 Greeks leaving Bulgaria in the first quarter of the twentieth century and as many Bulgars leaving Greece in the same period and under similar circumstances.

Emigrants and refugees from and into Romania moved in smaller numbers during the same period. Romania's drive to seize the extensive land properties of Greek monasteries, a heritage of endowments from wealthy and powerful Greek Phanariot governors of the Principalities and other donors, and to win over the Vlachs of Epirus and Macedonia and sever their bonds of loyalty to Greece, produced tension in Greek-Romanian relations after the 1860s which made the Greeks living in Romania an easy target for Romanian nationalism. Many of these left the country for Greece for the same reasons that some Vlachs of Macedonia and Epirus left their ancestral lands after these were incorporated into Greece in 1913, in search of a country presumed to be more friendly to them than the one they were leaving behind. Nationalism was destroying within a few decades the cohabitation of peoples of different tongues and creeds which had endured through many centuries of imperial rule.

When, in 1913, a nation-state come into being in Albania, Greeks from its southern part migrated south in search of a less precarious life than what they anticipated in the new state, although Albania officially recognised their minority status, and their minority rights were protected by international treaty. This migration was assisted by nationalist associations or by distant kinsmen in Greek West Macedonia and Epirus.

Other Greeks, mostly of Vlach descent, left their homes in Serbian Macedonia after 1913 to avoid assimilation. The authorities of Serbia and the future Yugoslavia, like those of other Balkan countries, were set on assimilating their inherited linguistic groups, including Vlachs who had long been hellenised through the Greek school system in operation in the Ottoman and Habsburg empires. The communal or private property assets of many of them—the product of many years of hard work and sound investment—were seized by the authorities to satisfy the needs of those they considered loyal citizens.

All these immigrant Greeks from the country's northern neighbours arrived in relatively small numbers and over a long stretch of time, and settled in many parts of the country on their own initiative with little or no support from the government. They were easily assimilated socially and economically, but this was not the case with the refugees of the First World War from Asia Minor, Pontus or Russia. Greeks from Turkey began arriving in Greece not long after the Young Turk revolt of 1908 which, in addition to setting the tottering empire on a reformist course, brought to power a set of army officers aiming at a complete Turkification of the empire. The resulting pressure on non-Muslims, especially Greeks and Armenians, increased as a consequence of the Balkan Wars of 1912–13 and the loss of almost all the Sultan's dominions. Greek merchants and other people who had movable property assets or were simply aware of what was to follow left Turkey for Greece and established themselves in the main cities.

The outbreak of the First World War increased pressure on the Greeks in Turkey, especially after Greece openly took sides with Turkey's enemies from 1917 onwards. Turkey's defeat in 1918, the landing of Greek troops in Smyrna the following year and the Greek-Turkish war that followed caused an exodus of Greeks fleeing the repressive measures of the Turkish authorities. Again, the first to leave were those who had the means to do so. However, most of these Greeks were ordinary people, and those living in particular at some distance from the coasts and the main communication centres stayed put, hoping against hope that Turkey would not come out of the war a clear winner or in a position to bring about what many people feared most.

The collapse of the Greek front in Asia Minor in August 1922 and the consequent retreat of the beaten army to the coast were followed by the first mass eviction of an unwanted population in the twentieth century. More than a million Greeks abandoned their homes in the wake of the retreating Greek army for the safety of the eastern Aegean islands, eventually to settle in mainland Greece. Prosperous cities with predominantly Greek populations, like Smyrna on the Ionian coast, were burned to the ground by the Turks. The Smyrna conflagration in particular symbolised dramatically the end of 'eastern' Greece. Its uprooted population was blown across the Aegean sea by the winds of war to 'western' Greece, a veritable shipwreck, barely able to stay afloat under the weight of so much destitute humanity. The Greek government tried as best it could to cope with a disaster of staggering proportions, and by the standards of the day it was quite successful. Under the Lausanne treaty of 1923, the Greek refugees from Turkey were exchanged for the Muslims of Greece, whose lands were given to the newcomers. Settled mostly in Greek Macedonia, where Greek-speakers were not everywhere in the majority, the newcomers radically changed that region's linguistic composition. Only the Muslims of Greek Thrace and the Greeks of Istanbul and two small islands at the Aegean entrance to the Straits, Imbros and Tenedos, were excluded from the mandatory exchange of populations. Most of these last Greeks of Turkey were uprooted in the mid-1950s as a result of tension between the two countries over Cyprus.

Other Greeks came from Russia, having been expelled by the Bolsheviks for sympathising with their enemies in the civil war that followed the October 1917 Revolution. Prosperous communities had grown up around old nuclei of Greek colonies with encouragement from the Romanovs in the eighteenth and nineteenth centuries, but these were dealt blows from which they never recovered. Their members, dispossessed and dispersed over southern Russia, were gathered together by a special commission headed by the novelist Nikos Kazantzakis, and transported to Greece.

Greeks from the crumbling empires of the Romanovs, the Ottomans and the Habsburgs or the rising nation-states in the Balkans streamed into Greece as refugees, just as others were emigrating to greener pastures. Emigration from the Greek kingdom had remained insignificant throughout most of the nineteenth century, and was not recorded, but by the end of the century and the first quarter of the twentieth it took the form of an exodus from certain provinces. Sharply declining family incomes in currant-producing districts of the Peloponnese in that period, and the protracted insecurity in bandit-ridden Macedonia, were factors that persuaded peasants to pack up and leave for places where life was less precarious. More than poverty or insecurity at home, it was the prospect of a life of plenty in the lands of promise outside Europe, in conjunction with easy access to ports like Piraeus, Patras and Thessaloniki and free passage for indentured labourers, which sent many young Greeks to Australia, Canada and above all the United States, intending to return home after making a small fortune as quickly as circumstances allowed. Indeed, almost half of those who emigrated in this first great wave did return home, some merely to fight in the Balkan Wars of 1912–13 or in the First World War.

Emigration virtually ended when the United States drastically cut the yearly quota of foreigners allowed into the country in 1921. Greek peasants were not exactly leading lives of plenty in the interwar period, and indeed many of them, especially the Asia Minor refugees, lived in extreme poverty. Yet relatively few were prepared to opt for counties such as Argentina or Brazil, although the government encouraged them to do so.

After the unprecedented movement of people in and out of the country in the first quarter of the twentieth century, Greece experienced more than twenty years of relative calm. Muslims had departed for Turkey and Bulgars for Bulgaria or the New World, while Greeks had arrived from Turkey, Bulgaria and Russia. A net population increase of more than 600,000 had to be assimilated and undoubtedly the incorporation of so many and varied destitute newcomers is one of the greatest Greek epics. The cost was immense, but the tremendous effort that had to be expended and the experience gained enriched

Greece in a unique way. It would not be an overstatement to say that, after a century of attempting to fashion its new national image while at the same time acquiring an acceptable national frontier, the country finally settled down to looking after the needs of its own people.

The Second World War and the Axis occupation in the first half of the 1940s produced a new wave of refugees and emigrants. Their active collaboration with the Axis occupiers extinguished what tolerance the Greeks had shown for the Muslim Albanians of Epirus and the Slav Macedonians: the former departed in the wake of the retreating Germans in 1944, and the latter drifted across the frontier in the second half of the 1940s, as the government forces fought against the Communist rebels in the Civil War. The Slav Macedonian community of Greece lost a sizeable part of its population as fugitives across the frontier or as casualties in a lost cause. The same community's surviving young people emigrated in the next two decades, along with other emigrants from Greece, to North America and Australia.

The factors behind this new and, presumably, final exodus of Greeks from their motherland in search of a better life and a more hospitable country than post-Civil War Greece have not been adequately researched and analysed. Such obvious causes as poverty and persecution of the defeated and vulnerable members of the society that came out of the Civil War do not fully explain the social and age groups of the emigrants. Why, for instance, did Slav Macedonians—mostly teenagers and young adults of both sexes-opt for Australia or Canada, while young Pontians chose to work in Germany as guest-workers? These were not random choices. Were the Slav Macedonians attracted to lands with an existing stock of their fellow-nationals from the first wave of emigration from Greece? Did the descendants of the refugees of the 1920s opt for Germany in the 1960s because it suited their objective of a temporary stay away from home?

Like the emigrants in the first great wave, most of those in the second wave left hoping to return home some day—with the exception, of course, of the Slav Macedonians, whose links with home had been weakened by their experience in the Civil War. Generally those, mostly young and unmarried, who went to Australia, did so in the expectation of finding a new homeland. It seems that the trauma of the 1940s, combined with the realistic prospect of a better life abroad, gave many young people in the 1950s and '60s the necessary impetus to make the leap away from family and home. Leaving home was no longer predominantly a family concern, as its had been at the time of the first emigration. The war, among other things, had loosened ties within families and allowed their members to think of themselves as individuals capable of making important decisions for themselves—something that had been unthinkable before the war, especially for women.

The late twentieth-century influx of political and economic refugees from the former Communist countries in the Balkans and the Soviet republics, as well as from Asia and Africa, shows a striking reversal of the pattern we have described of Greece as a refuge solely for the Greeks. For the first time in its modern history Greece has become attractive not only to Greeks uprooted from other countries and entering the only country open to them, but to a long list of people who would never before have considered Greece even as a place of transit.

This latest influx has not yet been analysed exhaustively. The great majority of the newcomers seem to be economic refugees from southern Albania—both Greeks and Albanians—driven by the collapse of the Communist regime in Albania and the subsequent dislocation of state services and the economy. Most have been destitute young men in their late teens and early twenties. Their numbers tend to increase in the summer months, when the cheap construction and agricultural work needing to be done exceeds the capacity of the indigenous labour supply. Almost 400,000 mostly illegal Albanian economic refugees or immigrants live at the margins of society, playing hide and seek with the authorities, trying to elbow out other contestants in the field of ill-paid work, robbing each other of their meagre earnings and contributing to an increase in crime. The issuing of temporary residence permits for a percentage of the immigrants has introduced a way of regulating and monitoring this type of immigration.

Greeks from the minority in southern Albania have had easier access to Greece and have received some support from the Church—which, incidentally, has led to many formerly Muslim Albanians converting to Christianity. Conversion through baptism facilitated the issuing of a visa by the Greek consular authorities in Albania, and secured an advantage over non-Christian and illegal immigrants in the search for better-paid work. In the census of 2001 the newcomers did cause a small increase in the population of Greece and perhaps further deprived the Greek minority in Albania of its demographic core. Another aspect of this crossing in and out of Greece and of the Greek ecclesiastical and economic presence in southern Albania has been this region's progressive hellenisation and differentiation from the more traditional and less developed northern part of Albania. It should be remembered that the Albanians were preserved from melting into the Greeks in the south and the Serbs in the north through their conversion to Islam in the fourteenth and fifteenth centuries.

The Greeks from the former Soviet republics of Russia, Georgia, Azerbaijan, Kazakhstan or Uzbekistan form a different category of economic refugees. These were driven away by the general deterioration of conditions following the collapse of the Soviet Union, in conjunction with the attraction of Greece as a prosperous, secure and accessible European haven. They were more welcome than the Greeks from Albania, perhaps because they have been associated with the refugees of the First World War and seen more as relatives in distress. Few Greeks in Greece knew of them before their arrival and even fewer knew why or when they had settled in these northern and little-known lands. The ancestors of most of them, it seems, had gone there as refugees from either Turkey or Greece: some were from Pontus, driven to Russia by the Turks in the nineteenth century or earlier, and others from Greece itself as defeated Communist guerrillas in the late 1940s. While suffering a crisis of insecurity due to a very low birth-rate, the Greek authorities welcomed this injection of new people without providing adequately for their settlement. Most of them were small traders and town-dwellers and as such mostly settled in densely populated Greek cities like Athens or Thessaloniki, where they were often made to feel no less excluded than in the countries they had come from. The authorities and their exploiters call them 'returning' (*palinostountes*) Greeks, while they are popularly referred to as 'Russo-Pontians'. But they would rather be called 'Greeks' and made to feel no different from the rest of their compatriots. With the exception of night schools to improve their poor command of Greek and some assistance to meet initial expenses, these economic migrants have been left to their own devices: the men do all kinds of low-paid work that indigenous Greeks shun.

Other newcomers, though no better treated, appear more appreciative of what little Greece is prepared to offer them, perhaps because they expected less than the ethnic Greeks or because they really had nowhere else to go. When Serbs from war-torn Bosnia found shelter with organisations or individuals sympathetic to their cause, state authorities did not make them feel very welcome. Kurds fleeing the drive by the Turkish authorities to crush Kurdish subversion have reached Greece in a steady stream from the Kurdish areas of south-eastern Turkey and northern Iraq. Leftist organisations gave the Kurds some assistance, and state authorities provided a camp at Lavrion (Attica) to house them provisionally, in the hope that international human rights organisations would take an interest in their future. The average Greek would be prepared to show some sympathy for these people provided they remained at some distance from his own home. Unlike most other illegal immigrants or refugees, who were prepared to work in order to survive, the Kurds have generally depended on handouts from local and state authorities or from the Red Cross and other humanitarian organisations.

Greek Socialist support for the Palestinian cause, dating from the years of military dictatorship in Greece, as well as the need to sustain Arab sympathy in the drive to keep UN General Assembly support over the Cyprus dispute with Turkey, opened Greece to all categories of Palestinians in the 1980s. But the Socialist government introduced a more restrictive policy in the second half of the 1990s, and Palestinian refugees later dwindled in numbers; also they are less likely to be seen as groups of young political activists.

Poles came to Greece mainly as economic refugees following their country's economic winter of discontent in the 1980s, but for them Greece was a staging-post to more prosperous countries. While awaiting the opportunity to move on to such a country, they took advantage of such opportunities as Greece offered and tried to raise some money mostly by working illegally in the fields. Their numbers, too, dwindled following Poland's signs of economic recovery.

Filipino and Sri Lankan women working as domestic servants for better-off families have become a noticeable feature of Greek society. They have entered the country through agencies directing young women from various Third World countries to Western cities, and are to be seen in public in the early morning and late evening as they journey to and from the houses where they work, or looking after a child in a park. As time has gone on, with little or no support from any source or authority, they have formed associations to keep in touch and exchange news from home. On Christmas Eve they bring new life to the Catholic cathedral in the centre of Athens.

By the year 2000 the economic immigrants in Greece had exceeded a million. Some will settle permanently, thus making up for the country's population deficit, and will face the difficulties of acculturation into a society which is culturally homogenous. The evolving content of Greek identity, treated elsewhere in this volume, will determine how far this process succeds or fails.

'*Diaspora*' is a Greek word meaning dispersion, and when used of people it implies either migration or flight. The phenomenon is caused by the inability of a land to support its population, the pursuit of trade and the establishment of commercial outposts. Greek colonies were created throughout the Mediterranean basin as early as the eighth century BC and were populated by the demographic surplus of mainland Greece. During the eastward thrust of Alexander the Great, Greeks migrated as far as India and after the Ottoman conquest they fled west and north. At the beginning of the nineteenth century, as we have already seem the Greek presence was conspicuous in Smyrna, Constantinople and Odessa, and in the trade centres of the Black Sea, the Balkans, Central Europe and southern France. It was though this commercial diaspora that Enlightment and revolutionary ideas entered the Balkan peninsula and the spark was lit that ignited the 1821 War of Independence.

In a study already mentioned in this chapter it is maintained that the educational system of the Greek state was designed, at least until 1922, in such a way as to cater to the commercial needs of the Mediterranean diaspora.[1] The Greek merchants of Asia Minor and Egypt became important benefactors of the Greek state and helped to shape its destiny.

As we have seen, the collapse of the European markets for Peloponnesian vine products in the 1890s (see p. 168) generated a mass exodus of surplus cultivators. The tide of migration between 1900 and 1930 took half a million Greeks to the United States. Unlike the Greek merchants of the eastern Mediterranean, the peasants who entered American society were ill-prepared to play an influential role in their new habitat. However, through hard work they eventually rose through the social strata of their adopted country, while the Greeks of the Mediterranean basin were compelled to abandon their homes altogether and return to Greece.[2]

The transformation, in the course of a generation, of Greek peasants into American shopkeepers and businessmen says much about their origin. Charles Moskos wrote: 'Even though late nineteenth-century Greek society was overwhelmingly rural, the cultural hegemony of its urban merchant class—both in the Greek state and in the Greek diaspora—fostered an individualistic outlook on economic activities which even permeated the countryside. The Greek villager was already eager to emulate consumer and city life styles ... There can be little

---

[1]See Konstantinos Tsoukalas, *Exartisi kai anaparagogi. O koinonikos rolos tou ekpaideutikou michanismou stin Ellada, 1830–1922* (Dependence and reproduction. The social role of the educational system in Greece), Athens: Themelio, 1977.

[2]Jenny Masur, 'Emigration' in *Greece: A Country Study*, Washington, DC, 1986, pp. 104–6.

Left, Ioannis Kapodistrias (1776–1831), first President of independent Greece. *Below*, early 20th-century members of the Diplomatic Corps.

Facing page, far left, Harilaos Trikoupis (1832–96). *Left*, Eleni and Demetrios Stavropoulos, an Athenian couple of 1885. *Bottom*, Athens, mid–19th century.

Above right, the actor Dionysios Tavoularis representing Rhigas, 1890. *Right*, the heroic image of Greece: a '*palikari*' from Delphi, 1880.

Thessaloniki burning on the night of 18–19 August 1917.

Eleftherios Venizelos
(1864–1936).

Constantinos Cavafis
(1863–1933).

Above, ship crowded with refugees from Asia Minor, 1922.

Below, first refugee housing in Halkidiki, northern Greece.

Above, Ioannis Metaxas reviewing a 4 August parade.

Below, 29 October 1940: volunteers enlisting at a recruitment centre.

Above, Greek forces in the Middle East, 1943.
Facing page, 29 October 1940: crowds celebrating with Greek and British flags.
Below, ELAS resistance troops with German prisoners, 1943.

Above, Liberation Day, 1944 (church and state have often merged in public perception).

Below, UNRRA relief for a devastated Greece.

Omonia Square, Athens, in the 1950s.

Above, a Russian dancer performs in front of the Parthenon. "Nelly's" (Ellie Seraidaris, 1899–1998) won international repute for her pictures; this one caused mixed reactions.

Right, Maria Callas (1923–77).

Left, George Papandreou
(1888–1968) and his son
Andreas (1919–96).
Below, the departure of
King Constantine and
Queen Anne-Marie for
the United States in
1967, bidden farewell
by the triumvirate of
Colonels.

Constantine Karamanlis signs the treaty for Greek accession to the European Community, Athens, 28 May 1979.

doubt that a satisfactory explanation of the genesis of Greek–American entrepreneurialism requires serious consideration of the cultural variables unique to Greek society and economy at the turn of the century.'[3] Another idiosyncrasy that distinguished the Greeks from other immigrants in the United States was, according to Moskos, their assimilation into American civic associations, social cliques and business life before they were acculturated to the norms and customs of the new society. The discrepancy between this early assimilation and delayed acculturation may explain why a distinct ethnic identity has survived among the Greek-Americans.[4]

Between 1950 and 1975, another half-million Greeks migrated to Western Europe, mostly to West Germany as *Gastarbeiter* (guest workers). The term indicates that the German state was not interested in assimilating this borrowed labour force, and few Greeks became German citizens. Proximity and cheap travel encouraged most to return to Greece and settle in the urban centres as small businessmen.[5]

The number of Greeks residing permanently outside the boundaries of the Greek state is difficult to compute. Mixed marriages have led to significant portions of older diasporas, such as those of Russia and the United States, entering the melting-pot of their adopted countries. Americans of Greek ancestry appear in official US statistics for 1980 as 980,000, although Greek-American sources make the number as high as 1,250,000. According to Greek statistics, there are today about 600,000 Greeks in Western Europe, mostly in Germany. In the last Soviet census in 1989, 358,000 people declared their Greek background: 104,000 in Ukraine, 81,000 in Russia, 100,000 in Georgia, 50,000 in Kazakhstan, 7,500 in Uzbekistan and 7,400 in Armenia.

Of the post-Second World War migrations the most significant was to Australia, where today there are 422,000 Greeks, followed by Canada with 192,000. Illegal immigrants may increase these numbers by half. There are about 120,000 Greeks in Africa and 50,000 in Latin America, half in Brazil and 20,000 in Argentina. The once thriving communities of the Middle East have declined to only a few thousands, but there are close to 30,000 Greek Jews in Israel.[6]

---

[3]Charles C. Moskos, *Greek Americans: Struggle and Success,* New Brunswick, NJ: Transaction Publishers, 1989, p. 140.

[4]Moskos, pp. 147–9.

[5]Masur, pp. 108–9.

[6]Yannis Hassiotes, 'Apodemos Ellinismos' (Diaspora Greeks) in *Istoria tou Hellenikou Ethnous* (History of the Hellenic world), vol. 16, Athens: Ekdotiki Athinon, 2000, pp. 538–45.

10

OF HEROES AND HEROIC DEEDS

A nation creates its own heroes and regards heroic deeds in the light of the values and principles it holds in highest esteem. Why certain actions are given prominence and others are neglected and forgotten is the result more of chance than of design. However, even here one sees in men's actions the elements expected to win the approval and applause of the nation.

Two instances of conventional heroic behaviour are indicative of the selective approach in the assessment of actions as heroic. The first concerns army Lieutenant Pavlos Melas, who left military service to fight the Bulgarian bands in Macedonia. In the autumn of 1904, on his third and final incursion into what was then Ottoman Macedonia, he and his band of irregulars were forced to give battle against Turkish troops in the village of Siatista, where he died in action. A comrade severed his head and carried it away, so that it should not fall into enemy hands. By his death Melas moved the Greeks of his day as no other modern Greek hero has done.[1]

Nearly forty years later, artillery Major Versis, when ordered by the Germans to surrender the guns of his battery after the collapse of the front in April 1941, collected them together and ordered his men to salute them. He then shot himself as his men sang the Greek national anthem. So runs the brief record of this officer's death after a week's desperate fighting against the invading German army in Greek Macedonia. This document was found in the course of research by

[1] *Pavlos Melas,* pp. 191 ff., letters to his wife Natalia from his first secret journey in Macedonia in 1904.

one of the present authors, buried under heaps of military reports in the country's War Archives, and does not even mention his first name.[2]

What made Melas but not Versis a national hero? Both men died honourably for their country, fighting its enemies—the latter by his own hand so as not to witness the dishonour of the nation's vanquished arms. Both died in a way for which their profession had prepared them; yet Melas was immediately seen as representing the nation's highest values and principles, while Versis was relegated to oblivion.

The difference in the two men's posthumous reputations has to be explained by the manner in which each tried to serve the nation. Versis lived and died as a professional soldier, while Melas left regular service to fight and die in the manner of the traditional irregular fighter and hero, the Klepht. On crossing into Ottoman Macedonia in 1904, he discarded his officer's uniform and, putting on the Klephtic apparel, tried as best as he could to act according to what it represented. His men were either local freebooters or Cretans of similar pursuits, and their movements and actions fit those of the traditional band of local brigands. What was seized upon by the Greek public then, and secured Melas a place in the nation's pantheon, was not his tragic death itself but death out of regular service and in a manner befitting the traditional Greek folk hero, the *pallikar*. Up till the Balkan Wars of 1912–13, the regular army was seen as being only good for ceremonial purposes, while the nation's battles were fought, and its glories won, by its 'true' army—the irregulars, the lineal descendants of the *Akritai* (lone soldiers who patrolled the borders of the Eastern Roman empire) and the Klephts of Turkish times.

The process of identifying the post-Independence irregulars with the pre-revolutionary freebooters of the Greek highlands is discussed in another context, but we should examine the values with which these traditional heroes were invested. The Klephts and their lineal descendants were supposed to represent freedom from all attachments and bonds save those of religion and family. They were portrayed not as the hunted outlaws they actually were—men who lived in a limbo and wished to ease their way back to law-abiding society by humbling themselves before the authorities and asking for their mercy—but as proud and brave men who could not bear to see themselves and their countrymen groaning under a foreign yoke like so many beasts of burden. Thus they broke with the authorities and took

---

[2]John S. Koliopoulos, *Greece and the British Connection, 1935–1941*, Oxford: Clarendon Press, 1977, pp. 292–3.

to the mountains to fight against them. Highland Greece became in this way 'free Greece'. All affiliations outside the family and the association of free men were so many compromises incompatible with their chosen identity and role. Corporate loyalties outside the family, on which modern regular civil society rests, were resolutely discarded.

If post-Independence highland outlaws were the lineal successors of the pre-revolutionary bandits, their enemies—the regular state authorities—were not qualitatively different from the Ottoman authorities. King Otto and the Bavarians and all those who became associated with that regime's efforts to establish regular state services were dismissed as so many foreigners—alien to the Greek 'way' of life and enemies of the 'nation's interests'.

The ways and values of pallikarism made Kapodistrias, Mavrocordatos and Trikoupis, who were opposed to them, look out of place, and made their efforts to institute and strengthen permanent state services and encourage the growth of civil society appear as the work of foreign agents bent on depriving the nation of its cherished ways and values. It was under the influence of the same values and ways that a traitor to the Greek cause in the War of Independence like Odysseus Androutsos was allowed a place in the nation's pantheon, while such staunch supporters of that cause as the newspaper editor Georgios Psyllas and the lawyer Anastasios Polyzoides were not. Furthermore, the band of brigands who opened hostilities against the Turkish army in northern Thessaly in 1897 and were the first to retreat and disperse were lionised by the public, while the regular army was blamed for the humiliating defeat. Under the same influence the populists Kolettis, Deliyannis and Andreas Papandreou have in their time succeeded in presenting the reformers Mavrocordatos, Trikoupis and Karamanlis in a negative light while winning for themselves immense if transient popularity.

Thus the pallikarist syndrome which consigned Versis to oblivion has also been responsible for the recent elevation of resistance to the Axis occupation forces in 1941–4 as 'national resistance', and the defeated rebels against the legally constituted government in the Civil War of 1946–9 as so many wronged and innocent victims of that government, and national heroes. Events and issues involved in the clashes of the 1940s have come to be seen in the light of the values associated with the alleged Greek 'traditional' hero, the pallikar. Even Markos Vaphiades, the commander of the 'Democratic Army' in 1946–9 which fought for a cause that, if successful, would have deprived Greece of its northern provinces, was made a parliamentary deputy by Andreas Papandreou in the 1980s.

In analysing people's values that are anchored in the past one always runs the risk of losing track of later developments and changes, due to influences since the time these values were formed, that have either been ignored or are imperceptible. In the Greece of today there are no bands of armed irregulars, and the highlands have lost much of their population to the lowlands; but for the fleeting Albanian illegal immigrant in search of agricultural work and the stray tourist, highland Greece appears to have been totally abandoned by humanity. The Greek village, that repository of what city people like to think of as traditional customs and values, has ceased to exist except in the minds of some anthropologists. However, even as people gradually overcome the old attraction of the ways of the pallikars, a reluctance to redefine the qualities and deeds of heroes in the light of the nation's present requirements lingers on like an afterglow or a hangover. Living and surviving under arbitrary foreign rule indeed called for guile and favoured dishonesty *vis-à-vis* authority, but why should men who exhibited these 'qualities' in their own time still be considered heroes to be emulated today when other qualities are required for the growth of civic society under a democratically elected government? Would an honest taxpayer or civil servant not be a more fitting hero for society today than yesterday's bandit? On the other hand, admitting that such a hero lacks appeal would be tantamount to admitting that the values which inspire heroes are no longer considered worth cultivating in society today.

To return to the two heroic officers already discussed, would not the inclusion in the nation's pantheon of the major who chose to die as a regular officer, instead of the one who left the colours to lead a group of armed irregulars, signify a preference for values better suited to for a society resting on and respecting law and order? Future historians of modern Greece should certainly be in a better position than their counterparts today to discern changes in the nation's hero-making and to see shifts of emphasis not visible to us.

Rhigas Velestinlis (1757–98)

Rhigas entered Greek history like a shooting star: he shone brightly for a moment and disappeared. His death in the cause of Greece's freedom secured for him an unassailable position in the national pantheon before Clio had a chance to take an interest in his life. Patriotic lore supplied almost all of the information about his early life, which neither he himself nor the annals of the time recorded. Most Greeks did not hear of him till long after his death in Belgrade in June 1798; indeed, most of those who were informed of the event knew very little of the circumstances. Only what the Austrian authorities chose to make public became known: Rhigas and a number of accomplices, all Greek subjects of the Ottoman Sultan, were arrested in Trieste in December 1797, having set out from Vienna to start a rising in Greece against Turkish rule. After lengthy and tortuous interrogations in Trieste, where Rhigas tried without success to commit suicide, and in Vienna, the Austrian authorities handed him and seven associates over to the Turkish authorities in Belgrade, where they were all murdered and their bodies thrown into the Danube. It is worth noting that of the fourteen suspects arrested, the six who were Austrian subjects were banished to Saxony while their Ottoman confederates were extradited. Two noteworthy aspects of the affair are that there was no extradition treaty between Austria and the Ottoman empire, and that no suspect was ever put on trial before an Ottoman court of law.

The Austrian position on the affair was weak. If the eight Ottoman subjects were guilty of conspiring against the security of a friendly state, so too were the Austrian subjects; and if the latter were not to be tried and punished, that was an admission that the eight were handed over to the Turks not because they were more guilty than the six, but because they were Ottoman subjects and the Porte had demanded their extradition. The Austrians had good reasons for satisfying the Turkish demand: in addition to the prospect of recovering Polish deserters who had escaped to the Danubian Principalities, they expected to obtain freedom of navigation for ships flying the Austrian flag off the North African cost. The shock expressed by the Austrian authorities on hearing of Rhigas's execution without trial in Belgrade and before reaching Constantinople could not have been more hypocritical.

Rhigas was born in 1757 at a village in Thessaly called Velestino, the ancient Pherae, capital of the tyrant Jason. Rhigas (meaning king— *rex*) was not an uncommon name in Greece at that time, and Velestinlis was the name he assumed on leaving his native village. He attended school at Zagora, a prosperous trading village on Mt Pelion, and possibly in another equally wealthier village on Mt Ossa, Ampelakia, both near Velestino. That such an education was well beyond the means of most Greeks of the time supports the hypothesis that his father was one of the better-off peasants of the locality. Before leaving Thessaly and while still under twenty, Rhigas is said to have worked for a time as a village schoolmaster.

The young man left home and went to Constantinople, following the example of most promising and ambitious young men of his time, and thence to the Danubian Principalities, which seldom failed to attract them. Commerce was the main attraction, but secretarial work for a merchant was equally attractive to the educated youth of backward Greece. In the second half of the 1780s Rhigas was in Wallachia, first in the service of the hellenised Brancoveanu family and later as secretary to the newly-appointed Hospodar of Wallachia, Nicholas Mavrogenis. Later he became a functionary in Craiova, getting to know the Pasha of neighbouring Vidin, Osman Pasvanoglou.

Working under Mavrogenis during the Russo-Turkish war of 1787–92, when many Greeks in the Principalities were crossing over to the Russians, must have put Rhigas's abilities to the test in view of the Hospodar's loyalty to the Sultan. Rhigas also transferred his loyalties to the Sultan's enemies after the defeat of the Ottoman armies in 1788 and the occupation of Bucharest by the Russians. There was nothing to keep him in Bucharest, and he had no reason to accompany Mavrogenis across the Danube, to be beheaded at the Sultan's orders. He attached himself in 1790 to a new patron, an expatriate Austrian and local magnate of Wallachia called Christodoulos Kirlianos, probably of Greek descent, who played an equivocal role in the war and was rewarded by the Habsburg Emperor with the title Baron von Langenfeld. The news from France in 1789 put Rhigas in a restless frame of mind, but it was not easy to interpret from remote Wallachia. Vienna, whither he followed Kirlianos, was home to one of the most prosperous and cultured Greek colonies of the Habsburg empire, numbering some 40,000; it was also closer to the events in France. Rhigas was profoundly shaken by these events, but his appraisal of the Revolution was influenced by its assumed implications for Greece's freedom. However, it was unclear what those implications would be.

In Vienna, during the six months he lived there, Rhigas published two books which he had no doubt prepared in Bucharest: an 'Anthology of Physics' and a collection of French novelettes, entitled 'School of Delicate Lovers', both translated into demotic Greek and reflecting two aspects of his conception of education: the moral and the scientific. Patriotism is their overriding characteristic. While in Vienna he also announced the publication of a Greek translation of Montesquieu's *Esprit des Lois*—which, however, never appeared.

Rhigas returned to Bucharest in early 1791 after quarrelling with Kirlianos; the war was practically over, and the Russians had evacuated the Wallachian capital. He now owned extensive property in Wallachia, notably an estate in Vlaska, where he installed his mother and younger brother from Greece. However, he lived in Bucharest, the most attractive Balkan city of the time, among rich and powerful Greeks. Like many of them, he was involved in various commercial enterprises: he invested in pig breeding and became involved in the export of hides. At the same time he served the Phanariot rulers of Wallachia as secretary or interpreter, having mastered French, Italian and German in addition to Greek and Turkish. As secretary he occupied much more than a clerical position: he conducted his employer's correspondence, commercial as well as political. He also found time to read extensively in the classics, natural sciences, poetry, history and geography.

It was believed at the time, and has been suggested ever since, that before leaving for Vienna once again in 1796 Rhigas travelled widely in Central and Western Europe to establish the network of his associates, but that can not be assumed; it also seems unlikely that after 1786 he ever visited cities in the Ottoman empire such as Smyrna, Thessaloniki and Ioannina, let alone Constantinople. However, there were no limits to the contacts he could pursue and establish while in Bucharest, working through his wide network of friends, relations and associates in the course of his normal business. His circle included merchants, schoolmasters, academics, poets, publishers and diplomats. It included such men as Osman Pasvanoglou, but Rhigas's relations with him are impossible to disengage from legend. Other acquaintances were Daniel Philippides and Gregorios Photiades, and two prominent men of letters, Joseph Moisiodax and Demetrios Katartzis.

Back in Vienna after years of absence, Rhigas embarked on the publication of a number of works, including his famous 'Map of Hellas'. The Poulios brothers of Siatista, who since 1790 had published the Greek gazette *Ephemeris*, issued in 1797 Rhigas's 'The Moral Tripod', a trilogy of Italian, French and German poems and romantic tales in demotic Greek. He also published in the same year a translation of volume IV of Abbé Barthélemy's 'The Voyage of the Young Anacharsis' and a series of maps, one each of Moldavia and Wallachia, and, much more important, twelve maps of Greece—inspired perhaps by the collection of geographical books donated by Ioannis Pringos to the school he had attended at Zagora as a boy. Finally, he published the 'New Political Order' and the 'Military Manual', both of which were seized and destroyed by the Austrian authorities, but some copies of the 'New Political Order' consisting of the 'Rights of Man', the 'Constitution of the Hellenic Republic' and the '*Thourios*' or war hymn escaped destruction. The 'Rights' and the 'Constitution' were based on the French revolutionary prototypes. Rhigas is also assumed to have had a hand in the publication of a book quite far removed from his liberal tendencies, a religious homily with the title 'The Prophesies of Agathangelos'; one of these prophesies was that the Greeks would be liberated by a 'blond race of the East'.

Rhigas was carried away by unrealistic optimism when he assumed that his constitution would be operative at all, let alone serve as a charter for the Greeks of his time. Equally unrealistic were the military manual, which was intended for a well-drilled regular army, and his address to 'the people descended from the Hellenes', by which he could have meant all the subjects of the Sultan. These 'descendants' were expected to heed his call and aid the establishment of the 'Hellenic Republic'. Here lay the fundamental weakness of his emancipatory efforts: the nation he had in mind—the 'Greek nation' of his political works—was not a national community but a political one which, he believed, could be roused to action by a national call. He could not have been aware that the supranational community to which he appealed was on the verge of being broken up into as many national communities as there were linguistic communities in the Empire. Whereas his French model was designed for a unitary and homogeneous nation, the 'Hellenic Republic' would house different languages, creeds, histories and myths. His political community was defined by such inconsistent criteria as the Greek language, Eastern Orthodox Christianity, exceptional services to the fatherland or exceptional merit. He somehow believed that all ethnic and religious differences would be reconciled under the heading 'Hellas', but not even such an illustrious name could have been a solvent for historic feuds embedded deeply in the lives of the different religious and linguistic communities he wished to reconcile in his new state.

These were the weapons Rhigas had with him when he set out from Vienna to launch an uprising in Greece. Probably the Austrian authorities regarded him, with his publications and his well-known eccentricities, as no more than a publicist with an inflated opinion of Osman Pasvanoglou or Ali Pasha of Ioannina; from his own passing references to them and from other indirect evidence it appears that he did. Both Pasvanoglou and Ali Pasha might indeed have supported Rhigas if he had succeeded in launching a rising, but only to further their own designs; neither could have been expected to let his own pashalik become part of Rhigas's 'Hellenic Republic'. It seemed that fate had chosen to put the rulers of a mighty empire to the test using a forty-year-old merchant from Thessaly who dreamed of a Hellas restored with French revolutionary methods, which would house all the oppressed subjects of the Sultan.[3]

[3]C. Perrhaevos, *Syntomos biographia tou aoidimou Riga Pheraiou tou Thessalou* (A brief biography of the famous Rhigas Pheraios of Thessaly), Athens, 1860; E. Legrand, *Anekdota engrapha peri Riga Velestinli* (Unpublished papers about Rhigas Velestinlis), transl. by S. P. Lampros, Athens, 1891; L. I. Vranousis, *Rhigas Velestinlis, 1757–1798* (in Greek), Athens, 1953; C. M. Woodhouse, *Rhigas Velestinlis*, Limni, Euboia, 1995.

11

CRIME AND IMPUNITY

Punishment has always been one of the primary defences of organised society. However, in modern Greece, which emerged from a revolt against arbitrary rule and was founded on the principle of the rule of law, crime and law-breaking have not always been punished according to the law of the land. The long centuries of illegitimate and arbitrary rule before Independence, and recurrent authoritarian rule ever since, no doubt helped to develop an attitude to crime at odds with the state's founding principles, but this by itself cannot explain what can only be described as a surprising laxity in administering justice. Behind these factors—or, perhaps because of them—there seems to be a general tendency to treat unlawful activities in the public domain far less severely than similar ones within the family. Occasionally such unlawful actions are not only treated by the authorities with excessive leniency, but also meet with society's approval.

Brigandage and public attitudes towards it are a case in point,[1] but abuse of power by state authorities, though often ill-documented and impossible to prove, also falls into this category. The swift-footed rural outlaws of modern Greece normally eluded their pursuers, who seldom sought their quarry in earnest; they have also eluded most of those who have attempted to study them. Contemporary Greek writers set on shoring up 'ethnic' truth (the term used in *The Dilessi Murders* by Romilly Jenkins, who really meant 'national') with reference to the problem of brigandage in the nineteenth century, and on silencing well-deserved criticism, were the first hostages of the country's brigands,

[1]See Koliopoulos, *Brigands with a Cause,* pp. 105 ff.

and moreover willing ones. They not only saw the post-Independence rural outlaws as lineal successors of the pre-Independence Klephts, but discerned in their pursuits a national mission to liberate all unredeemed Greeks.[2] Twentieth-century Greek and foreign writers anxious to meet the requirements of neo-Marxist historiography became the unwitting victims of Greece's rural thugs by trying to discern in their pursuits a primitive social rebellion.[3] Edmond About's brigand hero, the mischievous King of the Mountains, would have ridiculed the efforts of both groups of writers to elevate him and his comrades on to a stage far above that on which they pursued their simple objectives in the Greek highlands.[4]

Brigands entered the scene with qualifications that allowed them to outlive their time and outgrow their role. Their predecessors in rural outlawry, the Klephts, took part in the War of Independence with as many reservations, calculations and objectives of their own as their erstwhile bosses, the local magnates. A number of them, including such powerful and influential chieftains as Odysseus Androutsos and Georgios Varnakiotis, surrendered to their former Turkish overlords not long after the outbreak of hostilities, and kept out of the fray or even joined the enemy side until the end of the war. Those who did fight for the Greek cause also fought among themselves for positions or financial advantage. The brave, such as Georgios Karaïskakis, often died in action.

However, most Klepht captains survived to give their own accounts of their participation in the war. Romantic writers, indigenous and

---

[2]See Romilly Jenkins, *The Dilessi Murders,* London, 1961. For an eloquent defence of Greece see [John Gennadios], *Notes on the Recent Murders by Brigands in Greece,* London, 1870.

[3]The theme of the 'social bandit' as developed by E. J. Hobsbawn in two of his works—*Primitive Rebels,* Manchester 1959, and *Bandits,* London 1969—was used to describe pre-Independence Klephts and Armatoles by Spyros Asdrachas in 'Quelques aspects du banditisme social en Grèce au XVIII siècle', *Etudes Balkaniques,* VIII (1972), no. 4, pp. 97–112. For a less refined and rather facile analysis of the Klephts and the Armatoles along these lines, see Georgios D. Kontogiorgis, *I helladiki laiki ideologia* (Helladic popular ideology), Athens, 1979. For subsequent 'victims' of the Greek peasant outlaws see Stathis Damianakos, 'Banditism social et imaginaire pastoral en Grèce (XIXème—début XXème siècle)', *Études Rurales,* nos 97–9, pp. 219–40, and *Paradosi antarsias kai laikos politismos* (A tradition of rebellion and popular culture), Athens, 1987; and Riki van Boeschoten, *From Armatolik to People's Rule: Investigation into the Collective Memory of Rural Greece, 1750–1949,* Amsterdam, 1991.

[4]Edmond About, *Le roi des montagnes,* Paris 1853. See also the same author's *La Grèce contemporaine,* Paris 1854. About was Director of the French Archaeological School in Athens and a keen observer of Greek public life.

foreign, embellished these accounts, investing them with all the heroism and valour the country required to create its heroes. Theodoros Kolokotronis, the Moreot Klepht and famous warlord of the Revolution, found a superb story-teller in his war secretary Photakos Chrysanthopoulos.[5] Fact and fiction were mixed by another fine story-teller, Ambrosios Frantzis, to produce a history of the revolutionary war that represented Kolokotronis and the other captains as the dominant figures behind both the outbreak and the successful inclusion of the revolution[6] so much so indeed that a proud Moreot notable, Kanellos Deliyannis, whose family had employed many of the captains as its armed retainers before the war, felt obliged to complain to these authors of the grossly exaggerated role given to the captains in the accounts they had published.

The collections of Greek folk ballads published in Western Europe, and known since then as 'Klepthtic ballads', further enhanced the role of the Klephts as the nation's pre-war and war heroes. After the war 'Klephtic' ballads eulogising the deeds of established captains such as Kolokotronis were produced on demand. Most these came to be known among students of the genre as fakes, but this in no way affected the fame of the heroes they celebrated.[7] These songs extolled the deeds, real or fictitious, not of hunted robbers, who seldom survived long enough to perform the deeds that inspired the ballads, but of powerful captains or Armatoles in the service of local Turkish administrators, responsible for the security of communications over mountain passes. Post-war ballads praising captains who rose to fame in the War of Independence are similar. The ones praising the deeds or, more often, mourning the death of notorious brigands were well-known klephtic ballads adapted to the particular occasion.

Identifying pre-Independence Klephts with post-Independence robbers was unavoidable: both robbed vulnerable peasants and abducted wealthier people for ransom. It was also unavoidable that the sensation caused by a brigand's death should result in a song bewailing that death: peasants sang praises or mourned a violent death—not of some-

---

[5]Photakos (Photios Chrysanthopoulos), *Apomnimonevmata peri tis Hellenikis Epanastaseos* (Memoirs on the Greek Revolution), ed. by S. Andropoulos, Athens, 1899, 2 vols.

[6]Ambrosios Frantzis, *Epitomi tis historias tis Anagennitheisis Hellados* (Short history of regenerated Greece), Athens, 1839–41, 4 vols.

[7]For an authoritative analysis of the subject see Alexis Politis, *I anakalypsi ton hellenikon demotikon tragoudion* (The discovery of the Greek folk songs), Athens, 1984, as well as the same author's introduction to a collection of Klephtic ballads, Athens, 1973.

one who had robbed them, but of a young man whose life had been cut short by the agents of outside forces. However, it was strange that this identification on the part of peasants with the deeds of common robbers and the mourning of their violent deaths should also have an appeal to urban society.

Crime has always fascinated people, but in modern Greece brigandage exercises a different kind of fascination because of its association with qualities and objectives that differentiate it from other common crimes. Association with the pre-Independence Klephts gave brigands a measure of reluctant admiration, but the brigands' irredentist forays into Turkish-held Thessaly, Epirus and Macedonia made this admiration unreserved. As explained elsewhere, inability to use the regular army to promote the country's irredentist aims (because of the refusal by Greece's protecting powers to allow the dismemberment of the Ottoman empire) made the employment of brigands to incite revolt in the lands claimed by Greece an attractive possibility. The Greek authorities, while exporting lawlessness across the frontier, sustained the belief at home that the aim of liberating the unredeemed Greeks had not been abandoned. The press incited action across the frontier every time a crisis broke out in the Near East, and the authorities did all they could to satisfy public opinion. Brigands were released from prison in 1854 to take part in just such an engineered insurrection across the frontier in Thessaly and Epirus. Brigands were also conscripted twice subsequently—in 1878 in the same regions and in 1896–7 in Macedonia. In 1868 brigands were shipped to Crete to give a hand in the liberation of the island. On each occasion army officers facilitated the employment of these outlaws when they did not actually lead them in person; the authorities looked the other way and, as expected, denied any knowledge of such covert dealings.[8]

By the time of the struggle to displace Bulgarian agents and armed bands from the part of Macedonia claimed by Greece during the first years of the twentieth century, brigands acting as irregulars in the service of the nation's irredentist struggles were well entrenched in public esteem. Their employment and registration on the payrolls of army officers leading bands in the region appeared to all the sides that financed the struggle as integral national policy. Some officials resented the use of such means, believing that it undermined the credibility of the struggle and discredited their own motives, but

[8]Koliopoulos, *Brigands with a Cause*, pp. 145–6, 182–4, 200 ff.

these were an insignificant minority. The average official considered the employment of brigands not marely as a means to an end but almost as an end in itself.[9] The public, unintentionally but unavoidably, were educated to see in brigandage a constant feature of life: people complained only when they or their kin suffered its effects directly.

Similarly, abuse of public office for personal ends, though condemned in principle as morally reprehensible, has been pursued with determination and some pride—to the extent that, along with tax evasion, it should be ranked as one of the nation's most consistent pursuits. From gendarmes and soldiers extorting from peasants what little brigands had not taken already, to officers using their subordinates as domestic servants, and tax officials letting tax-evaders escape on payment of a fee—such acts were part of one of the country's most enduring traditions. Like banditry, abuse of public office for personal enrichment has seldom been punished, if at all, as severely as the law allows. Even when superiors are not prepared to show the expected understanding and leniency and take the culprit off the hook, politics has normally provided miscreants with a protective net. Again, as with banditry, arbitrary foreign rule in the past cannot possibly explain adequately the persistence of the habit of abusing office or the tendency to leave such abuses unpunished. A more satisfactory explanation should rather be sought in the way the public domain is organised, in the relations between individuals as citizens in this domain, and in their attitude towards the rule of law.

The rule of law and the institutions on which it rests were the primary objectives of modern Greece's founding fathers, but they have not developed as expected, perhaps because those who cared for them were too few and too weak to ensure their natural growth. The recipe was proper and tried, but the enzyme was in too short supply to raise the various groups of the country to the level of civic consciousness necessary to generate a self-sustained consensus on the basic principles. Confidence in the rule of law as the supreme and just guarantor of one's interests did not grow to the point of becoming the unassailable foundation for a civil society. Neither arbitrary rule from outside in the distant past, nor periodic lapses into authoritarianism at home, can convincingly explain this persistent lack of confidence in the rule of law, of which impunity for criminals is only one indication of a civil society stunted before it had a chance to mature.

[9] *Ibid.*, pp. 220 ff.

Part V. IDEOLOGY

12

SHAPING THE NEW NATION

'The present-day Greek', wrote the editor of a newspaper in insurgent Greece, 'is not reborn, as is commonly believed; he is born. He is the child of a famous and proud father, possesses the same features and constitution, the same functions, almost the same intellectual powers; in short, he is the living image of the father, a lion's cub. To grow and become like his father, he must have the same upbringing, the same conditions, those at least which are in accord with the spirit of the present century.'[1]

The notion of a new-born nation is a convenient starting-point for examining contemporary approaches to the identity of the Christian inhabitants of Greece who had revolted against the authority of the Sultan. The major themes here can be expressed in terms like *ethnos* (nation) and *genos* (stock), as well as the idea of the necessary space, referred to as *epikrateia* (realm), for the new nation-state. The true meaning of the term *ethnos* in insurgent Greece is elusive and more often than not misleading; it was frequently used in the sense of defining the Orthodox Christians, irrespective of their mother-tongue, or as a synonym for *genos* or for the nation-state. Religion and residence, as well as language and 'descent', were used in various combinations to define the identity of members of the insurgent nation. So too was active participation in the struggle against the Sultan.

Religion was one determinant on which everyone agreed, while residence was accepted only to determine citizenship. Language was grudgingly conceded for spreading Greek education to all Orthodox

[1] *Geniki Ephemeris tis Hellados,* 20 Feb. 1826.

227

subjects. One aspect of the early debates on defining the 'newly-born' nation was the lack of consensus on any combination of criteria. Two conflicting trends, 'modern' and 'traditional', clashed over the suitable criteria for defining the new nation and the identity of its members; the former favoured language while the latter insisted on religion. Eventually religion prevailed as the dominant criterion for defining the modern Greek nation, marking the beginning of irredentism. This was one of the most important and painful adventures in the history of modern Greece; it determined Greek national identity and has had a tremendous impact on relations with other Balkan peoples.

A related theme in the process of crafting the Greek nation was the belief in a 'mission'. As trustees of a great civilisation, but debased as they had been by servitude under barbaric rule, the Greeks were destined to civilise the East after first purifying themselves. Chastened by God 'for the dissensions of their rulers and the ensuing fratricidal strife', they were the 'chosen people', the 'new Israel', 'the first-born people of the Gospel', abandoned by the Christian peoples of Europe because of their government's policies. In 1825, after the destruction and suffering caused by the invading armies of Ibrahim Pasha in the Peloponnese, references to 'punishment' and 'abandonment' multiplied. Ibrahim was a scourge sent by God to facilitate the process of chastisement and purification, which had begun with the outbreak of hostilities in 1821. Thus purified in a 'bath of blood and tears', the Greeks would win a secure place among the civilised nations of Europe.[2]

The theme of joining the civilised nations of the European family was central for the Greeks to fulfilling their mission. 'The Greek people', proclaimed the president of the Third National Assembly in 1826, by 'taking up arms, did not break an oath of submission which, like a slave taken at the point of a spear [*doryalotos doulos*], they had never really given to the Sultan and which the Sultan, as an overlord ruling without consent, had never thought of demanding.' In another proclamation of the same Assembly it was maintained that the Greeks 'had been subjugated by force at the point of a sword. Never had they been asked by the Turks to pledge allegiance, never had they recognised their ruler, never had they sworn an oath to him, nor had they even invoked his name when taking an oath, because as Christians they possessed neither natural nor political rights.' The Greeks were the

---

[2]*Ibid.*, 22 Oct. 1827. Spyridon Trikoupis in a speech on the Battle of Navarino. See also *Salpinx Helleniki*, 5 Aug. 1821.

'remnants of a nation [which], though conquered and subjugated, had never really been incorporated into the Ottoman polity'. They were not rebels against a legitimate monarch, but were fighting against an illegitimate ruler to regain their kingdom from the Turks, who were merely 'encamped' in Europe.[3]

Also central to these early efforts to define the new nation and its 'mission' was the theme of a rightful and fitting 'realm'. The Greeks were called upon by Providence to 'redeem' the unredeemed brethren of 'Thessaly', 'Epirus', 'Macedonia', 'Bulgaria', 'Thrace' and all the Sultan's other 'Greek dominions', in both Europe and Asia. At the same time, they were called upon to 'enlighten' all these lands, which had been brutalised by long servitude while acting as a 'beacon' of light in the East.[4]

The declared self-confidence of insurgent Greece and the kingdom that emerged from it annoyed the West European powers more than it gratified them. This attitude was less the result of the unprecedented flattery heaped upon the insurgent Greeks by Western liberals and more the product of the deeply-felt duty of an elect and privileged people—as they perceived themselves—to deliver their brethren from tyranny and spread Western civilisation to the East. Here lay the root of so much disappointment suffered by the Greeks because of the refusal by the West to recognise such a role for them.

However, the Greeks had themselves to blame for the poor reception the West gave to their aspirations in the Near East which, in addition to being over-ambitious and unrealistic, were untenable because they rested on premises which most of their non-Greek-speaking fellow-Orthodox rejected as presumptuous and inimical to their

[3]*Hellenika Chronika*, 13 Feb. 1824 and May 1825; *Geniki Ephemeris*, 21 Apr. 1826 and 14 May 1827; Ioannis Philimon, *Dokimion peri tis Philikis Hetaereias* (Essay on the Society of Friends), Nauplion, 1834, p. 137; and the same author's *Dokimion historikon peri tis Hellenikis Epanastaseos* (Historical essay on the Greek Revolution), Athens, 1859, vol. IV, p. 3; Nikolaos Speliades, *Apomnimonevmata* (Memoirs), ed. by P. Christopoulos, Athens 1975, vol. II, p. 555; *Historikon Archeion Roma* (Romas Historical Archive), ed. by G. Kambouroglou, Athens, 1906, vol. II, pp. 146–7, 186–7; Adamantios Koraes, *Salpisma polemisterion* (War bugle), 2nd edn, Peloponnese, 1821 (reissue of 1801 edn published in Alexandria), p. 26.

[4]*Hellenika Chronika*, 23 Feb. 1824; *Geniki Ephemeris*, 6 Mar. and 10 Apr. 1826, 3 Sep. 1827; *Historikon Archeion Alexandrou Mavrokordatou* (Alexandros Mavrokordatos Historical Archive), ed. by E. G. Protopsaltis, vol. IV, Athens, 1974, pp. 59–60, 615; Adamantios Koraes, *Ti sympherei eis tin eleutheromenin apo tous Tourkous Hellada ... Dialogos dyo Graekon deuteros* (What is in the interest of Greece liberated from the Turks ... Second dialogue of two Greeks), Paris 1831, pp. 37–8.

own interests. Not all these *heteroglossoi* brethren of the Greeks, whom the founding fathers had assumed to be eager candidates for admission to the Greek nation-state, were willing to be incorporated. The position put forward in the national assemblies of insurgent Greece was that the domain of the new state would consist of imperial provinces, and these would take up arms against Ottoman rule.[5] Instead of placing Greek aspirations in the context of revolutionary policy, this plan of action, implying claims over all Ottoman territories inhabited by Orthodox Christians, created the impression of a new imperium in the making.

The all-encompassing and elusive notion of the Greek nation's domain nurtured the theory of the 'indivisibility' and 'unity' of the Greeks in time and space. This in turn favoured not language but culture as the chief determinant of modern Greek identity. Intimations of what was to come were discernible in unexpected quarters. Koraes's *Palaea Hellas* (Old Greece) as the nucleus of the future Greek state and the 'parts of Greece not yet freed'[6] was one such intimation. This 'Old Greece' represented only a small fraction of Greece, and in spite of having been liberated, it could easily have fallen back into slavery while the rest of the country remained subjugated.

This 'exterior Greece' remained an elusive notion because of imperfect knowledge of geography and conflicting views on the criteria for defining the new nation and its domain. Using language as the main determinant, representatives of the Enlightenment such as Athanasios Psalidas were reluctant to include in it the outer reaches of 'Greece', especially those in the north which had been 'de-hellenised' in terms of language and education during the centuries of foreign invasion and settlement. But although language had declined as a key factor of identity when the remnants of the Enlightenment were overshadowed by Romanticism, it was never really abandoned. The Greek nation-builders therefore launched and sustained an extensive school programme within 'exterior' Greece in order to re-claim it for the nation.

Were the Greeks arrogant to claim such a 'mission'? In the sense that the their claims rested not only on a generally admired heritage but on achievements in commerce and education that were recognised and admired in the Orthodox East, they presumed no more than their Balkan Orthodox brethren seemed to accept at the time. Before

[5] *Geniki Ephemeris,* 3 Sep. 1827.
[6] *Ephemeris ton Athenon,* 22 Oct. 1824, letter from Koraes to Odysseus Androutsos.

the challenge from the Bulgars took shape in the last quarter of the nineteenth century, the Greeks had reason to believe that they were best qualified to lead all their Christian brethren in the Balkans and Asia Minor and to inherit from the Ottoman Turks what they considered traditional Greek lands.

Perhaps most significant for the growth of a modern national identity and ideology, this initial conviction became an integral part of the independent Greek state's national ideology and policy in what came to be known as the 'Great Idea' (*Megali Idea*), which projected this state as the protagonist of Greek fortunes. Eventually the Greek nation–state secured unchallenged supremacy in the ideological restructuring of the traditional Greek world outside the state's boundaries, and succeeded in forcing the Ecumenical Patriarchate to relinquish its leading role throughout that world.

However, before this ideological imperium was established, the Greek nation–state first had to develop out of the various ideas put forward in insurgent Greece a coherent ideology and a credible identity that would correspond to the new realities. Religious differentiation from the Turks was no longer sufficient. It was essential, above all, to define modern Greek identity in relation to the other Orthodox peoples in the Balkans who had claims to the same lands. These 'others'—the Bulgars, the Albanians and the Vlachs—are discussed separately. But what was the relation of the Greeks to these people, and who were Greeks?

The name 'Hellenes' chosen for these Greeks was appropriate and perhaps unavoidable in view of the early and strong identification

---

The Great Idea

This term was used during a Greek parliamentary debate in 1844 to describe Greece's post-Independence irredentist aspirations. Since over three-quarters of Greeks at the time lived outside the borders of the Hellenic kingdom, it became the policy of most governments to unite and incorporate all territories which were home to unredeemed Greeks. In 1864 the Ionian Islands became part of the Greek state.

Thessaly and a section of Epirus followed in 1881. During the Balkan Wars and the First World War Greece reached its present size, with the exception of the Dodecanese ceded to it under the 1947 Paris treaty. The Great Idea expired in 1922 after the Asia Minor disaster. Since that time Greece has upheld the territorial *status quo* in the Balkans and the Aegean.

with ancient Hellas. '*Graecoi*' was also recommended as a conscious departure from '*Romaioi*' or '*Romioi*', terms still used in insurgent Greece but too closely identified with the nation's history of subjugation to the Ottomans. *Graecoi* was also favoured as being in accord with Western usage.[7] Finally 'Hellenes' prevailed because it was thought best for the 'descendants' of the ancient Greeks, but it undermined the potential appeal of the modern Greeks to their fellow-Orthodox in the Sultan's dominions, whose recorded cultural antecedents did not extend as far back as those of the people living in the Greek peninsula. This departure from tradition, reflecting the conscious effort to resurrect the classical past in as many ways as possible, together with the ungracious rupture with the Ecumenical Patriarchate, not only destroyed the vision of a Greek cultural imperium over the other Orthodox Christians of the East, but at the same time created a rift between popular culture and the new state culture.

How could the Greeks present themselves credibly as leaders of all the Eastern Orthodox when their choice of name placed language at the centre of national identity and made it the major determinant of that identity, if not the only one? Was language, even one as highly esteemed as Greek appeared to be at the time among non-Greek-speaking fellow-Orthodox, an adequate instrument by itself for establishing the new Greek empire? Were all the declarations that the insurgents had been fighting for—'the faith and the Cross' and the establishment of a 'Christian nation'—intended merely to deceive those who had been suspicious of Greek aims?

These were legitimate questions for non-Greek-speaking Orthodox Christians of the Ottoman empire to ask and for the Greeks at that time and subsequently to answer. The crux of the matter was: how could the Greeks possibly aspire to build a Western nation-state, with their own language as its primary determinant of identity, while at the same time aspiring to incorporate and accommodate the non-Greek-speaking Orthodox Christians in it as their equals? For more than fifty years no one had any particular cause to ask this question

[7]*Ephemeris ton Athenon*, 3 Aug. 1825; *Archeion Hydras* (Hydra Archive), ed. by A. Lignos, vol. VII, Piraeus 1934, pp. 312–13, 343; *Romas Archive*, vol. I, pp. 213, 765; Philimon, *Greek Revolution*, vol. IV, pp. 376, 377; Emmanouil Xanthos, *Apomnimonevmata peri tis Philikis Hetaerias* (Memoirs of the Association of Friends), Athens 1845, p. 188; Nikolaos Kasomoulis, *Enthymimata stratiotika tis Epanastasteos ton Hellenon 1821–1833* (Military reminiscences of the Revolution of the Greeks, 1821–33), ed. by G. Vlachogiannis, vol. I, Athens, 1939, p. 294.

or try to answer it. Albanian-speaking Suliots and Hydriots, Vlach-speaking Thessalians and Epirots, and Slav-speaking Macedonians had fought in insurgent Greece along with the other Greeks, and no one at the time had thought any of these non-Greek speakers less Greek than the Greek-speakers. When most of the northern Greek fighters settled in southern Greece as refugees, none of them thought, or was made to think, of himself as less of a Greek for speaking little or nothing of the language, notwithstanding the ongoing debate on Greekness and Greek identity. Essentially this question was never asked until the Greeks met the Bulgarians in the north as competitors, and even then the issue was circumvented by superimposing 'sentiments' or 'consciousness' on top of language.

However, the vision of a Greek Christian empire was no longer a driving force behind the objectives and actions of those holding power in the 'model' kingdom: at best it was a harmless hangover, at worst a show put on for the benefit of the masses who were still fascinated by that vision. The protagonists of the 'first' Greek war of liberation were now comfortably established as senators and ambassadors, and their sons were manning the services and were well on the way to endowing the country with an indigenous but Westernised intelligentsia. This generation of Greeks gave the nation a truly modern theory of Greek history and nationality. Building on existing scholarship and working in the changed atmosphere of the 1850s and '60s, Spyridon Zambelios and, especially, the country's foremost historian Konstantinos Paparrigopoulos were able to build a historical edifice that survived the onslaughts of many subsequent historiographers, and, when not distorted or misinterpreted, has served the rebuilding of the nation as no other theory has.[8]

Some of the major and lasting contributions of this historiographical school have been the reinstatement of Byzantium in the history of Eastern Christendom and of the Greek nation, the establishment of the cultural continuity of the Greek nation in time and space, and the convincing promotion of the modern Greek nation as a cultural community consisting of all the linguistic groups and peoples that it has incorporated in its long history from antiquity to modern times. All these three concepts reaffirmed the contemporary opinion that culture is the primary determinant of modern Greek

---

[8]The best account of the subject is that of Konstantinos Th. Dimaras, *K. Paparrigopoulos* (in Greek), Athens, 1986.

national identity, and placed that identity on what then appeared a safe and unshakeable course of national development.

Paparrigopoulos's concept of Greek history and the modern nation provided the main arguments in support of Greek claims to the Sultan's European and Asian dominions. It also strengthened the conviction of the generations of Greeks who confronted the Turks and the Bulgarians in the period between the Congress of Berlin (1878) and the Treaty of Lausanne (1923) that the Greek cause rested on solid historical and moral foundations. Later developments—particularly the insecurity associated with long and vulnerable borders, and the presence of minorities claimed by neighbours as their brethren—derailed these concepts and arguments from their original cultural tracks. The Greeks of the interwar period were led to believe that all inhabitants of Greece were, or ought to have been, Greek not only in sentiment due to sharing the same culture, but also in speech. Greek national ideology and assumptions about the Greek nation were led, under the influence of the threat from Bulgaria and international Communism, into a narrow path which did not allow for differences in language. The broad and all-embracing approach to national identity in the nineteenth century, which did not distinguish Albanian-, Vlach-, Slav- or Turkish-speakers from the dominant Greek-speaking component, had given way to the narrowest possible interpretation of modern Greek identity. Before setling down to the more modern approach, which defines the Greek nation as a cultural community embracing all the linguistic groups that have been incorporated and absorbed throughout its history, official Greece would look askance at what had come to be considered manifestations dangerous to the homogeneous nation. The Greeks of course did not invent assimilation, nor did they remain attached to such national visions longer than others in the West. Suppression of Slav Macedonian speech in Greece came much later than the ordeal of 'others' in the West, such as the Huguenots, Moriscos, Irish, Basques, Jews and Gypsies.

A disgruntled group of intellectuals, including Ion Dragoumis, who idealised a fictitious pre-Independence past, turned their backs on the Greek kingdom as the 'beacon' of the West in the East and searched in that past for guidance in reconstructing the Greek nation. This was only a subtle shift from the traditional position on the Greek nation, but it cast doubt on the Western liberal tradition as the proper basis for the nation. The fact that he met a violent death before the rise of fascism perhaps saved Dragoumis from seeing his ideas seized upon by the theorists of the Metaxas dictatorship of the 1930s. Greek nationalism under Metaxas generated the concept of the 'homogeneous and compact' nation described in a 1939 pamphlet for the country's youth. This 'compact' nation, kept together by 'physical, biological, psychological and historical bonds', became the ideological caricature of Paparrigopoulos's ideas.[9]

[9]See works by Ion Dragoumis: *O Hellenismos mou kai oi Hellenes, 1903–1909— Hellenikos politismos, 1913* (My Hellenism and the Greeks, 1903–1909: Hellenic civilisation, 1913], ed. by Philippos Dragoumis, Athens 1927; *Osoi zontanoi* [Those alive.), Athens, 1911, *Martyron kai heroon haema* (Blood of martyrs and heroes), 6th edn, Athens, 1973; and *Samothraki* (Samothrace), Athens, 1975 (reissue of 2nd edn of 1926). See also vol. IV of his *Phylla hemerologiou* (Journal leaves), ed. by Thanos Veremis and John S. Koliopoulos, Athens, 1985. Unfortunately there is no adequate study of Dragoumis, perhaps one of the most overestimated Greek men of letters. For the 'Fourth of August' fascist approach to the subject see E.O.N., *Ethnos* (Nation), Athens: E.O.N. Publications, 1939, p. 3.

13

DEMARCATING THE PAST

The 1992–4 crisis concerning the Macedonian Question showed that in Greece certain old ideas die hard, and that even when they seem to be dead and gone they reappear in various guises. One such idea is of a past that belongs by exclusive right to the modern Greeks alone. This past was never really felt to be coveted by others till recently, when it was suddenly thought to be in imminent danger. The Slavs of former Yugoslav Macedonia, after probing Macedonia's ancient Greek heritage for almost fifty years, finally adopted it completely—that, at least, was how it was seen in Greece.

The reaction of the Greeks to those they deemed northern inter-lopers has been to exclude them not only from territory claimed to be Greek by ancestral right, but from the history of that territory. The appropriation of certain aspects of the Greek past of Macedonia by the Slav Macedonians in the new state that came out of former Yugoslavia was greeted by demands for a 'demarcation' of the past and the cultural heritage associated with it, and of charges of 'misappropriation' of certain aspects of that cultural heritage. The arguments used to support these demands are, first, that these aspects of Greek antiquity, such as the name Macedonia, are the monopoly of today's Greeks by virtue of their ancestry and, secondly, that the use of the name poses a serious threat to Greek security, because the assumed—and thinly disguised—real intention behind it is to incorporate the whole of Macedonia, including Greek Macedonia, into the new Macedonian state.

The charge that this state harbours hostile intentions *vis-à-vis* Greek territorial integrity is impossible to refute. Irredentist claims against

Greek Macedonia form an integral part of its national ideology; they are at the core of the national identity of Greece's northern neighbour, and have been cultivated by its ruling élites since shortly after the Second World War. Most foreign onlookers argue that this threat, though distant, cannot be dismissed even if it is voiced by a state too small, compared to Greece, ever to implement it. Greece too was small and powerless in the nineteenth century compared to the mighty Ottoman empire and yet made a sizeable contribution towards dismembering it. What is at issue here is not politics, which has to come to terms will all kinds of uncertainties, but the exclusive claim to part of the past and the cultural heritage of Macedonia.

'Demarcation' means separation and limitation, and the intention of those who proposed it was to prevent the new state from trespassing on the cultural preserve and classical past of modern Greece. Behind all this lies the assumption that late-comers such as the former Yugoslav Republic of Macedonia cannot credibly lay claim to the cultural aspects of a heritage it only recently discovered, in the manner of the tenuous claim of one moving into another man's private home and eventually usurping not only the entire area but also its past. But a country is not a house, nor can peoples moving into that land be compared to owners or tenants. In the case of Macedonia the latecomers—namely the Slavs—moved into the territory in the sixth century AD, not as temporary sojourners but as fellow-occupants of the land, sharing it with its original inhabitants. They brought to that land their cultural contribution and received from others cultural influences they made their own. Such linguistic and other cultural traits they assimilated from those who lived there before them, as well as from others that came after them, bear witness to the fact that Slavs did not live in a cultural ghetto in Macedonia. They certainly lived side by side in a give-and-take relationship with all the other inhabitants of the area.

In the nineteenth century, when the provinces of the Ottoman Sultan that came to be known as Macedonia were claimed by the Greeks, the Sultan's non-Greek-speaking Christian subjects were never differentiated from the Greek-speakers on the basis of culture. Indeed, they were all considered as so many Greeks who had been denied the benefits of Greek education. The Slavs of Macedonia were seen as neither Bulgars nor Serbs, but simply as somewhat backward Christian brethren who had either 'un-learned' their Greek tongue or were in the process of hellenisation. In neither case were they strangers to Greece, and no Greek would ever think of denying them the right to that culture. The Greeks of the time did not see similar threats to their ancient cultural heritage. Indeed, it seems that they took a certain pride in the attraction of their culture to many non-Greek-speaking subjects of the Sultan.

So what happened to that self-confidence of 'little' Greece in the nineteenth century? What, in subsequent developments, caused the growth of the deep-seated insecurity displayed by the larger and more prosperous 'European' Greece? Was it their perceived enlightening mission as the 'chosen people' that made the Greeks of the nineteenth century feel and act in a manner that exuded confidence in their place and role in the Balkans? And is it the absence of a new mission, sensed by Greeks having lived in their traditional habitat for more than a century, that makes them regard their neighbours as scheming agents of conspiring foreign powers, intent on robbing them of both their land and their past simply by adoping the name 'Macedonia' for their nation?

Greece's inability to adjust to contemporary notions of nation and of people's identities has served it ill. Furthermore its intelligentsia, attached to the public purse as never before, have failed to produce original ideas and free their thinking from partisan shackles. It is ironic that, at a time when the country is experiencing unprecedented freedom of expression, so little use is made of it to rethink, redefine, review and revise traditional doctrines. Since the beginning of the 1980s university scholarship, which might have contributed such original ideas, has been unprecedentdly regimented by political mandarins, who owe their promotion to political parties and have been 'democratically' elected by the so-called 'academic community'. The press, on the other hand, which in the past was never short of new ideas, is now often run by barons who have one hand deep in the public p.irse while they keep the country's political leadership in a stranglehold with the other. The Church, finally, has never been so servile to the obsolete 'national' truths of yesteryear, with the result that the nation can expect no guidance from that quarter either.

Caught on the one side between the nationalists who considered any form of compromise over the name of former Yugoslav Macedonia treasonable and, on the otherside, foreign critics who had simply lost patience with the Greek government and were not prepared to take into consideration even its legitimate security concerns over the new name Macedonia, proponents of compromise have adopted the idea of 'demarcating' Macedonia's cultural heritage. The assumption is that the new state will eventually be persuaded to discard from its national ideology and history all cultural aspects that could identify it with the pre-Slav past of Macedonia. With the Greek past of the land thus safeguarded from Slav inroads, Greece could then be expected to welcome the new country as a good neighbour and even assist it against its Slav and non-Slav neighbours who do not disguise their wish to see part of it, or even the entire country, incorporated into their territory, while at the same time claiming certain sections of its population as their brethren. It is thus highly ironic that Greece, which has no claim either to the republic's land or its people, chose to start a quarrel with it over this issue which resulted in Greece being driven into a corner and turning European public opinion against its government and sometimes even against Greeks in general.

What the proponents of the 'demarcation' of Macedonia's cultural heritage fail to say is how the two neighbours, after dealing with its distant past, are to go about demarcating its recent past. This will certainly prove difficult, because it will eventually come up against the crux of the matter, namely the Slav Macedonians of Greece (mostly abroad) and their identity, which will prove a hard nut to crack. To tackle this controversial issue both sides will have to go about re-writing much of the history of Macedonia of the last century, because what each side considers this to be historical fact is actually each party's *national* version.

Drawing lines and limits on Macedonia's past and dividing its heroes and myths will doubtless prove an impossible task, basically because it is extremely difficult to divide a shared past and heroes of divided or undefined loyalties and identities. It should be particularly difficult, for instance, to decide what kind of state the Slav Macedonians who took part in the Greek War of Independence had in mind. They certainly did not join the struggle for a Greek national state like the one that emerged from it, because they fought as Christians, not as Hellenes. The Greeks of the new kingdom—and of today—would never accept that their state was not what most non-Greek-speaking Christians had had in mind when they took arms against the Turks. The Greeks almost certainly did not fight in 1821 for a Turkish-speaking Christian state, although Turkish was the *lingua franca* in the lands that took up arms against the Turks. Undoubtedly they did not fight for a Slav Macedonian or even a Balkan state, as is often asserted. Most likely, they, like the non-Greek-speaking Christians who fought along with the rest, did fight for a state under Greek leadership, but a leadership more like what they already knew from living together, and not like what developed soon after liberation:

'hellenically' nationalistic, even though a Greek education was admired and valued.

It should be even more difficult to decide on the objectives of more recent Slav Macedonian heroes like Kotas, whom the Greek side claims as one of its own national heroes and the Slav Macedonians consider as no more than a predatory local chieftain. His joining first the IMRO side and then the Greek side should not be regarded as proof that he was only pursuing the material benefits that a chieftain of his type might expect from joining such a cause. In both cases, perhaps, his chief goal was freedom from the Turks; but it was unlikely that his loyalties would remain undivided for long. Like other local warlords, Kotas is not an easy subject to 'deal with'. The problems of national histories in dealing with him after he was dead, and of those who tried to harness him to their cause when he was alive, were similar.[1]

Cultural heritages are a treasure-chest open to every human community, and not an exclusive preserve, and no one can be denied access to them. Claiming exclusive rights to a cultural heritage based on the right of descent from ancestors who created it contradicts this fundamental principle concerning the availability of past cultural achievements to all of humanity. Such a claim to exclusivity is not made any more acceptable even when it is advanced as a pretext for otherwise legitimate security reasons. Claims of that nature, even if they could ever be effectively defended, would eventually make national cultures and identities poorer and drive nations into postures of perpetual hostility over matters of culture.

---

[1]There are no reliable sources on the life and exploits of Kotas, who remains an elusive figure. What little is known about him comes from people who met him briefly. Metropolitan Germanos Karavangelis of Kastoria, who employed him as guard in the early years of the twentieth century, said in his Memoirs *O Makedonikos Agon. Apomnimonevmata* (The struggle for Macedonia: Memoirs), Thessaloniki, 1959, as little as he could and perhaps not what he would have wished to say. No doubt this was because by the time the book was written Kotas had won an unassailable place in the Greek pantheon. Douglas Dakin in *The Greek Struggle in Macedonia, 1897–1903*, Thessaloniki, 1966, handled Kotas with loving care. For a description of Kotas's captivating personality from an admirer see *Pavlos Melas*, ed. by Natalia P. Mela, Athens, 1964, pp. 233 ff. For a brief and timid attempt to explain his role in the events which led to his death in 1905, see Spyros Sfetas, 'I drasi ton kapetaneon Kota kai Vangeli Strebenioti san ekphrasi tis stasis tou slavophonou plethysmou sto Makedoniko Agona' (The activities of captains Kotas and Vangelis Strebeniotis as a reflection of the position of the Slav-speaking population in the Struggle for Macedonia), *O Makedonikos Agonas*, conference held by the Institute for Balkan Studies, Thesssaloniki, 1987, pp. 495–501. Like most Balkan heroes, Kotas was made to fit a prescribed model.

It is equally impractical to use history as a battlefield for the promotion of different agendas between explicit or covert exponents of state priorities and their opponents, or used as special pleading by advocates of various causes. Whether those advocates serve humanitarian or special ethnic and minority interests does not make them less culpable for manipulating history and using it to hoodwink unsuspecting audiences. Even scholars who are in one way or another engaged in promoting special causes often massage the facts to suit their case, or simply omit those that do not fit into their agendas. Regardless of the degrees of prejudice and partiality that often obscure the way it is presented by historians, the past has its own substance that needs to be discovered by the detached observer.

14

THE RETURN OF THE HELLENES

The ancient Hellenes were conquered by the Romans. Emperor Justinian destroyed the last vestiges of Hellenic civilisation, and state Christianity created a new civilisation on the ruins of the old. Traces of the Hellenes survive in popular lore, in literary manuscripts scattered in places of learning and in the visible ruins of their buildings—all paltry and 'sad relics' of a civilisation that perished and was held in contempt by its successor. Ancient Hellas was rediscovered in the Renaissance and its literary heritage was studied and admired in the centuries that followed. The resulting Classicism not only revived interest in the land of the ancient Hellenes, but Romanticism also contributed by assimilating its modern inhabitants with the revered ancient heroes and sages.

Identifying modern Greeks as descendants of the ancient Hellenes was unavoidable: the Greek language spoken by most of the country's inhabitants, and the physical remains of ancient Hellas, as well as the intellectual requirements of the age, made this identification irresistible. What was not unavoidable was turning this assumption of identity into one of the principal features of the national myth on which the modern Greek nation was founded. In the formative years of the modern Greek nation-state, ancient Hellas was only one of the ingredients available for the building of a new nation: Byzantium, Orthodoxy, the Ottoman empire and Europe were some others.

What helped to establish ancient Hellas as one of the principal parts of the formative myth of the new state was the fact that it was implicitly suggested by Enlightened Europe which, as seen elsewhere, played a decisive role as a legitimising factor. Had it not been for

Europe's espousal of ancient Hellas as one of the high-points of human civilisation and as one of its own three cherished antecedent heritages (the other two being the Roman empire and Christianity), it is not certain that the indigenous Greek élites of the time would have adopted it as their own. The very course of the War of Independence would have been in doubt without the influence brought to bear on it by the European factor.

This presumed continuity did not merely facilitate the adoption of Hellas by modern Greece; it also influenced the way Hellas was used as a founding myth. It would not be an overstatement to say that the Hellas adopted by modern Greece was a European Hellas—until much later, when modern Greeks were in a position to construct their own version of Hellas with materials that owed much to their own considerable powers of imagination.

The tools used for the regeneration of Hellas were, in addition to language, also history and geography and, from the end of the nineteenth century, folklore. In order to regenerate Hellas and the Hellenes, it was necessary first to locate them in place and time and eventually try to discover traces of them among their descendants, the modern Greeks. History and geography went hand in hand with classics and archaeology. Ancient historians and geographers were recruited for the purpose of identifying ancient regions and the sites of ancient cities. Albanian, Slav and Turkish place-names were in many cases abandoned and replaced by respectable Hellenic ones. Thus Vostitsa became Aigion, Leontari became Megalopolis and Koulouri Salamis. This hellenisation of place names, which annoys anthropologists so much that they use the non-Hellenic equivalents when doing their job, was an important aspect of the drive to efface the non-Greek vestiges of post-Hellenic times.

However, this early hellenisation of place-names was neither as thorough nor as extensive as subsequent efforts, when the Greek nation-state incorporated lands that had also been claimed by its northern neighbours. The changes affected principally the newly-formed municipalities and administrative districts and provinces. Names of places that had long been out of use and forgotten even by their inhabitants were unearthed from ancient texts to replace non-Greek names—the eminently forgettable legacies of foreign settlers or invaders. In contrast to subsequent hellenising drives, which aimed at refuting mainly Slav claims to northern Greek provinces, this initial hellenisation was not motivated by insecurity but as a response to the genuine admiration that Westernised Greeks and the Bavarian philhellenes felt for classical Greece. The production of Hellenic names for this Western nation-state in the southeastern fringe of Europe was part of the drive to turn this corner of the continent into the new Hellas.

Before looking at other aspects of the drive to hellenise the inhabitants and the territory of modern Greece, it would be useful to examine both the early and later efforts to replace non-Greek place-names with Greek ones, as well as the subsequent criticism of these efforts. The early phase of this drive in the 1830s, no less than the later phases in the 1910s and '20s, satisfied one of the basic requirements and priorities of the nation-state, namely the creation of a homogeneous national environment, both physical and human. Till recently this homogeneity has been considered not only an acceptable feature of a new state but a desirable one. Most Western nation-states nationalised their own environments, and this was never regarded as anything but appropriate. Spain, France, England and Germany did so, as did the United States of America. If a Moorish place-name could be hispanicised, or a Slavic one germanised or an American Indian one americanised, an Albanian or Slavic name could now equally well be hellenised. Hellas was an integral and important aspect of modern Greek nation-building, and the nation's inhabitants and geophysical environment had to follow this trend and become hellenised too.

The second wave of place-name changes, which satisfied different ideological needs, drew material from a much larger source. Following the restoration of Byzantium in the second half of the nineteenth century and its incorporation into the official national ideology as one of its integral components, what were thought of as modern Greek roots and traditions worth preserving and perpetuating expanded impressively. In renaming places and villages with foreign or 'barbaric-sounding' names, the modern Greeks drew from a wider range of place-names. Remains of ancient temples or city walls or simply their mention in classical texts or in subsequent accounts justified the renaming of the adjacent town or village, as did the local lore of miraculous icons or waters or the battlegrounds of Christian heroes against Muslim oppressors.

Excavations initiated by Western archaeological schools gradually expanded into ambitious operations to bring to light all the Hellenic and Byzantine remains hidden below ground. The drive to hellenise the country turned archaeology into a major discipline of national importance. Archaeology and history were seen not only as avenues leading to the past as a rewarding educational exercise, but as crucial in cultivating awareness of past civilisations and for solving modern problems. They thus became instruments in the ambitious project to reshape the present as much as possible according to what was thought to be the country's history.

The initial Hellas of the fledgling modern Greek nation-state was Europe's vision of it, i.e. classical Hellas south of Macedonia. This area was expanded towards the end of the nineteenth century to satisfy the country's new ideological requirements. History textbooks, which at first followed West European histories in the definition of ancient Greece's territorial limits, were subjected to significant changes. Demosthenes's arrogant attacks on King Philip II and his 'barbarian' kingdom of Macedonia were quietly omitted. Philip and Alexander the Great were not portrayed as the conquerors of ancient Greece; they only assumed leadership over it after the southern Greeks had squandered the vitality of the race in internecine quarrels and fighting. Macedonia was no less Greek than Attica or Lacedaemon, and the same was true of Epirus and Thrace.[1]

The restoration of Byzantium and Paparrigopoulos's theory of the continuity of the Greek nation as a cultural community in time and space, in addition to overcoming the shock of Jacob Philipp Fallmerayer's racial approach to modern Greece's medieval antecedents, assisted the hellenisation process in a decisive way. Ancient Hellenic civilisation was fused into the second stage of the Greek nation's march in history. The Byzantine civilisation attracted and assimilated the culturally inferior Slavs and Albanians, thus producing the modern Greek nation and its civilisation. The stones 'spoke' in Greek of a Greece that was everlasting; so in essence did the country's inhabitants, irrespective of the actual Greek idiom they used to proclaim their Greekness.[2]

Folklore came to the assistance of archaeology and history in the grand effort to silence foreign doubts about the hellenisation of the nation. The sources of popular customs, ballads and popular artifacts were 'traced' to the distant Hellenic or not so distant Byzantine past. Herderian ethnologists and linguists were presented with ancient 'findings' embedded in popular memory and everyday life. Hellenic customs and traditions were discovered, encouraged, cultivated and

---

[1]Christina Koulouri, *Historia kai geographia sta hellenika scholeia, 1834–1914* (History and geography in Greek schools, 1834–1914), Athens, 1988.

[2]Helli Skopetea, *Fallmerayer. Technasmata tou antipalou deous* (Fallmerayer. Tricks of the awesome adversary), Athens, 1997.

reworked to meet the country's ideological requirements. Folklore studies flourished, as did a wide range of supposed ancient customs and traditions.

Following the founding of the chair of History, chairs of Archaeology and Folklore were subsequently added to the faculties at the National and Kapodistrian University of Athens to assist in the hellenisation of the land and to defend the nation against all who questioned its ancient roots. The question of the future of Macedonia around the turn of the century provoked a revolution in modern Greek national ideology, such as was seen in other countries. The fierce and damaging attacks from linguists and ethnologists on the validity of Greek claims to the oldest historical rights to northern Greek lands such as Epirus and Macedonia, which bore the marks of medieval and subsequent changes in their original ethnological composition, added force to the hellenising process already under way. University professors were expected to participate in the nation's ideological battles against its enemies abroad. Most Greek academics proved willing at the time—as they have done ever since—to go along with what was considered to be the national ideology and policy, producing papers and monographs specifically designed to support them.

Despite unavoidable excesses, this hellenising drive produced some towering figures in the world of scholarship, namely Spyridon Zambelios, Konstantinos Paparrigopoulos, Nikolaos Politis, Georgios Chatzidakis and Stilpon Kyriakides. They and other scholars who took part in the nation's ideological battles did so in the firm conviction that they were working within the best traditions of Western scholarship, to which they unquestionably belonged and in which their work, on which official ideology and policy were based, was firmly rooted.

However, hellenising the present was not exclusively a state affair. The public seem to have responded with equal enthusiasm. Following the great flood of foreign names in use since the fourteenth century, which added Slav, Albanian, Turkish and Frankish names to the Christian Greek ones derived from Byzantium, Classical Greek proper names became fashionable during the Enlightenment and particularly after the War of Liberation to the dismay of the Orthodox Church. Second names were also influenced in the same fashion. Ancient Greek suffixes (-ides, -ades) were added to names with Italian (-poulos, -atos) or Turkish (-tzis, -lis) suffixes, especially after the arrival of the Asia Minor and Pontus refugees in the 1920s, who replaced their Turkish -oglu ending to become more acceptable in their new country.

Institutions were also given venerable names, even when their functions had little to do with their models. Thus the smallest administrative unit was called *demos*, even though most of these units consisted of as many as thirty or forty villages. When the country was granted a constitution in 1844, the lower chamber of deputies became the *Vouli*, and the highest court *Areios Pagos*.

Was it presumptuous of the modern Greeks to present themselves so assiduously as descendants of the ancient Hellenes? And did that posture have a price worth paying? In other words, did the modern Greeks gain little and lose much, as has often been implied by critics of the Hellenising drive, by labouring to transform Greek-, Albanian-, Slav-, Vlach- and Turkish-speaking Orthodox Christians into modern Hellenes? These are not questions for historians, who are trained to examine the developments and trends that give rise to these questions rather than answer them. These and other such questions have rested on the following three unspoken or little-elaborated assumptions. The first is that hellenisation, in the light of the general admiration of classical Greece in the West at the time, could have been avoided; secondly, that the modern Greek nation-builders could have chosen an alternative national myth—as attractive as classical Hellas and as effective in forging a modern nation—that would single them out from neighbouring nations; and thirdly, that what the modern Greeks gained by adopting this course was less than what they lost in the process.

Disappointment over the real achievements, irritation at the excesses of the hellenising drive, as well as nostalgia for what this drive undermined or made unpopular have sustained the above assumptions and the questioning of classical Hellas as the appropriate national myth for the modern Greeks. Disappointment over the new and nostalgia for the old were perhaps unavoidable and understandable; what is not easy to grasp is the total rejection of hellenisation, even as a myth, and the 'mythification' of the pre-hellenised modern Greek world. Critics of the hellenisation drive have underestimated its value as a goal and as a model for a subject people living under a despotic regime, which made them feel inferior to their masters and act accordingly. Equally, those critics have tended to idealise the supposed positive features of a world that fell into disrepute—such as the unpretentious simplicity, honesty and God-fearing virtue of the Orthodox peasants who lived in peace with each other during Ottoman times. This unpretentious simplicity, however, was as real as the supposed peace and cooperation within a traditional Orthodox peasant community. That community was a world where passions ran higher and tensions were more extreme than those of the world that grew out of it. The pre-national Orthodox peasant world was as insecure and divided in itself as that which succeeded it, without the sense of pride derived from membership in that new imagined community. No lore could ensure the pride of association with an illustrious and highly esteemed heritage, whose best proof was its linguistic vehicle.[3]

[3]Alki Kyriakidou,Nestoros, *I theoria tis Hellenikis Laographias.Kritiki analysi* (The theory of Greek folklore. Critical analysis), Athens, 1978.

15

OF GREEKS AND OTHERS

Defining modern Greek national identity has never been easy. Students of modern Greece have found the subject perplexing and elusive; so, for that matter, have those Greeks who felt responsible for shaping that identity. Of course, the analysis of any modern identity presents the student with problems, which have to do with the changing meaning of terms and the equally changing criteria for defining the identities of human communities. In the case of the modern Greeks these problems are compounded by the fact that the multiple terms and criteria which Greeks themselves have used to define their identity are not easily disentangled and examined separately. The modern Greeks, it seems, have been adding new terms or new meanings to old terms. They have also been playing around with more or less the same criteria from one generation to the next, adding new ones without dropping the old ones with which the new seemed to be in conflict. These shifts of meanings and definitions of terms and criteria were of course the result of changing needs and circumstances.

The concept of 'others' is useful in distinguishing and defining group self-perceptions. By identifying the others, or those who represent them on each occasion, one can expect to reach a relatively stable definition of a human group. In the case of the modern Greeks this approach is anything but safe because the 'otherness' of some has been deemed to be less significant than that of others, or to be absent altogether. The non-Greek Orthodox Christians, the Latin or Western Christians and the Muslims have been the three principal 'others' for the Greeks and are a convenient point of departure for a discussion of the subject.

The definition of the Greeks and the others in the first Constitution of the War of Independence, although this refers to them as citizens of the nation-state in the making, does provide some important clues to the criteria then in use for distinguishing them from each other. The relevant article (Art. 2) laid down that 'those indigenous inhabitants of the realm of Greece who believe in Christ are Greeks'. This definition, however, soon proved inadequate for the needs of the fledgling nation-state. Were the Catholic Greeks of the Aegean islands as Greek as the Orthodox Greeks? In political terms the answer would be a grudging 'yes', and in ideological terms it was also 'yes' but only with grave misgivings. Similarly, were non-indigenous Western Christians equally Greek if they chose to settle in the 'Greek domain' permanently? According to the Constitution they were, but were not in the eyes of the Orthodox Church. Lastly, were indigenous Muslim Turks as Greek as the rest if they chose to convert to Christianity, as many did to avoid being slaughtered or to keep their lands? Yes and no: Orthodox prelates welcomed such converts, but lay revolutionary leaders were reluctant to consider them as more than opportunists, who would turn against the Greeks as soon as the opportunity arose; only children converted under the age of twelve were thought to be meeting the qualifications of a Greek.[1]

Therefore, religion—or, more accurately, Eastern Christianity—was the principal qualification and criterion of Greek national identity. Residence in the 'Greek realm' was the second qualification, but no sooner was this laid down as a determining factor of Greek identity than it presented the Greeks with a series of questions which have never been answered to everybody's satisfaction. What, after all, constituted the 'Greek realm' during the War of Independence, when the fortunes of war changed radically and swiftly? Were the districts that had revolted against Turkish rule or would revolt in the future, as was specified in the same revolutionary charter, the only constituent lands of this realm? They were not, nor had they ever meant to be, as is seen in another chapter.

Another important determining factor of Greek identity—language—was introduced one year later by the second revolutionary constitution, no doubt as a major step in the desired Western orientation of the new nation-state on Europe's south-eastern fringe. The article already cited was amended to provide also for 'those coming

---

[1] *Prosorinon Politevma tis Hellados* (Preliminary Constitution of Greece), Corinth, 1822, Art. 2.

from abroad who have Greek as their mother tongue and believe in Christ'.[2] However, this amendment, by which it had been attempted to modernise the nation's effort to define its identity, was silently dropped in the next revolutionary constitution.[3] Yet language as a determining factor of modern Greek national identity would never cease to exercise a powerful influence on all subsequent efforts to come to grips with the intractable question under consideration here. Though never admitted openly, language became a powerful instrument in the hands of the Greek nation-state in the drive to hellenise the multilingual lands it gradually wrenched from the Ottoman empire in the course of a century.

The '*heteroglossoi*' or '*heterophonoi*' (heterolinguals) of the initial Greek nation-state—principally Albanians and Vlachs—caused no embarrassment to Greek state-builders; at the time no other Balkan nationalists claimed either of these as their kin. Besides, after many centuries of cohabitation, both the Albanians and the Vlachs of southern and central Greece had been thoroughly hellenised in most respects and sometimes in speech as well. Moreover, both had generously contributed to the making of the Greek nation-state in the southern Greek peninsula, the Vlachs in the Greek Enlightenment and the Albanians in helping to win the war against the Turks. Both identified with Greek national aims and future irredentist upheavals as perhaps no other linguistic community of the Orthodox Ecumene did. Finally, both Albanians and Vlachs were numerous enough to elicit respect and avoid discriminaion.

Other heterolinguals such as the descendants of the Slavs of Macedonia, of whom a fair number fought with distinction in southern Greece, and were given land on which to settle in the independent Greek nation-state, were again not differentiated—by others or by themselves—from the rest of the Greeks. These people were referred as 'Bulgarians' or 'Thracian-Macedonians', and were regarded as Bulgarian-speaking brethren. They too were not yet claimed as brethren by any other Balkan nationalists, and they too identified with the Greek nation-state no less than the Greek-speaking Greeks of the time. In any case, most heterolinguals of Greece, both then and later, had enough Greek not to feel excluded from the rest of the

---

[2]See correspondence of insurgent Greek government in *Archeia Hellenikikis Palingenesias* (Archives of Hellenic Regeneration), vol. I, Athens, 1971, pp. 289–90, 294, 389.

[3]*Nomos tis Epidaurou* (Epidaurus Charter), Hydra, 1824, Art. 2.

Greeks. The Greek-dominated Orthodox hierarchy and the dominant position that Greek education and the Greek language had in
the commerce of the Ottoman empire were trump cards that the
young nation-state was able to play for many decades to come.

The '*heterothreskoi*' or '*heterodoxoi*' (heteroreligionists), essentially the
Jews and the Muslim Turks and Albanians, were not discriminated
against politically or otherwise, although they were clearly differentiated from the other Greeks. Though free to exercise their religious
obligations, they—and indeed every religious community except the
Orthodox Christians—were not allowed to proselytise. On the status
of the heteroreligionists the Greek nation-state-builders—obviously
influenced by the Orthodox Church—displayed an insecurity dis-
proportionate to the threat these inhabitants of Greece posed to the
state religion. However, this insecurity seems to have had deeper roots
than the reluctance of Orthodox prelates to allow the heteroreligionists
complete freedom of action. Koraes, who opposed all restrictions
on political and human rights and was no admirer of protected state
religion, expressed the liberal position of the time on the subject as
follows: 'After letting them freely practise their religion, inside their
temples or temple precincts, we should encourage them to believe
that they would gradually be granted full political rights, as they prove
themselves capable of enjoying them; we can neither deny them these
rights, nor is it completely safe to grant them immediately. With such
gradual progress, instead of turning them into enemies, we shall make
them sincere friends of the commonwealth, so much so that we are
in a way offering them what we do not owe them.' This was because,
as he explained, neither the Jews nor the Muslims had fought for the
freedom of the land.[4]

'Others' were also the Gypsies, but they were the perpetual outcasts of sedentary society, and no more 'other' in newly-independent
Greece than they were everywhere in Europe then and later. Like the
transhumant Sarakatsan and Vlach shepherds, Gypsies were considered enemies of organised human society and state security; however,
unlike the Sarakatsans and the Vlachs, who were never thought to be
other than backward Greeks, Gypsies were never considered to be
members of the Greek nation.

---

[4]Adamantios Koraes, *Peri ton hellenikon sympheronton dialogos dyo Graekon* (A
dialogue of two Greeks on the interests of Greece), Hydra, 1825, p. 93; *Politikon
Syntagma tis Hellados* (Political Constitution of Greece), Troezen, 1827, Arts. 4 and
6. For these questions see Helli Skopetea, *To 'protypo basileio' kai i Megali Idea* (The
'model kingdom' and the Great Idea), Athens, 1988, pp. 41 ff.

Language as a determining factor appeared to be waning and religion to be waxing as the Enlightened and Westernised intellectuals gave way to the Romantics of post-Revolutionary Greece. Romanticism and a growing sense of superiority to the other peoples of the Ottoman empire—on account of commercial competence, accumulated wealth, more advanced education and a growing re-hellenisation of lands lost in the past to foreign invaders—brought the Greeks closer than ever to the Ecumenical Patriarch's spiritual domain. However, the challenge of the Bulgars in Macedonia forced Greek thinkers to come up with new arguments as the old ones showed their age. The Bulgars, by claiming the Orthodox Slavs of Macedonia as their brethren because of their Slav language, dealt a serious blow to Greek claims to the land. Language as a determining factor of identity was 'Western' and thus 'legitimated' and 'reliable', but as an argument in support of claims to unredeemed lands and their inhabitants it was dropped altogether. This was not the case with education for the 're-hellenisation' of Greeks who had 'lost' their mother tongue in the centuries of foreign invasion and rule. Greek education—or, more accurately, education in Greek schools for that purpose in the irredenta—was flourishing in an impressive way.

Religion as a determining factor was also no longer a convincing argument and had to be refined. The Slavs of Macedonia whom the Bulgars claimed as brethren were, like Greeks and Bulgars, Orthodox, but in the new situation what was important was not Orthodoxy as such but loyalty to the Ecumenical Patriarchate. The Bulgars and all those who had placed themselves under the Bulgarian Exarchate were so many 'schismatics'. The Ecumenical Patriarch was the true and legitimate head of the Ottoman Orthodox, the Ottoman Greeks; accepting the authority of the Ecumenical Patriarch was the unfailing proof of Greek identity.

Descent was another 'unfailing' determining factor of identity. This argument was thought to be unassailable. Who else but the Greeks could put forward the oldest and most illustrious titles to the land and its people? *Prior tempore, fortior iure.* The 'Bulgars' and 'Thraco-Bulgars' of past days now became 'Bulgarian-speaking Greeks' (*Voulgarophonoi Hellenes*) with striking 'Greek features'. They were Greeks by descent and by remaining loyal—at least those who did so—to the Ecumenical Patriarch.

In the case of the Slavs of Macedonia or the Slav Macedonians, a further and even more 'unfailing' determinant of identity was put forward at the time: 'consciousness' or 'sentiments' (*syneidesis* or *phronema*).

This marked a further departure from the initial course of national development charted by the men of the Greek Enlightenment. Consciousness was the most important determining factor of identity. It was a most useful tool, that was seized upon by modern Greek nation-state-builders and has never since been relinquished. Consciousness or sentiment was the ultimate proof of a person's identification with a community and loyalty to it. All the other determining factors, language in particular, were secondary.

This new Western import was thought to be modern, democratic and reasonable. Thus Greek identity rested on the paternal faith or the maternal tongue, on time-honoured customs, and above all on a person's right to choose it. Greek nation-state-builders were convinced that they possessed an irrefutable argument against all those who questioned the Greek identity of non-Greek speaking Orthodox in the irredenta and subsequently in the northern 'New Lands' of Greece. In cases where 'descent' was uncertain or impossible to prove convincingly, consciousness was the ultimate answer. Little did the Greeks think then of the inherent dangers in the concept of consciousness as a determining factor of identity; of the danger, in particular, of consciousness becoming a subject of interpretation, development, transformation or manipulation by agencies or people other than those immediately concerned; or of the danger of this concept being applied to define someone's 'correct' political affiliations.

For the time being, the Greeks of free Greece could indulge in identifying who were and who were not their brethren in unredeemed Greece among, first and foremost, the Slav Macedonians and, secondarily, the Orthodox Albanians and the Vlachs. Primary school students were taught in the 1880s that 'Greeks [are] our kinsmen of common descent, speaking the language we speak and professing the religion we profess'.[5] But this definition seems to have been reserved for small children, who could not possibly understand the intricate arguments of their parents on the question of Greek identity. It was essential to understand at that tender age that modern Greeks descended from the ancient Greeks. However, children must have been no less confused than adults over the criteria for defining modern Greek identity. Did the Greeks constitute a 'race' apart from the Albanians, the Slavs and the Vlachs? Well, yes and no. High school students were told that

---

[5]Christina Koulouri, *Historia kai geographia sta hellenika scholeia, 1834–1914* (History and geography in Greek schools, 1834–1914), Athens, 1988, p. 255.

the 'other races', i.e. the Slavs, the Albanians and the Vlachs, 'having been hellenised over the years in terms of mores and customs, are now being assimilated into becoming Greeks'.[6]

On the Slavs of Macedonia there seems to have been no consensus. Were they Bulgars, slavicised Greeks or early Slavs? They 'were' Bulgars until the 1870s and slavicised Greeks or hellenised Slavs subsequently, according to the changing needs of the dominant theory. There was no consensus, either, on the Vlachs. Were they latinised Greek mountain-dwellers or late immigrants from Wallachia? As in the case of the Slavs of Macedonia, Vlach descent shifted from the southern Balkans to the Danube, until the Romanians claimed the Vlachs as their brethren; this turned the latter into being countered irrevocably indigenous to the southern Balkan mountains. The Albanians or Arvanites were readily 'adopted' as brethren of common descent for at least three reasons. First, considerable numbers of Albanians had been living in southern Greece as far south as the Peloponnese for centuries. Secondly, many Christian Albanians had fought with distinction in the War of Independence. And thirdly, credible Albanian claims for the establishment of an Albanian nation-state materialised too late for Greek national theorists to abandon well-entrenched positions. Commenting on a geography textbook for primary schools in 1901, a state committee found it inadequate and misleading. One of its principal shortcomings concerned the Albanians, who were described as 'close kinsmen of the Greeks'. 'Such views are unacceptable from the point of view of our national claims and as far as historical truth is concerned. It must be maintained that they are of common descent with the Greeks (Pelasgians), that they speak a language akin to that of the Greeks, and that they participated in all struggles for national liberation of the common fatherland.'[7]

In 1908, just as the Young Turks were launching their pronunciamento that was intended to transform the decaying Ottoman empire, another national committee, mandated to decide on the content of geography textbooks for Greek children, gave the following definition for the Greeks of Asia Minor: 'Greeks are those who speak Turkish but profess the Christian religion of their ancestors. Greeks are also the Greek-speaking Muslims of Asia Minor, who lost their ancestral religion but kept their ancestral tongue. As far as the inhabitants of

[6]*Ibid.*, p. 378.
[7]*Ibid.*, p. 463.

Asia Minor who are Muslims and speak Turkish are concerned, only reliable historical evidence or anthropological studies can prove their Greek descent and that they are distinct from the non-Greek Muslims.'[8]

In that case, then, neither language nor religion was a reliable and decisive determinant of the modern Greek identity; what was reliable and decisive was descent—where it could be established through historical evidence or anthropological study. It was hoped, of course, that this would be descent from the ancient Greeks. History at first, and archaeology and folklore later, were mobilised to support this theory. The language and, when language was of no use, the ancient 'stones'—the mores and customs of the inhabitants—were reliable witnesses to the Hellenic past surviving into the modern Greek present. Conquerors and settlers of past centuries had been absorbed and assimilated by the culturally superior Greeks. The turbulent past of foreign invasion and conquest had left behind foreign place-names and linguistic pockets here and there to remind modern Greeks of the centuries of foreign captivity or settlement.

After a century of debate about the determining factors of modern Greek identity, who were the 'others'? The Osmanli Turks, who had invaded the Greek lands and were temporarily 'camping' in them, were certainly 'others'; so were Jews and Gypsies, who retained their particular identities, and foreign-born Catholics or Protestants. Greeks were all the rest, including the Hellenised Albanians, Slavs and Vlachs and not excluding even the '*heterothreskoi*' or '*heteroglossoi*', whose Hellenic descent could be safely established or whose Greek consciousness could be determined.

Interesting clues on the question of 'others' in the new Greek nation-state can be derived from the naturalisation provisions of its early and formative years. These reflect official views on who could be granted Greek citizenship and how. Initially, and before the question arose of who could and could not be appointed to higher state positions, foreign-born Greeks became Greek citizens on appearing before any local Greek authority and registering with it. Aliens (*alloethneis*) were required, before being granted Greek citizenship, to have resided for five years and acquired real estate in Greece, and to be of good character. The residence requirement was lowered in 1827 to three years, instead of five, no doubt in order to attract people to the country whose population was decimated by massacre, epidemics and famine.[9]

---

[8]*Ibid.*, 531.
[9]See *Archives of Hellenic Regeneration*, vol. I, p. 290.

As in all nation-states, naturalisation legislation in Greece has been based on *ius soli* or territory law and aimed at creating a homogeneous people. However, in Greece as in Germany and certain other European countries, *ius sanguinis* or blood law has always been decisive in defining citizenship—which provides a further clue to the question of Greek nationality and national identity. The 1823 and 1827 revolutionary constitutions, as well as the 1835 and 1856 laws—and the 1955 law— on Greek citizenship, clearly differentiated Greeks from the others. *Homogeneis* (ethnic Greeks) were—and still are—preferentially treated when it comes to citizenship.[10] In other words the Greek nation, although it created the Greek nation-state according to official theory, could not possibly be restricted to the confines of that state.

If others before them could have imagined, reconstructed or invented their modern identities, the modern Greeks could have done no less. What mattered for them, their neighbours and the 'others' was not so much the 'objective' or 'subjective' criteria the modern Greeks used as factors determining their national identity, but a certain nervousness and insecurity in the promotion of these criteria after the appearance of serious contenders for the lands of the Sultan in the last quarter of the nineteenth century. The chosen nation on the south-eastern fringe of Europe, which would be a beacon of light in the East and civilise its less fortunate brethren in the region, became the threatened, insecure and 'brotherless' nation of the late nineteenth century. Would the modern Greeks have felt more secure with language as the sole determining factor of their identity? Perhaps—but this would have required a different beginning from that which the Greeks had in the 1820s. It certainly required the nation to be less subservient to Orthodoxy and more anchored in the Enlightenment. Not that the two were incompatible; indeed, some of the more serious enlightened thinkers were Orthodox prelates. Orthodoxy was used by Greek Romantics to penetrate the world of Orthodox peasants and turn them into Hellenes with the Greek language as their instrument. Language, therefore, was both a medium and an end in itself. What surprises the student of modern Greece is not so much the grandiose and somewhat deceptive project of hellenising the Orthodox Ecumene of the southern Balkans as such, but that this project, as seen elsewhere, was largely realised, albeit at a high price. The imagined and imaginatively constructed Hellenic Ecumene in the southern Balkans may well

---

[10]Aimilios Bendermacher—Gerousis, *Hellenikon Dikaion Ithageneias* (Greek citizenship law), 3rd edn., Thessaloniki, 1975, pp. 15–18; Zoe Papasiopi-Pasia, *Dikaion Ithageneias* (Citizenship law), 2nd edn., Thessaloniki, 1994, pp. 27–30, 45–9.

Greeks and Jews

The Torah (Pentateuch) was, according to a dominant view, translated into Greek to make its content accessible to the linguistically Hellenised Jews of Egypt. In the Second Century BC the Old Testament was translated in its entirety by seventy Hellenised Jewish scholars.

The Jewish tradition and its Hellenic linguistic vehicle also facilitated the spreading of the word and the spirit of Christianity. Three of the four Gospels of the New Testament were originally written in the Greek *koine,* the lingua franca of the eastern Roman Empire, and were therefore made accessible to mankind. The Christian faith itself is a major point of convergence of the Hellenic and Judaic traditions.

The annexation of Thessaloniki in 1912 by the Greek state signalled the dawn of a new era in the life of the local Jewish community. Unlike the Romaniot Jews who merged into the Athenian environment, the Sephardic Jews from Spain formed a separate constellation within the decentralised Ottoman system. The highly centralised nation-state of Greece and its cultural homogeneity posed a significant challenge to this city with the largest Jewish community of the Balkans. Furthermore, the division of the European lands of the Ottoman Empire between Serbia, Greece and Bulgaria diminished the former role of Thessaloniki as a commercial hub and deprived it of its Balkan hinterland. Subsequent disasters struck the city—a great fire in 1917, the influx of refugees from Asia Minor in 1922–3, the Campbell Affair in 1931, and the final blow in 1943 when 60,000 Greek Jews died in the Holocaust. The saga of the Greek Jews in the resistance as well as the joint efforts of Archbishop Damaskinos, the resistance movement ELAS, Angelos Evert the police chief, and the population of Athens to save the Jews of Athens is yet another story partly told by Alex Kitroeff. Immediately after the Liberation, the Greek government appointed the Jewish communities as administrators of all property whose owners had died or been lost without a trace during the war.

A working hypothesis is being developed concerning the major question of anti-Semitism in modern Europe and the gradation of the phenomenon from the most cirulant forms in Central and Eastern Europe, to its minimal expression in South-eastern Europe (Serbia, Bulgaria and Greece). A first impression which requires much research and verification, is that the ideological basis of organised state and para-state anti-Semitism, rests on prototypes provided by societies with strongly entrenched *anciens régimes.* Although the Nazi extermination programme required the efficiency of a modern totalitarian state, the source from which Nazism, Fascism, the Iron Guard, the Ustasha and the Arrow

Cross drew their inspiration was the principle of every individual being predestined to a particular station in life—all alien to the Enlightenment and liberal middle-class thinking.

Bibliography

Alex Kitroeff, *War-Time Jews: The Case of Athens,* Athens: ELIAMEP, 1995, p. 126.

have trampled on the rights and sensibilities of the 'others' in the region. However, the Orthodox Ecumene was no less imagined, and the temporal state to which it was subservient—namely the Ottoman empire—was no paradise for subject peoples, the Greeks any more than their Orthodox 'brethren'. Two of the prime benefits of this hellenisation of the southern Balkan Orthodox Ecumene have been the modernisation it brought to backward areas and the sense of pride it gave to peasants in belonging to a community anchored in an illustrious past and set on a course towards a no less illustrious future. Orthodox diehards may curse the Greek nation-state as the instrument of the 'heretical' West, and neo-Orthodox thinkers may lament the loss of the supposed 'integrated' and orderly life of the pre-national Orthodox community of the southern Balkans. But both choose to ignore that this penetration and transformation of the Orthodox community of past days has primarily been achieved by means other than force or stealth.

Turkey in Greece

Modern Greece was formed by carving territory out of the declining Ottoman empire in the 1820s, just as modern Turkey one century later out of the ruins of the same empire. Greece, more than any other Balkan nation-state, undermined the ageing empire and accelerated its fall and, more than any of its other successor-states, contributed to the birth of Turkey. The little kingdom in the southern Balkans, which came into being by the forced agreement of the Porte, did all in its power to demolish the shaky empire, only to find it replaced by a more formidable adversary: a Turkish nation-state with a programme of homogenisation and a persistent imperial hangover. In more than one sense, Greece contributed generously to the creation of its eastern adversary.

In a different sense the Greeks constructed their 'own' image of the Turks. As the principal 'others', they were fashioned to suit the ideological and political requirements of the Greeks. The Turks had been foreign invaders in the dominions of the legitimate rulers of the land, the medieval Greek empire. This state had been conquered by force; it had not surrendered its sovereignty by its own will, nor had it treated with the conqueror. In this respect the Greeks had never recognised the Sultan as their legitimate ruler, notwithstanding the Orthodox Church's subservience to him.

According to the prevailing view among Greeks, the Turks were not only the latest of all arrivals in the region they occupied, but also total strangers to its history and civilisation. Moreover, they had not been able, in the centuries when they held sway over their subject peoples, to produce real wealth; they had adopted aspects of the civilisation of their subjects and were living as parasites on the wealth produced by them. They were temporarily camping in their lands until the inhabitants were in a position to evict them. Thus the Greeks have always thought of the Turks as usurpers of their sovereignty and temporary squatters, and have never accepted that these latest arrivals from Asia were co-habitants or had even acquired rights to the lands they had conquered by force.

As the independent Greek state distanced itself from its Ottoman antecedents, the estrangement between Greeks and Turks grew. The Greco-Turkish war of 1919–22 and the consequent Asia Minor Catastrophe and exchange of populations made the Greeks' Turkish neighbours not just strangers but feared enemies. The brief courtship of the Turks during the Greek struggle for Macedonia against the Bulgars at the turn of the nineteenth and twentieth centuries and the equally brief interlude of reconciliation and friendship initiated by Venizelos and Atatürk in the early 1930s made no appreciable change to Greek perceptions of modern Turkey and the Turks.

Turkey has also been demonised by the Greeks, who have endowed it with all the negative aspects of their own pre-Independence past, such as arbitrary rule, backwardness and corruption from which— as they would like to believe—they had moved on. The Turks were what the Greeks wished to leave behind; they represented the barbaric East, which had destroyed their 'own' idealised East. The West, in addition to everything else it has signified for the Greeks, became their refuge.

Another aspect of the modern Greek attitude towards the East has been a questioning of Turkey's Western orientation—that very orientation which most modern Greeks would readily accept for their own country. According to a widely-held view in Greece, the

Turks have not been able to build a Western nation-state because they are incapable of doing so. Also according to this view, the Western institutions Atatürk imported into Turkey have not taken root, while those who undertook to make them work have never been more than an insignificant and vulnerable minority.

This Greek image of modern Turkey has become deeply embedded in modern Greek national ideology. The perceptions that accompany it are regularly reproduced in Greece by the national school system and the press. This Turkey, scorned for its shaky and uncertain Western orientation and its backwardness, but feared all the same for the damage it is capable of inflicting on Greece, has become an essential and integral part of modern Greek identity. The Turk has not simply been one of the 'others'; while the Slavs, Albanians and Latins have all been 'others', the Turks were indissolubly associated with all the dark aspects of the past which the Greeks have shared with them and from which they want to believe they have at last freed themselves. Divesting Turkey of all its perceived negative features would require a redefinition of modern Greek identity on a scale much greater than that accomplished by the post-Second World War Germans over their own identity and their relations to the French. However, such a redefinition would require a corresponding redefinition of Turkish perceptions of modern Greece, like that pursued by the French *vis-à-vis* the Germans. It would also require a degree of stability in the region, because instability and provocative actions by either side make the perceptions from the other side appear as self-fulfilling prophecies.

A redefinition of Turkey's role in shaping modern Greece would require a reappraisal of the country's achievements as a nation-state, the political choices and courses of action that were necessary for these achievements, and the basic arguments behind these choices. What is required, in other words, is for the Greeks to come to terms with their real, not their imagined past by trying to see it in terms not only of Greek objectives but also of Turkish perceptions. Modern Turkey must be seen, first and foremost, as a nation-state pursuing national objectives as legitimate as those of modern Greece. Turkey's goal to turkify its past, its land and its inhabitants is no more objectionable or less legitimate than Greece's goal to hellenise its own past, land and inhabitants. It should be recognised that Turkey has been following a course no different, in terms of the principles involved, from that which Greece has followed since Independence. More important in this case than the obvious excesses committed in the drive to realise prescribed national objectives are the principles sustaining this drive—what could be described as the logic of the insecure nation-state.

It also needs to be recognised that a nation's 'historic right' to the past is the product of a national approach to that past—a process which involves the use of 'ethnic truth' and, as such, rights such as can be claimed by all nations that have shared the lands associated with it. In this sense the nineteenth-century preoccupation to put forward the oldest possible 'historic right' to land cannot be of any use in an international community which recognises effective possession as the most conclusive argument in any claim.[12]

[12]For the theme of the Turks as illegitimate rulers of the Greeks and as temporary campers in Europe see the following sources on insurgent Greece: *Geniki Ephemeris tis Hellados*, 21 Apr., 14 May and 23 June 1826; *Hellenika Chronika*, 2 May 1825; Koraes, *Clarion Call*, p. 26; *Romas Archive*, vol. II, pp. 146–7, 186–7; Philimon, *Society of Friends*, p. 137, and *Greek Revolution*, vol. IV, pp. 3, 95; Speliades, *Memoirs*, vol. II, p. 555.

16

EUROPE IN GREECE

Northern European liberals and Romantics constructed and promoted a view of modern Greece that corresponded to their own sensibilities and satisfied their Western intellectual requirements. Modern Greeks, for their part, created their own Europe. Those at least who chose the West European liberal nation-state as a model for Greek national development created a Europe that satisfied the ideological requirements of its creators. However, both westernised Greeks and Western liberals assumed more than the situation warranted. A disappointed Western observer, writing a century later under the weight of the traumatic 1919–22 Greco-Turkish war, discussed the liberal vision of a 'regenerated' Hellas as 'one of the extravagances of Western Philhellenism'. He added that the attraction of the West to Greece at that time was a 'curse which the West has set upon Greece', which had led to Greece's 'spiritual pauperisation' and was responsible for 'what Greece has lost, or failed to win'.[1]

Defenders of Greece's Eastern roots would readily agree with this interpretation of the Western impact on modern Greece, with the implication that an indigenous tradition provided a sound basis for the formation of a viable modern nation-state capable of securing for its inhabitants the freedom, prosperity and dignity with which the Western nation-state was associated throughout the nineteenth and twentieth centuries. But despite these misgivings about Greece and the West (and to put these misgivings into historical perspective), we should examine what appears to have been Greece's long Western

[1] Arnold Toynbee, *The Western Question in Greece and Turkey*, Boston and New York, 1922, pp. 351–2.

263

apprenticeship, as well as the related theme of a regenerated Hellas, which was suggested to the Greeks of the time by Western Philhellenes.

The principal thesis of this chapter is that the Western orientation of modern Greece, and the related drive to 'regenerate' ancient Hellas, have been at the core of a strong national myth that transformed the multilingual and multicultural Christian community of the southern Balkans into a modern nation and the fragmented geographical entity into a unified nation-state. This Western orientation also inspired within the community a pride of descent, which proved a cohesive and creative force, while securing acceptance of new institutions that have shown great resilience.

Critics of the national myth of modern Greece have always implied that the builders of the Greek nation-state in the 1820s and '30s were presented with a realistic alternative to the Western orientation, and that what the Greeks gained by turning to the West was not worth the losses they incurred in the process. However, this alternative course has never been expounded, nor have the losses suffered by the Greeks as the price of both their Western orientation and the drive to hellenise the pre-national Orthodox Ecumene ever been calculated.

Predictably, criticism of the liberal nation-state in modern Greece has come from conservative circles associated with the Orthodox Church. The modern Greek state is blamed not only for introducing the nationalist virus into the Orthodox Ecumene, but also for facilitating the introduction of Western mores, which have undermined traditional Greek values such as honesty, compassion and hospitality, and destroyed the sense of community created by the Orthodox form of worship.

Criticism of the state also came from an unexpected quarter. In the eyes of progressive political circles Koraes and the national vernacular he helped to fashion out of the written and spoken Greek of the time, as well as Kapodistrias and the centralised nation-state he and his Bavarian successors established, were no less damaging for Greek society. According to this view, the purified national vernacular broke the continuity of the Greek language and introduced linguistic elements alien to the language spoken by the people. The result has been an official language not understood by the uneducated and a popular language scorned by the educated. Even more calamitous, according to the same progressive view, has been the destruction of all indigenous political institutions and the concentration of power in the central government. One of the principal victims of this was local self-government, which is proved to have blossomed under Ottoman rule and offered a sound foundation for building a modern democratic polity.

Both these critical views of the Western liberal nation-state have rested on a number of shaky premises. Repetition and lack of rigorous questioning from its proponents have led to the growth of the enduring myth of a pre-national Shangri-La in which the Greeks enjoyed, under Ottoman rule and Orthodox spiritual guidance, not only local self-government but communal solidarity and a frugal existence devoid of the vicissitudes of modernity. This particular earthly paradise is supposed to have been shattered as soon as the disciples of Voltaire and Koraes set foot there.

It is worth examining briefly three of the premises of this 'Paradise Lost' construct: first, local left-government; second, tolerant temporal and religious rule; and, third, spoken and written Greek. These have been debated by such diverse critics of the modern Greek nation-state as Philorthodox politicians, unemployed nineteenth-century military commanders, conservatives like Ion Dragoumis, and left-wing activists in the twentieth century.

The critics of the modern Greek nation-state maintain that local self-government in pre-national Greece flourished under foreign rule as a proto-institution of representative government. However, they have kept very quiet about certain features of this institution not normally associated with representative government, such as the fact that communal councils functioned under Ottoman rule mainly as tax-assessing and tax-collecting organs of the foreign ruler and fostered the emergence of powerful families that used them to increase their wealth and influence. Another important and similarly overlooked aspect of these councils was that they were hardly representative in the Western sense. The community heads essentially represented the interests of the Sultan and not those of the community, and they received their mandate from him as his agents; they were appointed and recalled—or lost their heads—at his whim. Such were the local grandees of the Morea and islands like Hydra and Spetsae. What they represented was their own interests, wealth and power, and they held office because the local Ottoman administrator had so decided. In contrast to the Western concept of communal self-government, in which councils developed as nuclei of power antagonistic to the central government while deriving their authority from those they represented, communal councils in the Greek lands at that time grew out of the foreign ruler's practice of delegating the unpopular functions connected with taxation to the leaders of those they ruled. What representative or quasi-representative self-government developed among the Greeks of the time did so mainly outside the Sultan's dominions in the flourishing diaspora communities in Trieste, Venice, Vienna, Budapest and Odessa.

The second premise on which the critics of the Greek nation-state base their analysis of the pre-national Greek past is no less shaky. The Ottoman empire, as a multi-ethnic state, rested on toleration of non-Muslim and non-Turkish subjects—imposed on its rulers by the need to govern a multi-ethnic population. Non-Muslim subjects, in this case Orthodox Christians, were tolerated as long as they accepted the inferior status of the *raya* (flock) and were prepared to obey the ruler who had imposed that inferior status on them. In the effort to correct earlier views of Ottoman rule over the Christians of the Near East as a thoroughly intolerant and illiberal despotism, this has also been represented as wise and enlightened, indeed as securing a measure of peace and freedom for the various peoples of that region. However, this peace and freedom was only secured after all resistance to the imposition of this inferior status on the Sultan's non-Muslim subjects had been crushed. The toleration of Jews expelled from Western Europe (in particular Spain and Portugal) by intolerant Christian monarchs and their settlement in Thessaloniki and other cities of the empire satisfied the same imperial needs as the enforced transfer of other ethnic groups between its different parts.

Equally overstated its has been the benign nature of the spiritual rule of the Ecumenical Patriarchate and its metropolitans. The Patriarchate of Constantinople, as we have seen elsewhere, was essentially a hostage held captive by the temporal ruler of the empire. As such—and as an integral part of the imperial administrative machinery—it would never be able to play a role similar to the Vatican's. The Patriarch could only keep his position in the same way as he had won it: by buying the Sultan's favour for a vast sum of money. He collected this bounty from the metropolitans, who in turn put their hands deep into the pockets of the Sultan's Christian subjects.

The third premise of the attacks on the Western orientation of the Greek nation-state—the Western-inspired approach to the creation of its national vernacular—appeared to have an unassailable basis. The new official language was imposed from above in place of the spoken and written language of the people. Who could possibly deny it? Many did, questioning the way the issue of the national language was approached by its enemies. They would reply with the question implied in Demetrios Vyzantios's *Babylonia* (1836): which of the people's languages? What was often referred to as the popular language in the formative years of the modern Greek nation-state was lamentably poor and fragmented, and ill-suited to be the vernacular of a modern polity. It was sometimes described as a collection of idioms bearing the imprint of local historical developments. The only available alternative to the 'purified' language recommended by Koraes and other members of the lay intelligentsia of the time was the Greek of the Orthodox Church liturgy, but that was no more intelligible to uneducated people than the new official language and certainly no better able than the popular idioms to convey modern technical and scientific entities. Seen from the twenty-first century and after the main battles of the language question in Greece have been fought, the student of modern Greece is bound to wonder, not how the founding fathers of the new state came to forge an official language for the modern Greek nation and its polity, but how in the circumstances that decision could possibly have been avoided. The subsequent Atticising slant added to it was a symptom of ideological developments far removed from the objectives of Koraes and other enlightened Greeks of his time.

Looking at the institutions of the Ottoman administration and at the local petty tyrants and armed bands (Armatoles) who received their authority from the Sultan and looked after his interests and their own, and then at the one actually built on the model of a centralised, liberal Western democracy independent of a supranational church authority, and based on the concept of the sovereign people and on the legitimacy derived from recognition by its European peers which were its models, it is hard to imagine any elements of the former being grafted on to the latter.

The new nation-state was meant to represent a radical departure from all that was corrupt, unjust, inefficient, backward and inimical to the people's interests and will. To create this new polity it was necessary first to destroy the authority and influence of all who represented the old regime: the political and ecclesiastical administration and local communal councils that served and derived authority from the Sultan; then other local élites like the Armatole captains who were equally subservient to the local Turkish administrators and as exacting and tyrannical as they were; and powerful archons like the Hydriots and military entrepreneurs like the Maniots and Suliots.

The regime reflected in the revolutionary constitutional charters and the ones actually established by Kapodistrias and later by the Bavarian regency were thoroughly Western: centralised, efficient, free of institutionalised corruption, and sovereign. The departure from the initially proclaimed representative character of the regime was thought to be incidental and temporary: in fact it was necessary for the sheer survival of the fledgling new entity which was driven close to extinction by 1827. Kapodistrias's rule was the 'Directory' of the Greek War of Independence, established in response to the excesses perpetrated in the civil strife of 1824–5 by the entrenched local élites who were unwilling to relinquish power to a central revolutionary government. King Otto meanwhile was seen as a saviour sent by Providence to deliver the nation from the numerous petty tyrants who had arisen following the murder of Kapodistrias by a Maniote clan in 1831.

Most of the attacks on the new regime established in revolutionary and post-revolutionary Greece overlook the fact that the concentration of authority in a central lay government was the principal feature of the modern progressive state, associated with the French Revolution. A church independent of the administrative authority of the Patriarchate and subject to state authority was a progressive measure; so were the dissolution of the irregulars who had fought in the War of Independence and the formation of a regular army, the establishment of regulated justice and taxation, and civil administration answerable to the central government and not to local notables and captains. All these were steps leading in the same direction: the establishment of a modern polity similar to those of which examples were already in operation in the West. Alternatives to such a polity have been produced in Greece either by conservative reaction or by disillusionment with the way it has worked in practice. Its negative features mostly came about because the same élites, which it had aimed to break, gained access to the new system in a different guise.

The bid of the founding fathers of modern Greece to build a nation-state on Western lines was a bold and difficult undertaking, but it was the only possible option for the Greek people. Freedom from the Ottoman overlords and their underlings could be achieved only within the context of institutions that secured the rule of law— and these were the institutions that had been perfected in the West and used for similar purposes.

This bold bid for Western nation-statehood launched Greece on a great venture—its promising but troubled European apprenticeship— but the modern Greeks seem never to have made the sustained effort needed to fulfill all its requirements. Although the West has always had a powerful appeal to Greece, the influence of those who undertook to establish Western institutions seemed at times to be waning. The convinced and uncompromising Westernisers among the modern Greeks have always seemed to be outnumbered by the sworn enemies of the Western nation-state. The truly Enlightened liberals dedicated to the service of such a state have always been few compared to its opponents, i.e. the legion of those who favour an Orthodox or *opponents of western society* [handwritten annotation]

Balkan Greece, the Romantic dreamers and the not-so-romantic Pallikars, the strongmen or local power-brokers who did everything they could to strengthen their precarious position in the new state.

The Western-educated men who rushed to insurgent Greece to channel revolutionary action in the direction of Western liberal democracy numbered around 100: most of them had studied in German, Austrian, Italian and French universities, and represented the intellectual vanguard of the new Greece. They had a meteoric rise and a quick fall, but not before leaving their mark on the country's institutions. Some, like the Phanariot Theodoros Negris, died in the war. Others survived to tell of how they were pushed aside as 'Heterochthons' (Greeks from abroad). However, most were obliged to become players in the political game that resuscitated all the old, entrenched élites, clothed now in the legitimacy of Western institutions. Without a support base of their own in the country, Western-educated Greeks were too weak to challenge indigenous élites: they were simply tolerated for the Western legitimacy they brought to the insurgent country. Kapodistrias and the Bavarian regency used their talents and gave them appointments as officials in the state machinery, thus depriving them of their independence. Although the 'Pronunciamento' of September 1843 and the constitution of 1844 that it imposed represented a triumph for Western principles and representative institutions, this was nevertheless a constitution that limited the powers of the monarch and made possible the return of those whom both Kapodistrias and the Bavarian regency had tried to suppress, namely the powerful indigenous élites who were keen to use these institutions to rebuild their power-bases.

Though manipulated by indigenous élites nurtured in corrupt rule, those Western principles and institutions were never themselves attacked; they were too important as legitimising agents and links with the West. Gradually such principles and institutions allowed an indigenous class of parliamentarians to emerge. Men like Charilaos Trikoupis and Eleftherios Venizelos pushed the country forward, freeing it from its Eastern moorings, and their achievements have always been thought of as a vinndication of what the young Greek intellectuals from Western Europe stood for during the War of Independence.

However, the reforming efforts of men like Kapodistrias, Trikoupis and Venizelos were interrupted by either wars or internal upheavals—or by successors unable or unwilling to continue those reforming policies. The failure of a sustained effort and frequent reversals of policy have seldom been the result of men coming to power who had doubts about Greece's Western orientation being the only sound course for the country. Greek leaders have sometimes sided with one or more of the great Western powers against the others, but rarely, if ever, turned against the West as such. They did not lack conviction of the rightness of Greece's Western orientation; they merely lacked the courage to pursue it and the dedication to sustain public enthusiasm for it.

Questions about Greece's Western connection have mostly arisen when the Western powers have openly disapproved of the country's policies. For example, Western criticism of the employment of brigands and released convicts for irredentist action in Thessaly, Epirus and Macedonia in the second half of the nineteenth century fuelled anti-Western feeling. This was then exploited by leaders eager to capitalise on public disappointment in the inability of Greece to secure the territorial gains which the public had been led to believe were forthcoming. Well-merited criticism of the state hiring brigands in the pursuit of its foreign policy, and the understandable reluctance of Western powers to allow Greek territorial expansion to proceed faster than the need to maintain stability in the region and pursue their own interests allowed, played into the hands of populist leaders, who presented Greece in the role of victim of Western intervention as a means of winning popular support for themselves.

Irresponsible demagogues have not been an exclusively Greek phenomenon in modern politics. The peculiar contribution of modern Greece to the appraisal of Western liberal democracy in the contett of the modern nation-state has been sincere admiration of the West but a lukewarm acceptance of the need to model the country upon it. This in turn explains its troubled European apprenticeship, marked by bouts of courting Europe, followed by periods of searching for the supposedly unique features of modern Greek identity, at risk from too much modernisation. Orthodox prelates and Philorthodox intellectuals have always been at hand to anathematise the West and agitate for the Lord's 'chosen people' to return to the fold. Academics, with a keen sense of rewarded patriotism, have also excelled in the art of promoting ethnic myths as truth. All major crises surrounding the Eastern Question in the nineteenth century produced such lapses into patriotic hysteria. Consider for instance the Dilessi affair of 1870, when brigands abducted and killed Englishmen for ransom under the placid eye of the authories, the conflict over the future of Macedonia in the 1900s, and the issue of the name of the new nation-state to the north of Greece in the 1990s. The vociferous proclamation of 'ethnic truth' in each of these crises carried a considerable load of anti-Western feeling.

Despite periodic lapses into nationalistic hysteria, anti-Westernism and drummed-up nostalgia for the lost paradise of a pre-national

Orthodox Eden, modern Greece has been irrevocably cast off from its Ottoman Eastern moorings. However, disappointment over this still incomplete Westernisation of modern Greece has sometimes thwarted a realistic appraisal of how much has actually been accomplished by the disciples of Koraes, Voltaire and Locke despite strong opposition from the powerful enemies of what they stood for. Similarly, the disappointment caused by the excesses of modern Greece's pious national myth has led to an underestimation of the creative impact that this national myth has had on such an ethnically and linguistically diverse population as the one that formed the modern Greek state. The recent commendable sensitivity over the treatment of linguistic and other minorities by national governments in Greek history has tended to obscure the central achievement of securing for the shepherd, farmer, seaman and craftsman—whether Greek, Albanian, Vlach or Slav living in the southern Balkans—not only citizen rights in a modern liberal democracy, but pride in belonging to a historic nation and being the guardians of a great cultural heritage, revered by all 'enlightened' nations.

The occasional lapses of modern Greece into 'un-European' behaviour and practices have always drawn strong criticism from Western Europe. Equally, Western Europe's lapses into high-handed treatment of modern Greece have been met by cynicism on the Greek side regarding West European motives. To most Greeks the West has always appeared too willing to reach an understanding with dictatorial governments in Greece and to exploit friendly relations with them for reasons other than those offered for public consumption. Moreover, in its 150 years of independent statehood before joining the European Community in 1980, Greece had been blockaded several times by West European powers and twice partly or wholly occupied, in 1916–17 and again in 1941–4, by their armed forces.

Western approval has always been eagerly sought by the Greeks, but their addiction to philhellenic praise turned them sour when old friends turned into critics or even foes. Although flexible in their own domestic politics, most Greeks maintain a Manichean view of the outside world. The fact that foreigners pursue their own interests in relation to Greece, as they are entitled to, rather than hate or love Greece has rarely been prominent in Greek perceptions of the outside world.

Of all Westerners the British have observed the country most closely and they produced a significant body of literature. Some, such as E.M. Forster and Compton Mackenzie, came during the First World War on special missions and played an active role in the national schism between Venizelos and King Constantine. Others, such as Patrick

Leigh Fermor and C.M. Woodhouse, fought in the resistance against the Nazis and continued their love of the country with a scholarly view of Greek affairs in their own writings. Yet others, such as Romilly Jenkins, followed the policies of their own national governments and became detractors of all things Greek after the eruption of the Cyprus crisis in the 1950s.

Development has its down side and foreigners who enjoyed the environment and society of Greece when it was relatively underdeveloped are now faced with a new Greek phenomenon that is close to the Western norm. As Greece ceases to be fertile ground for anthropologists and the lure of its former picturesque poverty diminishes, scholars will have to adapt their tools of analysis to a new reality. This is now happening, mostly in Greece itself. The author of an anonymous commentary, published in London's *Sunday Telegraph* on 27 March 1994 offers an outdated sample of the arrogant foreign detractor that used to inflame Greek public opinion. The reply of a Greek official in the same newspaper on 3 April 1994 betrays a generational change of attitude towards the West.

In conclusion it could be said that more Greeks today than ever before are aware of the distance that still separates their country from the task set two centuries ago. Perhaps one of the greatest achievements of this seemingly endless apprenticeship in Europeanness has been a developing process of self-evaluation involving ever wide sections of the population. It is the result of tremendous strides in education, uninterrupted peace, democratic government for a quarter of a century, significant prosperity and, most important perhaps, the measuring of an increasing number of Greeks up against other Europeans in their own countries. The resulting self-assurance has convinced many Greeks that if they can excel in Germany, France or England they can be equally good Europeans just by being good Greeks. It is increasingly being realised that Greece's founding fathers set as a lasting goal an image of Europe that is an appropriate model for West Europeans no less than for the Greeks and other East Europeans. This model is based on the premise that in Europe the government is (or should be) accountable to the people, the rule of law is paramount, equality before the law is assured and so are equal opportunities for all, protection of the weak against the mighty, and the right to be different.[2]

---

[2] Hagen Fleischer, 'Europas Rückkehr nach Griechenland. Kulturpolitik der Grossmächte in einem Staat der Peripherie' in Harald Heppner and Olga Katsiardi-Hering, eds, *Die Griechen und Europa*, Vienna, Cologne, Weimar, 1998. pp. 125–91.

Europe's Trojan Horse

Excerpt from the anonymous 'Profile', *Sunday Telegraph* (London), 27 March 1994

What is the word for this obsessive pseudo-relationship of the Greeks with their country's past? (They even have a magazine, *Ellenismos*, devoted to the subject.) it is not quite pretentiousness, since there is too much passion for that.

No, the Greeks, the ancient ones, had a word for the modern Greek condition, paranoia. We must accept that Mr Andreas Papandreou and the current EC presidency are the sole legitimate heirs of Pericles, Demosthenes and Aristides the Just. The world must nod humbly at the proposition that in the veins of the modern Greek, with his dark glasses, car-phone and phantom olive groves attracting EC subsidies, there courses the blood of Achilles. And their paranoid nationalism is heightened by the tenuousness of that claim.

In the 1830s, an Austrian classicist called J.J. Fallmereyer made a study of the South Slav migrations and concluded not just that most Greeks are Slavs, but that not a drop of pure Greek blood was to be found in the modern Greek. In Athens, needless to say, his name is not much heard.

⌐Greece has been ruthless in erasing traces of ethnic diversity. The village of Marathon, scene of the great victory in 490 BC, the same Marathon where Byron looked out for an hour alone and dreamt that Greece might still be free, was, early last century, almost completely Albanian.⌐

Throughout the 1980s, Greece was mainlining $2 billion per year of EC funds, not forgetting the amazing 'Integrated Mediterranean Programme' of 1985, which gave the Greeks an extra £1.5 billion, as part of a deal with America. Mr Papandreou promised to shut up about American bases in Greece, while Washington gave ground to Brussels in a row over trade in corn gluten feed. Since December 1992 the Greek share has increased.

Then one could mention the EC's acquiescence in the Acheloos river dam project, a rampantly corrupt scheme to divert the river which Homer identifies as the source of all aquatic life, blasting a tunnel through the Pindus range to irrigate the plain of Thessaly, thereby drying up the Missolonghi wetlands and probably driving the Dalmatian pelican to extinction; or one could cite the EC's failure to punish Greece for inventing a fifth of its cotton crop in 1992, in order to claim extra subsidies.

Brussels has written some abusive letters, complaining of the Greek practice of exploiting its membership of the EC to run up vast public debts. Mr Delors has requested that Athens sack most of the 60,000 extra employees hired during the 1980s. He can whistle, as far as Athens is concerned.

The Greeks in short, have found in the EC a new kind of decaying Ottoman empire and, at least in some sense a new kind of slavery. If Byron were alive today, and looking at the ruination caused by the EC-funded Athens metro, he might dream again that Greece might be free; and perhaps that we in the rest of the EC might be free of them.

It's all Greek to the Greeks

Reply of the Greek Ambassador in London, Elias Gounaris, to the anonymous article of 27 March 1994. Published in the *Sunday Telegraph*, 3 April 1994.

Greece has not laid siege to Brussels and cannot, therefore, be Europe's Trojan horse ('Profile', March 27). If there is in the EC a member that wants to do to Europe what the Greeks did to Troy, it is not the country that I represent. By calling the EC 'a new kind of decaying Ottoman Empire' your writer at least leaves us in no doubt where he stands.

Modern Greeks are further accused of not being racially correct, i.e. 'genetically connected' with ancient Greeks. Such views were propounded by the Austro-German professor of history and part-time politician, Jacob Philipp Fallmerayer, in the 19th century when romantic notions about the 'soul' of nations were prevalent in Europe. Another Austro-German politician developed these concepts into a fully-fledged theory based on the primacy of 'blood and soil' (*Blut und Boden*).

Both Hitler and Fallmerayer were fairly consistent. The latter opined— as you repeat—that modern Greeks did not have 'a drop of pure Greek blood' in their veins because they were 'hellenised' Slavs. He meant this, however, as an insult because he considered Slavs racially inferior (Hitler called them subhuman—'*Untermenschen*').

Does your correspondent share this view? (He accuses Greeks of being a 'mixture of Slavs, Turks, Bulgars, Albanians, Vlachs, Jews and Gypsies', i.e. of purer stock than the Greeks since to admit to a 'mixture of mixtures' would ridicule the whole racially inspired argument. So it should.)

We think that racist theories are wrong and should be abandoned. Continuity in Greece is linguistic and cultural. This was proclaimed some 23 centuries ago by Isokrates, who said that 'we consider Greeks those who partake in our culture'. The Athenian taxi-driver mentioned in your 'Profile' would have heard of both Pindar and Homer. If he did not understand their verse, probably recited in the incomprehensible, to him, Erasmian pronunciation with a British accent to boot, he should be excused.

After 3,000 years, a language—even a remarkably stable language like Greek—does change. Try the verses 'And wel ye woot, agaynes kyndel Hyt were to lyven in thys wyse' on your average London taxi-driver and see how close he is to Chaucer, even though the medieval poet's language is only some 700 years removed from him. On the other hand, all churchgoing Greeks, including presumably your correspondent's 'toothless goatherd', understand the biblical Greek of 2,000 years ago.

There is, last but not least, a peculiar logic in your 'Profile'. You devote six columns to 'prove' that Greeks are not really Greeks, in terms of race, and end up with proposing that the European Union should 'free itself' from them, i.e. expel them. Would our alleged present turpitudes be forgiven if only we had a racially clean pedigree and if we could prove to your anonymous correspondent's satisfaction that we are indeed 'genetically connected' to the ancient Greeks? It seems to me that if ethnic cleansing has rightly become reprehensible of late, racial cleansing, be it by the somewhat milder method of expulsion, is definitely passé, in Europe at least.

Part VI. FOREIGN POLICY

17

GREEK FOREIGN POLICY
FROM INDEPENDENCE TO LIBERATION

The designation of the Greek state that emerged from the war against the Ottoman yoke determined the future course of its foreign policy. Greece inherited not only the responsibility of a tremendous cultural heritage, but also the daunting project of reconstituting the elusive realm of its classical antecedent. Although nineteenth-century irredentism was not invented by the Greeks, the historic landmarks that accentuated the presence of all things Greek in the southern Balkans became a compelling incentive for the new state's policy-makers.

The boundaries of the Greek state of 1832 embraced a population of 700,000, barely a quarter of the Greeks, the other three-quarters residing mostly in the European and Asian parts of the Ottoman empire.[1] Athens, a provincial town of 26,000 inhabitants in 1840, was a poor match for Constantinople with its 120,000 Greeks at the same period and the Ecumenical Patriarchate of the Orthodox Church commanding significant influence over a multinational Christian flock. The Ottoman Greeks, as well as the prosperous diaspora in Russia, the Danubian principalities, Vienna, Trieste and Egypt, provided the financial backbone of Hellenism. Although the irredentist ideology expounded by Greece was not always compatible with the interests

---

[1]See J. A. Petropulos, *Politics and Statecraft in the Kingdom of Greece, 1833–1843*, Princeton University Press, 1968, an analysis of the first decade of King Otto's reign. Katerina Gardika's *Prostasia kai engyiseis. Stadia kai mythoi tis ellimikis ethnikis oloklirosis (1821–1920)* (Protection and guarantees. Phases and myths of Greek national unification), Thessaloniki: Vanias, 1999, is an imaginative analysis of Western guarantees towards the Greek state and the international setting throughout its first 100 years of existence.

of the Great Church in Constantinople whose influence diminished with every new addition to the Hellenic realm, the Greeks in Crete, Cyprus, Epirus, Thessaly, Macedonia and the Ionian islands never ceased demanding union with the national centre. The last-named were ceded to Greece in 1864 by the British.

The Eastern Question went through many phases before assuming a more rigid configuration, with Britain upholding the *status quo* and Russia opting for dismemberment of the Ottoman empire. Although the latter option was naturally more compatible with Greek irredentist aspirations, Greece came firmly under British influence after a period of rivalry among the great powers in 1833–56. Britain's naval superiority in the Mediterranean during the Crimean war (1853–6) heralded its future influence in Greek affairs. When King Otto attempted to lead his feeble forces into Ottoman territory after provoking an uprising of the Greeks in Epirus, Thessaly and Macedonia, British warships, in a series of high-handed displays of power, blockaded the vital port of Piraeus and starved the unruly Greeks into submission.[2] With the conclusion of the war Otto suffered the penalty of his Russophile stance. The eclipse of Russian influence in the Balkans was followed by his deposition in 1862. Palmerston favoured the installation on the Greek throne of a prince of Denmark, who became King George I of the Hellenes, while Russia gradually substituted its traditional appeal to the Balkan Orthodox with a policy of wooing its Slavic brethren. By the last quarter of the century pan-Slavism had become a formidable antagonist of Greek irredentism.

In 1877–8 Russia made a forceful comeback in the Balkans. After a victory over the Turkish forces it obliged its defeated enemy to sign the San Stefano treaty, ceding most of its European territory to Bulgaria. The unredeemed Greeks, who had risen once more, looked on with dismay as their chief Balkan rival reaped the rewards of Russian patronage. Britain's intervention and the amending treaty of Berlin (1878) diminished these rewards, but it was becoming increasingly obvious to the British that because of its internal weaknesses the Ottoman empire would not be able in the future to fulfill the role of an effective buffer against Russian expansionism in which the West European powers had cast it.[3]

[2]M.S. Anderson, *The Eastern Question*, London: Macmillan Press, 1966, pp. 110–48.

[3]E. Kofos, *Greece and the Eastern Crisis, 1875–1878*, Thessaloniki: Institute for Balkan Studies, 1975, pp. 185–205, 226–56.

The 1880s and '90s witnessed developments of vital importance for Greece. The acquisition of the fertile plains of Thessaly in 1881 in the aftermath of the Berlin Congress alleviated the country's dependence on heavy imports of grain and added a vital source of revenue to the national treasury.[4] A policy of encouraging industrial growth, improving communications and reorganising the national administration and armed forces was financed largely through heavy borrowing from the international markets. By 1893 foreign loans exceeded 640,000,000 francs, only three-quarters of which had become available to Greece because these loans were issued below par.[5] In that year, in consequence of a prolonged mobilisation in 1885 and the dramatic decline in the price of that major export item, currants, the government declared the state bankrupt and imposed a moratorium on foreign debts (servicing of the debts required 33 per cent of budget revenues).

A new rising of the Cretans in 1896 obliged the Greeks to send military aid to the island, thus provoking hostilities with the Ottoman empire along their shared borders. In the war of 1897 their troops were defeated by a German-trained Ottoman army and the country was forced to accept an international control commission to guarantee that it paid a large war indemnity. The International Financial Control established itself in the country for several decades, ensuring that the Greek economy would yield enough to service its foreign debt. Crete, which had been an apple of discord between Greeks and Ottomans, was finally granted autonomy in 1898 after joint pressure on the Sultan from Britain, France, Italy and Russia.[6]

Meanwhile the management of the balance of power in Europe was assumed by Germany. Bismarck's efforts to stabilize relations with the other powers following his victory over the French in 1871 were accompanied by a general willingness to abstain from aggressive policies in the Balkans. When the young German Emperor Wilhelm II (who was set on asserting his power over Russia) obliged Bismarck to resign in 1890, his Chancellor's balancing act, which had secured peace for almost a generation, was fatally disrupted. 'The response of Britain to Germany's challenge was not immediate; with five major conti-

[4]M. Sivignon, 'The Demographic and Economic Evolution of Thessaly (1881–1940)' in Francis W. Carter (ed.), *An Historical Geography of the Balkans*, London: Academic Press, 1977.

[5]John Campbell and Philip Sherrard, *Modern Greece*, London: Ernest Benn, 1968, pp. 98–100.

[6]G. Papadopoulos, *England and the Near East, 1896–98*, Thessaloniki: Institute for Balkan Studies, 1969, pp. 195–224.

nental powers where previously there had been only four, it saw the making of an almost automatic balance of power. Having for so long regarded France or Russia, rather than Austria-Hungary or Prussia, as most likely to endanger an equitable balance in Europe, Britain was slow to appreciate the full implications of German ascendancy.'[7]

By 1869 the Ottomans had skillfully embarked on a policy of exploiting the inherent disputes among the Balkan states in order to preclude alliances that would threaten their European possessions. The independence (1870) of the Bulgarian Exarchate Church from the authority of the Ecumenical Patriarchate was encouraged and supported by the Porte. It initiated a conflict between Greece and Bulgaria, which was compounded by the Bulgarian annexation of Eastern Rumelia in 1885—a territory heavily populated by Greeks. Soon after that, the religious rivalry and competition to proselytise local peasants between agents of the autonomous Bulgarian Exarchate Church and the followers of the Ecumenical Patriarch developed into a full-scale nationalist struggle over the domination of Ottoman Macedonia.[8] Its two major and sometimes conflicting security concerns—the liberation of Greek territories from Ottoman rule and preventing the Bulgarians from dominating Macedonia—became the priority of Greece's foreign policy at the dawn of the twentieth century.

Efforts to recruit converts to the Exarchate Church were mainly focussed on the region from the river Haliakmon to the Shar and Rila mountains and from Mt Grammos to the river Nestos. The policy of ensuring that Macedonia would appear predominantly Bulgarian in a post-Ottoman settlement was generally pursued by both the conservative, Sofia-directed 'Supreme Committee' or 'Verhovists' and the more radical 'Internal Macedonian Revolutionary Organisation' (IMRO), which envisaged an autonomous status for the region. Responding to the challenge, Greece founded the 'National Society' in 1894 to protect the native population from forced conversion. The Patriarchate of Constantinople strove to maintain its spiritual authority over the Orthodox inhabitants, but was fast losing ground to the

---

[7]David Thompson, *Europe Since Napoleon*, London: Pelican, 1978, p. 524.

[8]'Since nationalism had begun to emerge, [...] the subject Christians had ceased to think themselves as simply members of the Orthodox Church. They thought of themselves primarily in national or linguistic terms. Now their Ottoman rulers proposed to exploit their national separatism for their own ends. Balkanisation thus became a calculated policy'. C.M. Woodhouse, *The Story of Modern Greece*, London: Faber & Faber, 1968. p. 183.

Exarchate Church and had to rely on the aid of Greek organisations.

However, it was the 'Ilinden' rebellion in 1903, a high-point of IMRO's activities, which alerted the Greek government to the danger of losing Macedonia to Bulgaria. The rebellion swept through a number of reluctant Greek towns and villages in Western Macedonia before being suppressed by the Ottoman army. In 1904 an ostensibly private society, the 'Macedonian Committee', was founded in Athens and given moral and material support by the government. The Greek consulate in Thessaloniki became the headquarters of the organisation and a number of young officers were granted indefinite leave of absence from their units in order to join the struggle. By 1908 the Greek bands had succeeded in checking Bulgarian infiltration into southern and central Macedonia.[9]

The Greek and Bulgarian bands in the field were joined by Serbian, Romanian and Albanian agents, each promoting its own nationalist and religious aspirations and adding to the confusion of the great powers. The Turkish authorities had done little to implement reforms proposed by the powers, and so in 1904 European police officers arrived in Macedonia to ensure that measures of pacification were carried out. However, except for the British the forces had little incentive to take their peace-keeping role seriously.

By 1904 Britain had finally overcome its traditional mistrust of France and in 1907 the Entente between the two was joined by Russia. Before settling its differences with Russia and finally abandoning its policy of buttressing the Ottoman empire, Britain had shown little sympathy for the predicament of Greece being forced to choose between a Balkan alliance against the Ottomans and co-operation with them to keep the Slavs at bay. Germany and Austria had instead taken the initiative of proposing the latter course in 1901 as part of a wider policy to bring the non-Slavic Balkan peoples (Greeks, Romanians, Turks) closer together. Although King George, consistent with his anglophile position, rejected the German overtures, he could not prevent a strong pro-German circle from developing within his own court. His eldest son and heir Constantine, married to Kaiser Wilhelm II's sister, sent a select number of his military clients to be educated in Berlin and aspired to secure German experts to reform the Greek army. By 1907 the main blocs of the First World War had already been formed—

---

[9]Douglas Dakin, *The Greek Struggle in Macedonia 1897–1913*, Thessaloniki: Institute for Balkan Studies, 1966, pp. 360–74.

with a predominantly military but defensive alliance between Germany, Austria and Italy (Italy later joined the Triple Entente) and a diplomatic alliance between France, Russia and Britain.[10]

The Ottoman reforms (Tanzimat) between 1839 and 1876 improved the lot of the Greek community in the empire, but the despotic rule of Abdul Hamid II after 1877, his treatment of minorities and his encouragement of a pan-Islamic movement posed a new threat to the prosperous but politically impotent Ottoman Greeks. The multi-ethnic membership of the clandestine 'Committee for Union and Progress' (the official name of what later became known as the Young Turks) and particularly the liberal branch of the organisation, which focused on a confederation of semi-autonomous Ottoman communities, was immediately attractive to the Greeks. According to the liberal Young Turks, a secular political ideology[11] would unite the citizens of the empire, and a parliamentary system would guarantee equal rights for all Ottoman citizens, irrespective of religion or race.

On the eve of an imposed solution in Turkey's European posses-sions promoted by Britain and Russia, Young Turk army officers staged a coup in Macedonia (June 1908) and obliged the Sultan to revive the short-lived constitution of 1876. Greeks, Bulgars and Turks embraced each other in the streets of Thessaloniki and vowed to patch up old feuds and to live happily together in constitutional harmony. The exhilaration of the Ottoman Greeks at the prospect of attaining the full benefits of modern citizenship coincided with the willingness of the Greek state to improve its relations with the Ottoman admin-istration in order to deal with the more pressing Bulgarian problem.[12]

The inability of the Young Turk regime to forestall Bulgarian inde-pendence and the annexation of Bosnia and Hercegovina by Austria, fanned the nationalism of its leadership.[13] Having reluctantly yielded to the Bulgarian and Austrian *faits accomplis*, the Young Turks were compelled to pursue a policy that would convince their compatriots

---

[10]For the attempt of Balkan states to counter the Slavic influence see Kostas Loulos, *I germaniki politiki stin Ellada 1896–1914* (German policy in Greece 1896–1914), Athens: Papazissis, 1991, pp. 57–76.

[11]The ideology was also known as 'Ottomanism'; see David Kushner, *The Rise of Turkish Nationalism 1876–1908*, London: Frank Cass, 1977. pp. 38–9.

[12]T. Veremis, *Istoria ton Ellinotourkikon Scheseon 1453–1998* (History of Greek-Turkish relations), Athens: ELIAMEP-Sideris, 1998, pp. 51–76.

[13]Bernard Lewis, *The Emergence of Modern Turkey*, Oxford University Press, 1968, p. 352.

of their power. The continued pressure from Crete, granted autonomy in 1898, for unification with the Greek mainland brought Turkish threats of armed intervention. Between 1908 and 1912 Greek governments discouraged the island's representation in the Greek parliament in order to avoid a confrontation with Turkey.

Eleftherios Venizelos, the Cretan statesman who had fought for the irredentist cause since his youth, entered Greek politics in 1910 and with his widely acclaimed social, political and military reforms inspired Greece as the new architect of irredentism. In May 1912 Greece and Bulgaria signed a treaty of alliance and, with Serbia and Montenegro, formed the league that would confront the Ottoman empire. This development came about partly in reaction to the menacing nationalism of the Young Turks and partly as the culmination of almost a century of Balkan struggle for independence and national unity.[14]

Russia's support for the Balkan League as a buffer to Austrian expansion, Britain's abandonment of Ottoman territorial integrity in view of the formidable German challenge, and the inability of the Young Turks to check Italian aggression in Libya in 1911, set the stage for a Balkan onslaught on the remaining Ottoman footholds in Europe. When war erupted in October 1912, Greece's main contribution was to prevent any reinforcement of the Turkish army by sea. The Greek fleet engaged Turkish warships in naval battles which forced them to remain inactive within the Dardanelles, and the Greek army in a frantic march almost without hindrance entered Thessaloniki in November 1912 only a few hours before Bulgarian troops closed in on the city. By the treaty of London (May 1913) Greece secured southern Epirus, a part of Macedonia, and Crete. Yet the old conflict between Greece and Bulgaria over which of them would rule Macedonia was left largely unresolved. While attacking Serbia and Greece, Bulgaria exposed itself to simultaneous offensives from Romania, Montenegro and Turkey. The treaty of Bucharest in August 1913 awarded Thessaloniki and the port of Kavalla to Greece. Serbia was given northern and central Macedonia, and Turkey reoccupied Eastern Thrace. Bulgaria's losses created chronic instability in the region; although it had signed away the greater part of Macedonia to Greece and Serbia, Bulgaria had hoped that future circumstances would allow a revision of the treaty. Austria and Russia were willing for this to happen, but Germany,

[14]E. Driault, M. Lheritier, *Histoire diplomatique de la Grèce de 1821 à nos jours*, vol. V, Paris, 1926.

which had supported Greek claims during the negotiations (boundaries with Albania, the islands and Kavalla), and France effectively opposed any revision.[15]

On the eve of the worst civil strife that the country had known since the War of Independence, Greece appeared to be in a state of fulfilment. Its territory had increased from 64,786 to 108,606 square km. and its population from 2,700,000 to 4,370,000.[16] The Balkan Wars marked the successful culmination of Cretan and Macedonian struggles for unification and the partial realisation of irredentist aspirations in Epirus and the Aegean islands. However, differences with neighbouring countries were exacerbated rather than resolved. Bulgarian hostility over the loss of Macedonia; Turkish reluctance to concede Greece's possession of Aegean islands, coupled with the persecution of Greeks in Asia Minor; and finally Italy's urge for self-aggrandisement in the eastern Mediterranean, meant that both the intensity and the number of causes of hostility towards Greece had increased. Although Serbian friendship and alliance (June 1913) partly compensated for these liabilities, in 1915 it became the focus of a clash between Venizelos—a friend of the Entente—and the neutralist King Constantine.[17] While Venizelos wanted to honour Greece's commitment to help Serbia militarily in case it was attacked by Bulgaria, the King was opposed to the involvement of Greece in the First World War. He advocated neutrality, a stance that would best serve the interests of his brother-in-law, Kaiser Wilhelm II, and Germany's allies. The ability of Greece to pursue an autonomous foreign policy was constrained by the prevailing bipolarity in European affairs. At the outbreak of the war, the pressure on the Balkan states exerted by the Triple Entente and the Triple Alliance became overpowering. With Turkey and Bulgaria joining the Central Powers, and a treaty that bound Greece to aid Serbia in case of Bulgarian aggression, there was, according to Venizelos, one course which the Greek government had no choice but to pursue: commitment to the side of the Entente.

---

[15]Helen Gardikas Katsiadakis, *Greece and the Balkan Imbroglio: Greek Foreign Policy, 1911–1913*, Athens: Syllogos pros Diadosin Ophelimon Vivlion, 1995, is the definitive work on the subject.
[16]Douglas Dakin. *The Unification of Greece 1770–1923*, London: Ernest Benn, 1972, p. 202.
[17]Although Venizelos and Constantine agreed that Greece was faced with both a Turkish and a Bulgarian danger, they differed widely in the remedies they prescribed. D. Portolos, 'Greek Foreign Policy, September 1916 to October 1919', PhD thesis, Birkbeck College, London, 1974.

Twice in one year Constantine's resolution to keep his kingdom out of the war forced his popular Prime Minister to resign, and the conflict between the two acquired wider national significance as Venizelos joined a revolt launched in Thessaloniki in the summer of 1916 and set up a 'provisional government' to bring Greece into the war.[18] An army made up of dissident troops and volunteers joined the Anglo-French forces on the Macedonian front. By the summer of 1917 Constantine was forced to abdicate in favour of his second son Alexander, and the entire Greek army joined the Entente war effort. The Greek divisions that took part in the Macedonian campaign of the autumn of 1918 contributed to the defeat of the German and Bulgarian forces, and Venizelos's eagerness to prove Greece a dependable ally of the West was further confirmed by the commitment of Greek units to the French expedition against the Bolsheviks in the Ukraine.[19]

At the Versailles peace conference of 1919 the Greek delegation argued before the Supreme Council of the Allies the Greek claims for the annexation of 'Northern Epirus' (Southern Albania), Thrace and the Dodecanese, and the internationalisation of Constantinople. Venizelos also demanded most of the *vilayet* (administrative region) of Aidin, including Smyrna, to ensure that the Greeks of Asia Minor,[20] who had been persecuted during the Balkan Wars and the years of Greek neutrality (1914–17), would 'be assured an undoubted security of life and an absolutely unmolested opportunity of autonomous development' (one of President Wilson's fourteen points). Of these claims 'Northern Epirus' was denied to Greece through Italian pressure, while the return of the Italian-held Dodecanese (with the exception of Rhodes), though included in the Venizelos-Titoni agreement of July 1919, was repudiated in 1922. The other claims, including the

[18]The revolt against Athens was triggered by the willingness of the King's puppet government to allow Bulgarian troops to occupy the Greek port of Kavalla. The definitive work on the Greece's role in the First World War is by George Leontaritis, *Greece and the First World War: From Neutrality to Intervention 1917–1918*, Boulder, CO: East European Monographs, 1990.

[19]For an accurate description of the expedition of Greek troops in the Ukraine, see Petros Karakassonis, *Istoria tis is Ukranian kai Krimaian yperpontiou ekstratias to 1919* (History of the Expedition to the Ukraine and Crimea in 1919), Athens: Lambropoulos, 1934.

[20]According to Leon Maccas, *L' Hellenisme de l'Asie Mineure*, Paris, 1919, p. 87, out oᶜa 10,685,574 Ottoman population 7,256,147 were Turks, 2,452,151 Greeks, 649,540 Armenians, 6,381 Bulgarians etc.

islands of Imbros, Tenedos and Lemnos (occupied by the British during the war), were conceded to Greece by the treaty of Sèvres (August 1920).[21]

In the light of subsequent developments, Venizelos's Asiatic adventure proved a grave error. However, at the time the Italian plans to occupy the central and southern coast of Asia Minor, and British readiness to counter Italian imperialism with a friendly Greek presence in the Aidin region, obscured fundamental considerations of strategy. The proposal of Lloyd George, the British prime minister, that Greek troops should be despatched to Smyrna to protect the Christian population was endorsed by President Wilson.

At the end of 1920 Venizelos was voted out of office by a war-weary electorate and King Constantine was restored. The return of the royalist party to power led to a reversal in French policy towards Greece. France's discontent with the treaty of Sèvres, which had significantly strengthened Greece, an ally of Britain, and thus created a potential threat to French interests in the Levant, was expressed openly after the change of government in Athens. At a conference in London in 1921 the representatives of Kemal Atatürk, resisting the concessions made by the Ottoman government, negotiated with the French and the Italians, and as the result the Italians evacuated their troops from Antalia. In June France signed a pact with Atatürk, abandoning Cilicia and giving large quantities of arms to the Turkish nationalist forces. In the mean time Atatürk had signed a treaty of friendship with the Soviet Union in March 1921. In August of that year the Greek army, having stretched its lines of comunication with the coast to the limit, was stopped by stiff Turkish resistance outside Ankara, the stronghold of the Kemalist movement. A year later a Turkish offensive broke the Greek defences, captured Smyrna and put an end to the Greek presence in Asia Minor.[22]

The treaty of Lausanne in 1923 signified the death of the Greek 'Great Idea'; of the remaining unredeemed territories Cyprus was officially ceded to Britain and the Dodecanese to Italy. The remaining Greek population in Asia Minor and Eastern Thrace were evacuated in a compulsory exchange with the Muslims of Macedonia, Epirus

[21]M. Llewellyn Smith, *Ionian Vision: Greece in Asia Minor, 1919–1922*, London: Hurst, 1999; prev. publ. 1973, pp. 284–311.

[22]The definitive work on the Greek claims at the Versailles Peace Conference is by N. Petsalis-Diomidis, *Greece at the Paris Peace Conference, 1919*, Thessaloniki: Institute for Balkan Studies, 1978.

and Crete. The Greeks of Constantinople, Imvros and Tenedos and the Muslims of Western Thrace were exempted from the exchange. More than one million Greeks descended upon a country of less than 5 million while about half a million Turks went in the opposite direction.[23] Rural refugees were settled mostly in Macedonia and Thrace. After the voluntary exchange of Bulgarian and Greek populations[24] and the compulsory exodus of the Macedonian Turks, minorities in Greece accounted for the lowest percentage in the Balkans. Furthermore, the impact of the refugees on national politics was unmistakable.[25] The addition of 300,000 voters to the 800,000 voting population played a decisive role in the plebiscite of 1924 which abolished the monarchy. Between 1924 and 1927 the Republic was shaken by military interventions, but the parliamentary system held to its course till 1936 when the restored monarch allowed the establishment of a dictatorship.

The power vacuum in the Balkans and the Eastern Mediterranean after the Great War gave Italy the opportunity to pursue its interests in that region. It had been among the victors, but was dissatisfied with the distribution of the spoils and, along with the defeated and the revolutionaries, assumed a revisionist stance towards the treaties.[26] Britain and France, the main defenders of the *status quo*, upheld the League of Nations as a peaceful instrument for resolving international conflict. Furthermore, France encouraged the formation of the 'Little Entente' and signed separate treaties with Czechoslovakia, Romania and Yugoslavia to ensure their loyalty and territorial integrity against a revived Germany and an expansionist Italy. While Yugoslavia became France's protégé in the Balkans, Italy wooed a defeated, isolated and revisionist Bulgaria, encouraging its hostility towards Yugoslavia and

[23]The most important work on interwar society and politics written in English is by George Th. Mavrogordatos, *Stillborn Republic: Social Coalitions and Party Strategies in Greece, 1922–1936*, Berkeley: University of California Press, 1983.

[24]See St. Ladas, *The Exchange of Minorities, Bulgaria, Greece and Turkey*, New York, 1932, pp. 27–8. According to the convention concerning reciprocal emigration of national minorities (Article 56, par. 2) of the Treaty of Neuilly (Nov. 1919), 'Bulgaria undertakes to recognise such provisions as ... the reciprocal and voluntary emigration of persons belonging to racial minorities'.

[25]D. Pentzopoulos, *The Balkan Exchange of Minorities and its Impact upon Greece*, Paris: Mouton 1962, pp. 95–119, 171–95.

[26]For Italy's grievances see Rohan Butler, 'The Peace Settlement of Versailles 1918–33' in C.L. Mowat, ed., *The New Cambridge Modern History (1898–1945)*, vol.12, Cambridge University Press, 1968, pp. 222–6.

Greece. Between 1923 and 1928 a revisionist Italy emerged as the most formidable threat to Greek security.[27]

After 1923 the main consideration for Greece was to secure the territorial *status quo* but there was little willingness on the part of France and Britain to guarantee it. Four years after the Versailles peace conference, Greece was isolated. The overwhelming pressure on the economy as the result of absorbing the refugees placed constraints on the military budget, and thus exposed the country to its hostile Balkan environment.[28] Relations with its old ally Serbia were strained by the Greek–Bulgarian protocol of September 1924 whereby Greece agreed to accept a League of Nations arbitration on matters concerning 'Bulgarian minorities' in its territory. By recognising the Slavic-speaking people of Greek Macedonia as Bulgarians, Greece also indirectly acknowledged the existence of a Bulgarian minority in Yugoslavia's Vardar province, the future republic of Macedonia. Yugoslavia insisted that a new protocol be drafted stating that the Slav-speakers in Greek Macedonia were Serbs—a demand which Greece flatly rejected. Although the protocol of 1924 was cancelled in March 1925, Yugoslavia had already repudiated the Greco–Serbian alliance of 1913, and relations between the two states had deteriorated.[29] Between 1924 and 1928 Belgrade made excessive demands concerning the free zone and the railway link with Thessaloniki. The pressure was accentuated by Yugoslavia's insistence that free passage of arms be guaranteed in time of war.

The abrogation of the Greek–Bulgarian protocol caused new tension between those two countries. The raids by IMRO irregulars in the 1920s caused frequent border incidents, the most violent of which, in 1925,[30] provoked the entry of Greek troops into Bulgaria. The League of Nations obliged Greece to withdraw its troops and bear the cost of the resulting damage.

The issue of compensation for the exchanged populations was an

[27]T. Veremis, *Ellada-Evropi. Apo ton Proto Polemo os ton Psychro Polemo* (Greece-Europe: From the First World War to the Cold War), Athens: Plethron, 1991, pp. 79–109

[28]P. Pipinelis, *Historia tis Hellenikis exoterikis politikis, 1923–41* (History of Greek foreign policy), Athens, 1953.

[29]Areti Tounta-Fergadi, *Elleno-Voulgarikes mionotites. Protokollo Politi-Kalfov* (Greek-Bulgarian minorities: the Politis-Kalfov Protocol), Thessaloniki: Institute for Balkan Studies, 1986.

[30]A Greek officer carrying a white flag and a few soldiers were killed by Bulgarian fire in September 1925. J. Barros, *The League of Nations and the Great Powers: The Greek-Bulgarian Incident, 1925*, Oxford, 1970.

issue that aggravated relations between Greece and Turkey. Furthermore, the Turkish government refused to recognise a substantial number of Constantinopolitan Greeks as being domiciled or 'established' and therefore exempt from the compulsory exchange. While Greece brought the case to the League of Nations in 1925, the Ecumenical Patriarch was expelled from Turkey on the grounds that he was not 'established' in Istanbul.[31]

In August 1923 Italian warships bombarded and occupied the island of Corfu in order to force Greece to accept humiliating concessions following the assassination of an Italian general in Epirus. The Greek government denied all responsibility before an investigation was conducted, and appealed to the League of Nations for arbitration. However, the League, reflecting the concern of France and Britain not to alienate Italy, refused to take up the case, pointing out that another international body (the Conference of Ministers) had already done so. Greece was therefore forced to accept the Italian terms in order to obtain the release of Corfu.[32]

By 1928 Greek enthusiasm for the collective security system had become considerably diluted. Furthermore, the improbability of a Balkan 'Locarno' guaranteeing the *status quo* in the area drove Greece into a series of bilateral agreements and treaties with its neighbours. The treaty of friendship with Italy, masterminded in 1928 by Venizelos (who made a triumphant comeback in Greek politics in that year), pulled Greece out of its diplomatic isolation, and gave the country the breathing-space it needed to deal with its other Balkan concerns. In 1930 a Greco-Turkish accord was signed by Atatürk and Venizelos, settling outstanding matters between the two countries and putting in place the cornerstone of a relationship which proved more durable than any other in the Balkans between the world wars.[33]

---

[31]The definitive work on Greek-Turkish Relations in the interwar period is by Alexis Alexandris, *The Greek Minority in Istanbul and Greek-Turkish Relations, 1918–74*, Athens: Center for Asia Minor Studies, 1983, pp. 144–73

[32]The other body was the 'Conference of Ministers' which had initially sent a committee headed by the assassinated Italian General Tellini to supervise the demarcation of the Greco-Albanian borders. The 'Conference of Ministers' could not therefore act simultaneously as the plaintiff and the judge of this issue. See James Barros, *The Corfu Incident*, Princeton University Press, 1965, pp. 297–315.

[33]Alexandris, op.cit., pp. 174–81. Also Evanthis Hatzivassiliou, *O E. Venizelos, I ellinotourkiki prosegisi kai to provlima tis asfalias sta Valkania, 1828–31* (E. Venizelos, the Greek-Turkish rapprochement and security problems in the Balkans, 1828–31), Thessaloniki: Institute for Balkan Studies, 1999.

While mending fences with Italy, Venizelos did not fail to assure Britain of his friendship, even at the price of discouraging Cypriot pleas for self-determination.[34] This was not difficult; Britain was engaged in a rapprochement (which lasted till 1935) with Italy, which it did not consider a threat to its interests in the Suez Canal and the Mediterranean. France, committed to the 'Little Entente', was less happy with these developments, but had confidence in the old Francophile Premier of Greece.[35]

Venizelos's bilateralism was reversed by his political opponents who obtained power in 1933. The treaty of February 1934 between Greece, Romania, Yugoslavia and Turkey was hailed as a triumph of Balkan cooperation; to France it was an answer to the growing menace of Nazi Germany, and provided a safeguard for the flank of the 'Little Entente', while Greece and Turkey were moved to participation by a budding rapprochement between Serbia and Bulgaria. However, instead of securing the Balkan states from external threats, the treaty—shunned by Albania and Bulgaria—caused the disputes of the European powers to move into the Balkans. Britain was sceptical of its effectiveness and Italy was against it—both were natural reactions.

Venizelos, whose policy had been to ensure Greek neutrality in case of any international conflagration, opposed the treaty, and his main concern therefore was to avoid a war with Italy if it were to attack Yugoslavia through Albania.[36] Although the treaty was later modified, Venizelos's fear of Italy was not unfounded. The rift between Britain and Italy after the Abyssinian crisis of 1935 and the Greek attachment to British interests (in spite of Britain's reluctance to guarantee Greek territorial integrity) paved the way for Mussolini's attack of October 1940. Ioannis Metaxas, appointed dictator by King George in 1936, displayed a loyalty towards Britain which can be explained partly by his dependence on his anglophile royal patron, but also by his conviction that Greek national security was linked to Britain's military presence in the region.[37]

---

[34]For a rare account of Venizelos' policy on Cyprus in 1931 see Yannis Pikros, 'O Venizelos kai to Kypriako zitima' (Venizelos and the Cyprus issue) in *Meletimata gyro apo ton Venizelo kai tin epochi tou* (Studies on Venizelos and his times), Athens: Filippotis, 1980, pp. 173–292.

[35]Costas Karamanlis, *O Eleftherios Venizelos kai oi exoterikes mas scheseis, 1928–32* (E. Venizelos and our external affairs, 1928–32), Athens: Evroekdotiki, 1986, pp. 11–176.

[36] C. Svolopoulos, *To Valcaniko symfono kai i elliniki exoteriki politiki 1928–1934* (The Balkan Pact and Greek Foreign Policy, 1928–34), Athens, 1974, p. 18–32.

[37]Besides Greece's enormous foreign debt to Britain, British economic interests

Thus Greece's capacity for maintaining an autonomous policy increased whenever the number of great powers participating in the balance of power system increased (1870–1913) or when their interest in its strategic position diminished (1923–35). On the contrary, whenever power blocs or a bipolar system prevailed (1914–18 and 1938–41), foreign interference and dependence grew.

In the winter of 1940 the Greek army repelled an Italian offensive, and after a successful counter-attack pinned down the enemy forces deep inside the territory of Italian-occupied Albania. Whether Metaxas could ultimately have succeeded in averting a German attack is open to conjecture; but he did resist inadequate British offers of help which he felt would provoke the Germans without substantially improving Greek defences. After Metaxas's death in January 1941, King George was persuaded that the forces Britain was willing to deploy in the Greek theatre merited Greece's total commitment to the Allied cause. Between April 6 and the end of that month German forces overran both Yugoslavia and Greece, and British troops, along with what could be salvaged of the Greek army and government, were evacuated to Crete. The King's choice in appointing the liberal Cretan politician Emmanouil Tsouderos as his prime minister came much too late to serve as concession to parliamentary politics. Crete too fell under a costly airborne German attack at the end of May. The King and his government-in-exile were established in London and Cairo for the duration of the war.[38]

Greece's winter campaign against the Italian army (1940–1) contributed to the Allied war effort by humbling Mussolini and forcing Hitler to intervene in the Balkans even as he was mustering his forces to invade Russia. Thus contemporary war rhetoric credited the Greek campaign with delaying the German move eastward.[39] The Greek resistance in the following years acquired for many, if not all, a double significance. It was not only a war against the occupying forces, but also a rebellion against authoritarianism in general. The Greek government-in-exile failed to recognise the scale of anti-monarchist sentiments at home, thus enhancing the influence of the Communist-led

---

were the most substantial in Greece during the interwar period. Thanos Veremis, *Dictatoria kai Iconomia 1925–26* (Dictatorship and Economy), Athens: MIET, 1982, pp. 91–118.

[38]John Koliopoulos, *Greece and the British Connection, 1935–41*, Oxford: Clarendon Press, 1977, pp. 263–93.

[39]C. M. Woodhouse, *The Story of Modern Greece*, London: Faber & Faber, 1968, p. 239.

EAM-ELAS movement and precipitating a devastating conflict between royalist and anti-royalist officers of the Greek army in the Middle East and North Africa.[40] Furthermore the privations suffered by the Greeks under the Axis occupation swelled the ranks of EAM-ELAS and made the KKE (Greek Communist Party) a formidable factor in wartime developments.

Following the German invasion Bulgaria, without bothering to declare war, annexed the eastern part of Greek Macedonia and Western Thrace. In Western Macedonia the Italian and German occupation authorities gave the exponents of the Bulgarian cause a free hand in their policy of intimidating the local population. Greek resistance forces were faced with the double task of opposing both the occupying army and the Bulgarian fascist Ohrana paramilitary forces. In 1943, at a meeting between Yugoslav and Greek partisans, Tito's representative used the term 'Macedonian nationals' for the first time and asked for the cooperation of EAM-ELAS to win Bulgarian collaborators back to the 'Macedonian' ideological camp. Throughout the war period ELAS resisted Yugoslav pressure to allow the 'Slav Macedonian National Liberation Front' (SNOF) to form separate bands and pursue its own policy in Greek Macedonia.[41]

An aggressive EAM-ELAS policy of monopolising the resistance, as well as the incompatibility of the KKE's political goals with British commitment to the constitutional monarchy, finally precipitated a confrontation, during which smaller resistance organisations sided with the British and the repatriated Greek government at the end of 1944. The first elections in ten years were held in 1946 under conditions not ideally suited to freedom of expression. The abstention of the KKE ensured the victory of the royalist party, which promptly carried out a plebiscite that resulted in the reinstatement of King George. Liberals, increasingly disoriented and isolated in the centre ground of a polarised political world, threw in their lot with the conservatives in the subsequent civil war between nationalists and Communists.[42]

[40]The military interventions were instigated by a loose coalition of cashiered republicans of 1935 and left-wing NCOs and soldiers. Hagen Fleischer, 'The anomalies in the Greek Middle East Forces, 1941–44', *Journal of the Hellenic Diaspora*, vol. V, no. 3, (autumn 1978), pp. 5–36.

[41]E. Kofos, *Nationalism and Communism in Macedonia*, Thessaloniki: Institute for Balkan Studies, 1964, pp. 121–33. See also the more specialized book by Johns Koliopoulos, *Plundered Loyalties: Axis Occupation and Civil Strife in Greek West Macedonia 1941–1949,*London: Hurst, 1999.

[42]For two different approaches on the period see Lars Baerentzen and John O.

Stalin who had honoured his 1944 agreement with Winston Churchill to allow Britain a free hand in Greece, demanded in 1947 a withdrawal of foreign troops and a revision of the Montreux convention of 1936 defining the regime of the Dardanelles, and raised claims on the Dodecanese islands ceded to Greece by Italy in 1947.[43]

The period of uneasy peace between liberation from the Axis occupation and the new fratricidal clash in 1946 offered the Greeks an opportunity for reflection and reconciliation, but the armed uprising of December 1944 had exacerbated division among them. Before the war Greece had been a country of small property-owners and shopkeepers, the exceptions being the dispossessed urban refugees from Turkey who became the recruiting ground for the Communist Party. The terrible hardships of foreign occupation introduced an element of desperation into Greek politics and swelled the ranks of left-wing resistance movements. It would take a civil war and a quarter of a century of turbulence before Greek society was able to find a new balance.

Iatrides, ed., *Studies in the History of the Greek Civil War, 1945–1949,* Copenhagen: Museum Tusculanum Press, 1987, and G.M. Alexander, *The Prelude of the Truman Doctrine: British Policy in Greece, 1944–47*, Oxford University Press, especially pp. 245–52. The latter's work counters the views of historical revisionism prevalent after 1974.

[43]In response to Soviet accusations that Greece was violating article 14, para. 2, of the 1947 Treaty concerning the demilitarisation of the Dodecanese, a top secret telegram was sent from the US Secretary of State, George Marshall, to the embassy in Athens (29 July 1948), advising that Communist pressure be ignored and urging remilitarisation of the islands. *US Foreign Relations Documents 1948,* vol. IV, pp. 116–17.

18

THE POST-WAR LEGACY

The years of division

Relations with the West. When President Harry S. Truman decided to launch his 'Truman Doctrine' in the US Congress, on 12 March 1947, the Soviet Union had already embarked on a radical reduction of the Red Army, from 12 million men in 1945 to about 4 million in 1947. The threat posed by Communism to the West was perceived as being linked not to military action, but to subversion from within; in the first cabinet of the new French Fourth Republic were four Communists, including the Minister of Defence. Across the globe the colonial empires—British, French and Dutch—were facing rebellions and campaigns for national independence.[1]

Britain's declaration in February 1947 that it could no longer provide the $250 million of military-economic support to Greece and Turkey was tantamount, in Secretary of State George Marshall's words, to 'an abdication from the Middle East with obvious implications as to their successor'.[2] Although the United States could have assumed the financial burden without publicising the fact, Truman chose instead to appear before Congress and inaugurate a global war against Communist influence. 'The President also won over Congress with assurances that the United States would not only control every penny of America's aid to Greece, but run the Greek economy by controlling foreign exchange, budget, taxes, currency and credit.'[3]

---

[1]Walter La Feber, *America, Russia and the Cold War, 1945–80.* New York: John Wiley, 1980, pp. 50–2.

[2]*Ibid.,* p. 52.

[3]*Ibid.,* p. 54.

The urgency of problems related to the Civil War, and the inability of a divided and paralysed government to handle the domestic situation effectively, disposed Greek politicians to allow the United States a role in Greek internal affairs. It was then that American aid agencies began to work in Greece for the first time. The US administration, faced with an isolationist Congress, took pains to convince Americans of an imminent Soviet threat not limited to Greece but with serious implications for Turkey and indeed for West European security generally. The Truman Doctrine inaugurated an era of US involvement in Europe and an overt American role in running Greek affairs. The Marshall Plan was proclaimed in June 1947. Greece's total share of the Plan was $1.7 billion in economic aid (loans and grants) and $1.3 billion dollars in military aid between 1947 and the 1960s.[4]

The fratricidal struggle that had raged in Greece for four years aggravated conditions in the already ravaged country. To the 550,000 (8 per cent of the population) who died between 1940 and 1944 were added another 158,000 deaths between 1946 and 1949.[5] Caught up in a war between the government army and Communist-leftist forces, Greek peasants and townspeople paid the highest price. Greece became the first testing-ground of the Truman Doctrine and indeed the first battlefield of the Cold War. At the UN the General Assembly condemned Albania, Yugoslavia and Bulgaria for aiding the Communist forces, but it was Tito's 1948 break with the Cominform which, by depriving the Communist-led 'Democratic Army', of Yugoslav support, ultimately led to its defeat. By the autumn of 1949 the government had won, while the 'Democratic Army'—including a substantial number of secessionist Slav Macedonians who had fought alongside it—fled into Albania and Yugoslavia.

American policy towards Greece, though primarily driven by defence considerations, was at first guided by liberal principles. The Department of State had discouraged admirers of authoritarian methods and viewed the Greek King as an obstacle to the reconstruction of a liberal democracy in the country. Yet, as the rift between the Soviet Union and the United States widened, the willingness of the US administration to soft-pedal its influence and to treat the Greek

[4]Stephen Xydis, 'The Truman Doctrine in Perspective', *Balkan Studies*, vol. 8, no. 2 (1967), pp. 239–62.

[5]T. Couloumbis, J. Petropulos and H. J. Psomiades, *Foreign Interference in Greek Politics*, New York: Pella, 1976, p. 117.

opposition with understanding diminished commensurately. As Cold War tensions heightened, Greece was increasingly seen as a bulwark against Communist expansion, and its administrative, military, economic and political institutions were shaped to serve that purpose. Efficiency and modernisation therefore acquired priority over democratic ideals. American missions favoured politicians eager to cooperate, irrespective of whether they might be lacking in stature and principles.

John Nuveen, head of the Economic Cooperation Administration (ECA), was an outspoken advocate of strong-armed efficiency, and the head of the military mission, General James Van Fleet, expressed his preference for an authoritarian government.[6] Representatives of the American Mission to Aid Greece (AMAG) sat on the most important committees and boards while Americans were employed in top administrative positions within Greek ministries and other government agencies. Members of the AMAG were granted extraterritoriality, inviolability of property and exemption from taxes, custom duties and currency controls.[7]

In March 1950 the Prime Minister, Sophocles Venizelos, was compelled to resign in favour of Nikolaos Plastiras following an open request from the US Ambassador. In June the same year, the departing General Van Fleet communicated to King Paul his preference for a strong government under Field-Marshal Alexander Papagos, who had been commander-in-chief of the government forces in the Civil War. Three months later the new US Ambassador, John Peurifoy, stated that 'while before the Korean conflict a centre-left government had been appropriate for Greece, a centre-right government is now necessary.'[8] Internecine strife among the Greeks therefore caused not only suffering and destruction but also foreign control because the nationalist victory over the Communist forces had only been possible because of US military aid, advice and diplomatic backing.[9]

There were three aspects to this particular dependence, which invited US control over the Greek policy-making process: strategic

[6]John Iatrides, 'American Attides toward the Political system of Postwar Greece' in T. Couloumbis and John Iatrides, eds, *Greek American Relations*, New York: Pella, 1980, pp. 60–5.

[7]A. Fatouros, 'Building Formal Structures of Penetration: the United States in Greece, 1947–48' in John Iatrides, ed., *Greece in the 1940s: a Nation in Crisis*, University Press of New England, 1981, pp. 252–3.

[8]Iatrides, *Greek-American Relations*, p. 65.

[9] Fatouros, *op.cit.*, p. 254.

concern over a Soviet and Balkan threat; the sorely needed economic aid to finance reconstruction; and the political weight that the stamp of US endorsement carried in the 1950s. American approval of a party or government carried with it the active promise of support and the passive guarantee of a term in office unobstructed by foreign interference.[10] In the 1950s Washington became convinced by the Korean War 'that the danger of Soviet expansion was strictly a military one, and that it could be resisted not by political and economic reforms achieved through the democratic left and centre, but by reliance on military elements not merely in strictly military matters but in politics as well.'[11]

Ambassador Peurifoy's involvement in Greek politics was so direct that few could doubt in 1951–2 which party the Americans favoured. Through his influence the life of the Centre coalition government under General Plastiras was shortened. The simple majority system endorsed by Peurifoy as a guarantee of stability facilitated the electoral success of Papagos; his Greek Rally (*Ellinikos Sinagermos*) conservative party secured 82 per cent of the seats in parliament with 49 per cent of the vote in the 1952 elections. Papagos's success proved somewhat more overwhelming than the ambassador had anticipated. Staunch in his friendship towards the United States and his anti-Communist sentiments, the Greek Field Marshal was also a nationalist who pursued the unification of Cyprus with Greece (*Enosis*) despite the damage it caused to relations among NATO members.[12] Although it is alleged that the United States did not initially oppose Papagos's *Enosis* policy, his stature within the conservative camp made him less controllable than his weak predecessors had been. However, US influence remained undiminished during and after his term in office, and advice and instructions continued to affect decisions concerning the economy, the armed forces and the gendarmerie. The reduction or termination of aid and the refusal of loans to correct imbalances provided leverage for pressure on the rare occasions of Greek obstinacy.

Greece's accession to NATO was initially obstructed by Britain's

[10]T. Couloumbis, 'The Greek Junta Phenomenon', *Polity*, vol. VI, no. 3 (spring), 1974.

[11]Maurice Goldbloom, 'United States Policy in Post-War Greece' in R. Clogg and G. Yannopoulos, eds, *Greece Under Military Rule*, London: Secker & Warburg, 1972, p. 231

[12]For details about Papagos' Cyprus policy see Ioannis D. Stefanidis, *Isle of Discord: Nationalism, Imperialism and the Making of the Cyprus Problem*, London: Hurst, 1999, pp. 260–80.

own concept of Western defence in the Near East and the opposition of the Scandinavian members to an over-extension of NATO's primary aims. When Greece and Turkey sent combat forces to South Korea in 1950, they were acting as members of the United Nations, but their motive was in fact to overcome objections to their entry into NATO. For the United States, Greek and Turkish participation would link its allies in NATO, the Central Treaty Organisation (CENTO), the Southeast Asian Treaty Organisation (SEATO), and the security treaty of Australia, New Zealand and the United States (ANZUS). For Greek politicians of the liberal coalition government which pressed for Greek membership, NATO provided not only an additional guarantee against Balkan Communism, but also a doorway leading to a community of democratic European states. In September 1951 NATO foreign ministers in Ottawa approved Greek and Turkish entry in principle. Two years later the American military presence in Greece was consolidated by the signing of a bilateral base agreement, which gave the United States the right to establish and supply its bases and to use Greek airspace. The agreement also set out the legal status of US forces in Greece.

The difference between conservatives and liberals on security issues and NATO was one of degree rather than kind. Both basically agreed that Greece's main security concern was its northern borders, that Communism threatened common cherished values, that NATO was indispensable for the defence of the country, and that America was Greece's natural ally and guarantor. The 1953 Greek-American agreement to lease bases and other facilities to the United States within the framework of NATO was accepted in general terms, not only by the conservatives but by the more prominent liberals as well. The latter recorded their opposition to the high level of military expenditure, and in 1958 against the installation of nuclear bases on Greek soil. They agreed that concessions on that issue could be made in a package deal which would include a favourable settlement of the Cyprus question, or if all other NATO members also decided to accept nuclear bases on their own soil.[13]

The issue which posed the greatest threat to the association of Greece with NATO was that of Cyprus.[14] The Karamanlis government that succeeded Papagos strove to secure self-determination for

    [13]T. A. Couloumbis, *Greek Political Reaction to American and NATO Influences*, New Haven: Yale University Press, 1966, pp. 33–89.
    [14]*Ibid.*, p. 201.

the island through the UN, but the cool or negative reaction of NATO members to the Greek cause came as a blow to the conservatives, who were thus faced with the predicament of having to choose between Greek national aspirations and their dedication to the Western alliance. The Centre Union party exhibited its full support for Cypriot independence after the conclusion of the Zurich–London agreements. George Papandreou made it the policy of his party to reject NATO involvement in Cypriot affairs and favoured arbitration by the UN General Assembly in the crisis that flared in 1963–4. US officials were clearly displeased.

The exclusive relationship between the Americans and the Greek ruling conservative party throughout the 1950s and early '60s estranged them from the liberal politicians waiting in the wings. The rise of the Centre-Union coalition under George Papandreou coincided with President John F. Kennedy's policy of reform as a deterrent to Communist influence. Papandreou's platform for 'democratisation' was in tune with the rising expectations of a Greek society experiencing a significant improvement of its living standards in the early 1960s.[15] Implicit in the notion of 'democratisation' was a promise of autonomy in the conduct of Greek foreign policy. Henry Labouisse, Kennedy's Ambassador in Greece, was a choice in keeping with the US administration's progressive ideas, but he could not dispel the strains between US officials in Greece and the Centre Union government. When the son of George Papandreou, Andreas, attempted as Minister to the Prime Minister to restrict the activities in Greece of the CIA and the USIA, the government's relations with the United States took a sharp down-turn. However, the Cyprus dispute was the most serious cause of irritation. According to Maurice Goldbloom (Labour Information Officer at the US Economic Mission in Greece, 1950–1): 'From the American point of view, the crucial thing about the quarrel was not the two communities on the island, but the damage it did to relations between Greece and Turkey, both allies of the United States.'[16]

This quarrel acquired a special significance for the US position in the Eastern Mediterranean when President Makarios of Cyprus joined the camp of the non-aligned, a policy requiring good relations with potential foes of the United States. Seizing the opportunity, the Soviet Union declared its support for the integrity of the island

[15]Thanos Veremis, 'Union of the Democratic Centre' in H. R. Penniman, *Greece at the Polls,* Washington, DC: American Enterprise Institute, 1981, pp. 84–104.

[16]Maurice Goldbloom, 'United States Policy in Post-War Greece', p. 236.

and in 1964 warned that it would not remain passive in case of a foreign intervention. Hence bringing Cyprus under the NATO umbrella by way of *Enosis* with elements of partition became an option of American policy in 1964. According to Dean Acheson's plan (allegedly drafted by George Ball), the island would be united with Greece, Turkey would acquire a sovereign military base, two Turkish cantons would be formed exercising local autonomy, and the Greek island of Kastellorizo would be given to Turkey. Both Greeks and Turks rejected the plan, but the diehards of *Enosis* on the one side and of the island's partition on the other drew their separate conclusions about American designs on the island—conclusions which precipitated the developments of 1974.

Identification with the right wing and the monarchy after 1965 limited the flexibility and scope of American policy in Greece. Throughout the conflict between Papandreou and the King over what the latter felt was a struggle for the control of the armed forces, American officials could not conceal their anxiety for the monarchy's future.

The coup of 21 April 1967, which prevented the Papandreous from winning the impending elections, was greeted by the Americans with undisguised relief. The Colonels who had staged the coup over the heads of their superiors were a breed of extreme right-wingers who in the early 1950s had identified with Papagos in his quarrels with King Paul. Their credentials included little besides skills in matters of intelligence and propaganda, and their instant, utterly fictitious justification of the coup was that it had prevented an imminent Communist take-over.

The rationalisations and cant used by US policy-makers to justify their friendly attitude to the Junta disappointed many of the Americophile parliamentarians in Greece who had hoped that the US administration would recognise the inherent limitations, not to mention the brutalities, of the unpopular regime. Congress imposed an embargo on heavy weapons (though not spare parts) for Greece in April 1967, but this was suspended in October 1968 due to the strain which the Soviet invasion of Czechoslovakia caused in the Balkans; it was only re-imposed in the early phase of the Nixon administration. Members of Congress as well as high-ranking officials made negative appraisals of the regime's value to the United States, yet the administration chose to formulate the ambiguous dilemma of 'how to deal with an ally with whose internal order we disagree yet who is a loyal NATO partner'.[17] In fact this was a non–existent dilemma. Since no possible parliamentary alternative in Greece would have upset the *status quo* in Greek–American relations, America's credibility suffered a steep decline, especially in the autumn of 1969 when the National Security Council under the chairmanship of Henry Kissinger advised the restoration of full-scale military assistance to the dictatorship. The successive visits to Greece of the NATO supreme commander General Goodpaster, Secretary of Defense Melvin Laird, Secretary of State William Rogers, the President's brother Donald Nixon, Secretary of Commerce Maurice Stans and finally Vice-President Spiro Agnew did more for the regime than any lifting of the embargo.[18]

In terms of short–term gains America's relationship with the dictators was rewarding. Its bases and Greek territorial and air space remained available during the June 1967 Arab-Israeli war and the September 1970 crisis in Jordan. In 1971–3 the Nixon administration negotiated important homeporting privileges for the Sixth Fleet in Piraeus and Eleusis. George Papadopoulos, the strongman of the Junta, not only displayed his loyalty to NATO but also held secret talks on the Cyprus question with Turkey and tried to coerce the 'renegade' Archbishop Makarios into line—failing which the Junta orchestrated a series of abortive attempts on his life. Over Cyprus the Colonels combined the irredentist line of Papagos with the conviction that the United States would be willing to bring the island into the NATO fold and remove Makarios's influence by supporting its union with Greece. The Junta felt that the obvious price for such a prize was the elimination of the Cypriot President. Far from being a 'Castro of the Mediterranean', Makarios was a political conservative practising balance of power diplomacy to avoid the partition of Cyprus, in which aim he ultimately failed.[19]

The problems of Greece received scant American attention throughout the period of the dictatorship, and there was a surprising lack of concern on the eve of July 1974. The Greek-Cypriot and Turkish policy desks were transferred in May 1974 from the Office of Near East Affairs to the Office of European Affairs, which had little experience of the Eastern Mediterranean. Kissinger's lukewarm reaction

[17]Goldbloom, *op.cit.*, p. 247

[18]T. Couloumbis, J.A. Petropulos and H. Psomiades, *Foreign Interference in Greek Politics*, pp. 129–39.

[19]Lawrence Stern, *The Wrong Horse*, New York: Times Books, 1977, pp. 81–2.

during the crisis, attributed to his distraction by major developments within the United States, was interrupted in only one instance; on July 23 'strong representations were made with the Colonels in Athens (...) with respect to a possible counter-offensive against Turkey in Thrace'.[20]

In his memoirs Kissinger vividly describes the international change of heart towards Greece following the Turkish invasion of Cyprus and the restoration of democracy in Athens. From the beginning of the crisis his own concern was to maintain NATO's southern flank intact, first by soft-pedalling American relations with the Greek military and then by counselling the Turkish Prime Minister, Bulent Ecevit, to show constraint. He criticises Karamanlis for lacking the courage to make concessions in order to regain occupied territory for the Republic of Cyprus. However, his argument is not convincing because a settlement based on some territorial transfer would have legitimised Turkey's attack without reversing the island's partition.[21] Three decades later, Cyprus remains divided, but the *de facto* partition, a Turkish goal since independence, has not prevented the extraordinary economic development of the Greek south or the stagnation of the Turkish-occupied north.

After the Turkish invasion was consolidated, there were allegations that the US intelligence establishment in Athens, in its effort to prevent a war between Greece and Turkey, was encouraging Greek officers to revolt against the Junta. The collapse of the military regime was precipitated by an ultimatum from General Davos, commander of the Third Army Corps in Macedonia.

Kissinger maintained a guarded optimism over the outcome of the discussions in Geneva between the guarantors of Cyprus, even though the terms of the ceasefire agreement were constantly being violated and he failed to provide backing for British efforts at conciliation. It appeared that Washington was prepared to let events run their course in Cyprus and would assume an active role only in case of war between the two NATO allies.

Greek-Turkish relations. In 1951 Greece and Turkey resumed friendly relations in the face of a common Soviet threat. Both were recipients

---

[20] The post-mortem of the intelligence community on Cyprus, released on 1 October 1975, quoted in Couloumbis *et al.*, *op.cit.*, p. 140.

[21] Henry Kissinger, *Years of Renewal*, vol. III, New York: Simon & Schuster, 1999, pp. 215–39. This well-written account clarifies its author's awareness of Turkish motives throughout the short history of the unified Cypriot state.

of aid under the Marshall Plan, and were formally admitted to NATO in 1952, at the height of the Cold War. A year later they signed, along with Yugoslavia, a treaty of friendship and co-operation followed by a formal alliance.

Cyprus had been occupied by Britain since 1878 and formally became a colony in 1925. With a population that was 80 per cent Greek and 18 per cent Turkish, and as a vital strategic location in the Eastern Mediterranean, the island became the bone of contention within the Western alliance. The Greek Cypriot claim for self-determination in order to unite the island with Greece—a mixture of traditional irredentism and contemporary anti-colonialism—was at first thwarted by Britain's reluctance to abandon its position in the Eastern Mediterranean. NATO became involved in the dispute in the 1960s but, having been designed to provide a defence against the Soviets and operating on the assumption that the notion of collective security took precedence over all other priorities, it was ill-equipped to resolve local conflicts.

In January 1950 a plebiscite among the Greek Cypriots organised by the Orthodox Church yielded a 96 per cent vote in favour of *Enosis*, and revived old pressures on the mother-country to take issue with Britain. Greek governments since 1931 had carefully avoided questions that would cause friction with Britain, and the Liberal coalition government of 1951 was no exception. However, with the United States having assumed a dominant position in Greece since the late 1940s, Greek inhibitions *vis-à-vis* Britain gradually diminished.[22]

When Archbishop Makarios, the political as well as spiritual leader of the Greek Cypriot community, began to steer the question into the international forum of the UN, the British decided to introduce Turkey into the matter as a counterweight to Greek demands. The Turkish government, which hitherto had been apathetic toward the conflict, now assumed responsibility for the welfare of the Turkish Cypriots and eventually full control over their destiny. Thus the foundations of the future intercommunal conflict were laid, and what began as an anti-colonial struggle gradually developed into a confrontation between Greek and Turk.

Relations between Greece and Turkey deteriorated in September 1955 when a mob in Istanbul demanding the annexation of Cyprus

---

[22]The bibliography on the Cyprus issue is vast. For a comprehensive account of the problem see P. Kitromilides and T. Couloumbis, 'Ethnic Conflict in a Strategic Area: The Case of Cyprus', *Greek Review of Social Research* (Athens), no. 24, 1975, pp. 271–91.

by Turkey attacked and destroyed Greek property and churches.[23] American efforts at conciliation were greeted with hostility on both sides, but by 1959 the Cyprus issue had become such a liability for Greece's relations with Britain and the United States that the Prime Minister, Constantine Karamanlis, felt compelled to seek a speedy solution to the entanglement. Makarios in the mean time had quietly abandoned the *Enosis* aspiration, which was countered by the Turks demanding partition of the island, and moved closer to Cypriot independence. Finally the British realised that retaining their military bases without the cost of quelling the Greek rebellion was the most expedient solution.

In 1959 Karamanlis and the Turkish Prime Minister Menderes drafted in Zurich an agreement for the creation of an independent republic of Cyprus, which was presented to the leaders of the two communities. It provided for British sovereign military bases in the island, and Britain, Greece and Turkey guaranteed the integrity and constitution of the state. Greece and Turkey would contribute a contingency force of 950 and 650 men respectively. A Greek Cypriot President and a Turkish Cypriot Vice-President were given veto power over vital legislation, and the Turkish minority were represented in the government and, the civil service in a proportion exceeding their actual size. The leaders of the two communities, who had played no part in drafting the Zurich agreement, signed the document in London.

After the defeat of Karamanlis in the election of 1963, the Centre Union coalition under George Papandreou was faced with a new phase in the Cyprus imbroglio, namely the protracted clash between the Greeks and the Turks in the island. Confronted with a deadlock in the passing of vital legislation, the President of the Republic, Archbishop Makarios, proposed to Dr Kütchük, the Vice-President, thirteen amendments to the 1960 constitution. Among the proposals was one that the veto powers of both the President and—more important to the Turks—the Vice-President would be abolished and the number of Turkish Cypriots in the administration reduced. Turkey and Dr Kütchük rejected the proposals, and fighting broke out between the two communities, which lasted well into the summer of 1964 and caused considerable hardship to the outnumbered Turkish Cypriots.

---

[23]The complicity of the Turkish government was established by the 1960–1 trials of the Menderes government. See Walter Weiker, *The Turkish Revolution, 1960–61*, Washington, DC: Brookings Institution, 1963, pp. 25–47.

It was thanks to a personal warning to the Turkish Prime Minister Ismet Inönü from the US President Lyndon Johnson that an invasion by Turkey was warded off that summer. An uneasy peace was restored by a UN peacekeeping force, but mutual hatred still smouldered between the two communities.

General George Grivas, who had been head of the most active anti-Communist band in the aftermath of German withdrawal from Greece, was the leader of the EOKA guerrilla movement in Cyprus which caused substantial harassment to the British forces between 1955 and 1959. A champion of the *Enosis* cause, he strongly disapproved of the Zurich settlement and Makarios's policy of pursuing independence rather than unification with Greece. In November 1967 Grivas, in command of the National Guard, attacked Turkish Cypriot villages, provoking a new threat of Turkish invasion—which American and NATO intervention once again averted by removing excessive Greek forces and Grivas himself from the island. Despite repeated clashes between the two communities, intercommunal talks persisted, and by the end of 1973 a ray of hope for a settlement appeared on the horizon. An attempt by the Greek Junta to assassinate Makarios triggered Turkey's invasion in 1974.[24]

Relations with the Balkans. The clash between Stalin and Tito in 1948 had a profound effect on the entire nexus of Balkan politics. Yugoslavia ceased supporting the Greek guerrillas, who remained obedient to Moscow's commands and were defeated. Bulgaria repudiated the Bled protocol, which it had signed a year earlier with Tito—this had provided cultural autonomy for the Pirin (Bulgarian) Macedonians, as a first step towards incorporating them into a Federated Macedonian Republic of Yugoslavia. The pro-Moscow Bulgarian government reverted to the 1924 Comintern position, namely that the three Macedonias would become an autonomous federal entity under Bulgarian influence.[25] By 1952, when Bulgarian claims against Greece were in full swing, Athens had been drawn closer to Belgrade. Commensurately with the growth of Yugoslavia's fear of Soviet-Bulgarian-Albanian encirclement, its relations with Greece improved. In 1953 a treaty of friendship and co-operation was concluded in Ankara

---

[24]For a detailed account of the 1974 Turkish invasion of Cyprus see Lawrence Stern, *The Wrong Horse, op.cit.*

[25]E. Kofos, *Nationalism and Communism in Macedonia*, Thessaloniki: Institute for Balkan Studies, 1964, pp. 196–9.

between the two states and Turkey, and in 1954 this was followed by a military alliance signed in Bled. However, with Stalin's death in 1953 relations between Belgrade and Moscow began to improve, and this was followed in 1955 by a Yugoslav-Bulgarian rapprochement. The suppression of the Hungarian uprising accounted for another deterioration in Soviet-Yugoslav relations, lasting till 1960.

Between 1956 and 1961 Greek-Yugoslav relations went through a 'golden age'. Free cross-border trade and military consultation were established and the Macedonian issue was not mentioned. In 1962 Skopje renewed its claims on Greek territory, and Athens revoked a border agreement it had made with Belgrade in 1959. As the feelings of insecurity in both states regarding the Soviet Union diminished, their bilateral relations became less constrained.[26] The more insistent the Macedonian issue became, the more relations deteriorated.

With Romania a rapprochement was highlighted by settlement of that country's financial obligations to Greeks whose property had been confiscated and by the Stoika plan to ban nuclear weapons from the Balkans. The latter, of course, was only adopted by the left-wing coalition (EDA) and never taken seriously by the Greek government. A further improvement in relations between Greece and its Communist neighbours was begun by the dictatorship of 1967, which was experiencing moral isolation from Western Europe. Sofia's favourable response to these overtures signified Soviet willingness to exploit Greek isolation, but it also reflected the spirit of international détente. However, relations with Yugoslavia foundered on bilateral reefs, and the Greek Colonels once again curtailed frontier crossing by the Yugoslavs.[27]

A major breakthrough occurred between the Greek military regime and Albania on 6 May 1971 when diplomatic relations, which had been completely severed since the war of 1940, were resumed. Greece's Balkan multilateralism began to take shape after democracy was restored in 1974.

[26]Evanthis Hatzivassiliou, 'The 1956 Reshaping of Greek Foreign Policy: The Balkans and the beginning of the "Detachment" Policy', *Journal of Modern Hellenism*, no.14, 1997, pp. 119–38.

[27]S. G. Xydis, 'Coups and Countercoups in Greece, 1967–1973', *Political Science Quarterly*, vol. 89, no. 3, fall 1974, pp. 534–5. For the foreign policy of the junta see Van Coufoudakis, 'Greek Foreign Policy, 1945–85: Seeking Independence in an Interdependent World. Problems and Prospects' in Kevin Featherstone and Dimitrios Katsoudas, eds, *Political Change in Greece before and after the Colonels*, London: Croom Helm, pp. 233–5.

After 1974

The conditions under which Greece's foreign policy was conducted after 1974 can be roughly classified into two periods: pre- and post-1989. During the first period the country's position on the southern flank of NATO gave it a vital role in the defence of Western Europe against the threat from the Soviet Union and its allies. The geostrategic importance of Greece and Turkey were mutually reinforcing, so that any disruption of their strategic continuum lessened their individual value to Western security.[28]

US complaisance towards the Greek military regime and subsequent inaction during the Turkish invasion of Cyprus opened the door to Andreas Papandreou's criticism of the West and his courtship of the Third World. Although Greece became a full member of the European Community in 1981, the election victory of the anti-Western Panhellenic Socialist Movement (PASOK) soon afterwards threatened to remove the country from the Western fold. Its founder Andreas Papandreou nevertheless chose to remain in both the EC and NATO. His plan was to milk the former and blackmail the latter at a time when the Western alliance still attached great importance to its southern flank. The deviation of Greece from its Western orientation after 1981 was a war of words rather than deeds.

With the collapse of Communism in the Soviet Union and its satellites, the geostrategic value of the southern flank appeared to decline. In the new security environment the United States demonstrated its unwillingness to maintain naval, airforce and monitoring bases in Greece, and thus PASOK's platform against its military presence lost its substance. Indeed the implications of global changes for South-Eastern Europe soon became clear. With Russia out of power politics and the European Union unable to play a decisive role during the bloody collapse of Yugoslavia, the United States was the only credible force capable of stabilising the volatile region.[29]

Papandreou's series of radical turns began in connection with his attitude to the EC during the second half of 1988. During Greece's second term in the seat of the rotating EC presidency he declared his unqualified support for European federalism, thereby effectively

---

[28]Thanos Veremis, *Greek Security: Issues and Politics,* Adelphi Paper no.179, London: IISS, 1982.

[29]Yannis Valinakis, *Greece's Security in the Post Cold War Era,* Ebenhausen: Stiftung Wissenschaft und Politik, April 1994.

committing Greece to the EC credo that challenged the traditional dependence of the Greek economy on the state and involved a significant trimming of the public sector.

Relations with the European Union are not classified in Greece under 'foreign policy' but belong to a special category with a profound input on domestic developments. The benefits of membership and the imperative of convergence have gradually created a re-alignment of political forces transcending the traditional right-left divide. With the collapse of Communism in Eastern Europe and, even more, the rise of technocrats in PASOK, the new 'modernisers' and 'traditionalists' have cut across the membership of both major parties in parliament. The new divide was nowhere more clearly visible than in the cross-party voting that contributed to the victory of Costas Simitis in the 1996 elections.

The restoration of democracy in Greece came about largely through a dramatic external event, the Turkish invasion of Cyprus on 23 July 1974, which triggered off the disintegration of the military regime and caused the return of Constantine Karamanlis as Prime Minister. Only one day after the second Turkish offensive in Cyprus, Greece withdrew from the military structure of NATO in protest against the alliance's failure to prevent the invasion. Another serious development consisted of the Turkish claims to a portion of the Aegean territorial waters, seabed and airspace, extending well to the west of the major eastern Aegean islands. According to Greek government assessment, this was a skillful diversion of international attention by Turkish diplomacy from the maintenance of its forces in Cyprus to a 'composite of directly and indirectly related and mutually reinforcing issues' in the Aegean.[30] A broad consensus was thus formed among Greeks of all political tendencies that the immediate threat to their national security no longer emanated from Greece's Communist neighbours but from Turkey.[31] The Karamanlis government took immediate measures to secure the fortification of the eastern Aegean islands.

[30]Van Coufoudakis, 'Greco-Turkish Relations and the Greek Socialists: Ideology, Nationalism and Pragmatism', *Journal of Modern Greek Studies,* I, no. 2 (October 1983), p. 375.
[31]Statements by senior Turkish officials confirmed public fears. The Turkish Prime Minister stated on 30 July 1974: 'The defence of the Aegean islands should be jointly undertaken by Greece and Turkey as allies within NATO.' Half a year later, on 4 April 1975, the Turkish Foreign Minister went even further: 'Neither the government nor Turkish public opinion can accept that the Aegean belongs exclusively to Greece. Half the Aegean belongs to Turkey and the other half belongs to Greece. This has always been the official view.'

Greece's withdrawal from NATO's military structure was more of a trial separation than a divorce since the country remained within the political arm of the alliance. Karamanlis repeatedly rejected the non-alignment option, and after the normalisation of the internal situation, expressed his willingness to re-enter the military structure of NATO. However, Greek reintegration attempts were vetoed by Turkey which, having raised a claim over the reallocation of the Athens 'FIR' (Flight Information Region), was in effect also demanding a reallocation of the operational control zones of the Aegean. According to pre-1974 arrangements, NATO had ceded military responsibility for the Aegean airspace (Greek and international) as well as the Aegean sea (Greek and international waters) to Greek command. Any other arrangement would have resulted in a situation where Greek territories (the eastern Aegean islands) would have been placed under Turkish protection.[32]

Negotiations on the country's re-entry proved long and arduous. Three reintegration plans with settlement proposals by the Supreme Commander Allied Forces Europe (SACEUR), General Haig, in 1978–9 and a fourth one by his successor General Rogers in 1980 were rejected. A solution was finally accepted in October 1980, with a provision that allowed the reallocation question to be settled later within the Alliance.

Throughout his post-Junta years as prime minister, Karamanlis accomplished the double feat of transforming himself into a true liberal politician and emancipating his political camp from its unqualified support for the United States and NATO. No doubt it took a disaster of the magnitude of that in Cyprus to shake up the Greek conservatives, both in Greece and the United States, and release them from their traditional loyalties. However, Karamanlis managed to temper such reactions into a constructive criticism of Western insouciance that proved effective both through the American embargo on weapons to Turkey, imposed in February 1975, and the plethora of UN resolutions over Cyprus.[33]

[32]A division of the operational control of the Aegean would make the co-ordination in times of war in such a restricted area difficult to achieve without violating national airspace or sea waters. This would be against a basic Military Committee principle (36/2) which provides that 'countries retain their sovereignty and are therefore ultimately responsible for the defence and security of their own territories and space.'

[33]T. Veremis, 'Greece and NATO: Continuity and Change' in John Chipman ed. *NATO's Southern Allies: Internal and External Challenges,* London: Routledge, 1988, pp. 269–70. Theodore Couloumbis, *The United States, Greece and Turkey: The Troubled Alliance,* New York: Praeger, 1983.

Greece's role as an interlocutor among Balkan states suspicious of each other's motives profited greatly from the July 1975 Conference on Security and Co-operation in Europe (CSCE) and the Helsinki Final Act. Although the spirit of Helsinki ultimately contributed to the erosion of authoritarian regimes in Eastern Europe, it still appeared in 1975 that the Communist *status quo* had been secured in exchange for 'unenforceable promises on human rights'.[34] This allowed the Balkan Communist leaders either to seek further emancipation from Soviet tutelage (Romania) or to be reassured that regional co-operation did not threaten their relations with Moscow (Bulgaria). In Helsinki Karamanlis secured the agreement of Romania, Bulgaria and Yugoslavia for an inter-Balkan meeting at the level of Deputy Ministers of Co-ordination and Planning.[35]

Of the three, Romania was traditionally the most positive toward political multilateralism and Bulgaria the least. Reluctant to enter even a limited multilateral relationship, Sofia attempted to dilute the Balkan initiative by including other East European states. A renewed effort by Karamanlis to make the summit meetings a recurring event was politely rebuffed by Bulgaria, reflecting Soviet fears that institutionalised Balkan co-operation might affect the cohesion of the Warsaw Pact. Belgrade took a middle position; without discouraging multilateralism, Tito felt that it presupposed a settlement of differences between such pairs of states as Greece and Turkey, Bulgaria and Romania, and Yugoslavia and Albania. Turkey agreed to participate once the meeting was fixed, and the inter-Balkan conference of Deputy Ministers of Planning took place in Athens between 26 January and 5 February 1976 with all the Balkan states participating except Albania, which remained adamant in its opposition to any multilateral arrangements.

In 1978 Bulgaria and the Soviet Union began to change their views on regional multilateralism. Karamanlis's visit to Moscow in 1979 was therefore well-timed for a significant rapprochement and for Soviet approval of a follow-up on Balkan multilateralism. After securing Zhivkov's agreement, Karamanlis proposed to the other Balkan leaders a conference of experts on telecommunication and transportation, which took place in Ankara on 26–29 November 1979.

---

[34]James E. Goodby, 'CSCE: The Diplomacy of Europe Whole and Free', Washington, DC: The Atlantic Council, July 1990, p. 2.

[35]C. Svolopolos, *Elliniki Politiki sta Valkania 1974–81*, Athens: Euroekdotiki, 1987, pp. 74–9.

However, from the second conference on inter-Balkan co-operation it became clear that questions of high politics could not be dealt with in a region divided into blocs. Nevertheless Karamanlis was not discouraged from approaching political cooperation indirectly, through confidence-building in fields of minor political importance.

While still living in Paris, in May 1973, Karamanlis had referred to a European orientation as being Greece's new 'Great Idea'. Full membership in the European Community, achieved in May 1979 after tortuous negotiations, was the reward for his dogged pursuit of an 'organic Greek presence in the West'. Yet the domestic debate between 1975 and 1981 on the merits and demerits of membership focused on the ideological and even security aspects of being part of the EC, 'rather than on the practical decisions needed to absorb the shock of accession and transform the institutional and administrative system into flexible and effective instruments capable of responding to EU policy requirements'.[36] The road to a sober assessment of Greek membership was still far in the future. In the mean time Greece would enter a new ideological phase with Papandreou in power.

During Papandreou's first term as prime minister (1981–5), Greece sought to pursue a more 'independent' foreign policy, but these were aspects of PASOK's policy that were no more than exercises in irrelevance. At a time when the non-aligned movement was in general decline Papandreou chose to establish ties with essentially anti-Western neutrals in North Africa and the Middle East, and when the Reagan-Gorbachev tug-of-war on disarmament was beginning to produce positive results, he joined the leaders of five other states (Mexico, Argentina, Sweden, India and Tanzania) in promoting world denuclearisation, and continued to press for nuclear-free zones in the Balkans. Finally, Papandreou's reluctance to join with the United States and Western Europe in condemning the Soviet Union on issues such as the introduction of martial law in Poland and the shooting down of the KAL airliner won his government points with Moscow but created ill-will in Washington, where support was far more important for Greek security.

Stripped of its rhetoric, however, PASOK's policy towards the West did not differ substantially from that of many Community

---

[36]Panayiotis Ioakimidis, 'Contradictions between Policy and Performance' in Kevin Featherstone and Kostas Ifantis (eds), *Greece in a Changing Europe*, Manchester University Press, 1996, p. 36.

members. Soon after his advent to power in 1981, Papandreou quietly abandoned his threat to withdraw from NATO and hold a plebiscite to decide on Greece's membership of the EC. Furthermore, instead of closing the US bases in Greece he signed a new defence cooperation agreement in 1983, prolonging the operation of the bases for five more years—although publicly he sought to portray it as a move towards their removal. Without any visible international benefit for the country, Papandreou consciously tried to create the impression of Greece being the maverick of the Western alliance, and it has been claimed that the electoral support he derived from his much-publicised rebellious image justified—in his own calculations—the damage it caused to Greece's position in the West. PASOK reflected a resurgent isolationism in certain segments of Greek society which sought to protect themselves from Western competition and the dislocations of adjustment posed by closer integration with Europe. Basing itself on a parochial sense of moral superiority but acknowledging the economic power and technology of the West, PASOK opted for a fantasy 'third way'.[37]

Both major parties, PASOK and New Democracy, shared similar perspectives regarding the problems between Greece and Turkey. Unlike Karamanlis, who had conducted bilateral discussions with Turkish officials without success, Papandreou insisted from the outset that any discussion with Turkey would be tantamount to jeopardising Greek security. Thus the February 1988 Davos meeting between Papandreou and the Turkish Prime Minister Turgut Özal represented a significant deviation from PASOK's basic foreign policy stand. Almost a year earlier Turkey's action in sending a research vessel escorted by warships into the disputed continental shelf region (around the islands of Lesbos, Lemnos and Samothrace) had caused a crisis which could have precipitated an armed clash, but was eventually defused—not before emphasising the delicate state of relations between the two countries in the Aegean.

Furthermore, the high level of defence spending, and the consequent burden on the Greek balance of payments, detracted from the government's populist image, and convinced Papandreou that he needed to reduce the prospect of a possible outbreak of fighting between Greece and Turkey. However, in the spring of 1988 the Turkish Foreign Minister Mesut Yilmaz raised the question of the 'Turkish' minority in Greek Thrace and dismissed any possibility of a Turkish

---

[37]Thanos Veremis, 'Greece' in Douglas Stuart, ed., *Politics and Security in the Southern Region of the Atlantic Alliance*, London: Macmillan, 1988, pp. 137–9.

military withdrawal from Cyprus before the two communities came to an agreement. Although some progress was made in developing a set of confidence-building measures to prevent dangerous incidents in the international waters of the Aegean, the 'Davos spirit' gradually lost momentum and ground to a halt in 1989.

After New Democracy won the election of 1990, its main task was to curtail the huge internal and external deficits and at the same time to improve Greece's image as a reliable partner of the West. Both priorities were connected to the country's two main foreign policy preoccupations: the evolving shape of the European Community, which would determine its economic future, and the forms of Western collective defence cooperation which would ensure its security. Greece, along with other southern EC members, favoured an acceleration of the Community's political union through a 'deepening' of its institutions.[38] In Greek eyes, broadening EU membership would blur the focus of the intergovernmental conference on political union and possibly diminish the prospects for economic and monetary union. Where security was concerned, Greek policymakers favoured the absorption over the long term of the Western European Union (WEU), the first post-war European attempt to create a unified security and defence system, by the EU.

The Maastricht treaty on the European Union, adopted in December 1991, was greeted with satisfaction in Athens and ratified in the Greek Parliament with the support of all parties except the Communists. At Maastricht Greece was also invited to become a member of the WEU. However, the EC's decision that Article 5 of the modified treaty of Brussels, which provides a security guarantee in case of attack on members, should not be applied between member-states of NATO and the WEU caused considerable irritation in Athens. At the same time the WEU's decision to invalidate Article 5 in case of Greek-Turkish conflict renewed Greece's interest in the United States and NATO as the more credible deterrents against threats to its security.[39]

[38]Jacques Delors, 'European Integration and Security', *Survival,* March/April 1991, pp. 99–110. See also Roberto Aliboni, ed., *Southern European Security in the 1990s,* London: Pinter, 1992.

[39]'After strenuous diplomatic efforts, the Greeks were accepted as full members of the Western European Union at the summit. Yet they were also asked to provide guarantees that they would never invoke some of the security provisions in this organisation. a requirement at best contradictory and at worst insulting to a full EC member.' Jonathan Eyal, 'A Force for Good in a Cauldron of Turmoil', *The European* (3 September 1992).

Relations with the United States improved as a result of the defence cooperation agreement in July 1990, which would regulate the operation of American bases and installations on Greek soil for the next eight years. Greece's naval support for the Allied cause during the Gulf War improved the positive climate of Greek-American relations and Mitsotakis was the first Greek Prime Minister to visit Washington since 1964. Stressing the necessity of decisively opposing invaders, Greece also made its airspace and bases available to the Western coalition's forces. Crete, in particular, was an important launch-pad for US operations in the Gulf.

The Balkans

The collapse of Communism in Eastern Europe was greeted with little enthusiasm in most Balkan states. Albania's Stalinist regime at first resisted change, despite the mass exodus of its people to Greece and Italy. Serbia considered Communism to be the only tissue that bound its different ethnic groups together. Romania's National Salvation Front, which won 66 per cent of the popular vote in the May 1990 elections, included a number of high-ranking former Communist Party officials, including President Iliescu. Bulgaria's Socialist Party, which secured 47 per cent of the vote in the June 1990 elections, was a modified version of the old ruling Communist party.[40]

With Communism in the Balkans collapsing, Greek foreign policy was well prepared to reap the resulting dividends. Following Karamanlis's record as the West's honest broker in the region, Papandreou pursued his own idiosyncratic multilateralism. He began his Balkan initiatives by reviving an old Romanian proposal for a regional nuclear-weapons-free zone and gradually became an exponent of all forms of regional cooperation.[41]

With Mikhail Gorbachev's devolution plans under way, the meeting of six Balkan foreign ministers in Belgrade in February 1988, dealing with confidence- and security-building measures and minority questions,

[40]Geoffrey Pridham, 'Political Parties and Elections in the New Eastern European Democracies: Comparisons with the Southern European Experience', *Yearbook 1990*, Athens: Hellenic Foundation for Defense and Foreign Policy, 1991, pp. 261–8.

[41]Evangelos Kofos, 'Greece and the Balkans in the '70s and the '80s', *Yearbook 1990*, Athens: Hellenic Foundation for Defense and Foreign Policy, 1991, pp. 217–20.

heralded a new phase of inter-Balkan relations. A further meeting of Balkan foreign ministers in Tirana on 18–20 January 1989 examined guidelines to govern relations between Balkan neighbours, while the meeting of experts in Bucharest on 23–24 May 1989 dealt with confidence- and security-building measures.[42]

Greece's bilateral relations with Bulgaria were institutionalised with the signing of a 'Declaration of Friendship, Good Neighbourliness and Cooperation' in September 1986. Bulgaria's decision to engage in this accord was motivated by its sense of isolation as Soviet influence waned in the region, while Greece for its part needed to secure its northern flank in the event of conflict with Turkey.[43] However, the advent of the Union of Democratic Forces (UDF) to power led to a shift in Bulgaria's policy toward Turkey. The October 1991 elections gave the UDF a narrow victory over the Socialists and made the Movement for Rights and Freedoms (MRF), a party representing the interests of the Turkish minority, the decisive factor in forming a government. This, together with strong US leverage on Bulgaria, increased Turkey's role in Bulgarian affairs.

A sensitive issue between Greece and Bulgaria was the UDF government's recognition in January 1992 of the Former Yugoslav Republic of Macedonia (FYROM) as an independent state with the name 'Macedonia'. However, the Bulgarian Foreign Minister Stoyan Ganev made clear that this did not entail recognition of a separate Macedonian nation.[44] While the threat to Greek security posed by this state was negligible, the sensitivities of the inhabitants of Greek Macedonia were stirred by evocations of past conflicts over the use of the term 'Macedonia'.

By August 1991 Yugoslavia had collapsed as a state. On 8 September 1991 a referendum was held in the Socialist Republic of Macedonia, in which the Slavic majority voted overwhelmingly for independence. However, in April 1992 the Albanian minority (25 per cent of the

[42]*Ibid.*, pp. 220–1.

[43]F. Stephen Larrabee, 'The Southern Periphery Greece and Turkey' in Paul S. Shoup and George W. Hoffman (eds),*Problems of Balkan Security* (Washington, DC: Woodrow Wilson Center Press,1990, p. 191: 'Noteworthy in this regard has been the expansion of military ties highlighted by the visit of Deputy Defence Minister and Chief of the Bulgarian General Staff, Atanas Semerdzhiev, to Athens in April 1988.'

[44] Duncan M.Perry, 'Macedonia: a Balkan Problem and a European Dilemma', *RFE/RL Research Report* 1, no. 25 (19 June 1992), p. 36.

total population) signalled its preference for becoming an autonomous republic. Greek public opinion only gradually became aware of the significance of these developments. At first Prime Minister Mitsotakis displayed flexibility on the question of the emerging state's name,[45] but the main concern in Greece was that the new state should not use the term 'Macedonia' without qualifiers—which, given the Socialist Republic of Macedonia's history of laying claim to Bulgarian and Greek territory, was considered essential. In an effort to block European recognition of the Republic, the Greek Foreign Minister Antonis Samaras recognised Slovenia and Croatia on 7 December 1991, and adopted a common EC declaration establishing conditions for recognition, which included a ban on 'territorial claims toward a neighbouring Community state, hostile propaganda and the use of a denomination that implies territorial claims'.[46]

Other Greek objections concerned the reference in the preamble of the constitution to the founding manifesto of the People's Republic of Macedonia in 1944, which stressed 'the demand to unite the whole of the Macedonian people around the claim for self-determination'.[47] The controversy over the terms of recognition hit the Greek media with full force. With a little help from politicians of all parties except the Communists, the public fear was aroused that Skopje would monopolise the term 'Macedonia'. Although privately Mitsotakis adopted a moderate position, his precarious majority in Parliament (two seats) significantly reduced his room for manoeuvre. When he dismissed Samaras and assumed the duties of Foreign Minister himself in April 1992, he was obliged by domestic pressure to maintain his predecessor's basic position. The saga of Greek foreign policy concerning the subsequently-named Former Yugoslavia of Macedonia (FYROM) has become a case-study of how diplomacy, when driven by an inflamed public opinion, is bound to fail. After many mishaps the Interim Accord of 13 September 1995 signed by Greek and FYROM Foreign Ministers Karolos Papoulias and Stevo Cervenkovski, and by Cyrus Vance (serving as a special envoy of the UN Secretary-General), though not a final agreement, cleared the way for a tacit normalisation between the two states.

[45]Interview in *Eleftherotypia,* 19 November 1991.
[46]Declaration on Yugoslavia, extraordinary EPC ministerial meeting, Brussels, 16 December, 1991. EPC press release, p. 129.
[47]Reference in Yannis Valinakis, *Greece's Balkan Policy and the Macedonian Issue,* Ebehhausen: Stiftung Wissenschaft und Politik, April 1992, p. 27.

The political significance of the Euro in Greece

by P.C. Ioakimidis, EU expert, Greek Foreign Ministry

The significance for Greece of accession to the single currency goes beyond mere economics. It is a political act of historic proportions for a number of reasons:

First, through accession to the single currency, Greece will secure its institutional place within the evolving political system of the European Union. Because this system is growing into a differentiated formation comprising an inner hard core of deeply integrated Euro-countries, which will take the most vital decisions, and a loosely integrated outer group, it is important that Greece succeeds in placing itself in the inner group.

Second, accession to the Euro represents a huge 'security investment' for Greece. Being a full member of the single currency means that Greece's external security is greatly enhanced. A country that shares the same currency with the most powerful countries of Europe (Germany, France, Italy, Spain) cannot fall prey to a hostile foreign attack or even be threatened by external powers. Such actions would amount to a challenge to the entire Eurozone.

Third, accession to the Euro will make Greece a player in the international economic and financial system. As a full member state of the European Central Bank and other European monetary institutions, it will be in a position to influence global economic policy and financial decisions, thereby further bolstering its international status.

Fourth, joining the Eurozone will be an additional factor for strengthening Greece's regional role as the countries of the Balkan region are eager to adopt the Euro as their own currency, or tie their national currencies to it in their attempt to underpin monetary stability and advance their cause for early accession to the EU.

Coupled with the adjustments in Greece's foreign and European policy that have occurred recently [this was written in 1999], the country is rapidly emerging as a respectable actor in European affairs. This is spectacular progress from the early 1990s when Greece was seen as the 'incurable sick man of Europe' heading for withdrawal from the European Union. To emphasise the political significance of accession to the Euro by no means implies a downgrading of the enormous economic benefits that Greece will derive in economic stability, low inflation, transparency in prices, investment activity and ultimately higher employment opportunities. Indeed the effort to qualify for joining the Euro has driven the process for economic consolidation, discipline and modernisation. As a result, the country has come for the first time in its modern history to sustain a stable macro-economic environment with virtually no budgetary deficits.

Ties between Greece and Albania were expanded through a cross-border trade agreement signed in April 1988. A year earlier, Greece had renounced its old claims to southern Albania and terminated the state of war that had remained in force since the Second World War. After the thaw during the Papandreou period, relations vacillated between the politics of the carrot and the stick. The fate of the Greek minority, which had been the main stumbling-block in Greek-Albanian relations in the past, persisted as a contentious issue.[48] The Albanian elections in March 1991 allowed the Socialists (formerly Communists) to retain power, but those that followed a year later gave the Democratic Party, headed by Sali Berisha, a clear mandate. The Greek minority was represented in the 1991 Albanian parliament by five deputies of the minority 'Omonia' party, but in 1992 its deputies were reduced to two and its name was changed under government pressure to 'Union for Human Rights'.

As economic and social conditions in Albania deteriorated, more than 400,000 of its nationals entered Greece as illegal immigrants. If this number is multiplied by four or five dependants who remained behind, it can be assumed that more than half of Albania's population came to be supported by remittances ($350 million a year on average) from the illegal workers in Greece. Despite this state of financial dependence, President Berisha chose to strain relations in 1994 by imprisoning five members of Omonia on shaky charges of conspiracy against the state, and although they were amnestied through American intervention, mutual suspicions persisted.[49] The 1997 'pyramid' scandal was followed by widespread upheaval that obliged Berisha to resign, and the coalition government under Fatos Nano inherited a collapsed state. Nevertheless relations with Greece improved and the members of the coalition cabinet who joined forces with the Socialists tried to restore order.

With Romania, Greece had no serious outstanding problems. The two countries have no common borders or old feuds to settle, and moreover they share a cultural history that goes back to Ottoman

[48]Estimates of the size of the Greek minority vary. The Albanians claim that there are only 40,000, while Greek estimates reach as high as 400,000; the number probably lies somewhere between the two estimates. For a discussion of the minority issue see Larrabee, 'Southern Periphery', p. 191; James Pettifer, 'Albania's Way out of the Shadows', *The World Today* (April 1991), pp. 55–7.

[49]Nicos Ziogas, 'Developments in Albania in 1994', *Southeast European Yearbook 1996–97*, ELIAMEP, 1995. p. 123.

times. After the overthrow of Ceauşescu, Greece was one of the first states to aid Romania, and continues to act as its intermediary *vis-à-vis* the EU and NATO.

From the outbreak of the Yugoslav crisis, Greece supported a form of confederation in the country that would guarantee the rights of its constituent parts and prevent the subsequent strife that would destabilise the region. Drawing on its ties with Serbia, it tried several times to act as an intermediary between the Serbs and the EU and sought to keep communications open. Greek mediation was instrumental in freeing the Bosnian President, Alija Izetbegovic, from Serbian captivity in Sarajevo during the spring of 1992 and maintaining contact between Ibrahim Rugova (leader of the Albanian Kosovars) and the government in Belgrade throughout the latter part of that year. In addition, Mitsotakis played a key role in brokering the Athens agreement on Bosnia in May 1993. The Bosnian settlement of 21 November 1995 in Dayton, Ohio, may not have solved the intractable problems between Croats, Bosnians and Serbs, but at least it put a stop to their bloody conflict.

Between 1974 and 1989 the Balkans had been a promising factor in Greek foreign policy, but throughout 1992–5 the regional credibility of Greece reached rock-bottom. After the interim accord between Athens and Skopje in 1995, the entire nexus of Greece's Balkan relations began to improve and the private sector made economic headway. The decision of NATO to bomb the Federal Republic of Yugoslavia in March–June 1999 over the conflict in Kosovo introduced an altogether new factor in regional politics and caused a devastation that will affect all future developments. The soft and hard protectorates of the West now include Bosnia, Kosovo, FYROM (to a lesser degree) and Albania. Thus NATO and the UN have been entangled in a region festering with irredentist claims, weak social and political institutions, and economic decline accelerated by the destruction of Serbia's infrastructure.[50] The open opposition of Greece to the military operation did not prevent the Simitis government from preserving the NATO consensus. Greek support for FYROM's integrity and the *status quo* of the borders between Kosovo and Albania

---

[50]See minutes of Halki International Seminars, 20–26 June 1999, 'Developing a Network of Young Leaders from Southeast Europe', especially keynote speech by Carl Bildt on 25 June. See also his article in the *Financial Times* of 21 June 1999: 'Rebuilding the Balkans'.

may cause tension with Albanian supporters of a greater Illyria, but it has won Greece the reputation of being an example of regional stability and a mainstream state within the EU.[51]

Turkey

The Aegean problems that erupted in the 1970s can largely be attributed to the waning of the Cold War. Although Turkey had demanded the exclusion of the island of Lemnos from NATO exercises as early as 1965, Greece's operational responsibility within the Aegean had not been challenged. Such issues as the continental shelf (CS), the Flight Information Region (FIR), and the incompatibility between the 10-mile limit of Greece's air space with the 6-mile limit of its territorial waters were raised by Turkey in 1973–4.[52]

The ambiguity that governed the transition from Cold War immobilism to the relative freedom of movement within the climate of détente spurred Turkey to pursue a more autonomous policy within NATO. The Middle East crisis of 1967 increased its value in the American agenda, and convinced policy-makers in Ankara that the vulnerable adjacent regions were no longer off-limits. Furthermore, the Soviet-American détente minimised the likelihood of Russian military involvement in regions of high priority for US interests, and therefore a Turkish invasion of Cyprus, which appeared unthinkable to President Johnson in 1965, was condoned by Kissinger as Secretary of State in 1974.[53]

The invasion of Cyprus in 1974 was a watershed in Turkish foreign policy because it was the country's first conquest since its army marched into the Syrian province of Alexandretta (now Hatay) in 1938. In both cases a *fait accompli* was established with little international protest. The lesson that war can accomplish foreign policy objectives by other means has thus made a lasting impression on the military and diplomatic establishments—two immutable factors in Turkey's policy-making.

---

[51]Van Coufoudakis, Harry J. Psomiades and Andre Gerolymatos, 'Greece as a Factor of Stability in the Post-Cold War Balkans' in *Greece and the New Balkans. Challenges and Opportunities*, New York: Pella, 1999, pp.423–31.

[52]T.Veremis, *Greek Security: Issues and Politics*. Adelphi Paper no. 179, London: IISS, 1982, pp. 14–19

[53]Van Coufoudakis, 'Turkey and the United States: The Problems and Prospects of a Post-War Alliance', *Journal of Political and Military Sociology*, vol. 9, no. 2, autumn 1981, pp. 179–94.

The invasion also opened a Pandora's Box of the Aegean's contested issues, and one after another in quick succession they flew out. As well as Cyprus, three of these caused serious tension between Greece and Turkey. The delimitation of the Aegean continental shelf brought the two countries close to war in 1976 and 1987, while control of air traffic over the sea and the allocation of operational responsibility for the Aegean and its air-space within the NATO framework were also important.[54] Subsequent efforts by Andreas Papandreou and Turgut Özal in 1988 to discover a *modus vivendi* based on a peaceful resolution of differences foundered on the EC's negative reply to the Turkish application for membership a year later. Deprived of a vital incentive to pursue a Greek-Turkish détente, subsequent Turkish governments were unwilling to revive the Papandreou-Özal initiative. Even moderate Turkish analysts did not escape the temptation to use power as the major factor in resolving Greek-Turkish differences,[55] and as the Cold War and its deterrent effect on regional conflict waned, the agenda of Turkish demands on Greece expanded. A sense of heightened self-esteem in terms of size, military strength and strategic value now determined the way Turkey viewed its western neighbour.

Prompted by the precarious state of affairs in the Balkans, Prime Minister Mitsotakis sought to improve relations with Ankara throughout the winter of 1991–2. His attempt to revive the Davos summit with Prime Minister Demirel and promote a non-aggression pact failed to bear fruit because no progress was made towards resolving the Cyprus question. The reluctance of the Turkish Cypriot leader Rauf Denktash to reach an agreement with the President of Cyprus, George Vassiliou, on the basis of UN General Secretary Boutros Boutros-Ghali's 'set of ideas', advanced during meetings in New York in August and September 1992, suggested that Turkey was not prepared to make concessions.

The Gulf War enhanced Turkey's strategic value in Western eyes, and the collapse of the Soviet Union opened up the possibility of renewing contacts with the Turkic peoples of Central Asia.[56] Although confronted with hostile eastern and southern flanks and a host of

---

[54]Andrew Wilson, 'The Aegean Dispute', *Adelphi Papers*, no.155, London: IISS, winter 1979/80.

[55]Tozun Bahcheli, *Greek-Turkish Relations since 1955*, Boulder, CO: Westview Press, 1990, p. 193.

[56]Shireen Hunter, *Turkey at the Crossroads: Islamic Past or European Future?*, CEPS, Paper no. 63, Brussels, 1995

formidable domestic problems, Turkey is encouraged by its Western allies to pursue a policy befitting its status as a regional power. The threat of military force has therefore become a standard Turkish bargaining ploy in Cyprus and the Aegean.

In March 1995 Greece lifted its objections to Turkey's entry into the EU Customs Union agreement, on the understanding that the application of Cyprus for EU membership would be discussed after the intergovernmental meeting of 1997. The Greek move elicited no positive response from the government of Ms Tansu Ciller. A series of incidents between the two states, beginning in 1994 over the right of Greece to extend its territorial waters from 6 to 12 miles, reached a climax on 8 June 1995 when the Turkish parliament granted the government a license to take whatever action that might be necessary—including military action—if Greece exercised its right (envisaged in the International Law of the Sea Convention) to extend its territorial waters.

In January 1996 a team of Turkish journalists removed the Greek flag from the barren islet of Imia which is part of the Dodecanese complex and hoisted the Turkish one in its place. Greek soldiers replaced the Greek flag and the incident was considered innocuous by the Greek Foreign Minister Theodoros Pangalos until Tansu Ciller herself presented an official claim to the islet and began a confrontation that almost led to war. The crisis was defused through US mediation, but a claim to actual land had been added to the overburdened agenda of Greek-Turkish problems.

Not only the United States but NATO too became involved in efforts to mediate between the Alliance's two member-states. Javier Solana, the Secretary-General, proposed confidence-building measures to avoid future crises. In July 1996 the EU Council of Ministers issued a declaration stating that relations between Turkey and the EU should be guided by respect for international law, international agreements and the sovereignty and territorial integrity of the EU member-states.[57] In April 1997 Greece and Turkey agreed with the proposal of the Dutch EU presidency to appoint a committee of experts to study bilateral problems. Of the two Turkish experts the former ambassador to Washington, Sukru Elekdag, had written an article with the title '2$^1/_2$ War Strategy' only a year before assuming this

---

[57]Carol Migdalovitz, 'Greece and Turkey: Aegean Issues-Background and Recent Developments', *CRS Report from Congress*, 21 August, 1997, Washington, DC: Congressional Research Service, 1997), 4–5.

new position. In it he suggested that Greece and Syria together, 'with their claims on Turkey's vital interests', prevented his country from enjoying the peace dividend. Unlike other officials who attributed the Turkish military build-up to eastern and northern threats, Elekdag promoted the view that Turkey must always be in a state of readiness to wage two-and-a-half wars (against Greece, Syria and the Kurds). That the Turkish government had chosen an exponent of such views to engage in discussions on Greek-Turkish détente was hardly encouraging.[58]

Throughout the Greek-Turkish disputes, Greece proposed that the continental shelf issue and, after 1996, the regime for Imia be referred for adjudication to the International Court of Justice in order to exclude confrontational attitudes and spare politicians on both sides from domestic embarrassment. However, Turkey insisted that all differences between the two states be discussed on a bilateral political basis. Although there had been similar talks in the past (1977–81), they had failed to produce results. Furthermore, Greece felt that Turkey was constantly burdening the agenda with new claims so that bilateral negotiations would only follow a Turkish agenda.

The government of Simitis that won the elections of October 1996 quietly disavowed the Papandreou tradition in domestic and foreign affairs, and indeed the leader of PASOK became the antithesis of his populist predecessor. His main priority, to which he subordinated all other considerations, was to achieve convergence with EU criteria in order to join the Economic and Monetary Union (EMU). On the Turkish side, the Necmettin Erbakan-Ciller coalition government of July 1996 was too preoccupied with opposition from its own military and Western criticism to resume pressures on Greece, but it did reiterate the allegation that there are 'grey zones' in the Aegean not covered by treaties. The coalition's removal from power allowed a new Greek-Turkish rapprochement to materialiee, engineered by the US Secretary of State Madeleine Albright at the Madrid NATO summit meeting of July 1997. An agreement signed by Simitis and the Turkish President Suleyman Demirel specified that the two sides would abstain from coercion and other initiatives that would affect each other's legitimate vital interests, and would respect the provisions of international treaties.[59]

---

[58]Sukru Elekdag, '2$^1/_2$ War Strategy', *Perceptions: Journal of International Affairs*, no. 1 (March-May 1996), Ankara, pp. 33–57.

[59]Migdalovitz, 'Greece and Turkey', 7–8.

Governing Greek-Turkish relations are the perceptions that each side has of the other. Where the Aegean is concerned, Turkey believes that Greece wants to transform it into a 'Greek lake', while Greece believes that Turkey aspires to make inroads at the expense of Greek sovereignty in the eastern Aegean islands. On the whole, Greece's policy is centred on defending the territorial *status quo*, while Turkey had appeared to challenge certain legal aspects regulating Greece's rights in the region.

Where Cyprus is concerned, attitudes to the *status quo* are reversed. The Turkish Cypriots and Turkey are not entirely unhappy with the situation as it has developed since 1974, while the Greek Cypriots would very much like to see Cyprus reunited. Security considerations weigh heavily in each side's willingness to find a solution. The Turkish Cypriots feel secure with 35,000 Turkish troops in the north of the island, while the Greek Cypriots feel insecure for the very same reason. Greek Cypriots hope that the prospect of EU membership may inhibit Turkey from using force in the future, and that if it achieves membership the chances of the island being re-unified will be increased. However, the Turkish Cypriots and Turkey believe that re-unification would remove Cyprus from Turkey's strategic control and enhance the position of the Greek majority.

The Cyprus and Aegean issues are not officially linked in Greece's current policy towards Turkey, but in fact Cyprus is a major catalyst in Greek-Turkish relations. The island has been divided ever since Turkey occupied the northern third in 1974 in the immediate aftermath of the coup organized by the Greek military dictatorship against the Republic's President, Archbishop Makarios. The Turkish forces displaced the Greek Cypriot element and established the whole Turkish Cypriot community—18 per cent of the population of the island—in a self-proclaimed state of Northern Cyprus. Repeated UN resolutions urging the withdrawal of foreign troops and the holding of intercommunal talks to re-unite the island have, up to the time of writing, been entirely fruitless.

The round of talks between the Turkish Cypriot leader Rauf Denktash and the President of Cyprus Glafcos Clerides began in New York in July 1997 and continued in Glion, Switzerland, under the UN's mediator and special envoy on Cyprus, Diego Cordovez. The objective of reuniting the island under a bi-zonal, bi-communal federation was overtaken by the prospect of discussions between the Cyprus government and the European Union in 1998 on the accesion of Cyprus to the EU. The Turks maintain that Cyprus cannot join the EU without the consent of the Turkish Cypriots unless Turkey itself is admitted. Even before the round of intercommunal discussions began, an agreement concluded for the closer integration of the Turkish Cypriot breakaway state with Turkey indicated the latter's readiness to hinder the accession of Cyprus to the EU by impeding the reconciliation of the two communities.[60]

At the EU summit meeting in Luxembourg on 12–14 December 1997, Turkey failed to be admitted to the list of candidates for the next round of accession negotiations due to its poor human rights record, its strained relations with Greece and its negative position on Cyprus. The EU's fifteen leaders did invite Ankara to attend the European conference to be held in Britain in 1998, but Turkey's reaction to this combined bitterness at its rejection with apparent dismissal of the idea of EU membership as unimportant. On 16 December the Turkish Foreign Minister Ismail Cem stated that Ankara would proceed with the integration of Northern Cyprus into Turkey proper whenever the EU began admission talks with the Cyprus government. Turkish violations of Greek airspace were stepped up, even within the 6-mile limit which Turkey recognises as belonging to Greece.

Throughout 1998 Ankara and Denktash continued to voice their anger over the rebuff. Denktash's decision not to return to the negotiating table until his own 'state' in the occupied north of the island was recognised on an equal footing with the Republic of Cyprus stopped the intercommunal talks in their tracks. On 31 August 1998 in a joint press conference the Turkish Foreign Minister Ismail Cem and Denktash announced a Turkish Cypriot proposal for a confederate relationship between two equal parts. The proposed entity implied partition in every sense except one: by not relinquishing its guarantor status (as defined by the 1960 agreement) Turkey hoped to secure a say on matters concerning Cyprus as a whole, and not just the north. With this initiative Turkey would naturally seek to block the island's entry into the EU until it too had been granted full membership.[61]

The clandestine entry of the PKK leader, Abdullah Ocalan, into Greece in February 1999, and the mishap of his passage to Kenya

---

[60] *War report*, no. 54, Sept. 1997, pp. 16–34.

[61] US analysts are impeded by their attempt to treat the two sides as equals, regardless of their profound differences in many fields of activity. For an American attempt at mediation, see James Wilkinson, *Moving beyond Conflict Prevention to Reconciliation: Tackling Greek-Turkish Hostility,* a Report to the Carnegie Commission on Preventing Deadly Conflict, New York 1999, p. 48.

with official Greek complicity, compounded the rift in Greek–Turkish relations, and when the Turkish elections in 1999 produced a coalition of right- and left-wing nationalists under Bulent Ecevit the future appeared bleak.

The EU summit in Helsinki on 9–10 December 1999 approved Turkey's 'candidacy' in the EU with Greek agreement, but Greece's terms for casting a positive vote included affirmation by the EU that the future accession of Cyprus would not be linked to resolution of the island's division. Up till the time of going to press, no progress towards a solution has been made, despite the many UN resolutions since 1974 and the talks between the two communities. Be that as it may, a new climate in Greek–Turkish relations was inaugurated in Helsinki, which may yet have a benign influence on the whole of the eastern Mediterranean.

Part VII. NATIONAL GEOGRAPHY

19

THE FRONTIER AND BEYOND

A boundary, as a demarcation line separating one domain from another and requiring special permission to cross, was a novel factor in the life of the Greeks. Ever since the Ottoman Turks had completed the conquest of the Greek lands and made them part of a single political unit, namely the Ottoman empire, few Greeks had ever crossed a border into a foreign country. Even those who ventured away from their homes in search of seasonal work or for longer spells seldom crossed into the jurisdiction of another monarch. Masons, millers, charcoal-burners, gardeners and other seasonal agricultural workers, muleteers, merchants and even seamen rarely had occasion to venture outside the Sultan's European and Asiatic dominions, but in time merchants began feeling their way northward into the lands of the Habsburgs and the Romanovs, as well as westwards.[1]

The Venetian, Genoese and, later, British island possessions in the Ionian and Aegean seas involved, of course, a kind of boundary, imaginary as it may have been except for merchants and seamen obliged by their calling to come into contact with foreign authorities; so too did the administrative jurisdiction of powerful pashas in the late eighteenth and early nineteenth centuries over well-defined districts. Ports of entry in the first instance and guarded passes in the second made the traveller aware, in the former case more than the latter, of approaching or departing from a land other than one's own, even

---

[1]This essay is based on material drawn from the book of John S. Koliopoulos, *Brigands with a Cause: Brigandage and Irredentism in Modern Greece, 1821–1912,* Oxford: Clarendon Press, 1987.

within the limits of the traditional Greek lands in the Balkans and Asia Minor.

The 1830 national boundary with Turkey was the first modern division between states in Greek national experience. For the first time in the modern era, the Greeks had their own nation-state, a realm defined by international treaty as independent and separate from others, and recognised as such by foreign monarchs and nations. Beyond that boundary lay the remaining dominions of the Sultan, suddenly inaccessible and uninviting because they were ruled by what was now perceived as an unfriendly power. Military posts denied all unauthorised crossing of the frontier in either direction, while customs officials levied import duties on goods carried by merchants and animals herded across the frontier.

Gradually the frontier developed into a significant factor of Greek life in more senses than one. It fulfilled the role of most frontiers in protecting the fledgling Greek kingdom from the Turks. Sanctioned by international treaty and guaranteed by three great powers of the time, Greece's frontier with Turkey precluded reconquest of the country by its former masters. After ten years of revolutionary war with its attendant carnage and destruction, the frontier represented peace and security; at least, this was what most foreign supporters of Greek independence, as well as many Greeks, believed and expected.

But at the same time the frontier penned the Greeks of the free fatherland into the southernmost tip of the Balkans, and separated them from their brethren inside the Sultan's dominions. For the first time in their modern history they were distinguished not only as western or European and eastern or Asiatic Greeks, but as northern or unredeemed Greeks and southern or free Greeks.

The first to feel the impact of the new frontier were all those whose livelihood depended on travelling the length of the Greek peninsula from north to south and from south to north. Artisans of every kind, soldiers of fortune, seasoned agricultural workers, monks on journeys to collect alms, pedlars, all kinds of merchants, and transhumant shepherds with their animals were obliged to cross the new frontier in and out of the Greek kingdom, and for most of them it was an unnecessary and often costly impediment. Expert millers from the rich waterways of the Macedonian mountains; stone-cutters and masons from the mountain villages of south-west Macedonia and Epirus; merchants in animal skins, wool and cheese from Thessaly, Macedonia and Epirus; transhumant shepherds wintering their flocks of sheep and goats on well-established winter pastures in the lowlands of Phthiotis and Aetolia—these and others whose professions required them to move along traditional routes now had to cross the frontier and enter the Greek kingdom as subjects of a foreign monarch.

Customs duties on the importation of goods and animals were a most undesirable novelty, but they represented only part of the cost of moving goods and animals across the frontier. Underpaid gendarmes and frontier guards supplemented their meagre and insecure salaries from the movable property of all those who were obliged to cross the border in either direction. When transhumant shepherds made their seasonal journeys, gendarmes and guards could delay the passage of their flocks until they were satisfied that the animals had not been stolen—which they often had been—and until their own needs were satisfied in the way sanctioned by custom: appropriation of quantities of goods and animals commensurate to the owner's need to reach his destination. All therefore had gifts for the gendarme and the guard. Some, like fugitives from the law, runaway servants, indebted peasants and artisans, rustlers, army deserters and brigands were always generous to the gendarmes and guards, thus satisfying them that everything was in order.

Southern Balkan pastoralists in particular saw their fortunes revolving around and dependent on the frontier, especially when Greece acquired Thessaly in 1881, while the frontier with Turkey denied them free access to the largest winter pastures of the entire region. It was little wonder that the Vlachs of the Pindus mountains should have petitioned the great powers to deny Greece the Thessalian lowlands, angering Greek nationalists who saw in this act of despair a conspiracy to prevent their nation from realising its manifest destiny of expanding northwards. Vlach shepherds of the mountain chain traversing the Greek peninsula and stretching into southern Albania were forced to pay the price of the new political realities. Incidentally, the incorporation of Thessaly into the Greek kingdom and its separation from the surrounding highlands, together with such other factors as the fragmentation of large estates in the plains and the relentless efforts of the state to end modes of life which it considered outdated and contary to the national interest, dealt a mortal blow to the pastoral economy of the region.

Another aspect of the 1830 national frontier was the creation along its Greek side of a number of refugee settlements from the Greek lands where revolts against Ottoman rule had been savagely suppressed. To the initial wave of demoralised northern Greek fighters who settled there were added the periodic waves of destitute refugees fleeing the Sultan's armies in Epirus, Thessaly and Macedonia after each unsuccessful round of irredentist unrest. These refugees were a sizeable and increasingly influential group who took part in the various irredentist upheavals of the nineteenth century, never failing to respond to captains on the look-out for hired guns. Northern Greek refugees, shepherds cast adrift by the disintegrating pastoral associations of central and northern Greece, and professional soldiers of fortune, once members of local Christian militias in the service of the Sultan, gave to the national frontier all the characteristics of a 'military' one similar to that which had grown up on the frontier between the Habsburg and Ottoman empires in the sixteenth century. It fostered lawlessness, since beyond the border there was a land open to plunder and eventual liberation. The width of the 'military border' increased at times of tension between the two neighbouring countries, whose laws were essentially unenforceable there. Bands of armed irregulars of various types and loyalties rubbed shoulders with units of frontier guards and gendarmes, and as clashes multiplied, the already blurred line between legality and lawlessness disappeared. This was a world apart, reproducing and nourishing the very values and practices which the modernisers in the Greek national state most wanted to see suppressed.

The generally unfriendly or hostile relations between the two neighbouring countries were a condition for the area's growth. Unfriendly or hostile relations alone, however, were not enough to produce such a state of affairs. What really gave the border belt the features described above was the fact that the Turks—despite their claims to the contrary—continued to use the contracting armatolic system of security on their own side of the border. Custom in this respect was too strong to change, while the military class that stood for that system was too powerful and influential to ignore, on either side of the border. Another no less important factor was Greek irredentism, which turned the frontier zone into a base of operations for the liberation of unredeemed brethren across the border. Irredentism provided the necessary ideological justification for the plundering raids launched from the frontier, and made the authorities turn a blind eye to such activities—or even incite them, especially when they too shared in the material returns from such raids. Irredentism sustained the forces that occupied so central a position in the military border.

This border and the irregulars associated with it tended to undermine reforming and modernising efforts in the region, channelling patriotic impulses into self-defeating ventures which gave patriotism a bad name. Like the Habsburg military border, it resulted in arrested development since it stood in the way of economic growth and the establishment of public order and security; not unlike the American Frontier, though for different reasons, it favoured lawlessness. The border belt—in 1881 no less than in 1830—was an integral part of what might be described as a system of manipulated lawlessness, which had developed ever since the Ottomans arrived in those lands, and was given a new lease of life after the establishment of the national state in the south.

Above all, the two nineteenth-century national land frontiers of Greece were gates leading to the unredeemed brethren and to the Greeks' 'promised land'. For most Greeks of the kingdom, Thessaly and Epirus until 1881 and Macedonia until 1913 were lands that were Greek by historic right and destined to join and enlarge the Greek state. The unredeemed provinces then acquired strange dimensions and qualities. Imperfect geographical knowledge, and information about the inhabitants that was either rudimentary or downright false, gave rise to flights of fancy about them. As might have been expected in a country where education had acquired a decisively classical bent, more was known about the past history of these lands than about the present. Greek travel books with relatively accurate information about the same lands appeared too late to influence Greek perceptions of them.

With the acquisition of Epirus and Macedonia in the Balkan Wars of 1912–13 the frontier was pushed so far to the north that the Greeks met and faced, in addition to their old opponents the Turks, new opponents such as the Bulgars and prospective ones like the Serbs and Albanians. As a national boundary the 1913 frontier proved short-lived, being superseded by an even more transient one, that of the Sèvres treaty of 1920—which in turn was superseded three years later by Greece's final frontier established by the Lausanne treaty of 1923. The frontier was no longer a gate leading to the promised land or a world beyond it that exercised irresistible attraction and fascination; the long and vulnerable new frontier was an outpost of Hellenism facing the Barbarians and keeping at bay enemies who coveted the Hellenic state; it was a medieval borderland requiring *akritai* (resident warriors) to defend the civilised Ecumene against incursions by anti-Christian hordes. The land beyond was no longer inviting; indeed, after the 1940–1 Axis invasion of Greece from the north and the 1946–9 Civil War, in which the country's Communists received political and military support from that quarter, the northen frontier and the north itself came to be associated with insecurity and war. The 'danger from the north' was no longer merely a slogan but the essence of Greek defence policy from 1923 onwards. This was the foreign policy doctrine that led the country always to keep on good terms with Britain as the great power controlling the eastern Mediterranean sea routes, and opened Greece to the world at large. Like the north-eastern gales that sweep over Greek Macedonia and Thrace and pound the Aegean archipelago and the country's eastern shores in winter, the north came to be associated with a sinister force threatening to extinguish precious life in the Greek fatherland, and pushed the Greeks into allying themselves with the seafating liberal democratic countries of the West, which were the source of all modernising ideas.

20

A NORTHERN BOUNDARY

The question of a northern boundary was first considered and discussed when the Greek Revolution of the 1820s became effectively limited to the southern Greek peninsula and the western Aegean islands, i.e. when all revolts in the northern Greek lands had been suppressed by the Turks. Up till then the very idea of a northern boundary, in the sense of a demarcation line separating two sovereign states, had been of little or no significance.

William Martin Leake, who had come to know the northern Greek lands, once observed how little most Greeks knew of places and people outside their own villages. He also criticised Meletios, the geographer-prelate of the eighteenth century, for his limited grasp of historical geography. The knowledge of the Greeks of his time about the region where their own people had come to live side by side with the Albanians and the Slavs, and which the ancient Greeks called Upper Epirus and Upper Macedonia, i.e. a region far from the sea, had not increased significantly since the time of Polybius.[1]

Around this time the term 'Hellas' meant different things to different people. Rhigas Velestinlis included the Balkan hinterlands in the 'Hellas' of his 'Charta' and considered its Christian inhabitants to be cultural descendants of the ancient Greeks and citizens of the Hellenic republic he aspired to establish.[2] Rhigas was convinced that its people 'descend

---

[1]W. M. Leake, *Travels in Northern Greece,* London, 1834, repr. Amsterdam 1967, vol. I, p. 204, and vol. IV, pp. 111–12. See also Georgios Papageorgiou, 'Oi Geographies', *Dodoni,* 26 (1997), p. 389.

[2]The best authority on Rhigas was the late Leandros Vranousis. See his *Rhigas Velestinlis—Pheraios* (in Greek), Athens, 1968, vol. II, pp. 681–727, for the text of

from the Hellenes' and 'inhabit Roumely, Asia Minor, the Mediterranean islands and Vlach-Bodgania'. This was also the Hellas of Philippides and Konstantas, who set its limits in the Black Sea, Bulgaria, Serbia and Bosnia, as well as that of *Logios Hermes*, one of the first Greek journals to be published abroad, but not the Hellas of the geographer Athanasios Stageiritis, whose classical approach left out Epirus and Macedonia.[3] This was also the 'Hellas' the insurgent Greeks vowed to liberate from Turkish rule. However, the fortunes of war obliged them to seek more realistic northern boundaries for the nation-state in the making on the basis of what at the time was considered to be 'Greece proper'.

Alexandros Mavrocordatos hoped that the latter would eventually become an 'independent power' with a buffer zone in the north of 'small but independent principatities': Vlach-Bogdania, Bulgaria, Serbia

---

Rhigas's 'Constitution' and the French Constitutions of 1793 and 1795, on which he drew. For his 'Charta' see pp. 569–644 and 762 in the same volume. See also the relative sections in his suberb book on the last volume (1797) of the Greek 'Gazette' of Vienna, published by the Brothers Markides Pouliou of Siatista, *Ephemeris, 1797. Prolegomena* (Gazette, 1797: Prologue), Athens, 1995, and A. P. Daskalakis, *Meletai peri Riga Velestinli* (Studies on Rhigas Velestinlis), Athens, 1964, and Nikolaos I. Pantazopoulos, *Rhigas Velestinlis* (in Greek), Thessaloniki, 1964. For a fine biography in English see C. M. Woodhouse, *Rhigas Velestinlis, the Proto-martyr of the Greek Revolution*, Limni: Euboea, 1995. For a critical evaluation of Rhigas's political works see see two recent books by an authority on political thinkers of the the Greek Enlightenment, Paschalis M. Kitromelides, *Rhigas Velestinlis. Theoria kai praxi* (Rhigas Velestinlis. Theory and practice), Athens, 1998, and *Riga Velestinli apanthisma keimenon* (Rhigas Velestinlis. A selection of his works), Athens, 1998.

[3]Most Greek geographers of the time followed Western writers on the lands of 'Greece' and meant *Graecia propria*, i.e. south of Thessaly. See the works of early nineteenth-century Greek geographers, especially Athanasios Stageiritis, *Ipeirotika, itoi historia kai geographia tis Ipeirou palaia te kai nea, kai bios toy Pyrrou* (Epirote studies, or history and geography of ancient and modern Epirus, and life of Pyrrhus), Vienna, 1819; Dionysios Pyrros o Thessalos, *Geographia methodiki apasis tis Oekoumenis* (Systematic geography of the world), Vienna, 1818; Kosmas Thesprotos and Athanasios Psalidas, *Geographia Albanias kai Ipeirou* (Geography of Albania and Epirus), ed. by Athanasios Ch. Papacharisis, Ioannina, 1964; Konstantinos Koumas, *Synopsis tis palaias Geographias* (Concise ancient geography), Vienna, 1819; *Neotati didaktiki Geographia* (Contemporary geography: A textbook), vol. II, Vienna 1838; Ioannis Valetas, *Geographia tis Hellados, archaias kai neas* (Geography of ancient and modern Greece), 2nd edn, Hermoupolis, 1841. See also Demetrios Philippides and Grigorios Konstantas, *Geographia neoteriki peri tis Hellados* (Modern geography of Greece), ed. by Aikaterini Koumarianou, Athens, 1970, for an 'expanded' Greece, as well as Argyris Philippides, *Meriki Geographia—Biblion ithikon* (Partial geography—book of ethics), edit. by Theodosis K. Sperantsas, Athens, 1978, for eastern continental Greece. Koraes's Greece also was *Graecia propria*. See his *Dialogue of two Greeks*, pp. 37–8.

and Bosnia. The northern boundaries of this independent country, though not specified, were perhaps those proposed by his close friend and adviser, Metropolitan Ignatius of Hungary-Wallachia: 'The natural and strong boundary is Souli, Ioannina, the Zagori mountains, Metsovon and the northern mountains of Thessaly and the villages of Makrynitsa', i.e. Mt Pelion.[4] This was indeed a 'natural and strong' boundary for the new state; certainly more so than the first northern boundary of the fledgling nation-state in the southern Balkans. However, it seems to have been no different from what was then thought of as the northern limit of Greek language and culture. The Fourth National Assembly excluded in 1826 the 'Olympus' representatives, i.e. the captains of the Armatoles of Mts Vermion, Pieria and Olympus, who had fought on the side of the southern Greek insurgents after the suppression of their revolt in 1822, and who were accepted six years later by the Fifth National Assembly as representatives of 'Macedonia, Edessa and Naousa'.[5]

Ioannis Kapodistrias, Greece's first head of state, had fewer doubts about the northern limits of the Greeks. In his reply to the question of Greece's three Protecting Powers in 1828 about a 'defensible frontier' for the new state, he proposed the river Aoos-Metsovon-Mt Olympus as a 'natural' demarcation line and explained: 'In ancient times this boundary also separated Greece from its northern neighbours. In the Middle Ages and in modern times, Thessaly was always kept Greek, while Macedonia was conquered by the Slavs and other races. Thessaly, thanks to its geographical position, avoided foreign peoples.'[6]

Kapodistrias's knowledge of historical geography was that of the educated Greek of his time. Evidence of this comes from two of his contemporaries: Georgios Gazis, the Epirot savant, member of the 'Association of Friends' in the Danubian principalities and secretary to the warlord Georgios Karaiskakis; and Athanasios Psalidas, the distinguished Epirot geographer, who taught for many years in various

[4] *Mavrokordatos Archive*, vol. IV, pp. 390–3, 614–15; Nikolaos Dragoumis, *Historikai anamniseis* (Historical reminiscences), ed. by Alkis Angelou, Athens, 1973, vol. II, pp. 119–120; *Ignatios Metropolitis Oungrovlachias* (Ignatius Metropolitan of Hungary-Wallachia), ed. by E. G. Protopsaltis, Athens 1961, pp. 203–4, 206–7.
[5] *Geniki Ephemeris tis Hellados*, 1 May 1826.
[6] *Archeia Hellenikis Paligenesias* (Archives of Hellenic Regeneration), *Ai Ethnikai Syneleuseis* (The National Assemblies), vol. II, Athens, 1973, pp. 233, 244–8, 264–5, 274, 275–6. See also Demetrios Vikelas, *I systasis tou Hellenikou Basileiou kai ta oria autou* (The establishment of the Greek kingdom and its boundaries), Athens, 1887, p. 42.

schools in Epirus and the Ionian islands. Gazis, in his 'Lexicon of the Revolution', wrote: 'Macedonia today is inhabited primarily by three Christian nations: Greeks, Bulgars and Albanians.' Psalidas, in his teaching notes, included the following on Macedonia, European Turkey's 'eighth province': 'Macedonia, the eighth province, which is famous for Philip and Alexander the Great, has today fallen low because it is inhabited by base people. The land is rich and produces cereals, wine, silk, cotton and other things. However, learning has vanished completely; its inhabitants are Bulgars, Turks and a few Greek and Vlach colonists from Albania.'[7]

The northern boundary proposed for the modern Greeks in the 1820s—granted fifty years later at the Congress of Berlin—seems to have reflected contemporary opinion among educated Greeks about the northern limits of the Greek language and learning. Knowledge of the Greek 'north', of course, was limited, as it was of other Turkish dominions in Europe. However, what is of significance is not knowledge of a land excluded from the Greek nation's 'realm', but the criteria used for excluding it. These were the Greek language and learning, i.e. ones associated with the Enlightenment.

The Greeks pushed their nation's northern frontiers deep into Slav-speaking Macedonia and, with considerable delay but with a vengeance, made themselves part of the Macedonian Question. At the same time, Greek views on modern Greek national identity and the criteria for defining that identity diverged from those advanced by the men of the Enlightenment.

The 'Great Idea' and the 'Greek empire' reflected the shift from positions concerning the 'domain' of the Greek nation held before and during the War of Independence. The call for irredentist action drowned out all voices questioning the wisdom and effectiveness of such action. Ioannis Kolettis's 'Great Idea' of 1844, and the war for the reinstatement of the 'Greek empire' proclaimed by the Philorthodox newspaper *Aeon* ten years late on the 400th anniversary of the fall of Constantinople, were significant—not only as departure from what till then had seemed the dominant national policy, but also because those who had stood for the course followed in the War of Independence did not seek to challenge them.

---

[7]Georgios Gazis, *Lexikon tis Epanastaseos kai alla erga* (Lexicon of the Revolution and other works), Ioannina, 1971, pp. 97–8 and Athanasios Psalidas, *I Tourkia kata tas archas tou ITH' aionos* (Turkey in the early nineteenth century), ed. by G. Charitakis, Ioannina, 1931, p. 55.

The Bulgarian challenge in the 1870s further strengthened the proponents of the 'Great Idea' and the 'Greek empire', and swept away what had survived from the days of the Enlightenment and the War of Independence. This challenge worked in different and unexpected ways. Language, of course, could no longer be used as a determinant of national identity and the national domain's northern limits, because it was also used by the Bulgarians to claim the Slav-speaking Christians of Macedonia and Thrace as their brethren. It was therefore silently dropped as an argument. Greek learning and education, on the other hand, were to become a powerful instrument in the hands of the Greeks who pushed the nation's northern frontier deep into Macedonia. Education was now instrumental not only in teaching the Greek language but also in shaping the identity of those who attended Greek schools to conform to the requirements of modern Greek national aspirations.

In place of language a 'less' fallible determinant of national identity was adopted, the '*phronema*' or '*syneidesis*' (i.e. the 'sentiments' or 'consciousness') of the people. What counted in determining the identity of Macedonia's inhabitants was not language but their Greek 'sentiments', their attachment to the Greek national tradition; language could be learned or unlearned, while 'sentiments' were more stable and less subject to outside pressure and manipulation. Moreover, the Greeks of the time, and of later times as well, had an additional argument on their side: their 'historic rights' to the land. Who else but the Greeks could possibly claim to possess the oldest titles to Macedonia? '*Prior tempore, fortior iure*' was a principle whose validity and strength few would question at the time. When the Ecumenical Patriarchate of Constantinople felt uneasy about letting the Orthodox Ecumene be identified with modern Greek national visions, it was coerced into bowing to the wishes of the Greek kingdom—the 'new centre' of the Greeks, as it came to be known.

The novel arguments for determining the identity of Macedonia's inhabitants and selective evidence on conditions prevailing there became the material for shaping a new Macedonia, a land after the Greek kingdom's own image. 'What if countless barbarian races fell upon the land, committed outrages, and settled upon the Greek areas like the sand of sea, and if the cities were enslaved? The Greek spirit and civilisation absorbed everything barbarian and un-Greek, everything that was inimical to the immaculate and beautiful idea of Hellenism.' So argued a pamphlet published in 1896 by a nationalist association with the title *Macedonia*. 'What has been left after the

Slavic deluge? Certain place-names, some ruins, bitter memories and dramatic stories. Nothing more.' The people's traditions, customs and manners, 'the inner life of the Macedonian people', testified to Macedonia's Greekness. It was further argued, regarding the position and significance of the Greek and Slav languages in Macedonia, that Greek was spoken in the cities, towns and villages of landed peasants, while Slav languages prevailed among the landless peasants. The economically and educationally superior status of the Greeks was invoked to prove that they were Macedonia's undisputed masters.[8]

If the British bore the 'White Man's Burden', the French their '*mission civilisatrice*', and the Americans their 'Manifest Destiny', the Greeks could not be denied a similar mission. With wealth, education, claims to illustrious ancestry and the powerful spiritual machinery of the Ecumenical Patriarchate, the Greeks had all the arguments they needed to claim a mission for themselves in the east. But of more interest here is not so much what preceded or followed this 'mission' of the late nineteenth-century Greeks, as the picture of Macedonia they invented and to which they made themselves captive. Without this picture of Macedonia and of the alleged '*phronema*' of the land's Christian inhabitants, irrespective of their language, it is difficult to explain the ferocity of the struggle that ensued in the hinterland of Macedonia. It was doubtless a Greek '*phronema*' that the young Greek officers from the kingdom were convinced they saw in the quiet resistance of Slav-speaking Christian peasants to the Bulgarian attempts to make them renounce their attachment to the Ecumenical Patriarch and declare for the Bulgarian Exarch. Pavlos Melas, the young Athenian army officer whose death in 1904 moved the Greeks of his generation to a unique degree, never for a moment doubted that those peasants whom he met deep inside Macedonia were as Greek as the Cretans he had with him. Ioannis Karavitis, a Cretan captain who fought with distinction in the same struggle and was one of thirty-four fighters from a single village of the Sphakia district who went over to Macedonia, was convinced that the Slav-speaking peasants around Monastir were more Greek than the Greek-speaking peasants of southern Macedonia. For Melas and Karavitis the Slav-speaking peasants whom they had vowed to deny to Bulgaria were either Greeks who had lost their Greek language in the dark centuries of foreign invasions, migrations and domination, or people of foreign origin

---

[8]Hetaria o Hellenismos, *Makedonia* (in Greek), 2nd edn Piraeus, 1896, pp. 80–2, 94–9, 102–3.

who, in spite of forming an organic part of the modern Greek nation, had been denied till then the benefits of Greek education.[9]

Firmly believing in the righteousness of their cause and the Greekness of Macedonia due to 'historical right', and the '*phronema*' of its Christian inhabitants, the generation of Pavlos Melas, Crown Prince Constantine and Eleftherios Venizelos pushed the northern border of Greece deep into Macedonia—so deep that the new border was no longer a gateway leading to the 'promised land'. The world beyond it no longer fascinated them as it had done till then. The long and vulnerable frontier deep inside mountainous and inhospitable Macedonia was now definitely the outer limit of Hellenism facing the Barbarians.

Had Greece over-extended itself by winning land also claimed by its northern neighbours? These neighbours had no better claim to the disputed land than Greece, but what is of interest to the historian is the outcome of Greece pushing its northern frontier inside Slav-speaking Macedonia and of the effort to demarcate the land according to a picture fashioned in the late nineteenth century. One aspect of this outcome was a kind of 'internal' frontier created by the Greek government's efforts to neutralise the impact of Bulgarian and Yugoslav claims against Greek Macedonia in the interwar period.

Both countries—Bulgaria more consistently than Yugoslavia—claimed the Slav-speaking inhabitants of Greek Macedonia, the Slav Macedonians, respectively as Bulgarians and as Serbs. Bulgaria's claims against Yugoslavia's slice of Macedonia as well, and the consequent rift between those two countries, reduced the real threat to Greece coming from them, but did not reduce the Greek perception of this threat. Greece's Slav Macedonians thus came to be identified as the enemy within. More intimate contact between official Greece and the newly-acquired land in the 1920s produced a less optimistic and benign view of the land and its inhabitants than the one produced by the protagonists in the struggle to deny Macedonia to the Bulgarians. A 1925 official report on the 'ethnological composition' of Greek Macedonia's population distinguished between three categories of Slav Macedonians: 'Slavophones of strong pro-Bulgarian sentiments', 'Slavophones of strong pro-Greek sentiments' and 'Slavophones lacking a national identity and not caring about such an identity'.[10]

---

[9]*Pavlos Melas*, pp. 239, 241, 242–3 and Ioannis Karavitis, *O Makedonikos Agon. Apomnimonevmata* (The Struggle for Macedonia. Memoirs), ed. by G. Petsivas, Thessaloniki, 1994, vol. I, 81 and vol. II, pp. 867–9.

[10] Historical Archive of Macedonia (Thessaloniki), Geniki Dioikisis Makedonias

There can be little doubt now that such distinctions were arbitrary, and only reflected growing doubts among Greek public servants concerning the Slav Macedonians' loyalty to Greece. There can also be little doubt that there was indeed pro-Bulgarian sentiment among them, probably not as strong as the pro-Greek sentiment in the same community, assuming the departure of most of those who had openly identified with Bulgaria in its long struggle with Greece to carve out spheres of exclusive influence in Ottoman-ruled Macedonia. The pro-Bulgarian, no less than the pro-Greek, Slav Macedonians of the official Greek position were those (perhaps a minority) who had for various reasons been able to make a leap into the nationalism of the twentieth century for which the rest, who remained attached to the identity secured by their Orthodox faith, were not yet ready.

Difficult as it may have been, however, the display of pro-Greek sentiment by Greece's Slav Macedonians became a major objective of Greek policy, as did their linguistic hellenisation. One may, of course, deplore the nationalistic onslaught on an unprotected local spoken language, but the Greeks of the 1920s and '30s did not invent assimilation, forced or otherwise, nor were they alone among European nations in the pursuit of such policies. The drive to hellenise the language and thoughts of the country's Slav Macedonians acquired a grim aspect when, in addition to the Bulgarian and Yugoslav challenges, a new threat appeared on the horizon. This was the adoption of the Slav Macedonians by Soviet-sponsored Communism in the 1920s and their promotion on the international political scene as members of a separate Macedonian nation, ostensibly striving for national self-determination. In the light of this new challenge, the Communist Party of Greece was seen as a dangerous agent of international Communism; because, small though the Communist following among Greece's Slav Macedonians may have been initially, the threat from that direction was perceived as being far greater than numbers suggested. For a quarter of a century, ever since the Greek Communist leadership was obliged to accept the Communist International line for a 'united and independent Macedonia' in 1924—and despite the abandonment of that line in 1935—the Greek Communists were seen as foreign agents bent on amputating

---

(Directorate General of Macedonia), F 108, report on the 'Ethnologiki synthesis tou plithysmou tis periochis tis Merarchias' (Ethnological composition of the population of the Division's area) by the chief staff officer of 10th Army Division, dated 9 April 1925.

Macedonia from the homeland. It was this last charge that further exposed the Slav Macedonians on Greek territory to the anger of the other Greeks, especially the Asia Minor refugees, who had been settled in Greek Macedonia in great numbers after the catastrophe of 1922. The ferocity of the Greek Civil War in the second half of the 1940s owed much of its ferocity to the Communist Party's association with a separatist movement in Greek Macedonia.

The Slav Macedonians of Greece were thus made to conform to the concept of Macedonia formed in the late nineteenth century. Their descendants—or those who could credibly be described as descendants of the Slav Macedonians—are now invited to fit the model fashioned in Skopje from raw material not very different from that used by Greek nationalist writers to support their own cause. Greek social anthropologists, journalists and some historians, quick to embrace what is considered politically correct, have contributed a new set of misconceptions about the identity and numbers of Greece's Slav Macedonians. In view of the Former Yugoslav Republic of Macedonia's tendency to nurture a view of Thessaloniki in its national policy similar to that of Constantinople in Greek national aspirations before 1922, the Greek tabloid press and champions of nationalist causes were quick to suggest that Greece's northern boundary was about to be pushed back into Thessaly. This national neurosis was largely responsible for the nationalist outburst of 1992–4.

21

WAR FOR LAND

Like most nation-states, modern Greece was born out of war, expanded through wars, and went to war to defend its territory. Favourable conditions abroad, successful diplomacy and the use of force secured extensive territories which the state's founding fathers could never have dreamed of acquiring for the new country. Ever since the First World War the Greeks have been struggling against predatory neighbours to keep possession of these territories.

The War of Independence (1821–30) was soon regarded as the first stage in a long struggle for the liberation of all lands claimed to be Greek that were outside the Greek state, and determined the course of national action. The independent Greek kingdom in the southern Balkans was the self-appointed homeland for all the Greeks of the Ottoman empire and at the same time the nation-state established by the decision of three great powers with conflicting interests in the region. As such, it was saddled with the role of a nationalist agent with a much restricted freedom of action. Britain's firm opposition to the dismemberment of the Ottoman empire until the advent of Germany as the declining empire's supporter, Russia's consistent championship of the claims for freedom of the empire's Orthodox subjects, and the opportunistic policy of France throughout this period, made Greece's role as an agent of freedom an extremely complicated one. Greece could take action to liberate the unredeemed Greeks as long as its three protecting powers were in agreement to allow such a drive for territorial expansion. Short of such agreement, Greek governments could at best prepare for the expected dismemberment of the Ottoman empire by inciting irredentist action within it. They would do this, first, to remind Greece's protectors of its claims to the Sultan's Greek dominions, and secondly to keep nationalist forces at home happy in the thought that the policy of liberation of the unredeemed brethren was being seriously pursued.

For eighty years from the time it was formed in 1833, the Greek regular army was instrumental in a number of unsuccessful attempts to put down brigands and in three successful coups, two against King Otto—in 1843 and again in 1862—and one against King George's government in 1909. It took the field twice to liberate unredeemed brethren—in Thessaly (1878) and Macedonia (1897). On the first occasion it withdrew into Greece before engaging the Turkish army, and on the second it was quickly and soundly defeated by the same army. Of the two territories acquired by Greece during this same period, the Ionian islands were granted to Greece by Britain in 1863, and the Sublime Porte ceded Thessaly by the decision of the great European powers at the Congress of Berlin in 1878.

The regular army in this period essentially satisfied two conditions. First, it secured for Greece a Western-style institution necessary for its Western orientation and legitimacy, and secondly, it produced an officer corps which proved invaluable in leading the expanded Greek army in the Balkan Wars and the First World War to the dramatic expansion of the country's territory in the space of ten years. National aspirations were fanned not by this army but by a different agent, the irregulars. Ill-paid gendarmes and frontier guards, drifting young transhumant shepherds seeking to augment declining family incomes, released convicts ready to oblige their patrons, and brigands eager for plunder made up the bands of irregulars which took up arms to promote Greece's national aspirations. They were not a national army but they symbolised a nation in arms. The continued existence of this irregular force was due to Greece's inability to use the regular army for the promotion of its irredentist programme. Irregulars could be sent across the Greco-Turkish border to stir up revolt among the Sultan's Christian subjects. The Ottomans were well aware that such irredentist escapades amounted to exported brigandage, and responded by letting loose their own irregulars, the Albanians, who were more than a match for the Greeks in the art of plunder. After each irredentist insurrection of this kind, everyone appeared satisfied but the unredeemed Christian subjects of the Sultan, whom both Greek and Albanian irregulars robbed with impunity. The Greek public were momentarily thrilled by the prospect of seeing their national aspirations realised, but the Porte presented itself as the innocent victim of Greece's irresponsible government and the Western powers became convinced that successor nation-states in the Near East were acting no more responsibly than the empire they were reluctant to dismantle.

Irredentist action of this type, in addition to keeping alive the impression that the political programme of the 'Great Idea' was being pursued, reproduced the irregular military element which sustained this action: an unofficial military class drawing on the tradition of the pre-independence Klephts. If the officers of the regular army represented and symbolised the Greek nation-state, the chiefs of the irregulars purported to stand for the Greek nation, both inside and outside the national state boundaries; they and those who benefited politically from their activities would have liked the rest of the Greeks to believe that they, not the government and the regular armed forces, were the true defenders of the nation's interests. Unlike the government and its regular army, these new Klephts would never cave in to pressure from the great powers. Indeed, they were outside the control of the government, and in many instances literally held it to ransom.

These post-Independence Klephts, who had outlived their usefulness by almost a century, were a striking symptom of modern Greece's inability to move on from the outworn practices of the past, even when it was clear to everyone that those practices were not only useless, but also dangerous. They projected the image of a Greece ruled by colourful thugs, and risked duping the Greek people into entrusting their national interests to those associated with such irregular and illegal practices. By the end of the nineteenth century, it seemed as if the whole country had slipped into 'klephtic' paranoia. The 1897 war with Turkey, which was precipitated by warlords and those who thrived on their exploits, shook the country out of its state of self-deception.

The struggle for Macedonia marked the high-point of this type of irredentist action—and its sudden end. In the space of some five years, hundreds of these swift-footed outlaws of continental Greece, and perhaps as many Cretan mountain-dwelling masters of the art of sheep-stealing, confronted Bulgarian irregulars of similar pursuits and Albanian irregulars in the service of the Ottomans. With the exception of the Ilinden insurrection of 1903 in Western Macedonia, in which mostly Slav Macedonian peasants were led by a handful of revolutionaries to rise against Turkish rule, all other actions in Macedonia during the following years up till the Young Turks' Revolt in 1908 were aimed at influencing the choice of national affiliations of the region's Slav- or Vlach-speaking inhabitants. Inability to dispossess the Sultan of his last dominions in Europe, forced the Greeks and their competitors to use all possible means to carve out spheres of exclusive influence in these fiercely contested provinces.

War and victories in the field eventually secured for Greece most of the lands which nationalists had claimed: the greater part of Epirus half of modern Macedonia including a Slav Macedonian minority; western Thrace which was home to a sizeable Muslim minority of Turks, Pomaks and Gypsies; Crete; and the eastern Aegean islands. These gains were the result of Greece's participation in four wars— the two Balkan Wars of 1912–13, the First World War and the Greco-Turkish war of 1919–22—and three international treaties, those of Bucharest (1913), Sèvres (1920) and Lausanne (1923).

Fighting the war obtained for Greece impressive territorial gains but not security. For the latter it was obliged, after ten years under arms (1912–22), to enter into several bilateral and multilateral defensive agreements with its neighbours or with one or more of the great powers, and to prepare to defend itself militarily against neighbours coveting different parts of these gains.

In particular it faced an over-sized and dangerous Yugoslavia, which pressed for a free zone in Thessaloniki and even for a land corridor

---

The Balkan Wars (1912–13)

The First Balkan War began when the smallest partner of the alliance, Montenegro, declared war against the Ottoman empire. Greece, Serbia and Bulgaria followed suit on 18 October 1912. The Greek navy played a vital role by blocking the supply of the Turkish forces by sea: headed by the heavy cruiser *Averoff,* it won a series of naval engagements which prevented the Turkish ships from leaving the Straits.

The Balkan allies made rapid progress. The Greeks advanced into Macedonia and captured its largest city, the port of Thessaloniki, in November 1912 and the capital of Epirus, Ioannina, in January 1913. The navy liberated the islands of Chios, Mytilini and Samos. The Ottoman government sued for peace and was obliged to accept the territorial gains of the Balkan allies by the London treaty of May 1913.

However, hostilities soon broke out between the Allies over the division of Macedonian territories. The Second Balkan War was initially fought between Bulgaria and the combined forces of Greece and Serbia, but the Bulgars were faced with attacks from Turkey and Romania and were obliged to negotiate. By the treaty of Bucharest in August 1913, Bulgaria ceded much of what it had gained in Macedonia to Greece and Serbia.

leading to it; a revisionist Italy acting as agent for Albanian claims to Epirus; an equally revisionist Bulgaria claiming Greek Macedonia and Thrace; and Turkey, in the ten-year Balkan wars.

In the period between the World Wars Greece signed a pact of friendship with Italy in 1928 to keep Yugoslavia at bay, similar pacts with Romania in 1928 and Yugoslavia in 1929 to neutralise the danger from Bulgaria, one more such pact and a full-blown military alliance with Turkey in 1930, and finally a regional pact in 1934 with the three Balkan states having common borders with Bulgaria: Yugoslavia, Romania and Turkey. Greece prepared for war against Bulgaria in the 1930s, but was obliged instead to go to war against two great powers, Italy and Germany, in the early 1940s. In October 1940, as a result of Italy's demand to occupy unspecified parts of the country, the Greeks chose to fight back in the firm conviction that to do this and fall united was preferable to submitting without a fight and inviting dismemberment. Submission to Italy was expected to lead to the partition of Greek territory by Italy, Bulgaria and Britain: Italy would seize western Greece, and Bulgaria Greek Macedonia and Thrace. It was expected that Britain would consider Greek territory fair game and seize Crete, key Aegean islands and perhaps the Peloponnese. After five months of successful war against Fascist Italy, Greece was obliged to fight Nazi Germany for the same reasons, with Britain's political and military support.

Greece was overwhelmed by the Axis, but its monarch and government did not recognise the defeat and left the country to pursue the war for the restoration of its independence and territorial integrity. After nearly four years of resistance to the Axis inside and outside the occupied country and as many years again fighting Communist insurgents backed by the Communist regimes of Albania, Yugoslavia and Bulgaria, Greece by the end of the 1940s was to enjoy a measure of security under American protection.

Security problems *vis-à-vis* its neighbours appeared to have been solved when Greece joined the Atlantic Alliance in 1952. For the first time in thirty years its territorial integrity was guaranteed by a mighty alliance, which considered the country's national borders as its own borders. It was, of course, security under great power protection, but security all the same. Greece had, in a sense, reverted in 1952 to its pre-First World War status of a Balkan state under institutionalised great power protection. This protection was enhanced in 1980 when it became a full member the European Union, but diminished after the fall of the Soviet and East European Communist regimes at the end of 1980s.

Diminished great power protection exacerbated Greece's fear of Turkish designs in the Aegean. Turkey's political instability, its strong Islamist movement, the Kurdish insurgency and an abysmal human rights record have made Greece suspicious of Turkish motives in the region. The tendency of Western powers to view, what Greece considers to be Turkish provocations as a dispute between two allies has been interpreted by the Greeks as Western tolerance of aggression. Given Turkey's enhanced strategic role in the region, most Greek politicians believe that the United States has adopted a policy of appeasement at the expense of the victim in the dispute. Although Greece played a positive role in the December 1999 Helsinki accord concerning Turkey's EU vocation, a significant gesture of reciprocity has (at the time of writing) yet to materialise from the other side of the Aegean.

Part VIII

22
CULTURE

The nineteenth-century Hellenic state adopted two great traditions that were to pose formidable challenges to its citizens: the linguistic heritages of a pagan and a Christian era. Although a live culture must draw 'for continuous sustenance on the great works of the past and the truths and beauties achieved by tradition'[1], the Greek state disrupted the continuity of the arts by interposing a wedge between the sacred content of painting and its own secular pursuits. Modern Greeks would have to reinvent a high tradition in the visual arts with a little help from their Western friends and their academies.

Unlike the visual arts, the Greek language maintained its existence and many of its forms throughout the Christian and Ottoman centuries. Its secular, religious, political and artistic users produced religious tracts, revolutionary diatribes, scholarly treatises and works of literary genius.

The post-Byzantine tradition of religious art that prevailed before Independence was challenged by a Western influence that came to Greece with the Bavarian administrators and technocrats who accompanied King Otto. Most of the important Greek artists of the nineteenth century studied or completed their education in Munich. The most prominent of these, Nikolaos Ghizis (1842–1901), became Professor at the Munich Academy and gained fame abroad. Others

---

[1]The icon 'is part and parcel of a usual system conveying and giving support to the spiritual fact and events that underlie the whole drama of the liturgy'—Philip Sherrard, *The Sacred in Life and Art*, Cambridge, England: Golgonooza Press, 1990, p. 72. Nathan A. Scott, Jr and Ronald A. Sharp, *Reading George Steiner*, Baltimore: Johns Hopkins University Press, 1994, p. 22.

such us Constantinos Volanakis (1837–1907), Nikiforos Lytras (1832–1904) and Georgios Iakovides (1852–1932) returned to Greece to take up appointments at the School of Fine Arts in Athens.

The talent of the 'Munich-period' Greek artists is seen at its best in their sketches and studies, while their finished work was often stilted, in common with most products of the Munich, Rome and Paris academies. The only Greek element in their work was the subject-matter, which might be drawn from folklore; the study of native light and colour came in the twentieth century with the 'Parisian' influence. A more indigenous though less influential tradition came from the Italianate school of the Ionian islands, which became part of Greece in 1864.

The Greek artistic diaspora discovered Parisian modernism after some delay. Impressionism never took root in Greece, but post-Impressionism influenced some of the work of Constantinos Parthenis (1878–1957), Constantinos Maleas (1879–1928) and Spyros Papaloukas (1893–1957). A Symbolist at heart, Parthenis became an influential exponent of modern trends, and the artistic generation that studied under him at the School of Fine Arts emulated his interest in Greek light and colour. A parallel though opposite influence came from Photis Kontoglou (1896–1965), a refugee from Asia Minor who sought to revive the tradition of Byzantine religious art: he rejected Western incursions and urged his students to seek out what had roots in Greek culture. After 1945 the cross-fertilisation of Parthenis and Kontoglou produced a generation of artists with a particular vision, of whom some of the more prominent were Yannis Tsarouchis, Nikos Hatzikyriakos Ghikas, Yannis Moralis and Spyros Vassiliou.

The Neo-Classical buildings depicted by Tsarouchis and his virile soldiers and sailors dancing solo, the scenery designs of Vassiliou and his view of the Acropolis spoiled by the construction boom, Ghika's kites and thorny suns over the maize of Hydra, even the youthful funerary figures of Moralis, refer to the picturesque aspects of isolation.[2] One may wonder-with the composer Manos Hatzidakis, an intelligent commentator on Greek culture-if this scavenging from Greek tradition was a genuine sign of creativity. Whether it was or not, the trend contributed to an image of modern Greece which was easily identifiable and marketable.

---

[2]For a comprehensive description of Greek art see *Istoria tou Ellinikou Ethnous* (History of the Hellenic nation), vol. 13, 1977, pp. 529–43; vol. 14, 1977, pp. 425–38; vol. 15, 1978, pp. 504–14.

Since the 1960s Greek artists have fallen under a cosmopolitan influence which has ceased to explore the native tradition. Sklavos, Takis, Chryssa, Samaras and Kounelis are celebrated diaspora figures, but even natives like Costas Tsoklis, Dimitris Mitaras and Kostas Varotsos belong to a West European mainstream. Alekos Fassianos, with his references to an ancient Mediterranean way of depicting figures, is a partial exception to this rule.

Modern Athens is the result of unforeseen circumstances—a sleepy village that was rapidly transformed into the capital of a new state. The influx of close to half a million destitute refugees from Asia Minor in 1922, and the unplanned movement after the Second World War of an agrarian population into the bloated centre of a centralised administration, were chaotic. Only a small part of the sprawling city is the result of planning, and its buildings lack the monumental qualities which are found in some other Balkan capitals. Exceptions to the absence of space and dignity are to be found in the area of the Parliament, the National Park, the Presidential Palace, Zappion and the reconstructed ancient Stadium. The rest is crammed and crowded, with few buildings of architectural merit.

How can an architect leave his mark amid such architectural anonymity? The visionary Dimitris Pikionis (1887–1968) was commissioned to reconstruct the archaeological walks to the Acropolis and the Philopappos monument on the hill opposite, and the two winding paths he produced are the products of hand-wrought marble and stone fragments that contain no reference to the industrial present. At the time when Athens and its natural environment were disappearing under the onslaught of the postwar building boom, Pikionis designed the monumental walks to preserve the fading memory of a pre-industrial habitat.[3]

Post-Independence architecture can be divided into three periods. First came the neo-classical style imported from the West and adapted to the modest scale of Athenian life. This was followed by the 'neo-vernacular' trend of the 1910s and '20s, drawing from popular tradition, and finally came the full adoption of modernism in the 1930s. A fourth period could be added to include the anonymous large-scale construction activity of the 1950s and '60s.[4] A significant exception

[3]Pegy Kounenaki, ed., *Dimitris Pikionis*, an issue of the *Kathimerini* supplement 'Epta Imeres', 16 October 1994.

[4]Helen Fessas-Emanouil, *Ideological and Cultural Issues in the Architecture of Modern Greece,* Athens, 1987; Spyros Amourgis, 'I architectonics tou mesopolemou, 1922–

to the post-war levelling was the work of Aris Constantinidis in the Greek Organisation of Tourism and his innovative series of 'Xenia' hotels.

In the 1950s and '60s the performing arts benefited greatly from the collaboration of artists, composers and stage directors. Revived productions of ancient Greek tragedies and comedies under the inspired guidance of Dimitris Rontiris (1899–1981), Alexis Minotis (1900–90) and Karolos Kuhn (1908–87), and chorodrama performances by Zouzou Nikoloudi (1917–) and Rallou Manou (1915–88), brought together such talented figures as Tsarouchis, Hatzidakis and Kuhn and created a new generation that included Dimitris Mitaras, Stavros Xarchakos and Spyros Evangelatos. The latter—along with Dimitris Papaioannou, Spyros Voyadjis and Vassilis Papavassiliou—were mainly responsible for stage productions in the 1970s and '80s that lifted the Greek theatre to a high level.

The Epidaurus and Athens festivals of the 1950s, '60s and '70s, the budding philharmonic orchestras in the tradition founded by the conductor Dimitris Mitropoulos, and the more recent 'Megaro Mousikis' concert hall, have made Athens an important European cultural centre.

Greek film productions became known internationally through the work of Michael Cacoyannis. Of his early muses Elli Lambeti in *The Girl in Black* haunts the screen with her melancholy eyes, and Melina Merkouri in *Stella* is the female equivalent of the indomitable *Zorba*. In the 1960s Nikos Koundouros produced his *Drakos* with Dinos Iliopoulos, a popular comedian turned dramatic actor. Another director who has made his mark internationally is Theo Angelopoulos. He won the *Palme d'Or* at the Cannes Film Festival for his *Eternity and One Day*, in 1998; he had already directed a series of film classics.

When Greece became independent in 1830, its musical tradition ran in two levels. There were the 'demotic' songs—strongly influenced by liturgical music—which had originated in the post-Byzantine period, and the mainly Italian school in the Ionian islands which had escaped Ottoman rule. Greece was cut off from the classical European musical tradition during the musical renaissance in the West between the sixteenth and nineteenth centuries. While polyphony was perfected in the West, the Orthodox Church, ever resistant to change, remained

---

40' (The architecture of the interwar period), *Architektonika Themata*, vol. I, 1967, pp. 146–9.

monophonic and used no instrumental accompaniment. Monophonic music developed into the 'Byzantine chant', and the sounds which emerged were a blend of psalmodic melody and folksongs, called *tragoudia*. In the twentieth century the folk tradition divided into the older demotic Klephtic songs of the countryside and a new type of urban song that appeared mostly with the Asia Minor refugees after 1922. Heard in prisons and in waterfront dens, the *rebetiko* was destined for wide success.

Many Greeks living in Europe returned home after Greece became an independent state, and became emissaries of a European musical culture. Kapodistrias and King Otto established bands, imported the first pianos, introduced musical education in schools, and invited musicians from Germany, Italy and the Ionian islands to perform in Athens. Opera was introduced, and many schools were founded and orchestras, choirs, musical societies and stage productions organised.

Among the better-known representatives of the European (mainly Italian) school were Pavlos Karrer (1829–96); Nicholas Mantzaros (1796–1873), who wrote the music for the national anthem; Napoleon Labelette (1864–1932); and Lavrangas (1860–1941), the creator of the Greek opera. With Manolis Kalomiris (1883–1962), a native of Smyrna, whose orchestration had a Romantic and Wagnerian character, Western and folk traditions merged. Modern Greece's claim to musical prominence owes much to Maria Callas, who had a brilliant career in Greek opera before being 'discovered' in Verona, and to Dimitris Mitropoulos, director of the New York Philharmonic Orchestra.

Working in the field of *avant garde* music, Yannis Christou (1926–70) transformed the concept of musical background to performances of ancient tragedies. Nikos Skalkotas (1904–49), a gifted composer who also died in his prime, became internationally known for his brilliant use of demotic tunes, of which his 'Greek Dances' are the best known. In his original modernist compositions, Ianni Xenakis (1921–2000) won international acclaim for his mathematically patterned musical creations. However, neither Skalkotas nor Xenakis worked from within the Greek musical tradition.[5]

Greece is nevertheless best known abroad for its popular music. Manos Hatzidakis (1925–94) was the first of a generation of composers who introduced themes from the *rebetika* in their compositions, and

[5]Mark Dragoumis , 'Music' in T. Veremis and M. Dragoumis, *Historical Dictionary of Greece*, Metuchen, NJ: Scarecrow Press, 1995, pp. 130–2.

drew the attention of the intelligentsia and ultimately the middle class to lowlife music. If an analogy is to be drawn between the domestication of the Argentine tango and the Greek *rebetico*, Greece's Gardel was Vassilis Tsitsanis (1915–84), although the latter excelled as a composer more than as a performer. Greek popular music became widely known through Hatzidakis's music for the film *Never on Sunday* and that of Mikis Theodorakis (1924–) for *Zorba the Greek*. Dionysis Savvopoulos (1944–) became the minstrel of the 1970s and '80s, drawing from pop and rock music.

Of all the aspects of culture inherited by the Greek state, everything connected with language was certainly the most lively and the most promising. Although literature depended mostly on the formal and stilted tradition of the Constantinopolitan Phanariots, the Ionian literati who entered the Greek kingdom in 1864 experimented with a vernacular which was unexplored and had many possibilities. The genius of Andreas Kalvos (1792–1869) from Zakynthos was 'discovered' many decades after writing his last ode, but his contemporary Dionysios Solomos (1798–1857) opened the way to poetic emancipation from a formal idiom. Although a master of unfinished verse, he laid the foundations for all creativity that followed. The Athenian Romantics and their purist form of *katharevousa* deserve little notice, but Emmanuel Roidis (1836–1904), with his corrosive irony directed against a pompous officialdom, created an important precedent in social criticism. George Vizyinos (1849–69) and Alexandros Papadiamantis (1851–1911) are the best craftsmen of the formal idiom, and the latter is a short story writer of genius. His innocent universe of devout Orthodox peasants remained neglected after his death.[6]

Preoccupation with the war between the exponents of *demotiki* (vernacular language) and *katharevousa* (formal language) throughout the first half of the twentieth century obscured the fact that talent, or lack of it, was to be found in both camps. Although the works of the champion of the vernacular, Yiannis Psycharis (1854–1929), appear as alien today as do those of the *katharevousa* supporters, the torrential *demotiki* of Kostis Palamas (1859–1943) gave free rein to his visionary verse. On the opposite side of the spectrum of temperaments is the understated poetry of the Alexandrian Constantinos Cavafis (1863–1933). His collected works, filling only a single volume, offer a grand

---

[6]For a concise presentation of Modern Greek literature see the brilliant work of Mario Vitti, *Istoria tis Ellinikis Logotechnias*, Athens: Odysseas, 1978.

Ode

A. Kalvos

As from the sun the hours
Like drops of fire
Fall into the sea of time
And vanish for ever

(translated by Philip Sherrard)

The God forsakes Antony

C. P. Cavafis

When suddenly at the midnight hour
An invisible troupe is heard passing
With exquisite music, with shouts—
Do not mourn in vain your fortune failing you now,
Your works gone astray, plans of your life
Turned out to be illusions.
As if long prepared for this, as if courageous,
Bid her farewell, the Alexandria that is leaving.
Above all do not be fooled, do not delude yourself.
It was a dream, your ears deceived you;
Do not stoop to such vain hopes.
As if long prepared for this, as if courageous,
As it becomes you who are worthy of such a city;
Approach the window with firm step,
And listen with emotion, but not
With the entreaties and complaints of the coward.
As a last enjoyment listen to the sounds,
The exquisite instruments of the mystical troupe,
And bid her farewell, the Alexandria you are losing.

(translated by Rae Dalven)

tour of Greek cultural history, and his subtle wisdom is conveyed in an idiom which is sparing of poetic effects. Palamas and Cavafis are two different incarnations of Greekness. The former heralded the territorial unity of Greece, the latter its unity in time.

Between the world wars, national attention, now freed from the 'Great Idea', was concentrated on the relief and integration of the

The King of Asine

George Seferis

We looked all morning round the citadel
starting from the shaded side, there where the sea
green and without luster—breast of a slain peacock—received
us like time without an opening in it.
Veins of rock dropped down from high above,
twisted vines, naked, many-branched, coming alive
at the water's touch, while the eye following them
struggled to escape the tiresome rocking,
losing strength continually.

On the sunny side a long open beach
and the light striking diamonds on the huge walls.
No living thing, the wild doves gone
and the king of Asine, whom we've been trying to find for
two years now,
unknown, forgotten by all, even by Homer,
only one word in the Iliad and that uncertain,
thrown here like the gold burial mask.
You touched it, remember its sound? Hollow in the light
like a dry jar in dug earth:
The king of Asine a void under the mask
everywhere with us everywhere with us, under a name:
'*Asinin te ... Asinin te ...*'
and his children statues
and his desires the fluttering of birds, and the wind
in the gaps between his thoughts,
and his ships anchored in a vanished port:

under the mask a void.

Behind the large eyes the curved lips the curls
carved in relief on the gold cover of our existence
a dark spot that you see travelling like a fish
in the dawn calm of the sea:
a void everywhere with us.

And the bird that flew away last winter
with a broken wing-
abode of life,
and the young woman who left to play
with the dogteeth of summer
and the soul that sought the lower world squeaking

and the country like a large plane-leaf swept along by the
torrent of the sun
with the ancient monuments and the contemporary sorrow.
And the poet lingers, looking at the stones, and asks himself
does there really exist
among these ruined lines, edges, points, hollows and curves
does there really exist
here where one meets the path of rain, wind, and ruin
does there exist the movement of the face, shape of the
tenderness
of those who've shrunk so strangely in our lives,
those who remained the shadow of waves and thoughts with
the sea's boundlessness
or perhaps no, nothing is left but the weight
the nostalgia for the weight of a living existence
there where we now remain unsubstantial, bending
like the branches of a terrible willow-tree heaped in
permanent despair
while the yellow current slowly carries down rushes up
rooted in the mud
image of a form that the sentence to everlasting bitterness
has turned to marble:
the poet a void.

Shieldbearer, the sun climbed warring,
and from the depths of the cave a startled bat
hit the light as an arrow hits a shield:
'*Asinin te ... Asinin te ...*' Could that be the king
of Asine
we've been searching for so carefully on this acropolis
sometimes touching with our fingers his touch upon
the stones

(translated by Edmund Keeley and Philip Sherrard)

---

uprooted Asia Minor refugees. The new crop of poets and intellectuals
vacillated between the utter despair of Kostas Karyotakis (1896–1928)
and the sober resignation of George Seferis (1900–71) to exaltation
of the senses with Odysseas Elytis (1911–96). The most important
intellectual product of that era was the group known as 'the generation
of the 1930s'. The common denominator of such writers George
Theotocas (1906–66), Constantine Dimaras (1904–92) and Kosmas

Politis (1888–1974) was their predilection for liberal democracy and political moderation. Their benign influence was soon eclipsed by dictatorship, war and civil strife, but their spirit was preserved for the return of more favourable circumstances in the future. The Surrealists Nikos Engonopoulos (1910–85) and, especially, Andreas Embirikos (1901–75) sought to relieve their contemporaries of their identity crisis and their psychological hang-ups. Thanks to their playful use of *katharevousa*, the capacity of the formal language for satire was once more exploited.

The Nobel prizes for Seferis and Elytis mark a highpoint achieved by the poetic medium in Greek culture. By the end of the century, however, the poetic muse appeared to have lost her momentum. The 1970s produced Manolis Anagnostakis and Lefteris Poulios, both vigorous poets who nevertheless failed to follow in the footsteps of the giants.[7] Other modes of artistic expression such as the cinema and certainly the performing arts are making an impact on the cultural life of Greece.

Nikos Kazantzakis (1885–1957) deserves special notice in this *tour d'horizon*. Thanks to Jules Dassin's film version of *Christ Recrucified*, Michalis Cacoyannis' *Zorba the Greek* and Martin Scorsese's *Last Temptation*, Kazantzakis achieved world recognition. His heroes—whether the sullen Cretan revolutionary Captain Michalis or the hedonistic Zorba—are larger-than-life figures who triggered fantasies of escape from post-industrial societies and contributed to the 'noble savage' archetype in the civilised West. Kazantzakis's celebration of man's irrational faculties and his cult of heroism are references to a Nietzschean creed favoured by a Western circle of intellectuals between the World Wars. In the 1950s, when his major works appeared, he represented a view of life that the 'generation of the 1930s' had already discarded two decades earlier. However, what made his work attractive to adolescent readers but alien to the Greek mainstream was not his proverbial clash with the religious establishment, but rather his fascination with excesses of personal behaviour. In one of his essays George Seferis claims that respect for balance is deeply embedded in a Greek folk tradition that goes back to antiquity.[8] Could the exaggerated characters of Kazantzakis outlive their hubris and defy this balance with impunity?

---

[7]See the collection of essays on Greek literature, *En lefko* (Athens: Ikaros, 1993), by the Nobel laureate Odysseas Elytis.

[8]Georgios Seferis, *Dokimes* (the title refers to studies made by a painter for a work in progress). Athens: Fexis, 1962, p. 197.

Other types of rebel, such as Stratis Myrivilis's (1892–1969) Vassilis the Arvanitis who, unlike the heroes of Kazantzakis, is humbled for his pride and acts of hubris, are more in keeping with a native concept of justice and balance. The defiant Arvanitis (the designation for fourteenth-century Albanian settlers in Greece), who even challenges divine authority, becomes a prototype of Greek valour in its hellenised Albanian incarnation. This indomitable figure, ultimately crushed by fate, is a subject closer to the heart of the Greek public.

CONCLUSION

This appraisal of the Greek nation and state since Independence has been written from a certain point of view-the liberal point of view. This is not so much out of personal preference as because the aims set by the founders of the Greek nation-state were those of Western liberal democracy. These aims were in a sense a yardstick for judging the performance of the renovated Greek nation and its newly-constructed state. Lapses into value judgements are not deliberately sought but are hard to avoid in this venture to observe and measure constructs such as nations and states.

The Greek state has been associated by different historians with the attributes and shortcomings of political personalities, the designs of the ruling classes and foreign arbiters, or the power structure of an organic entity with its own agenda. The nation-state is no different from any other man-made construct: conceived by individuals or groups of state-builders, it reflects their values and priorities. The final outcome bears the impress of its users: those who administer its institutions and the multitude of subjects who adapt their lives accordingly. Yet the latter have not been passive recipients of state authority. They slowly eroded official rules and made them conform to their own social norms and family priorities, while at the same time they themselves were transformed by the equalising benefits of the rule of law and willingly restructured their lives.

Did the renovated Greek nation fulfil the expectations of the founding fathers? In many ways it did, while in others it failed. The effort to fashion a homogeneous and functional national community out of a number of different linguistic groups at varying stages of development has succeeded–at some cost, though not as great a cost as is sometimes suggested. The success has been enhanced by the undeniable pride in a common descent which the renovated nation has inspired in this motley community. This pride in an ancient Greek heritage, which has often raised eyebrows and produced scathing criticism, not only proved to be the binding element necessary to hold society together, but also fostered a cultural revival worthy of nations with a much longer and less troubled independent nationhood.

The Enlightenment provided an intellectual framework well suited to the merchants of the Greek diaspora. It even stimulated the scholars of the Orthodox Church to produce works of striking originality. The French Revolution and its display of anti-clericalism put an end to the honeymoon between Church and Enlightenment, but the liberal seed had germinated by the time Greece gained independence, and its fruit became the staple food of all the constitutions formed between 1821 and 1864.

Adamantios Koraes, with his profound influence on the ideological underpinnings of the new state, provided the solid bridge between this isolated Ottoman province and the ideas of the West. Some may wonder why the Greek state turned its back on its Eastern past and embraced the West, and the answer is simple. Except for a reservoir of folk culture, the East had long ceased to provide the Greek élites with inspiration and purpose. The Bavarians endowed Greece with institutions and a modern administration shaped after an advanced French model. King Otto's regents passed on to Greece the system Bavaria had been given by its reforming statesman Maximilian Mongelas de Garnerin (1759–1838).[1]

The acid test of the country's path to modernity is to be found in the avatars of democracy in Greece. A society with an Ottoman (not indigenous) aristocracy had only the Church as a remnant of an *ancien régime* after Independence. A huge stratum of landless peasants and a small merchant élite made the future of parliamentary democracy hang in the balance, but Greek politicians proved wiser than their Balkan counterparts. The relatively bloodless expulsion of King Otto in 1862 deprived future monarchs of a dominant role in politics. The early distribution of public land to those who worked on it, and of deeds of ownership to squatters, helped to integrate the masses into the system and introduce them to the rituals of democracy.

[1] Eberhard Weis, *Montgelas, 1759–1799*, Munich, 1971.

Although the Greek 'segmentary society'[2] was not transformed into a civil society overnight, and separation between state and society is still a goal sought by modernisers in politics, the wild individualism bred by the family unit did not destroy the rule of law and parliamentary democracy. Throughout the formative years of state-building, distinguished parliamentarians such as Mavrocordatos, Deligiorgis, Koumoundouros and Trikoupis, who were keen to make democracy work, became the rule rather than the exception.

The role of the diaspora in facilitating Greece's transition to modernity cannot be exaggerated. The Western model was re-fashioned to suit Greece by such state-builders as Kapodistrias, Mavrocordatos, Koraes and Trikoupis and many others who had lived abroad for significant periods of their lives. No authoritarian reformer was therefore necessary to bridge the gap between a modernising state and a traditional peasantry. The apostles of change had already passed on to Greece the major trends then prevailing in Britain, France and the German states.

Why did the major disasters of the twentieth century not completely nullify Greece's journey to modernisation? How did the state manage to consolidate its territorial gains and integrate its own population into a mainstream ideology without violence? The disasters of the national schism in 1916–20, Asia Minor in 1922 and the Civil War in 1946 caused lasting divisions and placed obstalces in the way of Greece's path to modernity, but they did not derail the process. Of all the mishaps of modern times the military regime of 1967–74 is probably the most difficult to explain since it appears so utterly anachronistic in European affairs. Yet this last reincarnation of the Civil War helped to purge Greece of its heritage of a fratricidal cleavage.

Similarly the maverick politics of Andreas Papandreou in the 1980s slowed Greece's advance to the West, but also purged the Greeks from syndromes of victimisation and irrational suspicions of the motives of their Western partners. Expensive deviation as it may have been, PASOK's first term in power had the effect of a national psychodrama in which all kinds of underdogs were finally admitted to the tumultuous world of Greek politics as equals.

The effort to carve a relatively large territory out of the defunct Ottoman empire to house the renovated Greek nation and expand its limits with the means available to it was also generally successful.

---

[2]Ernest Gellner, *Conditions of Liberty: Civil Society and its Rivals*, London: Hamish Hamilton, 1994, pp. 97–102.

In many ways, the cost of this territorial expansion was high, but it was usually undertaken with the backing of a broad popular mandate.

The drive to define and create a public domain free from the incursion of familial and clientelistic networks in the nation's life has been less successful. Disentangling the private from the public sphere, and establishing a civil society that has not been penetrated by the state, are tasks that still have to be accomplished.

Yet the central government succeeded in divesting corporate groups of their power to cause mischief by offering them the opportunity to expend their energies in ways not inimical to the national interest. Success in the complex task of constructing viable and truly representative government and efficient administrative authorities has sometimes been marred by authoritarian rule in a variety of guises. Modernising Greece may be a task resembling that of Sisyphus, but with the difference that upward progress is greater than downward tumbles.

CHRONOLOGY

1821   The Greek War of Independence against Ottoman rule breaks out. The Ecumenical Patriarch, Grigorios, as head of the Christian Orthodox flock is held responsible by the Ottoman authorities and hanged.

1822   The first constitution for an independent Greece is drafted.

1827   The joint Ottoman–Egyptian fleet is destroyed at Navarino Bay (Pylos) by the combined fleets of England, France and Russia.

1828   Count Ioannis Kapodistrias arrives in Greece as its first president.

1830   France, England and Russia recognize the independence of Greece under the London Protocol of 3 February 1830. T he document consisted of three protocols: the first declared Greece's independence, its monarchical regime and its boundaries; the second concerned the accession of Prince Leopold of Saxe-Coburg to the throne (he declined the offer and later became the first King of the Belgians); and the third established religious toleration.

1831   Kapodistrias assassinated by members of a powerful clan in the Mani region of the Peloponnese.

1832   The Treaty of Constantinople (21 July) between Britain, France, Russia and the Ottoman empire, modifying Greece's boundaries.

1833   Arrival of Prince Otto of Bavaria in Greece as its first king. Because he was a minor, the affairs of state were managed by a Bavarian regency. The Greek Church declared 'autocephalous', i.e. independent from the administrative, but not the doctrinal, authority of the Patriarchate in Constantinople.

1834   Athens becomes the capital of Greece.

1835   End of regency on Otto attaining majority.

1843   Otto forced by troops of the Athens garrison and a popular demonstration in front of the palace to grant a constitution.

1844   The new constitution defines the regime as a constitutional monarchy.

1854   The occupation and blockade of Piraeus by French and British troops imposes neutrality on Greece during the Crimean War.

1862   King Otto forced to abdicate after an uprising against his rule in Nafplion and Athens.

1863   Prince George of Denmark becomes 'King of the Hellenes'.

1864   The Ionian islands incorporated into the Greek state through the Treaty of London (29 March). The new constitution defines the Greek political system as a 'crowned democracy'.

1866–9   An uprising in Crete against Ottoman rule fails to liberate the island.

1870   The Sultan recognises the autonomy of the Bulgarian Exarchate Church, which breaks all links with the Ecumenical Patriarchate.

1871   The government of Alexandros Koumoundouros grants legal title deeds to peasants squatting on public lands.

1875   Acceptance by King George of the principle that the leader of a party enjoying majority support in parliament should be given the mandate to form a government.

1878   Conclusion of the peace treaty of San Stephano, soon to be revised by the Congress of Berlin.

1881   The province of Thessaly and the region of Arta incorporated into the Greek state. The Convention of Constantinople signed between Greece and Turkey.

1883–93   Decade during which Harilaos Trikoupis and Theodoros Deliyannis alternated in power, marking the heyday of the two-party system. Trikoupis puts reforms into effect.

1895   Trikoupis defeated in the elections and retires from politics; he dies the following year.

1896   Another Cretan rebellion against Ottoman rule leads fo Greece being involved in the issue of Cretan liberation.

1897   A Greco-Turkish war breaks out. The Greek forces are defeated by the Ottoman army within three weeks in the Thessaly campaign.

1898   Prince George (second son of King George) appointed governor of Crete after the island is granted autonomy.

1903   A 'Macedonian Committee' founded by Greek officers to counter Bulgarian claims in Macedonia.

1908   A 'Sociological Society' established in Athens to support the collective action of workers. Outbreak of the Young Turk revolt in Thessaloniki.

1909   A group of officers organised in a Military League obliges the government to draft reforms in parliament. The Cretan politician Eleftherios Venizelos appointed by the officers of the League as their political adviser.

1910   Eleftherios Venizelos wins an overwhelming popular mandate in general elections and launches extensive reforms.

1911   A revised constitution comes into force. The Dodecanese islands in the Aegean occupied by Italy.

1912   Landslide victory in the election for the Liberal Party created by Venizelos. Greece and its allies Bulgaria, Serbia and Montenegro defeat the Ottoman empire in the First Balkan War.

1913   The Second Balkan War fought between former allies—Bulgaria against Greece and Serbia; Bulgaria defeated. King George assassinated in Thessaloniki. Greece granted significant territorial gains (Crete, Macedonia, Ioannina and islands of the Aegean), in the Treaty of London (30 May) and the Peace of Bucharest (10 August).

1915   Clash between Venizelos and King Constantine over Greek foreign policy during the First World War, Venizelos proposing a Greek alliance with the Triple Entente while the King opts for neutrality. Venizelos twice forced to resign.

1916   Greece divided between north and south with the revolutionary government under Venizelos, General Danglis and Admiral Kountouriotis in Thessaloniki, and the official government in Athens appointed by the King.

1917   Constantine forced to abdicate. His second son Alexander succeeds as king and Venizelos re-establishes his government in Athens. Thessaloniki devastated by a fire that started during the night of 18 August.

1918   Ten Greek divisions fight on the Macedonian front in the autumn campaign which defeats the German and Bulgarian forces.

1919   Greece takes its place among the victors of the First World War and expands the national territory through the Paris peace conference. The treaty of Neuilly (27 November) includes Bulgaria's renunciation of all rights to Western Thrace which is awarded to Greece.

1920   Under the treaty of Sèvres (10 August) Greece acquires Western and Eastern Thrace, the rest of the Aegean islands, and a mandate to administer the greater Smyrna area in Asia Minor, pending a plebiscite about its future.

1920   Death of King Alexander from the bite of a pet monkey. Venizelos defeated in the ensuing elections. The royalists return to power and restore Constantine to the throne.

1922   Greek forces defeated in Asia Minor and the ethnic Greek population flees to Greece. Constantine abdicates in favour of his eldest son, George II, and leaves the country.

1923   The treaty of Lausanne (24 July) fixes the boundaries between Greece and Turkey and imposes an exchange of populations. Close to 1.5 million destitute refugees arrive in a country of barely 5 million inhabitants.

1924   Greece becomes a republic following a referendum with George Kountouriotis as the first president.

1924–6   Military coups follow one another during a period of frequent interventions by the military in politics.

1926–8   An all-party government takes office.

1928–32   Venizelos' final four-year term in office.

1930   A Greek-Turkish treaty, signed by Venizelos and Atatürk, settles outstanding problems between the two states.

1933   Tsaldaris, leader of the Populist (pro-Royalist) party, wins the elections and Liberals fear restoration of the monarchy.

1934   Balkan Pact signed in Athens between Greece, Romania, Yugoslavia; Turkey attempts to create a federation of Balkan states.

1935   Failure of an anti-Royalist pre-emptive coup speeds up the process of King George's restoration.

1936   The leading Greek politicians Venizelos, Tsaldaris, Kondylis and Papanastasiou die in quick succession. On 4 August the King endorses the suspension of certain articles of the Constitution, enabling the caretaker Prime Minister, Ioannis Metaxas, to assume dictatorial powers.

1940   Greek resistance to the Italian Fascists' attack from Albania results in the first Allied victories in the Second World War.

1941   German armoured divisions overpower the Greek armed forces and occupy the country. British forces evacuate mainland Greece and, eventually, Crete in the face of an intensive German aerial assault. A Greek government-in-exile established in Cairo and London. Greek armed forces regroup in Egypt.

1941–4   Greece occupied by German, Italian and Bulgarian forces; Thrace and Eastern Macedonia annexed by Bulgaria. Greek resistance obliges the Germans to keep large forces in Greece and disrupts their transports to the Middle East. Internal strife between left- and right-wing resistance groups deepens divisions between Greeks. On 3 October 1944 the Greek Mountain Brigade distinguishes itself in the battle of Rimini on the Italian Adriatic coast.

1944   Athens liberated. The 'December events', an armed rebellion of the Communist-dominated resistance, further deepen ideological strife.

1946   A referendum on the future of the monarchy results in a 68% vote for its restoration.

1946–9   A fully fledged civil war called the 'third round' (the first being fought during the occupation and the second during the 'December events') is fought between the Communist-controlled Democratic Army in northern Greece and the National Army under a coalition government of 'Populists' (right-wingers and royalists). The Communist forces are defeated in 1949.

1947   In accordance with the Treaty of Paris (10 February) Greece acquires the Dodecanese islands. Under the Truman Doctrine massive aid is granted to Greece.

1952   Greece becomes a member of NATO. Elections are won by the Greek Rally, a new right-wing party led by Field-Marshal Alexander Papagos, who commanded the government forces in the Civil War. A reconstruction programme of a war-ravaged Greece is launched with American aid.

1955   In September a mob in Istanbul, demanding the annexation of Cyprus by Turkey, wreaks havoc in the areas of the city inhabited by Greeks.

1956   Elections are won by the newly-formed right-wing party called the 'National Radical Union' (ERE), led by Constantine Karamanlis, Minister of Public Works in the Papagos government. Archbishop Makarios of Cyprus deported to Seychelles by the British. The Greek Cypriots' struggle for self-determination reaches a climax.

1958   In the May elections, the ERE party under Karamanlis maintains its majority with 40% of the popular vote.

1959   Greece applies to the EEC for associate membership. Greek and Turkish Cypriot leaders sign the London agreement on the independence of Cyprus.

1960   Cyprus becomes an independent republic with Archbishop Makarios as President and Dr Fazil Kütchük as Vice-President.

1961   ERE wins 57% of the popular vote in general elections amid accusations of electoral fraud.

1963   Karamanlis loses the elections to George Papandreou, leader of the Centre Union, a party formed by the coalition of all the centre factions in Greek politics. Violence in Cyprus between Greek and Turkish Cypriot communities.

1964   In new elections the Centre Union turns its relative majority in the February elections into an absolute one, winning 52.7 per cent of the vote.

1965   King Constantine clashes with Prime Minister George Papandreou over the latter's appointment of himself as Defence Minister, leading Papandreou to resign in protest. An 'unrelenting struggle' is launched demanding new elections.

1966 (December)   The major parties agree to desist from attacks on the monarchy.

1967 (April)   A Junta of colonels launch a *coup d'état* and establish a military dictatorship. The King flees the country after an abortive effort in December to oust the military regime.

1968   Around 1,000 civil servants dismissed by the Junta; Junta officers in Cyprus try, but fail, to murder President Makarios.

1973   Abortive coup by navy units against the regime.

1974   The Turks invade Cyprus in two consecutive waves after a coup instigated by the Junta in Athens against Makarios replaces him with a nationalist stooge. The Junta collapses in July; democracy is restored in Greece; Karamanlis return as Prime Minister from his exile in Paris and wins the November elections by a landslide. Greece becomes a republic after a referendum (December).

1975   A new constitution replaces that of 1952, briefly restored after the abrogation of the Junta's 1973 constitution. A Turkish–Cypriot Federated State of Cyprus is proclaimed and recognised only by Turkey. There follows an influx of immigrants from mainland Turkey to northern Cyprus.

1976   Greek–Turkish relations go through a new crisis when a Turkish survey ship begins oil explorations in waters between the islands of Mytilini and Lemnos, claimed by Greece as part of its continental shelf.

1977 (November)   Karamanlis' New Democracy party wins a comfortable majority in the elections.

1979 (28 May)   Karamanlis signs a treaty of accession to the European Community with the nine EC members.

1980   Karamanlis becomes President of the Republic and George Rallis Prime Minister. Visit of Greek President to Moscow.

1981   Greece joins the EC. The Panhellenic Socialist Movement (PASOK), led by Andreas Papandreou, wins the October elections.

1982   Papandreou visits Cyprus—the first such visit by a Greek Prime Minister.

1983   The Turkish Cypriot Assembly unilaterally declares an independent Turkish Republic of Northern Cyprus, recognised only by Turkey. A Defence and Economic Cooperation Agreement (DECA) is signed between the United States and Greece, replacing that of 1953, together with other bilateral security arrangements.

1984   Constantinos Mitsotakis elected leader of the New Democracy party.

1985   Former judge Christos Sartzetakis elected President of the Republic. PASOK wins 45.82% of the popular vote in the June elections.

1987   A new crisis breaks out in relations between Greece and Turkey because of the Turkish intention to explore once again for oil in disputed areas of the Aegean seabed. Greece and Albania formally end the state of war which had technically existed between the two countries since 1940.

1988   Premiers Papandreou and Turgut Özal meet in Davos, Switzerland, to defuse tension between their two countries.

1989   A deadlocked June election leads to the formation of a government of 'limited duration' under the New Democracy deputy Tzannis Tzannetakis, with the support of the Communist Party. New elections in November 1989 also prove inconclusive. An all-party government is formed under Xenophon Zolotas, a non-partisan banker and economist.

1990   New Democracy, under Mitsotakis, wins the elections and Karamanlis again becomes President of the Republic.

1991   (16–17 October) The Brussels EPC (European Political Cooperation) meeting of the twelve Foreign Ministers decides that, before being granted recognition, the Former Yugoslav Republic of Macedonia ('FYROM') should 'adopt constitutional and political guarantees ensuring that it has no territonal claims towards a neighbouring Community state'. The Greek and Turkish Prime Ministers, meeting in Davos, agree to improve relations between their countries.

1992   The government imposes an austerity programme. The 'FYROM' issue dominates Greek foreign policy. There is an influx of ethnic Greek economic refugees from the former Soviet Union, Albania and Bulgaria.

1993   Former Foreign Minister Andonis Samaras leaves New Democracy and (September) instigates the defection of two deputies, causing the government to fall. PASOK voted back to power (October).

1995   End of Karamanlis's last presidential term. Constantine Stephanopoulos elected President of the Republic by Parliament.

1996   After a long illness, Andreas Papandreou replaced as Prime Minister by Constantine Simitis, and dies (June). Simitis wins elections (September) by a comfortable margin.

1997   The Simitis government pursues decisively its convergence policy, ensuring that Greece will meet the Maastricht criteria and thus qualify to participate in the Economic and Monetary Union.

1998   Death of Constantine Karamanlis. Clouds gather in Kosovo but Greece's relations with all its northern neighbours are good. Tension with Turkey grows over the efforts by Cyprus to enter the EU. Turkish allegations of 'grey zones' in the Aegean, and the Kurdish leader Ocalan's passage to Kenya, with Greek complicity, create an all-time low in Greek-Turkish relations.

1999   Greeks unanimously oppose the bombing of the former Republic of Yugoslavia by NATO aircraft, but the Simitis government maintains solidarity with its NATO partners. The Helsinki accord, acknowledging Turkey's eligibility as a full member of the EU, dispels the tension between the two Aegean neighbours.

2000   Stephanopoulos re-elected as President of the Republic by parliament. In general elections (9 April) PASOK under Simitis wins by a narrow margin. Greece accepted in the Economic and Monetary Union (EMU) of the EU.

BIBLIOGRAPHY

GENERAL AND BIBLIOGRAPHICAL

Admiralty Naval Intelligence Division (Geographical Handbook Series), *Greece* (3 vols), London, 1944.

Andronikos, M., M. Hadjidakis, V. Karayiorgis, *The Greek Museums*, Athens: Ekdotiki Athinon, 1975.

Beaton, Roderick, *An Introduction to Modern Greek Literature*, Oxford: Clarendon Press, 1994.

Brown, Anne, and Helen Dudenbostel, *Greece: A Selected List of References*, Washington, DC: Library of Congress, 1943.

Clogg, Richard, and Mary-Jo Clogg, *Greece* (World Bibliographical Series 17), Oxford: Clio Press, 1980.

Curtis, Glenn E., *Greece: A Country Study*, Washington, DC: Federal Research Division, 1995.

Dimaras, C. Th., C. Koumarianou, L. Droulia (eds), *Modern Greek Culture: A Selected Bibliography (in English, French, German, Italian)*, Athens: ANHCIASEES, 1974.

Divo, Jean-Paul, *Modern Greek Coins, 1828–1968*, Zurich: Bank Leu, 1969.

Garrett, Martin, *Greece: A Literary Companion*, London: John Murray, 1994.

Horecky, Paul, and David Kraus (eds), *East Central and Southeast Europe: A Handbook of Library and Archival Resources in North America*, Oxford: Cilo Press, 1976.

Iatrides, John, *Greece in the 1940s: A Bibliographic Companion*, Hanover, NH: University Press of New England, 1981.

Institut français d'Athènes, *Bulletin analytique de bibliographie hellénique*, Athens, first publ. 1945. Bibliographies of monographs, periodicals and journals of varying frequency.

Kitromilides, Paschalis, and Marios Evriviades, *Cyprus* (World Bibliographical Series 28), Oxford: Clio Press, 1982, 2nd edn, 1995.

Layton, Evro, *Five Centuries of Books and Manuscripts in Modern Greek*, Harvard College Library, Cambridge, MA, 1990.

Legrand, Emile, *Bibliographie Hellénique, ou description raisonée des ouvrages publiés par des Grèques au 18ème siecle*, Paris: E. Levoux, J. Maisonneuve Garnier Frères, 1918.

Mackridge, Peter (ed.), *Ancient Myth in Modern Greek Poetry*, London: Frank Cass, 1996.

Richter, Heinz, *Greece and Cyprus since 1920: Bibliography of Contemporary History*, Heidelberg: Wissenschaftlicher Verlag, 1984.

Schuster, Mel, *The Comtemporary Greek Cinema*, London: Scarecrow Press, 1979.

Sherrard, Philip, *The Pursuit of Greece: an Anthology*, London: John Murray, 1964.

Shinn, Rinn S. (ed.), *Greece: A Country Study*. Washington, DC: Foreign Area Studies, The American University, 1986.

Speake, Graham (ed.), *Encyclopaedia of Greece and the Hellenic Tradition*, 2 vols, London: Fitzroy Dearborn, 2000.

Spencer, Floyd, A., *War and Post-War Greece: An Analysis Based on Greek Writings*. Washington, DC: Library of Congress, 1952.

Stoneman, Richard (ed.), *A Literary Companion to Travel in Greece*, Malibu, CA: J. Paul Getty Museum, 1994.

Swanson, Donald, *Modern Greek Studies in the West: A Critical Bibliography of Studies on Modern Greek Linguistics, Philogy and Folklore, in Languages other than Greek*, New York Public Library, 1960.

Veremis, Thanos, and Mark Dragoumis, *Greece* (World Bibliographical Series, 17), Oxford: Clio Press, 1998.

———, *Historical Dictionary of Greece*, European Historical Dictionaries no. 5, Metuchen, NJ: Scarecrow Press, 1995.

Walton, Francis, *The Greek Book, 1476–1825*, Athens: I0ème Congrès International des Bibliophiles, 1977.

HISTORY

Before Independence

Angelomatis-Tsoungarakis, Helen, *The Eve of the Greek Revival: British Travellers' Perceptions of Early Nineteenth-Century Greece*, London: Routledge, 1990.

Augustinos, Olga, *French Odysseys: Greece in French Travel Literature from the Renaissance to the Romantic Era*, Baltimore: Johns Hopkins University Press, 1994.

Browning, Robert, *Medieval and Modern Greek*, London: Hutchinson University Liberty, 1969/Cambridge University Press, 1982, 1989.

——— (ed.), *The Greeks, Classical, Byzantine and Modern*, New York: Portland House, 1985.

Carras, Costas, *3000 Years of Greek Identity: Myth or Reality?*, Athens: Domus Books, 1983.

Cheetham, Nicholas, *Medieval Greece*, New Haven, CT: Yale University Press, 1981.

Clogg, Richard, *The Movement for Greek Independence, 1770–1821: A Collection of Documents,* London: Macmillan/New York: Barnes & Noble, 1976.

Constantine, David, *Early Greek Travellers and the Hellenic Ideal*, Cambridge University Press, 1984.

Cook, B.F., *The Elgin Marbles*, London: British Museum Press, 1977.

Dalrymple, William, *From the Holy Mountain: A Journey in the Shadow of Byzantium*, London: HarperCollins, 1997.

Forbes Boyd, Eric, *Aegean Quest: A Search for Venetian Greece*, London: Dent, 1970.

Geanakoplos, Deno John, *Greek Scholars in Venice*, Harvard University Press, 1962.

Gilchrist, Hugh, *Australians and Greeks*, 1: *The Early Years*, Sydney: Halstead Press, 1992.

Hadjiantoniou, George, *Protestant Patriarch: The Life of Cyril Lucaris (1572–1638), Patriarch of Constantinople*, London: Epworth Press, 1961.

Harris, Jonathan, *Greek Emigrés in the West, 1400–1520*, Camberley, Surrey: Porphyrogenitus, 1995.

Henderson, G.P., *The Revival of Greek Thought: 1620–1830*, Edinburgh: Scottish Academy Press, 1971.

Koromila, Marianna, *The Greeks in the Black Sea: From the Bronze Age to the Early 20th Century*, Athens: Panorama Cultural Society, 1991.

Mango, Cyril, *Byzantium: The Empire of the New Rome,* London: Weidenfeld and Nicolson, 1980.

Moutzan-Martinengou, Elisavet, *My Story*, translated by Helen Dendrinou Kolias, Athens, GA: University of Georgia Press, 1989.

Nicol, Donald, *Meteora: The Rock Monasteries of Thessaly*, London: Chapman & Hall, 1963.

Papadopoullos, Theodore, *Studies and Documents Relating to the History of the Greek Church and People under Turkish Domination*, Brussels, 1952.

Plomer, William, *The Diamond of Jannina: Ali Pasha, 1741–1822*, London: Jonathan Cape, 1970.

Runciman, Steven, *The Fall of Constantinople*, Cambridge University Press, 1965.

———, *The Great Church in Captivity: A Study of the Patriarchate of Constantinople from the Eve of the Turkish Conquest to the Greek War of Independence*, Cambridge University Press, 1968.

Stanford, W.B., and E.J. Finopoulos (eds), *The Travels of Lord Charlemont in Greece and Turkey, 1749*, London: Trigraph, 1984.

Stavrianos, L.S., *The Balkans since 1453*, repr. London: Hurst/New York University Press, 2000 (prev. publ. 1958).

Topping, P.W., *Studies in Latin Greece, AD 1205–1715*, London: Variorum, 1977.

Vacalopoulos, Apostolos, *History of Macedonia 1354–1833*, Thessaloniki: Institute of Balkan Studies, 1973.

Vrettos, Theodore, *The Elgin Marbles*, New York: Arcade Publishers, 1998.

Vryonis, Speros, *The Decline of Medieval Hellenism in Asia Minor and the Process of Islamization from the Eleventh through the Fifteenth Century*, Berkeley: University of California Press, 1986.

Woodcook, George, *The Greeks in India*, London: Faber & Faber, 1966.

Woodhouse, C.M., *Rhigas Velestinlis: The Proto-Martyr of the Greek Revolution*. Limni Evia: Denise Harvey, 1995.

Yiannias, John J. (ed.), *The Byzantine Tradition after the Fall of Constantinople*, Charlottesville: University of Virginia Press, 1991.

Zakythinos, D.A., *The Making of Modern Greece: From Byzantium to Independence*, Totowa, NJ: Rowman & Littlefield, 1976.

Nineteenth century

Augustinos, Gerasimos, *The Greeks of Asia Minor: Confession, Community and Ethnicity in the Nineteenth Century*, Kent, OH: Kent State University Press, 1992.

Bower, Leonard, and Gordon Bolitho, *Otho I, King of Greece: a Biography*, London: Selwyn & Blount, 1939.

Brewer, David, The Greek War of Independence, Woodstock, NY: Overlook Press, 2001.

Carabott, Philip, *Greek Society in the Making, 1863–1913: Realities, Symbols and Visions,* Aldershot: Ashgate, 1997.

Clogg, Richard (ed.), *The Struggle for Greek Independence: Essays to Mark the 150th Anniversary of the Greek War of Independence*, London: Macmillan, 1973.

Dakin, Douglas, *British and American Philhellenes*, Thessaloniki: Institute of Balkan Studies, 1955.

———, *The Greek Struggle for Independence, 1821–1833*, London: Batsford, 1973.

———, *The Unification of Greece, 1770–1923*, London: Ernest Benn, 1972.

Diamandouros, Nikiforos *et al.* (eds), *Hellenism and the First Greek War of Liberation (1821–1830)*, Thessaloniki: Institute for Balkan Studies, 1976.

Dontas, Domna, *Greece and the Great Powers 1863–1875*, Thessaloniki: Institute of Balkan Studies, 1966.

Driault, E., and M. Lhéritier, *Histoire diplomatique de la Grèce de 1821 à nos jours*, Paris, 1926.

Economopoulou, Marietta, *Parties and Politics in Greece 1844–55*, Athens: 1984.

Finlay, George, *History of the Greek Revolution and the Reign of the King Otto*, London: Zeno, 1971.

Gallant, Thomas W., *Modern Greece*, London: Arnold, 2001.

Hussey, J.M., *The Finlay Papers: A Catalogue*, London: Thames & Hudson, 1973.

Issawi, Charles, and D. Gondicas (eds), *Greeks in the Ottoman Empire: From the Tanzimat to the Young Turks*, New York: Darwin Press, 1997.

Jelavich, Charles, *Language and Area Studies: East Central and Southeastern Europe: A Survey*, University of Chicago Press, 1969.

Jenkins, Romilly, *The Dilessi Murders*, London: Longman, 1961.

Kofos, Evangelos, *Greece and the Eastern Crisis 1875–1878*, Thessaloniki: Institute for Balkan Studies, 1975.

Koliopoulos, John, *Brigands with a Cause*, Oxford: Clarendon Press, 1987.

Leontis, Artemis, *Topographies of Hellenism: Mapping the Homeland*, Ithaca, NY: Cornell University Press, 1996.

Levandis, John, *The Greek Foreign Debt and the Great Powers, 1821–1898*, New York: Columbia University Press, 1944.

Lidderdale, H.A., *The Memoirs of General Makriyannis, 1797–1864*, London: Oxford Uiversity Press, 1966.

McGrew, William W., *Land and Revolution in Modern Greece, 1800–1881*, Kent, OH: Kent State University Press, 1985.

Papadopoulos, G.S., *England and the Near East, 1896–1898*, Thessaloniki: Institute for Balkan Studies, 1969.

Pappas, Paul Constantine, *The United States and the Greek War for Intependence, 1821–1828*, New York: Columbia University Press, 1985.

Petropulos, John-Anthony, *Politics and Statecraft in the Kingdom of Greece 1833–43*, Princeton University Press, 1968.

Pratt, Michael, *Britain's Greek Empire: Reflections on the History of the Ionian Islands from the Fall of Byzantium*, London: Rex Collings, 1978.

Prevelakis, Eleftherios, *British Policy towards the Change of Dynasty in Greece 1862–63*, Athens, 1953.

Rossel, David, *In Byron's Shadow*, New York: Oxford University Press, 2001.

Stanford, W.B., and E.J. Finopoulos (eds), *The Travels of Lord Charlemont in Greece and Turkey, 1749*, 1994.

Strong, Frederick, *Greece as a Kingdom; or a Statistical Description of that Country from the Arrvial of King Otto in 1883 to the Present*. London, 1842.

Todorov, Varban N., *Greek Federalism During the Nineteenth Century*. Boulder, CO: East European Monographs, 1995.

Van de Kiste, John, *Kings of the Hellenic: The Greek Kings 1863–1974,* London: Sutton Publishers, 1999.

Woodhouse, C.M., *Rhigas Velestinlis: The Proto-Martyr of the Greek Revolution*, Limni Evias: Denise Harvey, 1995.

———, *Capodistria: The Founder of Greek Independence*, Oxford University Press, 1973.

———, *The Battle of Navarino*, London: Hodder & Stoughton, 1965.

———, *The Greek War of Independence: Its Historical Setting*, London: Hutchinson, 1952.

———, *The Philhellenes*, London: Hodder & Stoughton, 1969.

Twentieth century

Alastos, Doros, *Venizelos: Patriot, Statesman, Revolutionary*, London: Lund Humphries, 1942.

Alexander, G.M., *The Prelude to the Truman Doctrine: British Policy in Greece 1944–1947*, Oxford: Clarendon Press, 1982.

——, et al., *Greek-Turkish Relations, 1923–1987*, Athens: Gnosi, ELIAMEP, 1988.

Alexandris, Alexis, *The Greek Minority of Istanbul and Greek-Turkish Relations, 1918–1974*, Athens: Centre for Asia Minor Studies, 1983.

——, Argenti, Philip, *The Occupation of Chios by the Germans and their Administration of the Island: Described in Contemporary Documents*, Cambridge University Press, 1966.

Augustinos, Gerasimos, *Consciousness and History: Nationalist Critics of Greek Society 1897–1914*, Boulder, CO: East European Quarterly, 1977.

Auty, Phyllis, and Richard Clogg (eds), *British Policy towards Wartime Resistance in Yugoslavia and Greece*, London: Macmillan/New York: Barnes & Noble, 1975.

Averoff, Evangelos, *By Fire and Axe: The Communist Party and the Civil War in Greece, 1944–49*, New Rochelle, NY: Caratzas, 1978.

——, *Lost Opportunities: The Cyprus Question*, New Rochelle, NY: Caratzas. 1982.

Baerentzen, Lars, John Iatrides and Ole Smith (eds), *Studies in the History of the Greek Civil War 1945–49*, Copenhagen: Museum Tusculanum Press, 1987.

Baerentzen, Lars (ed.), *British Reports on Greece*, Copenhagen: Museum Tusculanum Press, 1982.

Barker, Elizabeth, *British Policy in South-east Europe in the Second World War*, London: Macmillan, 1976.

Barros, James, *The Corfu Incident of 1923: Mussolini and the League of Nations*, Princeton Univeristy Press, 1965.

——, *Britain, Greece and the Politics of Sanctions: Ethiopia, 1935–1936*, Atlantic City, NJ: Humanities Press, 1982.

——, *The League of Nations and the Great Powers: the Greek-Bulgarian Incident, 1925*, Oxford: Clarendon Press, 1970. 143p.

Beevor, Anthony, *Crete: The Battle and the Resistance*, London: Penguin, 1993.

Bitzes, John, *Greece in World War II to April 1941*, Manhattan, KS: Sunflower University Press. 1989.

Blinkhorn, Martin, and Thamos Veremis (eds), *Modern Greece: Nationalism and Nationality*. ELIAMEP/Sage, 1990.

Browning, Robert (ed.), *The Greek World: Classical, Byzantine and Modern*, London: Thames and Hudson.

Buckley, Christopher, *Greece and Crete, 1941*, London: HM Stationery Office, 1952.

Byford-Jones, W., *The Greek Trilogy: Resistance-Liberation-Revolution*, London: Hutchinson, 1945.

Calvocoressi, P., R. Clogg, D. Dakin *et al., Greece and Great Britain during World War I*, Thessaloniki: Institute for Balkan Studies, 1985.

Campbell, John, and Philip Sherrard, *Modern Greece*, London: Ernest Benn, 1968.

Cassimatis, Louis, *American Influence in Greece 1917–1929*, Kent, OH: Kent State University Press, 1988.

Casson, Stanley, *Greece against the Axis*, London, 1941.

Cervi, Mario, *The Hollow Legions: Mussolini's Blunder, 1940–1941*, London: Chatto & Windus, 1972.

Chandler, Geoffrey, *The Divided Land: an Anglo-Greek Tragedy*, London: Macmillan, 1959.

Charalambous, John, and Janet Warwick (eds), *Stefanos Sarafis: 60 years of Greek History*, London: PNL Press, 1992.

Clive, Nigel, *A Greek Experience, 1943–1948*, Salisbury: Michael Russell, 1985.

Clogg, Richard, *A Short History of Modern Greece*, Cambridge University Press, 1979.

———— (ed.), *Greece in the 1980s*, London: Macmillan, 1983.

————, *A Concise History of Greece*, Cambridge University Press, 1992.

————, *Greece, 1981–89: The Populist Decade*, London: Macmillan Press, 1993.

Close, David (ed.), *The Greek Civil War, 1943–1950*, London: Routledge, 1993.

————, *The Origins of the Greek Civil War*, London: Longman, 1995.

Couloumbis, Theodore, John A. Petropulos and Harry J. Psomiades (eds), *Foreign Interference in Greek Politics: An Historical Perspective*, New York: Pella, 1976.

Cruickshank, Charles, *Greece, 1940–1941: The Politics of Strategy of the Second World War*, London: Davis-Poynter, 1976.

Curtright, Lynn, *Muddle, Indecision and Setback. British Policy and the Balkan States: August 1914 to the Inception of the Dardanelles Campaign*, Thessaloniki: Institute for Balkan Studies, 1986.

Dakin, Douglas, *The Greek Struggle in Macedonia, 1897–1913*, Thessaloniki: Institute for Balkan Studies, 1966.

Dalven, Rae, *The Jews of Ioannina*, Philadelphia: Cadmus Press, 1990.

Despotopoulos, Alexandros, *Greece's Contribution to the Outcome of Two World Ware*, Athens: Ekdotiki Athinon, 1994.

Dontas, Domma, *Greece and Turkey: The Régime of the Straits, Lemnos and Samothrace*, Athens: G.C. Eleftheroudakis, 1987.

Dumanis, Nicholas, *Myth and Memory in the Mediterranean: Remembering Fascism's Empire*, London: Macmillan Press, 1997.

Eddy, Charles, *Greece and the Greek Refugees*. London: Geo. Allen & Unwin, 1931.

Essays in Memory of Basil Laourdas, Thessaloniki, 1975.

Eudes, Dominique, *The Kapetanios: Partisans and Civil War in Greece, 1943–1949*, London: New Left Books, 1972.

Falaci, Oriana, *A Man*, New York: Simon & Schuster, 1980.

Fleischer, Hagen, *Im Kreuzschatten der Maechte Griechenland, 1941–1944*, 2 vols, Frankfurt/Main: Peter Lang, 1986.

Fleming, Amalia, *A Piece of Truth*, London: Jonathan Cape, 1972.

Forbes-Boyd, Eric, *Aegean Quest: A Search for Venetian Greece*, London: J.M. Dent, 1970.

Forster, Edward, *A Short History of Modern Greece, 1821–1940*, London: Methuen, 1941.

Fortouni, Eleni, *Greek Women in Resistance*, New Haven, CT: Thelphini Press, 1986.

Frazier, Robert, *Anglo-American Relations with Greece: The Coming of the Cold War, 1942–47*, London: Macmillan. 1991.

Frederica, Queen, *A Measure of Understanding*, London: Macmillan, 1971.

Fromer, Rebecca, *The House by the Sea: A Portrait of the Holocaust in Greece*, Mercury House, 1998.

Gardikas Katsiadakis, Helen, *Greece and the Balkan Imbroglio: Greek Foreign Policy, 1911–13*, Athens: Syllogos pros Diadosin Ophelimon Vivlion, 1995.

Gerolymatos, André, *Guerrilla Warfare and Espionage in Greece, 1940–47*, New York: Pella, 1992.

Hadjipateras, C.N., and M.S. Fafalios, *Greece, 1940–41, Eyewitnessed*, Anixi Attikis: Efstathiadis, 1995.

Hammond, N.B.L., *The Allied Military Mission and the Resistance in West Macedonia*, Thessaloniki: Institute for Balkan Studies, 1993.

Hamson, Denys, *We Fell Among Greeks*, London: Jonathan Cape, 1946.

Hart, Janet, *New Voters in the Nation: Women in the Greek Resistance, 1941–1964*. Ithaca, NY: Cornell University Press, 1996.

Heckstall-Smith, Anthony, and H.T. Baillie-Grohman, *Greek Tragedy*, London: Anthony Blond, 1961.

Higham, Robin, *Diary of a Disaster: British Aid to Greece, 1940–41*, Lexington: University Press of Kentucky, 1986.

Higham, Robin, and Thanos Veremis (eds), *The Metaxas Dictatorship: Aspects of Greece, 1936–1940*, Athens: ELIAMEP/Vryonis Centre, 1993.

Hondros, John, *Occupation and Resistance: The Greek Agony, 1941–44*, New York: Pella, 1983.

Hourmouzios, Stelios, *No Ordinary Crown: A Biography of King Paul of the Hellenes*, London: Weidenfeld & Nicolson, 1972.

Housepian, Marjorie, *Smyrna, 1922: The Destruction of a City*, New York: Harcourt, Brace & World, 1968.

Iatrides, John (ed.), *Ambassador MacVeagh Reports: Greece, 1933–47*, Princeton University Press, 1980.

Iatrides, John, and Linda Wringley (eds), *Greece at the Crossroads: The Civil War and its Legacy*, Philadelphia: Pennsylvania State University Press, 1995.

Jones, Howard, *A New Kind of War: America's Global Strategy and the Truman Doctrine in Greece*, Oxford University Press, 1989.

Kaltchas, N., *Introduction to the Constitutional History of Modern Greece*, New York, 1940.

Kedros, Andri, *La Résistance Grècque, 1940–44*, Paris: Laffont, 1966.

Keeley, Edmund, *The Salonika Bay Murder Cold War Politics and the Polk Affair*, Princeton University Press. 1989.

Kesting, Jurgen, *Maria Callas*, Boston: Northeastern University Press, 1993.

Kitroeff, Alexander, *The Greeks in Egypt, 1919–1937: Ethnicity and Class*, St Antony's College, Oxford/London: Ithaca Press, 1989.

Kofas, John V., *Intervention and Underdevelopment: Greece During the Cold War*. Philadeliphia: Pennsylvania State University Press, 1989.

Koliopoulos, John, *Greece and the British Connection, 1935–1941*, Oxford: Clarendon Press, 1977.

Kondis, Basil, *Greece and Albania, 1908–1914*, Thessaloniki: Institute for Balkan Studies, 1976.

Koumoulides, John (ed.), *Greece in Transition: Essays in the History of Modern Greece, 1821–1974*, London: Zeno, 1977.

Kousoulas, George, *Revolution and Defeat: The Story of the Greek Communist Party*, Oxford University Press, 1965.

Leeper, Reginald, *When Greek Meets Greek*, London: Chatto & Windus, 1950.

Leon, George, *Greece and the Great Powers, 1914–1917*, Thessaloniki: Institute for Balkan Studies, 1974.

––––––, *The Greek Socialist Movement and the First World War: The Road to Unity*, Boulder, CO: East European Monographs, 1976.

Leontaritis, George, *Greece and the First World War: From Neutrality to Involvement, 1917–1918*, Boulder, CO: East European Monographs, 1990.

Llewellyn Smith, Michael, *Ionian Vision: Greece in Asia Minor, 1919–1922*, London: Hurst, 2000 (repr. of 1973 edn).

Mackenzie, Compton, *First Athenian Memories*, London: Cassell, 1931.

––––––, *Aegean Memories*, London: Chatto & Windus, 1940.

Marder, Brenda, *Stewards of the Land: The American Farm School and Modern Greece*, New York: Columbia University Press, 1979.

Martins, Percy F., *Greece of the Twentieth Century*, London: T. Fisher Unwin, 1913.

Mathews, Kenneth, *Memories of a Mountain War: Greece, 1944–1949*, London: Longman, 1972.

Mavrogordato, John, *Modern Greece: A Chronicle and a Survey*, London: Macmillan, 1931.

Mayes, Stanley, *Makarios: A Biography*, London: Macmillan, 1981.

Mazower, Mark, *Greece and the Inter-War Economic Crisis*, Oxford: Clarendon Press, 1991.

––––––, *Inside Hitler's Greece*, London: Yale University Press, 1993.

McDonald, Robert, *Pillar and Tinderbox*, London: Marion Boyars, 1983.

McNeill, William H., *The Greek Dilemma: War and Aftermath*, London: Gollancz, 1947.

––––––, *Greece: American Aid in Action, 1947–1956*, New York: Twentieth Century Fund, 1957.

————, *The Metamorphosis of Greece since World War II*, Oxford: Blackwell, 1978.

Mercouri, Melina, *I Was Born Greek*, London: Hodder & Stoughton, 1971.

Meyer, H.F., *Missing in Greece. Destinies in the Greek Freedom Fight, 1941–1944*, London: Minerva Press, 1995.

Miller, William, *Greece*. London: Benn, 1928.

Mitrakos, Alexander, *France in Greece During World War I*, Boulder, CO: East European Monographs, 1982.

Molho, Michael, and Joseph Nehama, *In Memoriam. Hommage aux victimes juives des Nazis en Grèce*, Thessaloniki, 1948, reprinted 1973.

Myers, E.C.W., *Greek Entanglement*, London: Hart–Davis, 1955; Gloucester: Alan Sutton, repr. 1985.

O'Ballance, Edgar: *The Greek Civil War, 1944–1949*, London: Faber & Faber, 1966.

Pallis, A.A., *Greece's Anatolian Venture and after*, London: Methuen, 1937.

Palmer, Alan, *The Gardeners of Salonika: The Macedonian Campaign 1915–1918*, London: André Deutsch, 1965.

Papacosma, Victor, *The Military in Greek Politics: The 1909 Coup d' Etat*, Kent, OH: Kent State University Press, 1977.

Papastratis, Procopis, *British Policy towards Greece during the Second World War, 1941–44*, Cambridge University Press, 1984.

Parish, Michael Woodbine, *Aegean Adventures, 1940–1943*, Lewes, Sussex: Book Guild, 1993.

Parker, Charles, *Return to Salonika*, London: Cassell, 1964.

Pentzopoulos, Dimitri, *The Balkan Exchange of Minorities and its Impact upon Greece*, London: repr. Hurst, 2002 (prev. publ. 1962).

Petsalis Diomidis, Nikos, *Greece and the Paris Peace Conference, 1919*, Thessaloniki: Institute for Balkan Studies, 1978.

Richter, Heinz, *British Intervention in Greece: From Varkiza to Civil War, 1945–1946*, London: Merli, 1985.

Sarafis, Marion (ed.), *Greece From Resistance to Civil War*, Nottingham: Spokesman, 1980.

————, Marline Eve (eds), *Background to Contemporary Greece*, 2 vols, London: Merlin Press, 1990.

Sarafis, Stefanos, *Elas: Greek Resistance Army*, London: Merlin Press, 1980.

Sciaky, Leon, *Farewell to Salonica: Portrait of an Era*, London: W.H. Allen, 1946.

Sevillias, Errikos, *Athens-Auschwitz*, Athens: Lycabettus Press, 1983.

Smith, Peter, and Edwin Walker, *War in the Aegean*, London: William Kimber, 1974.

Smothers, Frank, William Hardy McNeill and Elizabeth Darbishire McNeil, *Report on the Greeks: Findings of a Twentieth Century Fund Team which Surveyed Conditions in Greece in 1947*, New York: Twentieth Century Fund, 1948.

Stassinopoulos, Arianna, *Maria: Beyond the Callas Legend*, London: Weidenfeld & Nicolson, 1980.

Stavrakis, Peter, *Moscow and Greek Communism 1944–49*. Ithaca, NY: Cornell University Press, 1989.

Stavroulakis, Nicholas, *The Jews of Greece: an Essay*, Athens: Talos Press, 1990.

Stewart, I.McD.G., *The Struggle for Crete, 20 May–1 June 1941: A Story of Lost Opportunity*, Oxford University Press, 1966.

Sweet-Escott, Bickham, *Baker Street Irregulars*, London: Methuen, 1965.

Tatsios, Theodore George, *The Megali Idea and the Greek-Turkish War of 1897: The Impact on the Cretan Revolution on Greek Irredentism, 1866–1897*, New York: East European Monographs, 1984.

Toynbee, Arnold, *The Western Question in Greece and Turkey: a Study in the Contact of Civilisations*, London: Constable, 1922.

Trotter, William R., *Priest of Music: The Life of Dimitri Mitropoulos*, Portland, OR: Amadens Press, 1995.

Tsatsos, Jeane, *The Sword's Fierce Edge: A Journal of the Occupation of Greece, 1941–1944*, Nashville, TE: Vanderbilt University Press, 1969.

Tsouderos, Emanuel J., *Democracy or Monarchy? Why We Are Fighting*, Washington, DC, 1941.

Tsouderos, Emmanuel J., *The Greek Epic*, London, 1942.

Vacalopoulos, Apostolos, *A History of Thessaloniki*, Thessaloniki Institute for Balkan Studies, 1972.

Vatikiotis, P.J., *Popular Autocracy in Greece, 1936–41: a Political Biography of General Ioannis Metaxas*, London: Frank Cass, 1998.

Veremis, Thanos, *The Military in Greek Politics: From Independence to Democracy*, London: Hurst, 1997.

Vlavianos, Haris, *Greece 1941–49: From Resistance to Civil War*, London: Macmillan, 1992.

Vukmanovic, Svetozar, *How and Why the People's Liberation Struggle of Greece met with Defeat*, London: Merlin Press, 1985.

Ward, Michael, *Greek Assignments SOE 1943–1948*, Athens: Lycabettus Press, 1995.

Wittner, L.S., *American Intervention in Greece, 1943–1949*, New York: Columbia University Press, 1982.

———, *Modern Greece: A Short History*, London: Faber & Faber, 1977.

Woodhouse, C.M., *The Apple of Discord*, London: Hutchinson, 1948.

———, *The Rise and Fall of the Greek Colonels*, New York: Granada, 1985.

———, *The Struggle for Greece, 1941–1949*, repr. London: Hurst, 2002 (prev. publ. 1976).

Xydis, Stephen, *Greece and the Great Powers, 1944–1947: Prelude to the 'Truman Doctrine'*, Thessaloniki: Institute for Balkan Studies, 1963.

Zapantis, Andrew L., *Greek-Soviet Relations, 1917–1941*, Boulder, CO: East European Monographs, 1982.

Zervos, Stella Reader, *One Woman's War: Diary of an English Woman Living in Occupied Greece, 1939–1945*, Athens Centre Academic Press, 1991.

POLITICS

Alford, Jonathan (ed.), *Greece and Turkey: Adversity in Alliance*, London: Gower/ International Institute for Strategic Studies, 1984.

Aliboni, Roberto (ed.), *Southern European Security in the 1990s*, London: Pinter, 1992.

Allison, Graham, and Kalypso Nicolaidis (eds), *The Greek Paradox*, Cambridge, MA: MIT Press, 1997.

Amen, Michael Mark, *American Foreign Policy in Greece, 1944–1949: Economic, Military and Institutional Aspects*, Frankfurt-am-Main: Peter Lang, 1978.

American Hellenic Institute, *US Foreign Policy regarding Greece, Turkey and Cyprus*, Columbus: Ohio State University, 1989.

[The] Athenian (Rodis Roufos), *Inside the Colonels' Greece*, London: Chatto & Windus, 1972.

Attalides, Michael (ed.), *Cyprus Reviewed*, Nicosia: Zavalis, 1977.

_____ (ed.), *Cyprus: Nationalism and International Politics*, Edinburgh: Q Press, 1979.

Axt, H.J., *Griechenlands Aussenpolitik und Europa. Verpasste Chancen und neue Herausforderungen*, Baden-Baden: Nomos, 1992.

Bahcheli, tozun, *Greek-Turkish Relations since 1955*, Boulder, CO: Westview Press, 1990.

Barkman, Carl, *Ambassador in Athens*, London: Merlin Press, 1989.

Bitsios, D.S., *Cyprus: The Vulnerable Republic*, Thessaloniki: Institute for Balkan Studies, 1975.

Brown, James, *Delicately Poised Allies: Greece and Turkey*, London: Brassey's, 1991.

Carabott, Philip (ed.), *Greece and Europe in the Modern period: Aspects of a troubled Relationship*, London: Centre for Hellenic Studies, King's College, 1995.

Carmacolias, Demetrios, *Political Communication in Greece, 1965–1967: The Last Two Years of a Parliamentary Democracy*, Athens: National Centre of Social Research, 1974.

Chaconas, Stephen-George, *Adamantios Koraes: A Study in Greek Nationalism*, New York: Columbia University Press, 1942.

Chipman, John (ed.), *NATO's Southern Allies: Internal and External Challenges*. London: Routledge, 1988.

Clogg, Richard (ed.), *Greece under Military Rule*. London: Secker & Warburg; New York: Basic Books, 1972.

_____, *Parties and Elections in Greece*, London: Hurst, 1987.

Constas, D. (ed.), *The Greek Turkish Conflict in the 1990s*, London: Friedrich Naumann Institute/Macmillan, 1991.

Coufoudakis, Van, Harry Psomiades and Andre Gerolymatos (eds), *Greece and the New Balkans: Challenges and Opportunies*, New York: Pella, 1999.

Couloumbis, Theodore, *Greek Political Reaction to American and Nato Influence*, London: Yale University Press, 1966.

———, *The United States, Greece and Turkey: The Troubled Triangle*, New York: Praeger, 1983.

———, J.A. Petropulos and H.T. Psomiades (eds), *Foreign Interference in Greek Politics*. New York: Pella, 1976.

Couloumbis, Theodore, and Sallie M. Hicks (eds), *U.S. Foreign Policy toward Greece and Cyprus: The Clash of Principle and Pragmatism*, Washington, DC: Center for Mediterranean Studies and the American Hellenic Institute, 1975.

Couloumbis, Theodore, and John O. Iatrides (eds), *Greek-American Relations: a Critical Review*, New York: Pella, 1980.

Crawshaw, Nancy. *The Cyprus Revolt: An Account of the Struggle for Union with Greece*. London: Geo. Allen & Unwin, 1978.

Danopoulos, Constantine, *Warriors and Politicians in Modern Greece*, Chapel Hill, NC: Documentary Publications, 1984.

Deane, Philip, *I Should Have Died*, London: Hamish Hamilton, 1976.

Eaton, Robert, *Soviet Relations with Greece and Turkey*, Athens: ELIAMEP, 1987.

Economides, Spyros, *The Balkan Agenda: Security and Regionalism in the New Europe*, London: Centre for Defence Studies, no. 10, 1992.

EKEME, *The Third Greek Presidency of the Council of the European Union*. Athens: Estia, 1994.

Featherstone, Kevin, and Dimitrios Katsoudas (eds), *Political Change in Greece: Before and after the Colonels*. London: Croom Helm, 1987.

Featherstone, Kevin, and Kostas Ifantis (eds), *Greece in a Changing Europe*, Manchester University Press, 1996.

Frazier, Robert, *Anglo-American Relations with Greece: The Coming of the Cold War*, London: Macmillan, 1991.

Gianaris, Nicholas, *Greece and Turkey: Economic and Geopolitical Perspectives*, New York: Praeger, 1988.

Gourgouris, Stathis, *Dream nation: Enlightment, Colonization and the Institutions of Modern Greece*, Stanford University. Press, 1996.

Hart, T. Parker, *Two NATO Allies at the Threshold of War: Cyprus, a Firsthand Account of Crisis Management 1965–68*, Durham, NC: Duke University Press, 1990.

Helsinki Watch, *Denying Human Rights and Ethnic Indentity: The Greeks of Turkey*, New York: Human Rights Watch, 1992.

Hitchens, Christopher, *Cyprus*, London: Quartet Books, 1984.

Iatrides, John, *Revolt in Athens: The Greek Communist 'Second Round'*, Princeton University Press, 1972.

——— (ed.), *Greece in the 1940s: A Nation in Crisis*, Hanover, NH: University Press of New England, 1981.

Ioannides, Christos, *In Turkey's Image: The Transformation of Occupied Cyprus into a Turkish Province*, New Rochelle, NY: Caratzas, 1991.

———, *Realpolitik in the Eastern Mediterranean*, New York: Pella, 2001.

Jecchinis, Christos, *Trade Unionism in Greece: A Study in Political Paternalism*, Chicago: Roosevelt University, Labor Education Division, 1967.

Karakatsanis, Neovi M., *The Politics of Elite Transformation: The Consolidation of Greek Democracy in Theoretical Perspective*, Westport, CT: Praeger, 2001.

Kariotis, Theodore (ed.), *The Greek Socialist Experiment. Papandreou's Greece, 1981–1989*, New York: Pella, 1992.

Kazakos, Panos, and P.C. Ioakimidis (eds), *Greece and EC: Membership Evaluated*. London: Pinter, 1994.

Keridis, Dimitris, and Dimitris Triantaphyllou (eds), *Greek-Turkish Relations in the Era of Globalization*, Everett, MA: Brassey's, 2001.

Kitromilides, Paschalis, *The Enlightment as Social Criticism: Iosipos Moisiodax and Greek Culture in the Eighteenth Century*, Princeton University Press, 1992.

———, *Enlightment, Nationalism, Orthodoxy: Studies in the Cultural and Political Thought of Southeastern Europe* Aldershot: Variorum, 1994.

——— and Peter Worsley (eds), *Small States in the Modern World*, Nicosia: Zavallis, 1979.

Kofos, Evangelos, *Nationalism and Communism in Macedonia*, Thessaloniki: Institute for Balkan Studies, 1964.

———, *The Impact of the Macedonian Question on Civil Conflict in Greece, 1943–1949*, Athens: ELIAMEP, 1989.

Kohler, Bete, *Political Forces in Spain, Greece and Portugal*, London: Butterworth Scientific, 1982.

Kourvetaris, George A., *Studies in Modern Greek Society and Politics*, Boulder, CO: East European Monographs, 1999.

Kuniholm, Bruce, *The Origins of the Cold War in the Near East: Great Power Conflict and Diplomacy in Iran, Turkey and Greece*, Princeton University Press, 1980.

Lavdas, Kostas, *The Europeanization of Greece: Interest Politics and the Crises of Integration*, London: Macmillan, 1997.

Lazakis, Christopher T., *The Steering of Greece in the Last Fifty Years: From the Epoch of the Civil War to the Epoch of Neoliberalism*, Ciel Trappe Books, 1996.

Legg, Keith, *Politics in Modern Greece*. Stanford, California: Stanford University Press, 1969.

——— and John Roberts, *Modern Greece*, Boulder, CO: Westview Press, 1996.

Lesser, Ian, *et al.*, *Greece's New Geopolitics*, Santa Monica, CA: RAND, 2001.

Loulis, John C., *The Greek Communist Party, 1940–1944*, London: Croom Helm, 1982.

———, *Greece under Papandreou: NATO's Ambivalent Partner*, London: Institute for European Defence and Strategic Studies, 1985.

Macridis, Roy, *Greek Politics at a Crossroads*, Stanford, CA: Hoover International Studies, 1984.

Markesinis, Basil, *The Theory and Practice of Dissolution of Parliament: A Comparative Study with Special Reference to the United Kingdom and the Greek Experience*, Cambridge University Press, 1972.

Mavrogordatos, George, *Rise of the Green Sun: The Greek Election of 1981*, London: King's College, 1983.

———, *Stillborn Republic: Social Coalitions and Party Strategies in Greece, 1922–1936*, Berkeley: University of California Press, 1983.

Melakopides, Costas, *Making Peace in Cyprus*, London, Ontario: Queen's University, Martello Papers 15, 1996.

Meynaud, Jean, *Les Forces Politiques en Grèce*, Paris: Etudes des Sciences Politiques, 1965.

Mitsos, Achilleas, and Elias Mossialos (eds), *Contemporary Greece and Europe*, Aldershot: Ashgate, 2000.

Mouzelis, Nicos, *Politics in the Semi-Periphery*, London: Macmillan, 1986.

Munkman, C.A., *American Aid to Greece: A Report on the First Ten Years*, New York: Praeger, 1958.

Nachmani, Amikam, *Israel, Turkey and Greece: Uneasy Relations in the East Mediterranean*, London: Frank Cass, 1987.

Papandreou, Andreas, *Democracy at Gunpoint: The Greek Front*, London: André Deutsch, 1971.

Papandreou, Margaret, *Nightmare in Athens*, Englewood Cliffs, NJ: Prentice-Hall, 1970.

Pappas, Takis, *Making Party Democracy in Greece*, London: Macmillan, 1998.

Pelt, Mogens, *Tobacco, Arms and Politics: Greece and Germany from World Crisis to World War, 1929–41*, Copenhagen: Museum Tusculanum Press, 1998.

Penniman, Howard, *Greece at the Polls: The National Elections of 1974 and 1977*, Washington, DC: American Enterprise Institute, 1981.

Pfaltzgraff, Jr., Robert L., and Dimitris Keridis (eds), *Security in Southeastern Europe and the U.S.-Greek Relationship*, London: Brassey's, 1997.

Poulantzas, Nikos, *The Crisis of the Dictatorships: Portugal, Greece, Spain*, Atlantic Highlands, NJ: Humanities Press, 1976.

Reddaway, John, *Burdened with Cyprus: The British Connection*, London: Weidenfeld & Nicolson, 1986.

Ricks, David, and Paul Magdalino (eds), *Byzantium and the Modern Greek Identity*, Aldershot: Ashgate, 1998.

Roubatis, Yannis, *Tangled Webs: The U.S. in Greece, 1947–67*, New York: Pella, 1987.

Salem, Norma (ed.), *Cyprus: A Regional Conflict and its Resolution*, New York: St Martin's Press, 1992.

Sotiropoulos, Dimitri, *Populism and Bureaucracy: The Case of Greece under PASOK, 1981–89*. Notre Dame, IN: University of Notre Dame Press, 1996.

Spourdalakis, Michalis, *The Rise of the Greek Socialist Party*, London: Routledge, 1988.

Stavrianos, L.S., *Balkan Federation: A History of the Movement toward Balkan Unity in Modern Times*, Northampton, MA: Smith College, 1941.

———, *Greece: American Dilemma and Opportunity*, Chicago: Henry Regnery, 1952.

Stavrou, Nikolaos, *Allied Politics and Military Interventions: The Political Role of the Greek Military*, Athens: Papazissis, 1988.

Stavrou, Nikolaos (ed.), *Greece under Socialism: A NATO Ally Adrift*, New Rochelle: Caratzas, 1992.

Stearns, Monteagle, *Entangled Allies: US Policy toward Greece, Turkey and Cyprus*, New York: Council on Foreign Relations Press, 1992.

Stern, Laurence, *The Wrong Horse: The Politics of Intervention and the Failure of American Diplomacy*, New York: Times Books, 1977.

Stivachtis, Yannis, *The Enlargement of International Society and Greece's Entry Into International Society*, London: Macmillan, 1998.

Stuart, Douglas (ed.), *Politics and Security in the Southern Region of the Atlantic Alliance*, London: Macmillan Press, 1988.

Sweet-Escott, Bickham. *Greece: A Political and Economic Survey 1939–1953*, London: Royal Institute of International Affairs, 1954.

Theodorakis, Mikis, *Journals of Resistance*, London: Hart Davis, MacGibbon, 1973.

Tsoucalas, Constantine, *The Greek Tragedy*, Harmondsworth: Penguin, 1969.

———, *The Greece of Karamanlis*, London: Doric Publications, 1973.

Tsoukalis, Loukas (ed.), *Greece and the European Community*, Farnborough: Saxon House, 1979.

Tzannatos, Zafiris (ed.), *Socialism in Greece: The First Four Years*, Aldershot: Gower, 1986.

———, *Greece's Balkan Policy and the 'Macedonian Issue'*, Ebenhausen: Stiftung Wissenschaft und Politik (SWP), 1992.

Tziampiris, Aristotle, *Greece, European Political Cooperation and the Macedonian Question*, Aldershot: Ashgate, 2000.

Valinakis, Yannis. *Greece and the CFE Negotiations*, Ebenhausen: SWP, 1991.

———, *Greece's Security in the Post-Cold War Era*, Ebenhausen: SWP, 1994.

Vatikiotis, P. J., *Greece: A Political Essay*, Beverley Hills, CA/London: Sage, 1974.

Veremis, Thanos, *Greek Security: Issues and Politics*, London: 1155, Adelphi Papers no. 179, 1982.

———, *Greece's Balkan Entanglement*, Athens: ELIAMEP, 1995.

——— and Michael Thumann, *The Balkans and CFSP: The Views of Greece and Germany*, Brussels: Centre for European Policy Studies, 1994.

Veremis, Thanos, and Yannis Valinakis (eds), *U.S. Bases in the Mediterranean: The Cases of Greece and Spain*, ELIAMEP, 1989.

Vryonis, Speros (ed.), *Greece on the Road to Democracy from the Junta to PASOK, 1974–1986*, New Rochelle, NY: Caratzas, 1991.

Wilson, Andrew, *The Aegean Dispute*, London: International Institute for Strategic Studies, 1979.

Woodhouse, C.M., *Karamanlis: The Restorer of Greek Democracy*, Oxford: Clarendon Press, 1982.

Xydis, Stephen, *Modern Greek Nationalism*, Seattle, WA: University of Washington Press, 1969.

Yannopoulos, George (ed.), *Greece and the EEC: Integration and the Convergence*, London: Macmillan Press, 1986.

Zaharopoulos, Thimios, and Manny E. Paraschos, *Mass Media in Greece: Power, Politics and Rivalization*, Westport, CT: Praeger, 1993.

THE ECONOMY

Alexander, Alec, *Greek Industrialists: An Economic and Social Analysis*, Athens: Centre of Planning and Economic Research, 1964.

Alogoskoufis, George, Lucas Papademos and Richard Portes (eds), *External Constraints in Macroeconomic Policy: The European Experience*, Cambridge University Press, 1991.

Break, George, and Ralph Turvey (eds), *Studies in Greek Taxation*, Athens: Centre of Planning and Economic Research, 1964.

Candilis, Wray, *The Economy of Greece, 1944–66: Efforts for Stability and Development*, New York: Praeger, 1968.

Coutsoumaris, George, *The Morphology of Greek Industry: a Study in Industrial Development*, Athens: Centre of Economic Research, 1965.

Demopoulos, G., *Monetary Policy in the Open Economy of Greece*, Athens: KEPE, 1981.

Evans, Peter, *Ari: The Life and Times of Aristotle Socrates Onassis*, London: Jonathan Cape, 1986.

Freris, A.F., *The Greek Economy in the Twentieth Century*, London: Croom Helm, 1986.

Georgakopoulos, Theodore, *Economic Effects of Value-added-tax Substitution: Greece*, Athens: Centre of Planning and Economic Research, 1976.

Germidis, Dimitrios, and Maria Negreponti-Delivanis, *Industrialisation, Employment and Income Distribution in Greece: A Case Study*, Paris: OECD, 1975.

Gortsos, Christos, *The Greek Banking System*, Athens: Hellenic Bank Association, 1998.

Halikias, D.J., *Money and Credit in a Developing Economy: The Greek Case*, New York University Press, 1978.

Harlaftis, Gelina, *Greek Shipowners and Greece, 1945–1975: From Separate Development to Interdependence*, London: Athlone Press, 1993.

Hellenic Industrial Development Bank, *Greek Industry in Perspective*, Athens, 1967.

Hitiris, Theodore, *Trade Effects of Economic Association with the Common Market: The Case of Greece*, New York: Praeger Publishers, 1972.

Jouganatos, George, *The Development of the Greek Economy, 1950–91: An*

Historical, Empirical and Econometric Analysis, Westport, CT: Greenwood Press, 1992.

Krengel, Rolf, and Dieter Martens, *Fixed Capital Stock and Future Investment Requirements in Greek Manufacturing*, Athens: Centre of Planning and Economic Research, 1966.

Munkman, C.A., *American Aid to Greece: A Report on the First Ten Years*, New York: Praeger, 1958.

Papandreou, Andreas, *A Strategy for Greek Economic Development*, Athens: Centre for Economic Research, 1962.

Pepelasis, Adamantios, *Labour Shortages in Greek Agriculture, 1963–1973*, Athens: Centre for Economic Research, 1963.

Pirounakis, Nicholas, *The Greek Economy: Past, Present and Future*, London: Macmillan, 1997.

Psilos, Diomedes, *Capital Market in Greece*, Athens: Centre for Economic Research, 1964.

Shaw, Lawrence, *Postwar Growth in Greek Agricultural Production: A Study in Sectoral Output Change*, Athens: Center of Planning and Economic Research, 1969.

Tsakalotos, Euclid, *Alternative Economic Strategies: The Case of Greece*, Aldershot: Avebury, 1991.

Tsoukalis, Loukas, *The European Community and its Mediterranean Enlargement*, London: Geo. Allen & Unwin, 1981.

———, *The New European Economy*, Oxford University Press, 1991.

Vouras, Paul, *The Changing Economy of Northern Greece since World War II*, Thessaloniki: Institute of Balkan Studies, 1962.

Wallden, Sotiris, *Integration of Southeastern Europe into the World Economy and Balkan Economic Cooperation*, Athens: ELIAMEP, 1999.

Xydis, S., *The Economy and Finances of Greece under Axis Occupation*, Pittsburgh: Hermes Printing Co., 1943.

Zolotas, Xenophon, *Monetary Equilibrium and Economic Development, with Special Reference to the Experience of Greece, 1950–1963*, Princeton University Press, 1965.

———, *The Positive Contribution of Greece to the European Community*, Athens: National Bank of Greece, 1978.

———, *Monetary and Economic Essays, 1961–1991*, Athens: Bank of Greece, 1997.

SOCIETY

Aschenbrenner, Stanley, *Life in a Changing Greek Village: Karpofora and its Reluctant Farmers*, Dubuque, IW: Kendall Hunt, 1986.

Berggreen, Brit, and Nanno Marinatos (eds), *Greece and Gender*, Bergen: Norwegian Institute in Athens, 1995.

Blum, Richard, and Eva M. Blum, *The Dangerous Hour: The Lore of Crisis and*

Mystery in Rural Greece, London: Chatto & Windus/New York: Scribner's, 1970.

Boulay, Juliet du, *Portrait of a Greek Mountain Village*, Oxford: Clarendon Press, 1974.

Burke, John and Stathis Gauntlett (eds), *Neohellenism*, Canbema: Humanities Research Centre, Australian National University, 1992.

Campbell, J.K., *Honour, Family and Patronage: a Study of Institutions and Morals in a Greek Mountain Community*. Oxford: Clarendon Press, 1964.

Carabott, Philip (ed.), *Greek Society in the Making, 1863–1913*, Brookfield, VT: Ashgate, Variorum, 1997.

Cassia, Paul Sant, and Constantina Bada, *The Making of the Modern Greek Family: Marriage and Exchange in 19th-Century Athens*, Cambridge University Press, 1994.

Cowan, Jane K., *Dance and the Body Politic in Northern Greece*, Princeton University Press 1990.

Damianakos, Stathis *et al.*, *Brothers and Others: Essays in Honour of John Peristiany*, Athens: National Centre for Social Research (EKKE), 1994.

Doxiadis, Constantinos A., *Ekistics: An Introduction to the Science of Human Settlements*, London: Hutchinson, 1968.

Dubisch, Jill, *In a Different Place: Pilgrimage, Gender and Politics at a Greek Island Shrine*, Princeton University Press, 1955.

—— (ed.), *Gender and Power in Rural Greece*, Princeton University Press. 1996.

Durrell, Lawrence, *The Greek Islands*. New York: The Viking Press, 1978.

Dimen, Muriel, and Ernestine Friedl (eds), *Regional Variation in Modern Greece and Cyprus: toward a Perspective of the Ethnography of Greece*, New York Academy of Sciences, 1976.

Eddy, Charles, *Greece and the Greek Refugees*, London: Geo. Allen & Unwin, 1931.

Friedl, Ernestine, *Vasilika: A Village in Modern Greece*, New York: Holt, Rinehart & Winston, 1963.

Gage, Nichols, *Portrait of Greece*, New York Times, 1971.

Herzfeld, Michael, *The Poetics of Manhood: Contest and Identity in a Cretan Mountain Village,* Princeton University Press, 1985.

——, *A Place in History: Social and Monumental Time in a Cretan Town*, Princeton University Press, 1991.

Kain, Hart Laurie, *Time, Religion and Social Experience in Rural Greece,* Lanham, MD: Rowman & Littlefield, 1993.

Karakasidou, Anastasia, *Fields of Wheat, Hills of Blood: Passages to nationhood in Greek Macedonia, 1870–1990*, University of Chicago Press, 1997.

Katsanevas, Theodore, *Trade Union in Greece*, Athens: National Centre of Social Research, 1984.

King, Francis, *Introducing Greece*, London: Methuen, 1956.

Lambiri, Ioanna, *Social Change in a Greek Country Town: The Impact of Factory Work on the Position of Women*, Athens: Centre of Planning and Economic Research, 1965.

Lambiri-Dmiaki, Jane, *Social Stratification in Greece, 1962–1982*, Athens: Sakkoulas, 1983.

Larrabee, Stephen, *Hellas Observed: The American Experience of Greece 1775–1865*, New York University Press, 1957.

Lazarou, G. Achille, *L'Aroumain et ses rapports avec le grec*, Thessaloniki: Institute for Balkan Studies, 1986.

Leontidou, Lila, *The Mediterranean City in Transition: Social Change and Urban Development*, Cambridge University Press, 1990.

Levi, Peter, *The Hill of Kronos*, London: Harvill Press, 1981.

Loizos, Peter, *The Heart Grown Bitter: A Chronicle of Cypriot War Refugees*, Cambridge University Press, 1981.

———— and Euthymios Papataxiarchis (eds), *Contested Identities: Gender and Kinship in Modern Greece*, Princeton University Press, 1991.

Mackridge, Peter, *Ourselves and Others. The Development of a Greek Macedonian Cultural Identity since 1912*, Oxford: Berg, 1997.

McNeil, William H., *The Metamorphosis of Greece since World War II*, Oxford: Blackwell, 1978.

Mazower, Mark (ed.), *After the War was over: Reconstructing the Family, Nation and State in Greece, 1943–60*, Princeton University Press, 2000.

Megas, A.G., *The Greek Calendar Customs*, Athens, 1963.

Michaelides, Constantine, *Hydra, a Greek Island Town: Its Growth and Form*, University of Chicago Press, 1967.

Miller, William, *Greek Life in Town and Country*, London: George Newnes, 1905.

Moss, W. Stanley, *Ill Met by Moonlight*, London: Harrap, 1950.

Mouzelis, Nicos, *Modern Greece: Facets of Underdevelopment*, London: Macmillan, 1978.

Peristiany, J.G. (ed.), *Contributions to mediterranean Sociology: Mediterranean Rural Communities and Social Change*, Paris: Mouton, 1968.

Peristiany, J.G., *Sociology in Greece*, Rome: Istituto Luigi Sturzo, 1968.

Pettifer, James, *The Greeks*, London, Viking, 1993.

Ruprecht, Louis Jr, *Hellenism, Modernism and the Myth of Decadence*, Albany: State University of New York Press, 1996.

Salamone, Stephen, *In the Shadow of the Holy Mountain: The Genesis of a Rural Greek Community and its Refugee Heritage*, East European Monographs, New York: Columbia University Press, 1987.

Sanders, Irwin, *Rainbow in the Rock: The People of Rural Greece*, Cambridge, MA: Harvard University Press, 1962.

Sherrard, Philip, *The Wound of Greece—Studies in Neo-Hellenism*, London: Rex Collings, 1978.

Sicilianos, Dimitrios, *Old and New Athens*, London: Putnam, 1960.

Sifianou, Maria, *Politeness Phenomona in England and Greece*, Oxford: Clarendon Press, 1992.

Somonsen, Thordis, *Dancing Girl: Themes and Improvisations in a Greek Village Setting*, Denver, CO: The Fundamental Note, 1991.

Spinellis, Calliope D., *Crime in Greece in Perspective*, Athens: A. Sakkoulas, 1997.

Spyropoulos, Diana, *Greece: A Spirited Independence*, London: Dillon Press, 1990.

Stahl, Paul, *Household, Village and Village Confederation*, New York: East European Monographs, Columbia University Press.

Triantafyllidou, Anna, *The Social Psychology of Party Behaviour*, Aldershot: Dartmouth, 1997.

Tamis, Anastasios M. (ed.), *Macedonian Hellenism*, Melbourne: River Seine Press, 1990.

Travlos, John, and A. Kokkou, *Hermoupolis*, Athens: Commercial Bank of Greece, 1984.

Thompson, Kenneth, *Farm Fragmentation in Greece: The Problem and its Setting, with Eleven Village Case Studies*, Athens: Centre of Economic Research, 1963.

Vermeulen, Cornelis J., *Families in Urban Greece*, Ithaca, NY: Cornell University Press, 1970.

Vlachos, Evangelos, *Modern Greek Society: Continuity and Change (an Annotated Classification of Selected Sources)*, Fort Collins: Colorado State University, 1969.

Vryonis, Speros (ed.), *The 'Past' in Medieval and Modern Greek Culture*, vol. 1: 'Byzantina and Metabyzantina', Malibu, CA: Undema, 1978.

Walcot, P., *Greek Peasants, Ancient and Modern: A Comparison of Social and Moral Values*, Manchester University Press, 1970.

Weintraub, D.M. Shapira, *Rural Reconstruction in Greece: Differential Social Prerequisites and Achievements during the Development Process*, Beverly Hills, CA: Sage, 1975.

Winnifrith, Tom, and Penelope Murray (eds), *Greece Old and New*, London: Macmillan, 1983.

———, *The Vlachs: The History of a Balkan People*, New York: St. Martins Press.

———, *Shattered Eagles: Balkan Fragments*, London: Duckworth, 1995.

DIASPORA

Bardis, Panos D., *The Future of the Greek Language in the United States*, San Francisco, CA: R and E Associates, 1976.

Bottomley, Gillian, *After the Odyssey: A Study of Greek Australians*, St Lucia: University of Queensland Press, 1979.

Burgess, Thomas, *Greeks in America*, Boston, MA: Sherman, French, 1913.

Callinicos, Constance, *American Aphrodite: Becoming Female in Greek America*, New York: Pella, 1994.

Calvocoressi, Peter, *Threading my Way*, London: Duckworth, 1994.

Catsiyannis, Timotheos, *The Greek Community of London*, London, 1993.

Chimbos, Peter D., *The Canadian Odyssey: The Greek Experience in Canada*, Toronto: McClelland and Stewart, 1980.

Clogg, Richard (ed.), *The Greek Diaspora in the Twentieth Century*, London: Macmillan, 1999.

Contopoulos, Michael, *The Greek Community of New York City: Early years to 1910*, New York: Aristide D. Caratzas, 1992.

Contos, Leonidas, C., *2001: The Church in Crisis*. Brookline, MA: Holy Cross Orthodox Press, 1982.

Cutsumbis, Michael. *A Bibliographic Guide to Materials on Greeks in the United States, 1890–1968*. New York, Center for Migration Studies, 1970.

Efthimiou, Miltiades B., and George A. Christopoulos. *History of the Greek Orthodox Church in America*, New York: Greek Orthodox Archdiocese, 1984.

Fairchild, Henry Pratt, *Greek Immigration to the United States*, New Haven, CT: Yale University Press, 1911.

Georgakas, Dan, and Charles C. Moskos (eds), *New Directions in Greek American Studies*. New York: Pella, 1991.

Hellenic Studies Forum, *Greece in English Speaking Countries*, Sydney: Ellinikon Fine Printers, 1993.

Karas, Nicholas, V., *The Greek Triangle of the Acre*, Lowell, MA: Meteora, 1984.

Kourvetaris, G.A., *First and Second Generation Greeks in Chicago*, Athens: National Centre of Social Research, 1971.

Leber, George J., *The History of the Order of Ahepa*, Washington, DC: Order of Ahepa, 1972.

Litsas, Fotios K., *A Companion to the Greek Orthodox Church*, New York: Greek Orthodox Archdiocese of North and South America, 1984.

Marketou, Jenny, *The Great Longing: The Greeks of Astoria*, Athens: Kedros, 1987.

Monos, Dimitri, *The Achievement of the Greeks in the United States*, Philadelpia: Centrum, 1986.

Moskos, Charles, *Greek Americans: Struggle and Success*, Englewood Cliffs, NJ: Prentice-Hall, 1980.

Orfanos, Spyros, Harry J. Psomiades and John Spyridakis, *Education and Greek-Americans: Process and Prospects*, New York: Pella, 1994.

Panagopoulos, E.P., *New Smyrna. An Eighteenth-Century Greek Odyssey*, Gainesville: University Press of Florida, 1966.

Papaioannou, George, *From Mars Hill to Manhattan: The Greek Orthodox in America under Athenagoras*, Minneapolis: Light and Life, 1976.

Papanikolas, Helen Zeese, *Toil and Rage in a New Land: The Greek Immigrants in Utah*, Salt Lake City: Utah Historical Society, 1974.

———, *Aimilia-Emily; Georgios-George*, Salt Lake City: University of Utah Press, 1987.

Psomiades, Harry, and Alie Scourby (eds), *The Greek American Community in Transition*, New York: Pella, 1982.

Rostovtzeff, M., *Iranians and Greeks in South Russia*, New York, 1969.

Saloutos, Theodore, *They Remember America: The Story of the Repatriated Greek-Americans*, Berkeley, Los Angeles: University of California Press, 1956.

_____, *The Greeks in the United States.* Cambridge, MA: Harvard University Press, 1964.

_____, *The Greeks in America: A Student's Guide to Localized History*, New York: Teachers College Press, Columbia University, 1967.

Tamis, A., *The Macedonian Greeks in Australia*, Melbourne: La Trobe University Press, 1994.

Tavuchis, Nicholas, *Family and Mobility among Greek Americans*, Athens: National Centre of Social Research, 1972.

Vatikiotis, P.J., *Among Arabs and Jews: A Personal Experience, 1936–90*, London: Weidenfeld and Nicolson, 1991.

Vlachos, Evangelos, *An Annotated Bibliography on Greek Migration*, Athens: Social Sciences Centre, 1966.

_____, *The Assimilation of Greeks in the United States, with Special Reference to the Greek Community of Anderson, Indiana*, Athens: National Centre of Social Research, 1968.

Vryonis, Speros, *A Brief History of the Greek-American Community of St. George, Memphis, Tennessee, 1962–1982*, Malibu, CA: Undena, 1982.

Watanabe, Paul, *Ethnic Groups, Congress and American Foreign Policy: The Politics of the Turkish Arms Embargo*, Westport, CT: Greenwood Press, 1974.

Xenides, J.P., *The Greeks in America*, New York: George H. Doran, 1922.

Zotos, Stephanos, *Hellenic Presence in America*, Wheaton, IL: Pilgrimage, 1976.

EDUCATION

Browning, Robert, *Medieval and Modern Greek*, London: Hutchinson, University Library, 1969.

Dawkins, R.M., *Modern Greek in Asia Minor: A Study of the Dialects of Silli, Cappadocia and Pharasa, with Grammar, Texts, List Translations and Glossary*, Cambridge University Press, 1916.

Faubion, James D., *Modern Greek Lessons: A Primer in Historical Constructions*, Princeton University Press, 1993.

Gennadius, J., *A Sketch of the History of Education in Greece*, Edinburgh: World Federation of Education, 1925.

Holton, David, Peter Mackridge and Irene Philippaki-Warburton, *Greek: A Comprehensive Grammar of the Modern Language*, London: Routledge, 1997.

Horrocks, Geoffrey, *Greek: a History of the Language and its Speakers*, New York: London, 1997.

Kazamias, Andreas, and Byron G. Massialas, *Greece: Tradition and Change in Education: A Comparative Study*, Englewood Cliffs, NJ: Prentice-Hall, 1965.

Massialas, Byron G., *The Educational System of Greece*, Washington, DC: GPO, 1981.

Mackridge, Peter, *The Modern Greek Language: Descriptive Analysis of Standard Modern Greek*, Oxford University Press, 1987.

Moleas, Wendy, *The Development of the Greek Language*, New Rochelle, NY: Aristide Caratzas, 1889.

Moustaka, Calliope, *Attitudes, Sociometric Status and Ability in Greek Schools*, The Hague: Mouton, 1967.

Newton, Brian, *Cypriot Greek: Its Phonology and Inflections*, The Hague: Mouton, 1972. 186p.

_____, *The Generative Interpretation of Dialect: A Study of Modern Greek Phonology*, Cambridge University Press, 1972.

Oliver, E. Eugene, *Greece: A Study of the Educational System of Greece and a Guide to the Academic Placement of Students in Educational Institutions in the United States*, Washington, DC: American Association of Collegiate Registrars and Administration Officers, 1982.

Palmer, L.R., *The Greek Language*, London: Faber & Faber, 1980.

Ricks, David, *The Shade of Homer: A Study in Modern Greek Poetry*, Cambridge University Press.

Seaman, David, *Modern Greek and American English in Contact*, The Hague: Mouton, 1972.

RELIGION

Adeney, W.F., *The Greek and Eastern Churches*, New York, 1928.

Amand, Emmanuel, *Mount Athos: The Garden of the Panaghia*, Amsterdam, 1972.

Benz, Ernest, *The Eastern Orthodox Church*, New York: Doubleday, 1963.

Frazee, Charles, *The Orthodox Church and Independent Greece, 1821–1852*, Cambridge University Press, 1969.

Hammond, Peter, *The Water of Marah: The Present State of the Greek Church*, London: Rockliff, 1956.

Harper, Ralph, *Journey from Paradise: Mount Athos and the Interior Life*, Baltimore: Johns Hopkins University Press, 1987.

Hasluck, F.W., *Athos and its Monasteries*. London: Kegan Paul, 1924.

Hore, A.H., *Eighteen Centuries of the Orthodox Greek Church*, London, 1899.

Hussey, J.M., *The Orthodox Church in the Byzantine Empire*, Oxford: Clarendon Press, 1986.

Kanellopoulos, Panayotis, *Ascent to Faith*, New York: Exposition Press, 1966.

Kitromilides, Paschalis, and Thanos Veremis (eds), *The Orthodox Church in a Changing World*, Athens: ELIAMEP-CAMS, 1998.

Neale, John, *A History of the Holy Eastern Church*, 2 vols, London, 1851.

Papademetriou, George C., *Essays on Orthodox Christian-Jewish Relations*, Bristol: Wyndham Hall, 1990.

Papadopoullos, Theodore H., *Studies and Documents Relating to the History of the Greek Church and People under Turkish Domination*, Brussels, 1952.

Rinvolucri, M., *Anatomy of a Church: Greek Orthodoxy Today*, London, 1966.

Sherrard, Philip, *Athos: The Mountain of Silence*, Oxford University Press, 1960.

Waddington, George, *The Conditions and Prospects of the Greek or Oriental Church*, London, 1854.

Walker, Andrew, and Costa Carras (eds), *Living Orthodoxy in the Modern World*, London: SPCK, 1996.

Ware, Timothy, *The Orthodox Church*, Harmondsworth: Penguin, 1963.

_____, *Eustratios Argenti: A Study of the Greek Church Under Turkish Rule*. Oxford, 1964.

Zizioulas, John D., *Being as Communion*, Crestwood, NY: St Vladimir's Seminary Press, 1993.

LAW

Eddy, Charles, *Greece and the Greek Refugees*, London: Geo. Allen & Unwin, 1931.

Kariotis, Theodore C. (ed.), *Greece and the Law of the Sea*, The Hague: Kluwer, 1997.

Pazarci, Huseyin and Costas Economides, *Two Views on Legal Questions Concerning the Greek Islands of the Aegean Sea* (in Greek), Athens: Gnosi, ELIAMEP, 1989.

Rozakis, Christos, and C. Stephanou (eds), *The New Law of the Sea,* Amsterdam: North-Holland, 1983.

Rozakis, Christos, *Analysis of the Legal Problems in Greek-Turkish Relations 1973–88*, Athens: ELIAMEP, 1989.

Syrigos, Angelos M., *The Status of the Aegean Sea According to International Law*, Athens: Sakkoulas-Bruylant, 1998.

Tassopoulos, John, *The Constitutional Problem of Subversive Advocacy in the United States and Greece: A Comparison of the Legal Guarantees of Political Speech in Time of Crisis*, Athens: Sakkoulas, 1993.

JOURNALS AND YEARBOOKS

Aegean Review, New York Wire Press, 1989.

Anglo-Hellenic Review, London, 1990.

Balkan Studies, Thessaloniki: Institute of Balkan Studies, since 1960.

Byzantine and Modern Greek Studies, Oxford, 1975.

Charioteer, The, Annual Review of Modern Greek Culture, Greek Cultural Society of New York (Parnassos), 1958.

Dialogos, King's College London, 1994.

Emphasis, Hellenic Resources Institute, Boston, MA, 1995.

Epitheorisis Koinonikon Erevnon (The Greek Review of Social Research), Athens: Social Science Centre, 1969.

Epsilon: Modern Greek and Balkan Studies, University of Copenhagen, Dept. of Modern Greek and Balkan Studies, 1987.

Etudes Helléniques—Hellenic Studies, Outremont, Quebec, 1992.

Greek Economic Review, Athens, Oxford, 1979.

Greek Letters (a journal of Modern Greek literature in translation), Athens, 1987.

Hellenic Review of International Relations, Thessaloniki: Institute of Public International Law, 1981.

Hellenika: Jahrbuch für die Freunde Griechenlands, Ausgaben Neugriechische Studien, Bochum, 1964.

Italoellinika. Rivista di Cultura Greco-moderna, Istituto Universitario Orientale, Naples, 1989.

Journal of Modern Greek Studies, Johns Hopkins University Press, 1985.

Journal of Modern Hellenism. New York, 1985.

Journal of the Hellenic Diaspora. New York: Pella, 1974.

Journal of Southeast European and Black Sea Studies, London: Frank Cass and ELIAMEP, 2001.

Lychnari, Adamantios Koraes Foundation, Styx Publishers, Groningen.

Mandatophoros: Bulletin of Modern Greek Studies, Byzantijns-Nieuwgrieks Seminarium University of Amsterdam, 1972.

Modern Greek Society: A Social Science Newsletter. Providence, Rhode Island, 1973.

Modern Greek Studies, Australia & New Zealand, 1993.

Modern Greek Studies Yearbook, University of Minnesota, Minneapolis, 1985.

Paralos: A Journey into Hellenism, Hellenic Students Association of Princeton, 1995.

Philia, Zeitschrift für wissenschaftliche, ekonomische und kulturelle Zusammenarbeit der Griechisch-Deutchen Initiative, Würzburg, 1987.

Revue des Etudes Neo-Helléniques, Faculté des Lettres et Sciences Humaines, University of Aix-en-Provence, 1968.

Scandinavian Studies in Modern Greek, Gothenburg, Sweden, 1977.

Synthesis, Review of Modern Greek Studies, London School of Economics, 1996.

Tetradio, Institute for Greek Studies, University of Ghent, Belgium, 1992.

The South-East European Yearbook, Athens: ELIAMEP, 1988.

Thetis, Mannheim, Germany, 1994.

Yper, Van Nuys, California, 1994.

INDEX

Abdroutsos, Odysseas 22, 214, 222
Abdul Hamid II, Sultan 282
About, Edmond 222
Academy of Athens 198–99
Acheson, Dean 300
Aegean Sea and islands 53, 58, 119, 163,
    201, 231, 250, 284, 286, 287, 308–9,
    312–13, 320–4, 327, 345, 369, 370–1
Africa 211
Agathangelos 26
Agnew, Spiro 301
agriculture 165–73, chapter 7 passim, 210
Aitolikon 20–1
Albania, Albanians 71, 80, 99, 106, 112,
    116, 129, 135, 136, 159, 163, 183,
    184, 201, 203, 206, 207–8, 215, 231,
    233, 234, 243, 245, 246, 247, 251–2,
    254–6, 271, 281, 285, 290–1, 295,
    305–6, 310, 314, 318–20, 331, 333,
    343, 344, 346
Albright, Madeleine 323
Alexander I, King of Greece 285
Alexander the Great 210, 245, 337
Ali Pasha of Ioannina 219
Anagnostakis, Manolis 358
Anagnostaras (Papageorgiou Anagnostis)
    19, 30
Andriadis, André 170, 198
Andrianopoulos, Andreas 199
Angelopoulos, Theo 352
Anthimos VI, Patriarch 144

archaeology 244–5
architecture 350–51
archons 33, 37
Areios Pagos 14, 21–2, 24, 247
Argentina 205, 211, 311
Armansberg, Joseph Ludwig von 166
Armatoles 21, 122, 195, 201, 223, 267,
    330, 335
armed forces 93, 101–2, chapter 4 passim,
    188, 196, 343–4
Armenians 203
Arsakes, Apostolos 160
art 349–51
Arvanites 137, 359
Association of Friends 13, 15, 18
Atatürk see Kemal
Athens 22, 38, 50, 70, 77–9, 115, 149,
    150–1, 154, 195, 201, 208, 258, 277,
    351, 364, 368
Athens College 199
Athos, Mount 57
Attica 183, 245, 267
Australia 206, 211
Austria 12, 24, 206, 216–19, 280, 282,
    283
Axis see World War, Second

Balkan Pact (1934) 290, 346, 367
Balkan Wars (1912–13) 34, 127–8, 131,
    132, 202, 204, 205, 213, 283–4, 285,
    345, 366

Ball, George 300
banks 174
Barthélemy, Abbé 218
Bavaria 49–50, 142, 145, 166, 196, 264,
    269, 349, 361, 364
Benakis, Emmanouil 197
Berisha, Sali 318
Berlin, Congress of 202, 234, 278–9, 336,
    343, 365
Bismarck, Otto von 279
Bolivar, Simon 32
Bonaparte, Jerome 23
borders, chapter 19 *passim*, 364
Bosnia-Hercegovina 208, 282, 319
Boutros-Ghali, Boutros 321
Brazil 205, 211
brigands 51, 188, 213–15, 221–25, 270,
    343
Britain 38–9, 47–8, 50–1, 55, 56, 63, 70,
    72–3, 76, 78, 81, 85, 123, 129, 130,
    153, 171, 271–5, 278, 279, 281–2,
    284, 287–93, 294, 298, 302–3, 332,
    342, 343, 346, 362, 367
Bucharest 217–18
Bulgaria, Bulgarian language 65, 71, 74,
    75, 80, 99, 112, 136, 138, 147, 161,
    184, 202, 205, 212, 224, 229, 231,
    233, 234, 237, 251–3, 258, 278, 280–
    1, 282–5, 287, 288, 295, 305–6, 310,
    314–15, 331, 337, 338–40, 344–6
Byzantine Empire 4–5, 6, 7, 149, 213,
    233, 244–5, 350

Cacoyannis, Michael 352, 358
Callas, Maria 353
Canada 205, 206, 211
Carbonari 18, 23–4, 33
Catastrophe (in Asia Minor, 1922) 129–
    32, 152, 204, 231, 260, 362; *see also*
    Great Idea
Catholic Church 163, 250
Cavafis, Constantine 135, 354–5
Ceauşescu, Nicolae 319
Cem, Ismail 325
Centre Union 56, 57, 98, 101, 102, 104,
    299, 368
cereals 19, 171, 185
Cervenkoski, Stevo 316
Chams of Epirus 138

Charalambis, Soteris 325
Chatzidakis, Georgios 246
Chaucer, Geoffrey 275
children's deportation in civil war 94–5
Christodoulos, Archbishop 151
Christou, Yannis, 353
Chrysanthopoulos, Photakos 223
Chryssa (Vardea Mavromihaki) 351
Church, Greek Orthodox 1–3, 129,
    chapter 3 *passim*, 158–60, 162–3,
    184, 187, 207, 227–8, 230–33, 238,
    242, 246–8, 250, 252–3, 257–9, 260,
    264–6, 267, 270, 277–8, 280, 303,
    338, 352–3, 361, 365
Churchill, Winston 78, 293
Ciller, Tansu 322–3
cinema 352, 358
citizenship 52, 201, 250, 256–7
civil service 48, 58–61, 99–100, 225
Civil War (1946–9) 55–6, 68, 69–102,
    107, 108, 153, 154, 155, 206, 208, 293,
    295, 331, 341, 346, 362, 368
class structure, chapter 8
classical Greece 1, 4–5, 7–8, 38, 242–7,
    254, 263–4, 273, 352
Clerides, Glafcos 324
Colonels, regime of the 57, 101–2, 105,
    124–5, 140, 149–50, 153–4, 174, 300–
    2, 306, 362, 369
Comintern 88, 110, 112–17, 120, 123,
    133–6, 152, 340
Committee of Union and Progress 282
Communism 55–6, 135–6, 177, 234,
    314–16, 340
Communist Party of Greece, *see* KKE
Conference on Security and Co-
    operation in Europe (CSCE) 310
Conservative Party 118
Constantine I, King of Greece 54, 66,
    127, 128, 132, 271, 281, 284–6, 339,
    366–7
Constantine II, King of Greece 57, 100,
    101, 102
Constantinides, Aris 139
Constantinople 26, 141, 149, 159, 195,
    197, 204, 210, 277, 287, 289, 336
constitutions 21–2, 29–43, 44–52, 57,
    129, 166, 102, 250, 257, 269, 365,
    366, 367

Cordovez, Diego 324
Corfu 120, 289
coups d'état 123, 153, 367; *see* also Colonels, regime of the
Crete 127, 163, 201, 205, 224, 279, 283, 284, 287, 291, 314, 338, 344–5, 365, 367
crime, chapter 11
Croatia 316
Crusades 5, 6
currants 165, 166–8, 171, 279
Cyprus 56, 98, 102, 163, 204, 286, 297–305, 307–9, 313, 320–6, 368–9
Czechoslovakia 124, 287, 300

DAG (Democratic Army of Greece) 89, 91–5, 138, 295, 368
Damaskinos, Archbishop 258
Daniilides, Dimosthenis 136
Dassin, Jules 358
Davos, Ioannis 302
debt 167, 170, 279
Deligiorgis, Epaminondas 66, 362
Deliyannis, Anagnostis 32
Deliyannis, Kanellos 13–14, 25, 27, 223
Deliyannis, Theodore 65, 67, 128, 214, 365
Delors, Jacques 273
Deltas, Stephanos 199
Demirel, Suleyman 321, 323
Denktash, Rauf 321, 324–5
diaspora, *see* emigration and diaspora
Dichasmos, *see* National Schism
Dikaios, Gregorios 18, 25, 30, 35, 37
Dikaios, Nikitas 25
Dimaras, Constantine 357
Dimitrov, Georgi 85
Dodecanese islands 99, 285, 286, 293, 322, 365, 368
drachma 170, 171, 172, 173
Dragoumis, Ion 234, 265

EAM 70, 76–7, 78, 81, 82, 83, 85, 86, 87, 92, 292
Ecevit, Bulent 302
economy 65, 99, chapter 6 *passim*
Ecumenical Patriarch, Patriarchate 141–2, 145, 146–7, 149, 158, 181, 231, 232, 253, 277–8, 289, 337, 338

EDA (United Democratic Left) 56, 101, 124, 138, 306
EDES 70, 71–2, 74, 78, 79
education chapter 5 *passim*, 197, 269, 337
Egypt 12, 46, 291
EKKA 70–1
ELAS 70–92, 292
electoral systems 63–7
Elekdag, Sukru 322–3
Elytis, Odysseus 357–8
Embirikos, Andreas 358
emigration and diaspora 156, 167, 168, 174, 195, 197, chapter 9 *passim*, 217–18, 266, 277, 351, 353, 361–2
Engonopoulos, Nikos 358
Enlightenment 163, 230, 254, 268, 361
Epirus 29, 50, 53, 62, 70, 78, 79, 111, 138, 159, 183, 184, 201, 203, 206, 224, 229, 231, 233, 278, 283, 286, 289, 328, 330–31, 335–6, 345
Erbakan, Necmetin 323
ERE (National Radical Union) 368
European Monetary Union and euro 109, 177–9, 317, 323, 370, 371
European Union (EU; EEC, EC) 61, 103, 104, 105, 106, 108, 109, 139, 174–7, 198, 271, 273–4, 307–8, 311–13, 317, 319–26, 346–7, 368–70
Evangelatos, Spyros 353
Evert, Miltiades 109, 199

Fallmerayer, Jacob Philipp 245, 274
Farakos, Grigoris 77
Fassianos, Alekos 351
Fermor, Patrick Leigh 272
Flamiatos, Kosmas 146
Forster, E.M. 271
France 7, 22–4, 47–8, 50–1, 63, 130, 168, 210, 279, 281–2, 284, 286, 287, 294, 342, 362
Frantzis, Ambrosios 223
Frederica, Queen of Greece 94, 100
French Revolution 7, 22–4, 143, 217, 219, 268, 361

Gallina, Vicente 17
Ganev, Stoyan 315
Gazis, Anthimos 17
Gazis, Georgios 335

Gemistos Plethon 6
gendarmeire 81–2, 95, 188, 196
Gennadios, Ioannis 167
Genoa 163, 327
George I, King of Greece 127–8, 132, 278, 281, 343, 365–6
George II, King of Greece 55, 71, 72, 76, 290, 291, 292, 295, 367
Germanos, Palaion Patron 15, 32
Germany 120, 171, 206, 211, 258, 279–80, 281–5, 287, 290–3, 342, 346, 362, 367; *see also* World War, Second
Ghizis, Nikolaos 157, 349
Glezos, Manolis 125
Goldbloom, Maurice 299
Goodpaster, Andrew J. 301
Gorbachev, Mikhail 311, 314
Gounaris, Dimitrios 130
Gounaris, Elias 274
Gouras, Ioannis 22
Great Idea (*Megali Idea*) 130, 135, 231, 286, 336
Greco-Turkish war (1919–22) 112, 114, 260, 263, 286, 367
Greek language 1, 4–5, 129, 158, 159, 161, 162–3, 227–8, 254, 256, 257, 258, 264, 267, 273–5, 336, 337, 349, 354
Gregory V, Patriarch 144
Grivas, General George 305
Gulf War 314, 321
Gypsies 53, 252, 256, 345

Haig, Alexander 209
Hansen, Christian 164
Hatzidakis, Manos 350, 352–4
Hatzikyriakos-Ghikas, Nikos 199, 350
hellenisation, chapter 14 *passim*
Helsinki Final Act 310
Hitler, Adolf 274, 291
Hobbes, Thomas 27, 42–3
Homer 273
Hungary 306
Hydra 12, 18–19, 28, 34, 233, 265, 267
Iakovidis, Georgios 350
Ibrahim Pasha 12, 24, 46
Ignatius, Metropolitan 33, 335
Iliopoulos, Dinos 352
IMRO 240, 280–81, 288

India 210, 311
industry 169–70
inflation 60, 171–2, 174, 175, 177
Ionian Islands 52, 163, 183, 197, 198, 278, 343, 350, 352, 353, 354, 365
irregular fighters 83–4, 212–15, 221–4, 330–1
Iskos, Andreas 21, 27
Islam, Muslims 137, 163, 250, 252, 255–6, 286–7, 345
Isocrates 7, 135
Israel 211
Italy 76, 78, 99, 120, 122, 127, 135, 171, 231, 246, 280, 283, 284, 286, 287–9, 290–3, 346, 36; *see also* World War, Second

Jenkins, Romilly 221, 272
Jews 116, 137, 211, 252, 266
Joachim II, Patriarch 147
Johnson, Lyndon B. 105, 305
justice, chapter 11 *passim*

Kafandaris, George 170
Kaklamanis, Apostolos 150
Kalomiris, Manolis 353
Kalvos, Andres 354–5
Kanaris, Constantions 64
Kanellopoulos, Panayotis 139, 198
Kapodistrias, Ioannis 12, 23, 26, 28, 29, 31, 32, 34, 40–1, 46–9, 50, 164, 165–6, 264, 267–8, 269, 364
Karaiskatis, Georgios 31, 222, 335
Karamanlis, Constantine 56, 57, 61, 68, 101, 102–4, 107, 109, 125, 139, 150, 154, 174–5, 298, 302, 304, 308–11, 314, 368–70
Karatheodori, Constantine 199
Karavangelis, Germanos 145
Karavitis, Ioannis 338
Karrer, Pavlos 353
Karyotakis, Kostas 135, 357
Katartzis, Dimitrios 218
Kazantzakis, Nikos 205, 353–9
Kemal, Mustapha (Atatürk) 130, 260–1, 286, 289
Kennedy, John F. 299
Kenya 325
Khuri, Karolos 352

Kiepert, Heinrich 159
Kirilianos, Christodoulos 217
Kissinger, Henry 301–2, 320
KKE 55–6, 57, 61, 68–98, 107, 108, 110–26, 133–4, 138, 153, 292, 293, 340
Kleanthis, Shamatis 164
Klephts 25, 122, 213, 222–5, 344
Kolettis, Demetrios 17, 51, 63, 67, 214
Kolokotronis, Theodoros 4, 12, 13, 14, 19, 25, 31–2, 223
Kondoglou, Photis 350
Kondyles, Georgios 367
Konstantas, Gregorios 17, 22, 334
Kontakes, Petros 31
Koraes, Adamantios 8, 22–3, 26, 27, 30, 32, 38, 41, 42, 230, 252, 264–7, 271, 361
Kordatos, Ioannis 134
Korean War 296–7, 298
Kosmas of Aitolia 159, 163
Kosovo 319, 370
Kotas, Constantinos 240
Koumoundouros, Alexandros 64, 66, 166, 192, 362, 365
Koundouros, Nikos 352
Kounelis, Yannis 351
Kountouriotis, Georgios 31
Kountouriotis, Pavlos 366–7
Kouremenos, Yarmoulis 24
Krimas, Vassos 198
Kurds 208–9, 323
Kütchük, Fazil 304, 368
Kyriakides, Stilpon 246

Labelette, Napoleon 353
Laird, Melvin 301
Lambeti, Elli 352
Lambrakis, Grigoris 103
land tenure 111, 165–6, 169, 188, 192–3, 365
Lausanne, Treaty of 204, 234, 286, 331, 345, 367
Lavrangas, Dionysios 353
Lavrion mines 167
League of Nations 202, 287–9
Leake, William Martin 333
Leopold of Saxe-Coburg 364
Liberal Party 53, 118, 127, 132–3

literature 354–8
Locke, John 27, 42, 271
Louriotis, Nikolaos 20
Lytras, Nikiforos 350

Maastricht Treaty 313, 370
Macedonia 50, 53, 70, 71, 73, 74–6, 79, 83, 85, 86, 87–9, 93, 95, 97, 106, 109, 111, 112–17, 133–4, 137–8, 159, 162, 179, 183, 193, 201, 202–5, 206, 213, 224, 229, 233, chapter 13 *passim*, 245, 251, 253–5, 260, 270, 278, 280–1, 283–5, 286–7, 292, 305–6, 315–16, 319, 328, 330–31, 335, 336–41, 343, 344–5, 346, 365–7, 370
Mackenzie, Compton 271
Makarios, Archbishop of Cyprus 102, 299, 301, 303–5, 324
Makedontski 87–9, 95
Makriyannis, Ioannis 135, 140
Maleas, Constantinos 350
Manos, Stephanos 140, 177, 199
Manou, Rallou 352
Mantzaros, Nikolaos 353
Markezinis, Spyros 172, 294
Marshall Plan 172, 295, 303
Marshall, George C. 172, 294
Maurer, Georg von 141
Mavrogenis, Nicholas 217
Mavrocordatos, Alexandros 17, 20–1, 24, 28, 34–6, 45, 51, 63, 67, 214, 334, 362
Mavrocordatos, George 214
Mavromichalis, Petros 16
Maximos, Seraphim 134
McDonald, Robert 177
McNeil, W.H. 4, 154, 156
Megali Idea see Great Idea
Melas, Ioannis 23
Melas, Lt Pavlos 212–13, 338–9
Meletios 333
Menderes, Adnan 304
merchants 29, 158, 160, 194–5, 196, 197, 200, 204, 210, 217–18
Mercouri, Melina 352
Metaxas, Andreas 31, 51
Metaxas, Ioannis 55, 72, 77, 80, 82, 119, 124, 129, 130, 135, 136–7, 171, 235, 290–1, 367

Metternich, Count 24
Miaoulis, Andreas 12
migration 53, 154, 156, 167, 168, 184–5, 187–90, 195, chapter 9 *passim*, 277, 318, 328–9, 351, 353, 361–2
Mihailovic, Draga 72
military dictatorship, see Colonels, regime of the
Minotis, Alexis 352
Missolonghi 20, 64, 201
Mitaras, Dimitris 351–2
Mitropoulos, Dimitris 352–3
Mitsotakis, Constantine 107, 108, 109, 177, 314, 316, 321, 370
Moisiodax, Iossipos 218
monarchy 22–4, 30–1, 32–8, 100, 117, 127, 365
monasteries 57, 145–6
Mongelas, Maximilian 301
Montenegro 283
Moralis, Yannis 350
Morea, see Peloponnese
Moskos, Charles 210–11
mulberry growing 186
music 352–4
Mussolini, Benito 135, 171, 290
Myrivilis, Stratis 358

Nano, Fatos, 318
Napoleon 28
nation-state idea 264–71, 360–1
National Bank of Greece 170, 173
National Guard 80–2, 95
national identity, chapters 14 and 15 *passim*
National Radical Union 56
National Schism (*Dichasmos*) 54, 128, 271, 284–5, 362, 366
nationalisation 174, 176
nationalism 135–6, chapter 12
NATO 104, 106, 108, 297–303, 305, 307–9, 319–23, 368, 370–1
Nauplion 195
Navarino, battle of 47, 364
Negris, Theodoros 17, 20, 21, 28, 31, 269
Nemours, Duc de 24, 32, 34
New Democracy Party 102, 107–9, 110, 150, 174, 177, 312–13, 369, 370

Nikoloudi, Zouzou 352
Nixon, Donald 301
Nixon, Richard 300–1
Nuveen, John 296

Ocalan, Abdullah 325, 371
occupation (German-Italian), see World War, Second
Odessa 195, 210
Oikonomos, Konstantinos 146
olives 186
Olympic Airways 174, 178
Olympic Games 65
Olympus, Mount 335
opium 186
Orthodox (Greek) *see* Church
Otto, King of Greece 49–50, 141, 164, 166, 201, 268, 278, 343, 349, 353, 361, 364–5
Ottoman empire, *see* Turkey
Özal, Turgut 312, 321, 340

PAK (Panhellenic Resistance Movement) 124
Palamas, Kostis 354
Palestinians 209
Pallikars 213–15, 269
Pangalos, General Theodoros 115, 120, 131
Pangalos, Theodoros 322
Panourgias, Panourgias 154
PAO (Panhellenic Liberation Organisation) 70–1, 74
Papadiamantis, Alexandros 354
Papadopoulos, George 301
Papagos, Field-Marshal Alexander 100, 103, 173, 296–8, 300, 368
Papaioannou, Dimitris 352
Papaligours, Panaghis 174–5
Papaloukas, Spyros 350
Papanastasiou, Alexander 367
Papandreou, Andreas 57, 68, 102, 104, 105–9, 124–5, 150–1, 155, 175–6, 178, 199, 214–15, 273, 299, 300, 307–8, 311–12, 314, 321, 362, 369–70
Papandreou, George 56, 57, 74, 84, 101–4, 107, 125, 299, 300, 304, 368–9

Paparrigopoulos, Konstantinos 5, 7, 135, 233–5, 245–6
Papavassiliou, Vassilis 352
Papoulakos, Christophoros 26, 146
Papoulias, Karolos 316
parliament 52–6, 67, 118, 136, 196
Parthenis, Constantine 350
parties, political, 62–3, 67–8; *see also names of parties*
PASOK 98, 102, 104, 105, 107–9, 110, 124–5, 150, 154, 155, 174–5, 307–8, 311–12, 362, 369–70, 371
Pasvanoglou, Osman 217–19
Patras 195, 205
Paul I, King of Greece 100, 296, 300
peasants 51–2, 82, 92–3, 95–6, 111, 146, 154, 165–73, chapter 7 *passim*, 195, 210, 223–5, 247–8, 338
Pelion, Mount 335
Peloponnese (Morea) 12–20, 25, 35, 52, 80, 90, 129, 146, 165, 166, 168, 183, 196, 205, 265
Peurifoy, John 296–7
Phanariots 17, 45, 160, 181, 195, 218, 269, 354
Pharmakidis, Theokletos 141–2, 151
Philip II of Macedon 7, 245, 336
Philippides, Daniel 218, 334
Photiadis, Grigoris 218
Pikionis, Dimitris 139, 199, 351
Pindus mountains 159, 187, 329
piracy 201
Piraeus 167, 205, 278
Plapoutas, Kolias 25, 27
Plastiras, Nikolaos 84, 172, 296, 297
poetry 354–8
Poland 209, 216, 311
Politis, Kosmas 358
Polybius 333
Polychroniades, Konstantinos 17, 24, 27–8, 36
Polyzoides, Anastasios 4, 39, 214
Pontians 74, 79–80, 111, 114, 137, 186, 203, 206, 208, 246
Poulios, Lefteris 359
Praïdis, Georgios 20–1, 35
press 32, 34, 35–6, 37, 39, 40–2, 238
Pringos, Ioannis 218

Psalidas, Athanasios 230, 335–6
Psaros, Dimitris 71
Psycharis, Yannis 354
Psylas, Georgios 31

Rallis, George 369
Raphael I, Patriarch 158
refugees: 125–6, 129, 200–10, 329–30; (post-1922) 74, 111–12, 114, 117, 129–34, 137–8, 170, 186, 188, 193, 204, 246, 260, 293, 341, 351, 353, 347
Rogers, Bernard 309
Rogers, William 301
Roïdes, Emmanuel 57–8, 354
Roman Empire 1–2, 4–5, 7
Romania 12, 65, 127, 161, 162, 202, 203, 216–19, 281, 287, 290, 306, 310, 314, 318–19, 346
Romas, Dionysios 23, 33
Rontiris, Dimitris 352
Rousseau, Jean-Jacques 27, 42
Rumelia 52, 196, 202, 280
Russia 12, 18, 47–9, 63, 65, 146, 204–5, 217–18, 278, 279–80, 281–2, 283, 342

Samaras, Antonis 109, 199, 316, 370
Samaras, Lukas 351
Sartzetakis, Christos 370
Savopoulos, Dionysis 352
Scholarios, Metropolitan Dorotheos 159, 163
Scorsese, Martin 358
Seferis, George 140, 356–8
Senate 14–15, 16, 19–22
Seraphim, Archbishop 151
Serbia, Serbs 64, 65, 72, 114–15, 158, 203, 208, 258, 281, 283–4, 288, 319, 331, 345
Siantos, George 80
Sikelianos, Angelos 135
Simitis, Kostas 109, 140, 151, 177, 178, 319, 323, 370–1
Skalkotas, Nikos 353
Sklavos, Gerasimos 351
Slavs 135, 147, 159, 163, 233, 234, 237–40, 245, 246, 247, 253–5, 271, 278, 333, 336, 339–41, 344; *see also* Macedonia

Slovenia 316
Smyrna 32, 130, 195, 204, 210, 285, 286
Solana, Javier 322
Solomos, Dionysios 354
Sophoulis, Themistocles 84
Sotiropoulos, Sotirios 166
Speliades, Nikolaos 24, 34
Stageiritis, Athanasios 334
Stalin, Joseph 78, 85, 99, 123, 124, 293, 305–6
Stephanopoulos, Constantine 370–1
stockrearing 53, 184–5, 186–9, 252, 328–9
Sweden 311
Syngros, Andreas 167, 197
Syria 323
Syros 165, 167

Takis (Vassilakis) 351
Tanzania 311
territorial expansion 134–5, 270, 277–8, chapter 21 *passim*
theatre 352
Theodorakis, Mikis 354
Theotokas, George 135, 139, 140, 357
Theotokis, Georgios 128
Theotokis, Ioannis 17, 32, 33, 40
Theotokos, Georgios 128
Thessaloniki 56, 133, 169, 201, 205, 208, 258, 268, 281, 283, 285, 288, 341, 345, 366
Thessaly 50, 90, 111, 126, 138, 159, 167, 168–9, 183, 193, 197, 201, 214, 216, 224, 229, 231, 234, 278–9, 328, 329, 330–1, 335, 343, 365
Thrace 114, 115, 117, 134, 183, 193, 202, 229, 245, 251, 253, 283, 292, 312, 337, 346
Thucydides 181
Tito, Josip Broz 75, 85, 87, 93, 123, 292, 295, 305, 310
tobacco 171, 186
Trichopoulos, Dimitris 198
Trieste 195, 216
Trikoupis, Charilaos 53, 59, 61, 64–6, 67, 127, 128, 197, 214, 269, 362, 365
Trikoupis, Ioannis 21
Trikoupis, Spyridon 45, 141, 142

Tripolista 18–19
Tritsis, Antonis 150–51
Truman, Harry S. 294, 368
Truman Doctrine 294–5
Tsaldaris, Panagis 367
Tsarouchis, Yannis 350, 352
Tsatsos, Constantine 139, 198
Tsitsanis, Vassilis, 354
Tsoklis, Costas 351
Tsouderos, Emmanouil 291
Tsoukalas, Constantine 210
Turkey, Turks 3, 7–8, 11–12, 25, 26, 27, 30, 52, 65–6, 111, 116, 117, 122, 127, 129–30, 144, 147, 157–8, 163, 182, 195, 200–3, 208, 214, 216–20, 221–4, 227–32, 233, 237, 239, 240, 242–3, 246, 247, 255–6, 259–62, 277–87, 289–90, 298, 299–300, 301–6, 307–10, 312–13, 314, 320–6, 327–8, 330–1, 342–7, 364–71
Tzannetakis, Tzannis 370

United Nations 82, 91, 295, 298, 303, 305, 311, 316, 324–6
United States of America 38–9, 42, 70, 85, 123, 153, 168, 171, 172, 205, 210–11, 285, 286, 294–305, 307–9, 311–14, 346–7
University of Athens 160–1, 164, 197, 246
urbanisation 4, 154, 156, 189–90
USSR 70, 78, 85, 93, 110, 112, 115–16, 120–24, 126, 204–5, 207, 208, 211, 285, 286, 291, 293, 294, 299, 300, 305–6, 307, 310–11, 320–21, 340; *see also* Russia

Van Fleet, James 296
Vance, Cyrus 316
Vapheiadis, Markos 86, 123, 125, 214
Varkiza accord 70, 80, 82, 87
Varnakiotis, Georgios 21, 22, 222
Varotsos, Kostas 352
Varvaresos, Kyriakos 172–3
Vassiliou, George 321
Vassiliou, Spyros 350
Velestinlis (Feraios), Rhigas 30, 215–20, 333

Velouchiotis, Aris (Athanasios Klaras) 80, 86, 119
Venice 195, 327
Venizelos, Eleftherios 53–4, 59, 61, 67, 116, 117, 126–34, 197, 260, 269, 271, 283–6, 289, 290, 339, 366–7
Venizelos, Sophocles 296
Versis, Major 212–14
Vienna 195, 217, 219
vine growing 186, 210
Vizyinos, Georgios 354
Vlachs 112, 129, 135, 138, 159, 161, 163, 183, 202, 203, 231, 234, 246, 247, 251, 255, 256, 271, 329, 344
Volanakis, Constantinos 350
Voltaire 265, 271
Voulgaris, Demetrios 66, 67
Voulgaris, Petros 84
Voyadjis, Spyros 352
Vyzantios, Demetrios 266

Wallachia, *see also* Romania 217–18
War of Independence 11–23, 61, 142–4, 167, 214, 239, 243, 250–1, 255, 268, 277, 336, 342–3, 364
Washington, George 32
West, relations with chapter 16 *passim*
Western European Union 313
Wilhelm II, Kaiser 279, 281, 285
Wilson, Woodrow 285

Woodhouse, C.M. 272
World War, First 54, 66, 203, 271, 284, 343, 345, 366
World War, Second 55, 60, 70, 71, 72–81, 87, 97, 119, 120–1, 138, 153, 171–2, 212, 258, 272, 291–3, 295, 331, 346, 367–8

Xanthos, Emmanuel 23
Xarchakos, Stavros 352
Xenakis, Iannis 353

Yannopoulos, Pericles 136
Yilmaz, Mesut 312
Yugoslavia 71–2, 75, 76, 80, 84, 93, 112, 123, 127, 136, 203, 236, 287–8, 290, 295, 303, 305–6, 307, 311, 315–16, 319, 339, 345–6, 371

Zachariadis, Nikos 80, 86, 116, 120–24, 134
Zaimis, Andreas 32, 35
Zambelios, Spyridon 233, 246
Zervas, Leonidas 198
Zervas, Napoleon 70
Zhivkov, Todor 310
Zoe 148
Zolotas, Xenophon 109, 370
Zurich-London agreements 299, 304–5